CAMBRIDGE GREE

GENERAL EDITORS

P. E. EASTERLING
Regius Professor Emeritus of Greek, University of Cambridge

PHILIP HARDIE
Senior Research Fellow, Trinity College, Cambridge

RICHARD HUNTER
Regius Professor of Greek, University of Cambridge

E. J. KENNEY
Kennedy Professor Emeritus of Latin, University of Cambridge

S. P. OAKLEY
Kennedy Professor of Latin, University of Cambridge

HORACE

ODES

BOOK I

EDITED BY

ROLAND MAYER

Professor of Classics, King's College London

CAMBRIDGE
UNIVERSITY PRESS

CAMBRIDGE
UNIVERSITY PRESS

University Printing House, Cambridge CB2 8BS, United Kingdom

Cambridge University Press is part of the University of Cambridge.

It furthers the University's mission by disseminating knowledge in the pursuit of education, learning and research at the highest international levels of excellence.

www.cambridge.org
Information on this title: www.cambridge.org/9780521671019

© Roland Mayer 2012

First published 2012
5th printing 2014

A catalogue record for this publication is available from the British Library

Library of Congress Cataloguing in Publication data
Horace.
[Carmina. Liber 1. English]
Odes, book I / Horace ; edited by Roland Mayer.
p.   cm. – (Cambridge Greek and Latin classics)
Includes bibliographical references and indexes.
ISBN 978-0-521-85473-3 (hardback)
1. Horace – Translations into English.   2. Odes, Latin – Translations into English.
3. Rome – Poetry.   I. Mayer, Roland, 1947–   II. Title.
PA6395.M39   2012
874′.01 – dc23   2012002646

ISBN 978-0-521-85473-3 Hardback
ISBN 978-0-521-67101-9 Paperback

CONTENTS

PREFACE

The date of the informal commissioning of this commentary is easy for me to recover, since 6 July 2004 was when the Horatian Society held its annual dinner in the Old Hall of Lincoln's Inn, London. It also happened that the editorial board of this series had met earlier that afternoon, and decided that one title the series needed was Horace's first book of odes. Our Society's then President, Ted Kenney, showed some art in snaring his commentator. Pre-dinner drinks on a summer evening under the shade of plane trees, views over perfect lawns to flower borders and fine brick buildings naturally lower one's resistance, especially when a good dinner with good friends is in prospect. It was at some point during these convivial proceedings that Ted proposed that I should undertake the present work. Oiled as I was, and able to deny him nothing anyway, I naturally assented. Only the next day did the enormity of that assent become evident, but as Reason began to totter back to her throne, the enormity was reduced to a more manageable scale. As an undergraduate I had read Nisbet and Hubbard's indispensable commentary shortly after its appearance, but in later years, using it as a university teacher, I often wondered what I can have made of it, since it was clearly not designed with me in mind. The basic aim of the present commentary is to provide the student reader with the sort of information that will facilitate the construe of the text. Beyond that, guidance is provided for an appreciation of Horace's craft, his use of language, metre, and his construction of his poems. Interpretation of each poem posed a rather more difficult issue, about which something has been said at the end of the Introduction.

Over the years assistance with queries on many matters has been cheerfully and authoritatively provided by friends and colleagues. My especial thanks are owed to E. L. Bowie, G. D'Alessio, A. Dyck, N. Holzberg (especially for his bibliographical information), J. North, D. W. Rathbone, M. L. West, W. Wootton, and two MA groups who vetted portions of the commentary at various draft stages. Mr N. Bryant Kirkland drew my attention to Heaney's poem based on *Carm.* 24.

April 2011   R.G.M.

ABBREVIATIONS

Bo Index	Bo, D., *Q. Horati Flacci Opera*, vol. III *De Horati poetico eloquio* (Turin, 1960)
Bo Lexicon	Bo, D., *Lexicon Horatianum*, 2 vols. (Hildesheim 1965–6)
CAH	Bowman, A. K., E. Champlin, and A. Lintott, eds., *The Cambridge ancient history*, 2nd edn. Volume X *The Augustan empire, 43 BC–AD 69* (Cambridge 1995)
CIL	*Corpus inscriptionum Latinarum* (Berlin 1863–)
CLE	Buecheler, F. and E. Lommatzsch, eds., *Carmina Latina epigraphica* (Leipzig 1895–1926)
D–S	Daremberg, C., and E. Saglio, eds., *Dictionnaire des antiquités grecques et romaines d'après les textes et les monuments* (Paris 1877–1919)
E–J	Ehrenberg, V., and A. H. M. Jones, *Documents illustrating the reigns of Augustus and Tiberius*, 2nd edn (Oxford 1976)
EO	Mariotti, S., ed., *Orazio: Enciclopedia oraziana* (Rome 1996–8)
FLP	Courtney, E., *The fragmentary Latin poets*, 2nd edn (Oxford 2003)
G–L	Gildersleeve, B. L., and G. Lodge, *Gildersleeve's Latin grammar*, 3rd edn (London 1895)
GEP	Gerber, D. E., ed., trans., *Greek elegiac poetry* (Loeb classical library 258) (Cambridge, Mass., and London 1999)
GIP	Gerber, D. E., ed., trans., *Greek iambic poetry* (Loeb classical library 259) (Cambridge, Mass., and London 1999)
GL	Campbell, D. A., ed., trans., *Greek lyric* (Loeb classical library 142, 143, 461, 476, 144; 5 vols.) (Cambridge, Mass., and London 1982–93)
GLK	Keil, H., ed., *Grammatici Latini* (Leipzig 1857–80)
GP	Gow, A. S. F., and D. L. Page, eds., *The Greek Anthology* II: *The Garland of Philip* (Cambridge 1968)
HE	Gow, A. S. F., and D. L. Page, eds., *The Greek Anthology* I: *Hellenistic epigrams* (Cambridge 1968)
H–S	Hofmann, J. B., and A. Szantyr, *Lateinische Syntax und Stilistik* (Munich 1965)
K–H	Kießling, A. and R. Heinze, *Q. Horatius Flaccus Oden und Epoden*, 10th edn (Berlin 1960)
K–S	Kühner, R., and C. Stegmann, *Ausführliche Grammatik der lateinischen Sprache*, II *Satzlehre*. 2 vols. 5th edn rev. by A. Thierfelder (Hanover 1976)
LIMC	*Lexicon iconographicum mythologiae classicae* (Zurich 1981–97)
LTUR	Steinby, E. M., ed., *Lexicon topographicum urbis Romae* (Rome 1993–2000)

N–H	Nisbet, R. G. M. and M. Hubbard, *A commentary on Horace: Odes Book I* (Oxford 1970)
N–H	Nisbet, R. G. M. and M. Hubbard, *A commentary on Horace: Odes Book II* (Oxford 1978)
NLS	Woodcock, E. C., *A new Latin syntax* (London 1959, repr. 1985)
NP	Cancik, H. and H. Schneider, eds., *Der neue Pauly: Enzyklopädie der Antike* (Stuttgart, 1996–2003) (the English edn, *Brill's New Pauly*, may be consulted, but the translations sometimes distort the original)
N–R	Nisbet, R. G. M. and N. Rudd, *A commentary on Horace: Odes Book III* (Oxford 2004)
N–W	Neue, F., and C. Wagener, *Formenlehre der lateinischen Sprache*, 3rd edn (Berlin 1892–1905)
OCD	Hornblower, S., and A. Spawforth, eds., *The Oxford classical dictionary*, 3rd edn rev. (Oxford 2003)
OLD	Glare, P. et al., eds., *Oxford Latin dictionary* (Oxford 1968–82)
RE	Pauly, A., G. Wissowa, and W. Kroll, eds., *Real-Encyclopädie der classischen Altertumswissenschaft* (Stuttgart 1893–1980)
Roby	Roby, H. J., *A grammar of the Latin language*, 2 vols. (London 1871–4)
Roscher	Roscher, W. H., ed., *Ausführliches Lexicon der griechischen und römischen Mythologie* (Leipzig 1884–1937)
TLL	*Thesaurus linguae Latinae* (Stuttgart, Munich, and Leipzig 1900–)

INTRODUCTION

1. LYRIC IMPULSE AND LYRIC CHALLENGE

me doctarum hederae praemia frontium
dis miscent superis, me gelidum nemus
Nympharumque leues cum Satyris chori
secernunt populo, si neque tibias
Euterpe cohibet nec Polyhymnia
Lesboum refugit tendere barbiton.

These lines of Horace's first and programmatic ode suggest to us at least one reason why he tackled the challenge of composing lyric poems in Latin. His earliest success had been in the native Roman genre of satire. The subject matter of satire was everyday life, and its characteristic tone was critical. The writer of satire – he might not even regard himself as a poet (cf. *S.* 1.4.39–42) – had therefore to keep his feet on the ground. The lyric poet on the other hand escaped the world of everyday (*secernunt populo*), he removed himself to a cool grove, far away from the heat of the town, where he joined the dance with nimble Nymphs and Satyrs. Nymphs and Satyrs of course only exist in an imagination nurtured on literary tradition (*doctus*), not in the satirist's real world. The imagination of the lyric poet, who now dons the persona of the *uates* (cf. 31.2),[1] is inspired by Muses (Euterpe and Polyhymnia); the satirist needed no such assistance, nor was he *doctus*, in the way that a lyric poet was. Lyric is thus presented in these lines as something both liberating and demanding.

The liberating power of lyric was generated above all by its diversity as a genre. To a Roman reader and poet the Greek tradition of lyric song was presented as a 'canon' of nine poets,[2] whose range of themes and tones answered human experience far more fully than the restricted scope of Roman satire. On transforming himself into a lyric *uates*, Horace could deal with more varied issues and situations, which all had different and appropriate tones of voice for him to develop. This variety was part and parcel of the tradition of lyric composition which he appropriated from Greece. Greek lyric was polymorphous, thanks to the service of song in occasions public (praise, lament, prayer) and private (love and friendship, the symposium). The lyric tradition thus kept Horace linked to a realistic world in which men and women fall in love, enjoy a drink together

[1] Here and in the commentary poems within the first book are referred to by their number, and where needed line number.
[2] For the so-called canon of lyric poets see Pfeiffer 1968: 182–3. For a handy overview of Horace's exploitation of the canonical singers see G. Burzacchini, art. 'melica' in *EO* 1 68–76.

(*Carm.* 20),[3] need consoling for the loss of loved ones (*Carm.* 24), pray to the gods (*Carm.* 21, 30, and 31), or are moved either to celebrate congenial divinities in hymns (*Carm.* 10, 21) or to secure the favour of a potentially dangerous one (*Carm.* 35). Such situations are common, but lyric treatment invited greater refinement than the satires; in the satires, for instance, men have dinner together, in the lyrics they meet for symposia (*Carm.* 20 and 27).[4] Fantasy too is liberated and refined by the lyric: in the fourth ode, Horace envisages a springtime in which Venus dances beneath the moon with her retinue of Nymphs and Graces, engaging figures who had not appeared in Latin poetry before Horace. Satire could not rise above a farting Priapus (*S.* 1.8.46–7).

Even where satire shared themes with lyric, such as the charms of the country-side or sex, the lyric treatment will appeal more to the imagination or fancy. This is achieved for instance by the introduction of the religious or divine element, which was excluded from the realistic genres of satire or invective.[5] In *Carm.* 17 Horace does not hesitate to claim that his country estate is under the direct protection of Faunus, a figure who would have no place in an account of the farm in the satires. Moreover, the girl he welcomes into this protected landscape, Tyndaris, is a musician, whereas in satire Horace's girlfriends of choice are hardly so congenial and attractive (cf. *S.* 1.2.123–4 and 5.82–5). Love could be explored in lyric more sympathetically and more variously (albeit idiosyncratically).[6]

But the appropriation of lyric, if it was to prove relevant, presented the poet with particular challenges: Horace had to remodel the Alcaean tradition for Roman conditions.[7] These conditions were fundamentally different from those of the smaller, simpler, and poorer world of the Greek. Horace's world was altogether grander. His readers were masters of a vast territorial empire, and one of his addressees, Iccius, is off to conquer Arabia (poem 29). The Romans' private life was altogether more luxurious, and so it is impossible to imagine Alcaeus listing anything comparable to the *grands crus* which we find in poem 20. Contemporary political conditions at Rome were far more momentous than anything Alcaeus had been involved in. Granted he had been active in the political life of his own community (cf. *Lesbio ciui* 32.5), his historical activity looks like little more than turf-wars when compared to the recent civil conflicts of the Romans. Thus Horace

---

[3] Murray 1993 is fundamental on Horace's adroit adaptation of symposiastic song to Roman social practices.

[4] N–H 1970: 20 observe with reference to the extravagance of the second ode that Horace 'allows himself a licence in an ode that would have been impossible in a prosaic epistle'.

[5] See Krasser 1995: 13.

[6] The old battle over the 'Pyrrha' ode highlights Horace's bewildering 'take' on erotics: see Quinn 1963 = Rudd 1972: 103–21 and West 1967: 99–107.

[7] This issue is discussed in more detail by N–H 1970: xii: 'the differences between the two poets are in fact more illuminating than the resemblances' and Hubbard 1973: 9–15; similarly, Wilkinson 1968: 11 speaks of the 'small amount of spirit' Horace derived from his models.

had to overhaul the lyric tradition comprehensively so that it could adequately accommodate Roman experience, or more specifically Horatian experience. For instance, by the time he started writing the odes Horace's engagement in civic life had settled firmly into the private sphere. To be sure, in the epodes he had tackled contemporary civic concerns, but his tone had had to suit the genre: it had to be critical, as in epodes 7 and 16, where he addressed his fellow Romans as criminals, *scelesti* (7.1), and was unrelievedly pessimistic. Lyric provided a different platform for Horace's engagement with the events of the day. For instance, Alcaeus composed a song to be sung at a symposium on the occasion of the death of his personal political enemy, the tyrant Myrsilus. Horace, acknowledging by means of a motto or quotation in the opening line of *Carm.* 37 a debt to this model, reconfigured his own celebrations after the defeat of Cleopatra as religious and national. Incidentally, he can praise her vanquisher, Octavian, but without tipping over into propaganda: Cleopatra's husband, the outlawed Marcus Antonius, is nowhere mentioned. More generally, Horace again combines the civic note with the religious in *Carm.* 21, following perhaps in the footsteps of Anacreon, *GL* II 348, who had described Artemis' attachment to the city of Magnesia. But concern for the collapsing state (*ruentis imperi rebus* 2.25–6) demanded a more specific remedy, through the help of a saviour, and here the poetry of civic concern embraces panegyric, a matter we may now turn to.

Sometime during the second century the Roman aristocracy began to cultivate literary men as heralds of their own renown, adopting a long-standing Greek cultural practice. Ennius (not at first a Roman citizen) was an early exponent of the panegyric of successful generals in epic (see Cicero, *Pro Archia* 22). Greek poets too provided what was wanted, as we see in the figure of Archias. Cicero makes it plain in defending that poet (*Pro Archia* 19–21) that he was much in demand for his laudatory epics (none of which has survived). Praise presented the Roman citizen however with something of a challenge. A Greek or other non-citizen could be expected to attach himself to a high-ranking member of the dominant power, but a freeborn Roman had to watch his step more carefully when praising a superior; it could seem overtly self-serving. Lyric tradition opened up several honourable paths to tread. As White 1993: 82–3 demonstrated, occasional verse cast flashes of publicity onto the individuals whose activities could be brought into the field of lyric discourse. He offers as an example *Carm.* 36, in which Horace celebrates on behalf of a superior friend, Lamia, the return to Rome of Numida. Nothing is said about Numida, and very little about Lamia, so the poem focuses upon the return as an occasion for a party, with incense, sacrifice, music, drink and crowns and girls: all central to the lyric tradition. Occasional verse enabled a poet to praise decently without loss of his own self-respect. A specific occasion also allowed praise by indirection, as we see in *Carm.* 31: the dedication of the temple of Apollo on the Palatine in October of 28 is heralded at the outset,[8]

---

[8] Here and in the commentary dates are 'before Christ', unless otherwise indicated.

and that obliquely praises the temple's dedicator, Octavian; but the poem (unlike Propertius 2.31, which celebrates the same occasion) veers off into a personal prayer for well-being. The public occasion is thus restricted to its impact on the private world of the poet, but the public figure is implicitly acknowledged. The Greek lyric tradition had heavily invested in praise, which had taken its grandest form in choral song. Appropriation of that more solemn voice (minus of course the song and the dance) allowed Horace to develop a poetry in praise of national figures. He took up that challenge in the twelfth ode (and, again by indirection, in the sixth). The manner of the choral lyric of Pindar, however, was something which at this stage he was reluctant to attempt (cf. *Epist.* 1.3.12–13), though he would make amends in his final book of odes.

Horace owes a great deal to the varied tradition of early Greek song, but his own lyric voice has characteristics which are much less prominent, perhaps even non-existent, in his models. One such characteristic is moralizing and the giving of advice.[9] Very little of this is found in Alcaeus; in one poem, *GL* I 38A, he recommends drinking while he and his companion are young, because death will put a stop to it. Such melancholy advice is rare in him,[10] but common in Horace, whose eye is often on the right use of time and on its passage (*Carm.* 4, 9, 11, 16, 23, 25).[11] The now aged Sappho also comes close to such a sentiment in her advice to young girls to dance,[12] but her focus on time's passage is less sharp. Anacreon once advises moderation in drinking, *GL* II 356B, a song that provides the germ of *Carm.* 27, but Horace advises moderation in many other situations (*Carm.* 18, 31, 33, 38). The admonitory or paraenetic tone of the lyrics is the reverse of the critical voice of the satires. In short, one way or another, Horace's persona is invariably that of the moralist. Throughout his works there is a steadiness and integrity of his observation of the workings of human nature, and from his work generally we derive the hope that life makes sense.[13] He gives his observations poetic shape so as to teach the masters of the world how to be its citizens as well.

Other individual traits of the poet's persona are irony and humour, neither prominent features of early Greek lyric.[14] David West has long emphasized Horace's humour (though sometimes he goes further than some can follow him, e.g. in his account in 1995: 167 of the 'largely humorous' *Carm.* 34). Humour is prominent in *Carm.* 22, which starts so seriously but soon descends to puns and oxymora; its successor, *Carm.* 23, is tenderly humorous. For a poem which

[9] Not his most attractive feature according to Hubbard 1973: 7–9.
[10] Fraenkel 1957: 178 noted that the advice given by Alcaeus was, so far as we can tell, different in character from Horace's.
[11] Barchiesi 2009: 325 provides a crisp résumé of how Horace exploits time; more generally cf. F. Citti, art. 'tempo' in *EO* II 645b–653a.
[12] West 2005 offers a completion of *GL* I 58.11–22, now to be seen as a complete poem.
[13] As Syndikus 2001: 6 puts it, song for Horace represents the spirit of a well-ordered life, in which disharmonies are resolved.
[14] For Alcaeus' lack of humour see MacLachlan 1997: 154.

is rightly seen as one of Horace's most original experiments, *Carm.* 27, 'one of the cleverest that Horace ever wrote' (N–H 1970: 311), he devised a technique of dramatic presentation unprecedented either in early Greek lyric or even in Hellenistic poems which narrate an ongoing series of events.[15] But what makes the poem is its ironical exaggerations and its bantering tone, a tone adopted too in *Carm.* 29, to Iccius, whose dreams of military glory are comically overdrawn and ironically deflated.

Summing up, with Feeney 1993: 43, we may say that 'the relationship which Horace establishes between himself and Greek lyric . . . develops his own vision of what being a lyric poet means in the place and time in which he found himself'. Horace would seem to have chosen to exploit 'civic' themes precisely because of their absence in Catullus.[16]

2. TECHNICAL CHALLENGES OF LYRIC

The challenge to the imagination was not all that Horace had to contend with by any means. He had also to naturalize the principal metres of Greek monodic song and to devise appropriate registers of language, a matter for which he had very little guidance since, as he claimed, he was the first to transplant lyric from Greece to Rome.[17]

A. Metre

In spite of Horace's claim to have naturalized Greek lyric metres, earlier Roman poets had experimented with the adaptation of some lyric verse lengths. In the early first century, for example, the bizarre Laevius had composed with an eye on Anacreon and Sappho,[18] but it is significant that his lyrics were not reckoned to have conformed to the 'lyric stamp' in accordance with the 'rule of the Greeks'.[19] Nonetheless he acclimatized the hendecasyllable (a line of eleven syllables), which was to become the lyric verse of choice for Catullus. Catullus experimented with other metres, some of which Horace too adopted, for instance the so-called glyconic, pherecratean, and greater asclepiad; twice he used the sapphic in its

---

[15] See Martin 2002.

[16] It is worth noting that Horace did not celebrate weddings, arguably because Catullus had done that so well before him. Perhaps for the same reason he did not express his own grief at the death of a friend or family member.

[17] Rossi 2009: 376–7 not only supports this claim, but demonstrates the degree to which even Horace's 'Greek colleagues' had lost the feel for lyric.

[18] For his work see Courtney 2003: 118–20, and the appreciation by Barchiesi 2009: 320–1.

[19] So Porphyrio on *Carm.* 3.1.2: *uidentur illa [lyrica] non Graecorum lege ad lyricum characterem exacta.* Possibly third-century AD Porphyrio wrote a commentary on Horace, which has survived, though not in its original form; for discussion of his commentary see N–H 1970: xlvii–xlix, S. Borzsák, art. 'esegesi antica' in *EO* III 17–23, Herzog–Schmidt 1997: 259–61, Diederich 1999, and Kalinina 2007.

stanzaic form. And that brings us to a capital difference between Horace and his predecessors: Laevius presumably, and Catullus manifestly, did not establish the four-line stanza as the cornerstone of lyric composition.[20] Most of their lyrics were composed in continuous lines of the same metre (κατὰ στίχον). Horace composed in this way too (the first ode, for example, repeats exactly the same verse length in thirty-six lines), but he broke decisively with the Roman lyric tradition and reverted to the stanzaic structure found above all in Alcaeus and Sappho.

Horace also imposed greater regularity on the metrical patterns of the individual lines which make up his lyric stanzas. His Aeolic models, Sappho and Alcaeus, had composed lyric to be sung, and so their metrical patterns still showed considerable flexibility.[21] Whilst it would be rash to exclude categorically the possibility that Horace intended his poems to be sung, it is clear that their publication in book form presupposes reading rather than singing.[22] The reading voice expresses metrical patterns better if they are more regular,[23] and regularity is what Horace imposed upon the Aeolic verse lengths.[24] For instance, he decided that the first two syllables, the so-called 'base' of asclepiads, glyconics and pherecrateans, should invariably be spondaic.[25] Catullus before him had been as liberal as the Greek lyric poets in admitting short syllables to the base, which could thus be either an iamb or a trochee (though he does show a preference for the spondee). Catullus had written two poems in the sapphic stanza, and like Sappho he had allowed the fourth syllable of the long lines to be either long or short, nor had he felt any need for a regularly recurrent place in the line where a word should end. Horace however made it a rule that the fourth syllable should be long and that a word should end after the fifth syllable (or just occasionally after the sixth).[26] He seems to have had no predecessor in the use of the alcaic stanza, but here too he imposed upon himself the sort of restrictions

---

[20] Catullus could of course compose in stanzas or strophes whenever he wanted, as can be seen in the hymn, *Carm.* 34, and the wedding song, *Carm.* 61, in which four glyconics are followed by a pherecratean, a structure found in Anacreon. But generally he preferred not to do so. It is also significant that the lyric poems of Callimachus were composed in continuous lines of the same verse length.

[21] See West 1992: 147–50.

[22] For the issue of singing the odes see G. Milanese, art. 'Musica' in *EO* II 921–5, Lyons 2006 and Rossi 2009. The *Carmen saeculare* was surely at least chanted.

[23] The point is stressed by Rossi 2009: 369: 'reading valorizes all the more the virtuosity of the caesurae (however monotonous)'.

[24] In fact, regularization started well before Horace, as West 1992: 148 notes for the treatment of the 'base' even by Sappho and Alcaeus. The tightening-up process continued when these metrical schemes were adopted by later Greek poets (not that there were many successors). Horace builds on a tradition of growing strictness. We see a similar movement in the stricter Roman adaptation of the dactylic hexameter, and in the restriction of the last word in the elegiac pentameter to two syllables.

[25] See Raven 1965: 141 and Wilkinson 1968: 10–11.

[26] For this tightening up see Raven 1965: 144 and N–H 1970: xliv.

already noted, but not found in his Greek model:[27] Alcaeus treated the fifth syllable of the first three lines as *anceps*, but Horace made it invariably long, and he insisted that a word generally end after the fifth syllable in the first two lines. These adjustments give Horace's alcaic stanzas a much more weighty effect than that of the original, especially in the third line.[28] The regular position in the lines of word-endings also helped to produce clearly defined blocks of words, which facilitated their artful placement, a feature which again is appreciated more by reading than by singing. It will be discussed more fully below.

We may now look in more detail at the metrical schemes of the odes in the first book.[29] We begin with those constructed out of the asclepiad and its briefer partners, the glyconic and the pherecratean. The asclepiad consists of the 'base' (two long syllables) followed by two choriambs, rounded off by two more syllables (one short, one *anceps*); there is always word-end (marked thus: |) after the first choriamb. The scheme is represented thus:

$$- - - \cup \cup - \mid - \cup \cup - \cup \times$$

An extra choriamb can be added to produce the so-called 'greater' asclepiad, thus:

$$- - - \cup \cup - \mid - \cup \cup - \mid - \cup \cup - \cup \times$$

A choriamb is removed from the asclepiad to produce the glyconic, thus:

$$- - - \cup \cup - \cup \times$$

And finally to produce the pherecratean, the penultimate short syllable is removed from the glyconic, thus:

$$- - - \cup \cup - \times$$

Metrical schemes based on the asclepiadic lines have been numbered from first to fifth, but without consistency. Here the numbers assigned by Klingner, and adopted by N–H and West, are followed. The numbers of the poems composed in these systems are given in brackets.

First asclepiad: a series of asclepiad lines written κατὰ στίχον. (1)
Second asclepiad: three asclepiads followed by a glyconic. (6, 15, 24, 33)
Third asclepiad: two asclepiads followed by a pherecratean and a glyconic. (5, 14, 21, 23)

---

[27] For these see Raven 1965: 145–7, and the fuller analysis in N–H 1970: xl–xliii.
[28] See Page 1895: xxvii with n., and Wilkinson 1966: 110–11; West 1995: 128 helpfully illustrates the effect of the difference of weight between the third and fourth lines in *Carm.* 27, and N–H 1970: xli–xliii illustrate the favoured patterns of word length in the third line.
[29] Important discussion of details of Horace's treatment of these metres will be found in N–H 1970: xxxviii–xliv and by M. Rosellini, art. 'metri lirici' in *EO* II 912–19.

Fourth asclepiad: a glyconic and an asclepiad form distichs (it is not necessarily the case that the distichs should be doubled to form stanzas). (3, 13, 19, 36)
Fifth asclepiad: a series of 'greater' asclepiad lines written κατὰ στίχον. (11, 18)

The alcaic stanza is composed of four lines.[30] The first two have eleven syllables (hendecasyllables), with word-end normally after the fifth; the third has nine syllables (enneasyllable) and the fourth ten (decasyllable). The scheme is represented thus:

$$\times - \cup - - \mid - \cup \cup - \cup \times$$
$$\times - \cup - - \mid - \cup \cup - \cup \times$$
$$\times - \cup - - - \cup - \times$$
$$- \cup \cup - \cup \cup - \cup - \times$$

The sapphic stanza is also composed of four lines. The first three have eleven syllables (hendecasyllables), with word-end normally after the fifth; the fourth line has five syllables, and is called the adonius. The scheme is represented thus:

$$- \cup - - - \mid \cup \cup - \cup - \times$$
$$- \cup - - - \mid \cup \cup - \cup - \times$$
$$- \cup - - - \mid \cup \cup - \cup - \times$$
$$- \cup \cup - \times$$

One poem, the eighth, is composed in a related metre, called the 'greater' sapphic. This consists of distichs, the first line of which is an aristophaneus, and the second a Sapphic hendecasyllable to which a further choriamb has been added. The scheme is represented thus:

$$- \cup \cup - \cup - -$$
$$- \cup - - - \mid \cup \cup - \mid - \cup \cup - \cup - -$$

Finally three poems in the first book are composed in what metricians call 'epodic' metres. The metre of the fourth ode consists of distichs, a greater archilochian followed by an iambic trimeter catalectic (i.e., one syllable in the final metron has been suppressed). The greater archilochian is composed of two metrically different cola, a dactylic tetrameter and an ithyphallic; resolutions may be found in the first three dactyls, and there must be word-end after the fourth one. The iambic trimeter has a normal caesura after the fifth syllable. The metrical scheme is represented thus:

$$- \underset{\smile\smile}{} - \underset{\smile\smile}{} - \underset{\smile\smile}{} - \cup \cup \mid - \cup - \cup - -$$
$$\underset{\smile}{} - \cup - - \mid - \cup - \cup - -$$

---

[30] Strictly speaking the original alcaic and sapphic stanzas consisted of three lines; the four-line layout is owed to Alexandrian editorial practice (Rossi 2009: 375, n.64).

The metre of the seventh and twenty-eighth odes is the same: a dactylic hexameter is followed by a dactylic tetrameter, and the scheme is represented thus:

$$- \smile\smile - \smile\smile - \smile\smile - \smile\smile - \smile\smile - \times$$
$$- \smile\smile - \smile\smile - \smile\smile - \times$$

B. Linguistic register and style

A further, more complex task which Horace faced in his creation of Latin lyric was forging a lyric style, or rather styles.[31] Looking back to his Greek models, we find in Anacreon a refined elegance that is the polar opposite of the sublime intricacies of Pindar; Alcaeus, Horace's chief model, might be said on the other hand to have no clear style at all.[32] Yet all were in the 'canon', and all might be laid under contribution for the development of Latin lyric (cf. for Anacreon *Carm.* 23, and for Pindar *Carm.* 12). So unlike his Greek models, who could stick to a fairly uniform and individual manner of their own devising, Horace had to become something of a chameleon, adopting different styles for different lyric situations. His success was duly recognized by Quintilian, a teacher of rhetoric in the late first-century AD, when he said (*Institutio oratoria* 10.1.96) that Horace was 'occasionally elevated' (*insurgit aliquando*), and that he was 'full of agreeable charm' (*plenus est iucunditatis et gratiae*).

If once again we glance briefly at his Latin predecessors, we will have a better idea of how he faced up to the challenge of producing his varied lyric styles. Laevius, if the excerpts from his lyrics that are all we have to go on are not eccentric, was addicted to unusual word-forms, especially compound words,[33] but he also used urbane colloquialisms, like *bellus* (20), and diminutives. These linguistic features are still prominent in Catullus' styles too, though with a difference.[34] Catullus furthermore allowed a colloquial word-form, *mi* for *mihi*, in one of his sapphic odes (51.1, 7). Horace set his face against all such things. Compound words, for instance, are few and formed in more restricted ways; diminutives are severely limited; and word-forms that were more at home in

[31] See the careful account of F. Muecke, art. 'Lo stile lirico oraziano' in *EO* II 775–83. N–H 1970: xxii offer a paragraph on the issue.

[32] For Alcaeus' amateur writing see Campbell 1924: 198 and Bowra 1961: 173–5; for the neat, urbane style of Anacreon see Bowra 1961: 296–7 and MacLachlan 1997: 202–3, who stresses his gracefulness.

[33] See the résumé in Courtney 2003: 118.

[34] Simpson 1879: 182–5 provides a handy list of 'familiar' expressions and at 185–6 a list of diminutives. Ross 1969: 19–22 discusses Catullus' compound adjectives, and at 159 he notes their difference from Laevius'; at 110–11 he discusses *bellus* in the poet's urbane style, and at 158–9 the diminutives (where again he notes their difference from Laevius'). Jocelyn 1999 however further refines upon Ross's distinctions, and insists that Catullus' 'lyric' styles are highly artificial, and do not reflect the ordinary conversation of the élite as much as is sometimes supposed.

the spoken language are generally banned from the patently 'textual' poems. In short, the style is in general further removed than that of his predecessors from the spoken language, and given greater formality. It needs however to be added that some features of his diction are not fairly described as 'prosaic'. Words like *condicio* or *delecto*, for instance, are more properly described as 'neutral', since they were available for use in a wide range of genres, even the most elevated (tragedy, history). Perhaps what needs to be borne in mind is that an ode is generally speaking framed as an address by the persona of the poet to an individual within his own society; much of the language normally used by the élite in familiar conversation ought to be entirely at home in lyric.[35]

In contradistinction to the restrictions placed upon the sorts of words that might be allowed into lyric, the door was opened to a range of words and syntagms which marked the poems off from even the most formal Latin prose. Such features as archaism (the revival of old words), coinage, metaphor, poetic diction (the use of a lexicon peculiar to poetry), and grecism (both lexical in the borrowing of Greek words, and syntactical in the creation of Latin constructions based upon a Greek model) all contributed to the literariness of the style.[36] It should be borne in mind however that many of these devices are something more than ornaments. The aim of a special poetic syntax for instance was to produce a dense and economical style, often by dispensing with words or constructions, normal in prose, that clog the expression, e.g., prepositions or subordinate clauses. Especially prominent is the extended use made of the infinitive and of the genitive case with adjectives (again, a glance at the Index will establish this point). A peculiar virtue of the 'figure' grecism is that the lexicon was as a rule standard Latin, but the resulting construction was novel, as we see at 15.18 *celerem sequi* 'swift to pursue/in pursuit'.

C. Word order and placement

More artificial than the language of lyric is the placement of the words in the sentence and in the stanza. Wilkinson 1966: 218–19 noted that Catullus had only just begun to show the way to more elaborate word placement in his own stanzaic lyrics (the hymn to Diana, 34, and the first epithalamium, 61). It was left to Horace to exploit the possibilities of artistic arrangement to the fullest, and there are numerous studies of his achievement, among which Naylor 1922 must take pride of place.[37] Three factors were to be taken into account by the poet: metrical exigency must have played some part in the position a word might

---

[35] It is worth remembering that even in epic everyday words, like *sane*, or word-forms, like *mi*, will be found in the speeches of the characters.

[36] The Index should be consulted for these features.

[37] See Smith 1894: lxi–lxviii, Wilkinson 1968: 146–7 and 1966: 218–20, Collinge 1961: 1–35, Nisbet 1999 = 2009: 378–400, Talbot 2007–8.

occupy in a given metre, but aesthetic pattern and semantic emphasis were the chief objects (Wilkinson 1966: 219, n. *).

Aesthetic pattern was a feature peculiar to Roman poetry. The so-called 'golden' line of the dactylic hexameter, for instance, is hardly exploited by Greek poets; we find examples of the basic pattern (two epithets + a verb + the two nouns with which the epithets agree) even in Horace's lyrics.[38] Thanks to the flexibility of an inflected language, Horace can produce 'iconic' or 'representative' patterns of words, illustrated in the note to 5.1, which picture what they describe. Artful patterns were particularly facilitated by the introduction of a regular word-end in aeolic lines after the fifth syllable. Marouzeau 1946: 319 drew attention to the common placement of an epithet at that point in agreement with the last word of the line, thus: *piscium et* summa *genus haesit* ulmo (2.9, sapphic) and *uelox* amoenum *saepe* Lucretilem (17.1, alcaic). Likewise in asclepiads, there may be an epithet ending as usual with the sixth syllable, in agreement with a final noun, thus: *hunc si* mobilium *turba* Quiritium (1.7). The aesthetic function of the word-end in the alcaic has been amply illustrated by Talbot 2007–8.

Semantic emphasis was achieved primarily by word placement within the line, taken as a unit, beginnings and endings being the marked positions. Line-beginnings are exploited at 7.28–9 so that *certus* and *ambiguus* are highlighted. As an instance of the force of line-ends, Marouzeau 1949a: 214 drew attention to the neat placement of three epithets, *aestuosus, inhospitalis,* and *fabulosus,* at the end of successive lines in 22.5–7, thus enhancing the exotic character of the places named. When Horace wanted to discourage unruly behaviour at a symposium he placed the deterrent words *barbarus* and *impius* at the end of their lines (27.2 and 6) to point his disapprobation. Clustering of words can underscore their significance. At 22.9, for example, the explanatory anecdote is crisply, but teasingly, introduced with three simple words: *me silua lupus,* all of which will be developed in the sequel. The opposite sort of placement, terminal, is found in the much admired 9.21–2, where the descriptors come first and the sense is only solved at the end of the phrase by the three nouns *puella, risus,* and *angulus.* Juxtaposition (for which the Index should be consulted) is another way of emphasizing the force of words, especially if there is contrast, as for instance at 6.9 *tenues grandia* or 9.17 *uirenti canities.* Horace was himself later to enunciate an important principle of juxtaposition, when in the *Ars Poetica* 46–8 he said that 'clever combination' (*callida iunctura*) makes a well-known word new. Wilkinson 1968: 126 explained that for the Roman this included the innovation of the metaphorical use of words hitherto taken in only the strict sense. As an example we might point to 22.8 *lambit Hydaspes.* Roman poets had already used *lambo* metaphorically of licking flames, but Horace seems to be the first to extend the image to the water of a river gently lapping against its banks.

---

[38] See the Index, s.v. 'word order' and 2.11–12n.

3. THE ARCHITECTURE OF THE ODE[39]

Since Richard Heinze's indispensable essay on the defining characteristics of the Horatian ode is now readily available to anglophone readers,[40] focus may here be directed upon an equally fundamental issue, the construction of the poem. Tyrrell 1895: 192–3 in his iconoclastic way threw out a challenge in declaring that 'no reader of the Odes, however careless, can have failed to notice the extraordinary difficulty of discovering in them anything like a connected train of thought'. That challenge has been met by many careful readers since, e.g., Tracy 1951, Cordray 1956, Collinge 1961, Commager 1962: 58–88, Cupaiuolo 1967: 52–62, Quinn 1980 (who equips each ode with an account of its structure in an introductory note), and works cited below. Indeed the challenge was actually anticipated by Mitscherlich 1800, whose work Tyrrell presumably did not know.[41] One fact is established by all such investigations into structure: Horace's poetic architecture is highly varied, and equally variously described and analysed. Indeed, the reader must be flexible in offering analyses of structure, for as Tarrant 1995: 35–6 fair-mindedly cautioned, diverse descriptions of any poem's structure can co-exist, and a relativist will be loath to declare alternative interpretations invalid.

Before proceeding to a description of the strategies Horace favoured for the construction of his odes, it is worth noting that here too he imposed something of a burden upon himself as an artist that had not existed for most of his Greek models. So far as we can tell early Greek lyric poems were generally short. Of course, we have very few complete poems, but the consensus is that the dimensions lay between eight and thirty-two lines; Anacreon's songs seem to have been very short.[42] Given that these poems were designed for performance at a symposium or some such gathering where others were expected to sing as well, brevity was a courtesy. But Horace composed to be read, so there was no external restraint upon the scale of his composition. The first three odes therefore, all possibly longer than was normal for Greek lyrics, show something of Horace's ambition to build in large dimensions. Such scale however produced problems in the management of the ideas and transitions which the poet had to resolve aesthetically. His models provided no guidance.

---

[39] The discussion of this issue is of course wide-ranging: see F. Serpa, art. 'struttura' in *EO* II 750–2, esp. for its bibliography; N–H 1970: xxiii.

[40] Heinze 2009 in Lowrie 2009a: 11–32.

[41] Mitscherlich 1800: v: 'in eo potissimum mihi elaborandum intellexi, ut . . . universum cuiusque carminis habitum et incessum expedirem, dispositionis artem enodarem'. His analyses remain attractive, and remind us that it was not just within living memory that Horace started to be read intelligently.

[42] So Kirkwood 1974: 60, and 176 for Anacreon. But Professor E. L. Bowie notes that Alcaeus, *GL* I 298, reached at least forty-eight lines.

A. *Linear progression*

The most straightforward manner of proceeding was unilinear (so Brink 1971a: 450–1),[43] whereby the thought moves forward in a connected series of statements, images, and propositions. A neat example is ode 18 (cf. Campbell 1924: 227): Horace advises Varus to plant vines (1–2), and then provides him with reasons to do so (3–6). Wine-drinking is a blessing, but since Horace is aware that it can be taken to excess, he warns, in a general way, against substance-abuse, providing examples (7–11). Lyric being subjective, he has something to say about himself: he will not meddle inappropriately with a god (11–13), and he prays to be free of the bad effects of excess (13–16). Ode 19 is equally linear in its layout: Horace declares that he is unexpectedly back in love (1–8), and that its effect is overpowering (9–12); he bids his slaves prepare a propitiatory sacrifice to Venus (13–16). The famous Cleopatra ode, 37, is more elaborate, but essentially linear in movement. Horace tells his companions to prepare a celebration; the self-contained initial stanza is characteristic (Wilkinson 1966: 208). He then explains why good cheer was previously inappropriate: Rome was menaced by an enemy, but (*sed* 12) she has now been driven back to her homeland, where she has shown surprising mettle by committing suicide. The whole poem is one great period (Wilkinson 1966: 210).

The grand twelfth ode is equally linear in its construction (Brink 1971a: 451–2 provides an analysis). Horace asks in the opening lines what man or hero or god he should sing of. The poem then works its way through various candidates in reverse order: gods (13–24), heroes (25–32), men (33–48). It closes with a prayer to Jupiter (49–60), the first divinity Horace had hymned, in which the focus is also on concern for the last mortal alluded to, Augustus Caesar.

But it is also possible for there to be some sort of return to the starting point. We see this in the very first poem, which begins with an address to Maecenas and then proceeds in a linear fashion (thanks to the priamel and its cap) until the initial address is as it were completed by the appeal to Maecenas in the last two lines.

B. *Situation and response*

A large number of the odes begin by positing a situation, the speaker's response to which forms the body of the poem. The movement of the response may or may not pick up the initial situation.

i. There may be a linear movement away from the initial situation, which is thus entirely forgotten as the poem develops; Commager 1962: 315 defined this structure as 'centrifugal' and Brink 1971a: 453 as 'open-ended'. Many odes are

---

[43] Brink revised his position on the structure of the first ode in the Addenda of vol. 3, p. 596. This is another useful reminder, that such analyses can prove hard to confine to one category.

constructed so that the movement is from a concrete situation or reflection to advice or more generalized reflections, from the ostensible to the real subject (Syndikus 1995: 27). This construction is seen in the second and third odes. The first three stanzas of the second poem describe a prodigious flood; the next three deplore the danger posed to Rome, and the wickedness that prompted this expression of divine disapproval. At the mid-point of the poem, Horace asks what is to be done, where is help to be sought (25–30). The poem ends with suggested solutions to the problem: various divinities are canvassed as potential saviours.

The third poem begins with a prayer for the safe voyage to Greece of Virgil (a particular situation), then at line 9 Horace launches into a more general diatribe against the transgressive daring of mankind, which merits divine punishment (see Syndikus 1995: 27 and Schmidt 2002: 306–7). The ninth ode is similar, though it focuses more tightly on the addressee: the opening description of wintry weather segues into advice suitable to the character of the young addressee from line 9; Horace himself stays out of the picture. Finally, the situation and response of the thirteenth ode unfold in linear fashion: Lydia is making the poet jealous, so he warns her against the young thug she has set her heart on, and he concludes with a paean to untroubled constancy.

It is also worth noting that the linear movement away from the initial situation allows the poet to change the mood of the poem (Campbell 1924: 224), the movement often being from gloomy to cheerful. Syndikus 1995: 20–1 finds this movement in the second, ninth (for which cf. again Campbell 1924: 224–5), and thirteenth odes (for which cf. yet again Campbell 1924: 227); he identifies a similar movement in the twenty-fourth ode, from the distress of grief to the resigned acceptance of the inevitable.[44]

The reverse direction is also possible: a general reflection or proposition is enunciated at the outset, and Horace then moves to personal application or considerations, a manner of proceeding found in the tightly integrated seventeenth ode. The poem opens with descriptive statements about the poet's estate, which suggest divine protection of the landscape. Once the addressee's name, Tyndaris, has been introduced into this descriptive opening, Horace begins to focus on himself, as poet, and on her, as singer, so that it becomes clear that the poem is effectively an invitation to the woman to join the poet in this special place. The poem then seems to move away to another theme, the girl's jealous boyfriend, but he in fact provides the foil, as Campbell 1924: 227 saw, to the protected landscape and the gentle poet. There is thus again a contrast of mood between the opening (the restful atmosphere of the country estate) and the close (rowdy parties of Rome) (Wilkinson 1966: 209). The progression is here linear, but the poem forms a complex unity (see Brink 1971a: 461–2 for a sound analysis).

---

[44] The analysis of the *Epist.* 1.16 by Mayer 1994: 36–9 may be compared for the gradual change of tone by the end of the poem.

ii. Alternatively there may be some sort of return to the initial situation in a circular movement. Clearly articulated examples of this are provided by odes 22 and 31. In the twenty-second ode Horace postulates the immunity from harm of the pure in heart and illustrates it by an (imaginary?) incident in his own experience. By evoking in the final stanzas the geographical extravagance of the opening, he offers what Tarrant 1995: 36–7 calls a 'da capo' structure, but with a goofily warped conclusion: Horace will be safe wherever he is not because of his moral virtue, but because he sings of love.

In *Carm.* 31 Horace wonders at the outset what he should ask of the god Apollo (1–3); by means of an embedded priamel he rejects a range of possible options (3–15), and stresses the simplicity of his own way of life (15–16). This prepares for the substance of the prayer to Apollo with which the poem closes (Syndikus 1995: 22). Ode 16 is similar: a young woman is assured that she has the means to put an end to Horace's invectives. The body of the ode (5–21) is a meditation upon the power and destructiveness of anger. At line 22 he reverts to the particular situation of the opening, the call to restraint (Syndikus 1995: 28–9, Tarrant 1995: 37).

iii. A number of odes move by contrast, what might be called thesis–antithesis. The opening situation of the eleventh ode, for instance, is an injunction to Leuconoe to give up prying into the future. The rest of the poem, the response to astrology, offers advice on what she should be doing instead, both as regards the future (*ut melius, quidquid erit, pati* 3) and, more pressingly, the present (*carpe diem* 8). The twentieth ode too opens with a situation: Maecenas is offered a cheap wine of Horace's own in the first two stanzas; in the third, by way of contrasting response, he is reminded of the grand vintages he can command, but Horace cannot. The thirty-third ode, addressed to Albius, who has been dumped by Glycera, has a similar pattern. The situation is that Albius is much upset by this turn of events, but Horace responds with a dose of realism when he points out how mismatches are a constant feature of love affairs, including his own (a subjective close). The final ode, 38, is constructed along similar lines: in the first four lines Horace tells his slave-boy what he does not want in the way of preparations for a drinking session, the implication being that the boy is keen to provide these fripperies. In the second stanza Horace indicates instead what simple arrangements suit them both in the circumstances. A less obvious variant of this contrasting mode is seen in ode 29: the situation is that Iccius is preparing to go on campaign in the East, with a view to securing the prizes of victory (1–10). By way of response, the long final question (10–16) expresses Horace's surprise and dismay: Iccius has reprehensibly given up philosophy for the pursuit of wealth.

C. *The parts of the Ode*

In addition to analysis of the ode as a complex whole, attention has been directed to two parts or sections of the poems, the middles and the endings.

i. Middles

Both Moritz 1968 and Williams 1968: 122–3 drew attention to some functions assigned to the centre of a number of the poems, and they described the varied roles that the centre (or the beginning of an ode's second half) might perform. At 9.13, for instance, Horace delivers his moral message, 'quid sit futurum cras fuge quaerere' (Moritz 1968: 117), the burden of the poem. The central point also serves as a hinge, connecting the two halves of an ode: Moritz 1968: 117 cited as examples 2.25–30, 17.13–14, and 25.9–12; Williams 1968: 123 independently cited 2.25–8 as marking the transition between the descriptive opening and the concluding prayer, and 17.13–16 as connecting the hymnic and sympotic halves of the ode. The centre also serves as the privileged place for the addressee's name at 24.10 and 26.8, or for that of an important person, such as Caesar at 6.11 and 37.16 (Moritz 1968: 119 and 122). Harrison 2004: 82 also recognized the middle (or roughly the middle) of the poem as a formal or thematic turning point, a fulcrum or pivot where an important notion might be enunciated in a gnome (practical maxim), as for example at 3.21, or where the poem might move in a new direction, as at 7.15–19, where sympotic advice is given to Plancus.

ii. Endings

Rutherford 1997: 61 rightly felt that as a student of Greek lyric, Horace could be expected to make use of some of the closural devices he found in his models. His hunch can be supported by reference to the useful work of Esser 1976 (cf. its critical résumé by Nisbet 1979), who drew attention to some common strategies for ending odes: prayers (2, 31), or the mention of crowns (1 and 38), myths (7 and 8), or moralizing maxims (13.17–20, 24.19–20) are all to be found. Commonest of all is the final focus upon the poet, Horace (or the speaker or the persona) himself; odes 1, 5, 6, 14, 16, 18, 20, 31, 33, and 38 all end in this way (what Esser called the 'Ich-Schluß', personal ending). The detailed account of the range of lyric endings by Schrijvers 2009 (originally 1973) also repays study, since his categories sometimes anticipate, sometimes supplement Esser.

It was noted above in discussion of the overall structure of the ode that the tone of the ending might be the polar opposite from its beginning, so that there is a more or less gradual evolution of feeling as the poem unfolds. The second ode illustrates this: we move from fears prompted by foul weather, a sign of heaven's anger with mankind, to a confident prediction of Caesar's vengeance on Rome's enemies. Syndikus 1995: 17–20, esp. n. 4, with bibliography, noted the contrast between light-weight personal endings and the more serious content of the body of the poem in, e.g., 6 and 19, or in the case of 38 a serene ending of the book after the grandeur of 37.

4. THE ARRANGEMENT OF THE BOOK

As if Horace had not shouldered enough of a burden in mastering unusual metres, devising satisfactory linguistic registers, and excogitating situations along with a management appropriate to lyric poetry, he added yet more to his artistic load by organizing, to some extent, the miscellany of poems into a book (and then the book itself had to be co-ordinated, again to some extent, with the two which were to follow it). In so doing he was following the lead of Catullus, Virgil, and indeed his own earlier published works.[45] Arrangement had thus become an established part of the aesthetic of the poetry book in the late Republic. It needs however to be remembered that the poems were composed over an unknown period of years, and that some, perhaps most, may well have circulated as individual pieces before collection into their books. The point of this warning is that each poem is an autonomous artistic entity which does not require knowledge of its neighbours for an understanding of itself: there is no meta-text.[46] We may now turn to a brief account of what would probably be common ground among those who have addressed the issue of arrangement.[47]

Only the first poem appears to be composed for its place in the collection, since it is addressed to Maecenas (as are the first poems of the first book of *Sermones*, the *Epodes*, and the first book of *Epistulae*), and it announces the poet's fresh initiative as a lyricist (rather as the first of the *Epistulae* announces his retirement from poetic composition). Two factors are widely agreed to have influenced the choice of the poems to follow. First, Horace decided to continue at the outset with honouring significant addressees. The second poem ends with the encomium of (and quasi-address to) Octavian, the third (addressed to a ship) is occasioned by Virgil's journey to Athens, and the fourth is addressed to the man who was suffect consul in the year in which the collection is generally reckoned to have been published, 23. The second factor in the choice of poems to succeed the first seems to have been metrical variety: the first nine odes are all in different metres, and only with the tenth is a metrical scheme repeated (the sapphic). Thereafter, clear signs of organization are much more patchy.

---

[45] For discussion of the organization of the book(s) of Catullus see Gaisser 2009: 22–44, for Virgil's *Eclogues* see Clausen 1994: xx–xxvi, and for Horace's *Epodes* see Watson 2003: 20–30 and Lyne 2007: 314–40. Watson fairly notes that such analyses have often been unsatisfactory or have yielded mixed results.

[46] This point is also made by Barchiesi 2009: 329–30: 'poems are regularly autonomous'.

[47] Discussion of this issue was initiated some time ago: see Sellar 1891: 142 and Wickham 1896: 26–30. Typically, discussion becomes longer and more sophisticated over time: see Collinge 1961: 36–55, Mutschler 1974, and Minarini 1989, who reviews discussions to date of the arrangement of the poems in the collection. Helpful are the articles by A. Barchiesi, 'proemi e chiuse' in *EO* II 727–32 and 'sequenze' *EO* II 741–2.

Lowrie 2009b identifies a cluster of poems, from the twelfth to the eighteenth, which allude successively to a range of lyric predecessors: Pindar, Sappho, Alcaeus, Bacchylides, Stesichorus, Anacreon, and Alcaeus. Rather as with the metrical virtuosity displayed in the opening sequence, we would here find the poet demonstrating the varied scope of his lyric themes: encomium, erotic passion, civic concern, mythological narrative, to name but a few. Thematic links may have prompted the juxtaposition of some poems, e.g. Bacchus and Venus in 18 and 19, or divine power (more specifically Fortuna) in 34 and 35. Griffin 1994: 77, among others, recognizes a trio of sympotic odes, 36, 37, and 38, to close the first book. They are moreover carefully differentiated one from another: ode 36 celebrates a private occasion shared with friends, whilst 37 seems to be more public (certainly the occasion is one for public rejoicing), and an anonymous group is addressed (each refers to Salian priests as well). Ode 38 is private and solitary, in marked contrast especially with the grand poem which precedes it. Formal presentation, on the other hand, may have suggested that the two dramatic monologues, 27 and 28, be juxtaposed. Looser configurations (i.e., not juxtaposition) may also be detected: Quinn 1980: 162 observed that the arrangement of the first six love poems in the collection – 5, 8, 11, 13, 17, and 19 – is obviously planned, without being chronological.[48]

Number may be significant. Since there are thirty-eight poems in the first book, or nineteen in two halves, the twentieth, which begins the second half, might seem to deserve some prominence: indeed, it is dedicated to Maecenas, so he receives poems that initiate both halves of the book. The middle poem of the first half, the tenth, as we saw, is the first to repeat a metre, but it is a hymn, possibly based on one by Alcaeus, and certainly dedicated to a divinity to whom Horace seems to have had a particular devotion. On the other hand, the middle poem of the second half, the twenty-ninth to Iccius, does not seem to be especially significant (charming though it is).

The influence of the Alexandrian edition of the poems of Alcaeus has also been canvassed as a factor in the arrangement of the poems in the first book by Lyne 2007: 293–313 and Cucchiarelli 2006: 73–113. Lyne, however, wryly notes (2007: 306) that such discussions are always more persuasive and more interesting to the writer than to the reader.

In case the foregoing discussion strike some readers as undernourished it is worth drawing attention to the withering dismissal of the inventiveness of some analysts by Nisbet 1995: 423–4, who later scouted the whole notion of sequential reading (see N–R 2004: xxviii). But even those who fancy such elaborate structures might be prepared to agree with Williams 2004: vi that a commentary is not the best place to argue the case for such a reading.

---

[48] But Quinn seems to feel that *Carm.* 16 is not a love poem; it might however be included in the list, since it ends with an appeal for affection.

5. DATES OF COMPOSITION AND PUBLICATION

The odes in the first book, with the exception of the very first, may well have been the earliest to be written; certain metrical considerations strongly suggest this.[49] But it is impossible to determine when exactly Horace began to write the lyrics that would make up the book. Some believe he began composing in the thirties, whilst he was working on the epodes. The first poem to have a clear historical reference is the thirty-seventh, which celebrates the death of Cleopatra in 30 (but the poem need not have been written in that year). *Carm.* 6 alludes to the production of Varius' tragedy *Thyestes* in 29 (it was part of Octavian's triumphal celebrations), and *Carm.* 31 refers to the dedication of the temple of Apollo on the Palatine in 28; the Arabian expedition of Aelius Gallus, the occasion of *Carm.* 29, probably took place in 26–25, which was also roughly the time when king Tiridates took refuge with Augustus in Spain (26.5n.). In the year 25 Marcellus married Julia, an event which seems to have prompted the combination of the families' names at 12.45–8. Finally, the suffect consulship of Sestius in the latter half of 23 accounts for the prominent placement of the fourth poem, which is dedicated to him, and indeed 23 is generally taken to be the year of publication of the first three books of odes. That they were published together is inferred from *Epist.* 1.13, in which Horace consigns *uolumina* (2) of lyric poems (*carmina* 17) to Vinnius for delivery to Augustus. Hutchinson 2008: 140 (originally in *CQ* 52 (2002) 517–37) however has argued for publication of the first book all on its own before 24, but his case has not convinced N–R 2004: xix-xx or Nisbet 2007: 13–14. Since Horace had probably known the dedicatee for some time, the ode need not have been written to honour his suffect consulship in 23, but its prominent position is hard to explain otherwise.

6. TRANSMISSION OF THE TEXT AND THE TRADITION OF COMMENT

Until the invention of printing in the fifteenth century Horace's poems were transmitted in manuscripts. The manuscripts on which modern critical editions of his texts are based are all mediaeval, the oldest dating to the ninth century. They have been divided into two groups, each of which is reckoned to depend upon a different ancient codex. This bipartite division is however somewhat untidy, because a MS which belongs largely to one camp may nonetheless exhibit a reading characteristic of the other camp. The reason for this is that manuscripts do not always present a straightforward text; variant readings are sometimes transmitted as well, in the margin or between lines, and subsequent copyists may decide to accept the variant rather than the main reading. Thus the tradition

---

[49] See N–H 1970: xxviii and xliii, and R. G. M. Nisbet, art. 'La vita' in *EO* I 220–1.

becomes contaminated. Additionally, errors of transcription were made, and those too could be transmitted. The text of the odes may however have been better protected from error thanks to its metrical and linguistic difficulty; it seems that the lyrics were less read in the Middle Ages than the hexameter poems (which anyway offered more satisfactory moralizing). It is therefore reassuring to be told by Tarrant 1986: 185 that 'the text of Horace has been relatively well preserved: ancient variants are not excessively numerous, interpolated verses are rare'. In fact, there are no interpolated verses in the first book of odes. Ancient variants, on the other hand, for example *crines* and *cultus* at 15.20, can be difficult to decide between. There are also cases where no transmitted reading is satisfactory, and a correction or emendation by a modern scholar (i.e., from the Renaissance to the present day) is accepted into the text; examples will be found at 2.39, 7.27, 12.46, 23.5–6, 25.20, and 31.18.

7. INTERPRETATION: A NOTE

The aim of the series in which this commentary has the honour to appear is to provide readers with literary guidance to classical texts. The commentary is a necessary foundation for an informed appreciation of the text as a work of literature, and indeed it can itself give the reader considerable help with wider issues of interpretation. But there must also be an interpretative overview of the text, which the commentary itself usually cannot provide. So each poem has been equipped with an end-note, which is designed to draw attention to available interpretations and to provide some measure of critical assessment of their value. But there is an obvious difficulty in doing anything like justice to thirty-eight very different works of poetic art and their interpretations in reasonable compass. It has only to be remembered that West 1995 devoted a whole book to interpretation of just the first book of odes, and that Syndikus 2001 is the third edition of a main-stream reading of the odes; half of the first volume, over one hundred and fifty pages, is devoted to book one. Yet neither West nor Syndikus attempted to canvass all shades of opinion. So abundant is the scholarly writing on these poems that there can be no question of doing so (and to be frank some readings are unrewarding). And so a policy for citation was needed for this commentary. Elaine Fantham, herself a practised commentator in this series, provided such a policy when she took a firm stand on this difficult matter: 'commentators have a responsibility to privilege literal or traditional interpretation' (2002: 408). Thus the fourteenth ode, to name probably the most debated in this book, is taken to be a political allegory, though alternatives (excluding football matches) are noted. At any rate it is hoped that no important reading has been overlooked.

Q. HORATI FLACCI
CARMINVM LIBER PRIMVS

QUINTI HORATI FLACCI
CARMINVM LIBER PRIMVS

I

Maecenas atauis edite regibus,
o et praesidium et dulce decus meum:
sunt quos curriculo puluerem Olympicum
collegisse iuuat, metaque feruidis
euitata rotis palmaque nobilis   5
terrarum dominos euehit ad deos;
hunc, si mobilium turba Quiritium
certat tergeminis tollere honoribus,
illum, si proprio condidit horreo
quidquid de Libycis uerritur areis.   10
gaudentem patrios findere sarculo
agros Attalicis condicionibus
numquam demoueas, ut trabe Cypria
Myrtoum pauidus nauta secet mare.
luctantem Icariis fluctibus Africum   15
mercator metuens otium et oppidi
laudat rura sui; mox reficit rates
quassas indocilis pauperiem pati.
est qui nec ueteris pocula Massici
nec partem solido demere de die   20
spernit, nunc uiridi membra sub arbuto
stratus, nunc ad aquae lene caput sacrae.
multos castra iuuant et lituo tubae
permixtus sonitus bellaque matribus
detestata. manet sub Ioue frigido   25
uenator tenerae coniugis immemor,
seu uisa est catulis cerua fidelibus
seu rupit teretes Marsus aper plagas.
me doctarum hederae praemia frontium
dis miscent superis, me gelidum nemus   30
Nympharumque leues cum Satyris chori
secernunt populo, si neque tibias
Euterpe cohibet nec Polyhymnia
Lesboum refugit tendere barbiton.

quodsi me lyricis uatibus inseres,   35
  sublimi feriam sidera uertice.

2

Iam satis terris niuis atque dirae
grandinis misit Pater et rubente
dextera sacras iaculatus arces
    terruit Vrbem,

terruit gentes, graue ne rediret   5
saeculum Pyrrhae noua monstra questae,
omne cum Proteus pecus egit altos
    uisere montes,

piscium et summa genus haesit ulmo,
nota quae sedes fuerat columbis,   10
et superiecto pauidae natarunt
    aequore dammae.

uidimus flauum Tiberim retortis
litore Etrusco uiolenter undis
ire deiectum monumenta regis   15
    templaque Vestae,

Iliae dum se nimium querenti
iactat ultorem, uagus et sinistra
labitur ripa Ioue non probante u-
    xorius amnis.   20

audiet ciues acuisse ferrum,
quo graues Persae melius perirent,
audiet pugnas uitio parentum
    rara iuuentus.

quem uocet diuum populus ruentis   25
imperi rebus? prece qua fatigent
uirgines sanctae minus audientem
    carmina Vestam?

cui dabit partes scelus expiandi
Iuppiter? tandem uenias precamur   30
nube candentes umeros amictus
    augur Apollo;

siue tu mauis, Erycina ridens,
quam Iocus circum uolat et Cupido;
siue neglectum genus et nepotes   35
    respicis auctor,

heu nimis longo satiate ludo,
quem iuuat clamor galeaeque leues
acer et Marsi peditis cruentum
    uultus in hostem;   40

siue mutata iuuenem figura
ales in terris imitaris almae
filius Maiae, patiens uocari
    Caesaris ultor,

serus in caelum redeas diuque   45
laetus intersis populo Quirini,
neue te nostris uitiis iniquum
    ocior aura

tollat; hic magnos potius triumphos,
hic ames dici pater atque princeps,   50
neu sinas Medos equitare inultos
    te duce, Caesar.

3

Sic te diua potens Cypri,
    sic fratres Helenae, lucida sidera,
uentorumque regat pater
    obstrictis aliis praeter Iapyga,
nauis, quae tibi creditum   5
    debes Vergilium; finibus Atticis
reddas incolumem precor
    et serues animae dimidium meae.

illi robur et aes triplex
   circa pectus erat, qui fragilem truci   10
commisit pelago ratem
   primus, nec timuit praecipitem Africum
decertantem Aquilonibus
   nec tristes Hyadas nec rabiem Noti,
quo non arbiter Hadriae   15
   maior, tollere seu ponere uult freta.
quem mortis timuit gradum
   qui siccis oculis monstra natantia,
qui uidit mare turbidum et
   infames scopulos Acroceraunia?   20
nequiquam deus abscidit
   prudens Oceano dissociabili
terras, si tamen impiae
   non tangenda rates transiliunt uada.
audax omnia perpeti   25
   gens humana ruit per uetitum nefas.
audax Iapeti genus
   ignem fraude mala gentibus intulit;
post ignem aetheria domo
   subductum macies et noua febrium   30
terris incubuit cohors
   semotique prius tarda Necessitas
leti corripuit gradum.
   expertus uacuum Daedalus aera
pennis non homini datis;   35
   perrupit Acheronta Herculeus labor.
nil mortalibus ardui est:
   caelum ipsum petimus stultitia neque
per nostrum patimur scelus
   iracunda Iouem ponere fulmina.   40

4

Soluitur acris hiems grata uice ueris et Fauoni
   trahuntque siccas machinae carinas
ac neque iam stabulis gaudet pecus aut arator igni
   nec prata canis albicant pruinis.

iam Cytherea choros ducit Venus imminente luna   5
   iunctaeque Nymphis Gratiae decentes
alterno terram quatiunt pede, dum graues Cyclopum
   Volcanus ardens uisit officinas.
nunc decet aut uiridi nitidum caput impedire myrto
   aut flore terrae quem ferunt solutae,   10
nunc et in umbrosis Fauno decet immolare lucis,
   seu poscat agna siue malit haedo.
pallida Mors aequo pulsat pede pauperum tabernas
   regumque turres. o beate Sesti,
uitae summa breuis spem nos uetat incohare longam;   15
   iam te premet nox fabulaeque Manes
et domus exilis Plutonia; quo simul mearis,
   nec regna uini sortiere talis
nec tenerum Lycidan mirabere, quo calet iuuentus
   nunc omnis et mox uirgines tepebunt.   20

5

Quis multa gracilis te puer in rosa
perfusus liquidis urget odoribus
   grato, Pyrrha, sub antro?
    cui flauam religas comam

simplex munditiis? heu quotiens fidem   5
mutatosque deos flebit et aspera
   nigris aequora uentis
    emirabitur insolens

qui nunc te fruitur credulus aurea,
qui semper uacuam, semper amabilem   10
   sperat, nescius aurae
    fallacis. miseri, quibus

intemptata nites! me tabula sacer
uotiua paries indicat uuida
   suspendisse potenti   15
    uestimenta maris deo.

6

Scriberis Vario fortis et hostium
uictor Maeonii carminis alite,
qua rem cumque ferox nauibus aut equis
    miles te duce gesserit.

nos, Agrippa, neque haec dicere nec grauem   5
Pelidae stomachum cedere nescii
nec cursus duplicis per mare Vlixei
    nec saeuam Pelopis domum

conamur, tenues grandia, dum pudor
imbellisque lyrae Musa potens uetat   10
laudes egregii Caesaris et tuas
    culpa deterere ingeni.

quis Martem tunica tectum adamantina
digne scripserit aut puluere Troico
nigrum Merionen aut ope Palladis   15
    Tydiden superis parem?

nos conuiuia, nos proelia uirginum
sectis in iuuenes unguibus acrium
cantamus uacui, siue quid urimur,
    non praeter solitum leues.   20

7

Laudabunt alii claram Rhodon aut Mytilenen
    aut Epheson bimarisue Corinthi
moenia uel Baccho Thebas uel Apolline Delphos
    insignes aut Thessala Tempe;
sunt quibus unum opus est intactae Palladis urbem   5
    carmine perpetuo celebrare et
undique decerptam fronti praeponere oliuam;
    plurimus in Iunonis honorem
aptum dicet equis Argos ditesque Mycenas:
    me nec tam patiens Lacedaemon   10
nec tam Larisae percussit campus opimae

quam domus Albuneae resonantis
et praeceps Anio ac Tiburni lucus et uda
   mobilibus pomaria riuis.
albus ut obscuro deterget nubila caelo   15
   saepe Notus neque parturit imbres
perpetuos, sic tu sapiens finire memento
   tristitiam uitaeque labores
molli, Plance, mero, seu te fulgentia signis
   castra tenent seu densa tenebit   20
Tiburis umbra tui. Teucer Salamina patremque
   cum fugeret, tamen uda Lyaeo
tempora populea fertur uinxisse corona
   sic tristes affatus amicos:
'quo nos cumque feret melior fortuna parente,   25
   ibimus, o socii comitesque.
nil desperandum Teucro duce et auspice Phoebo.
   certus enim promisit Apollo
ambiguam tellure noua Salamina futuram.
   o fortes peioraque passi   30
mecum saepe uiri, nunc uino pellite curas;
   cras ingens iterabimus aequor.'

                          8

Lydia, dic, per omnes
   te deos oro, Sybarin cur properes amando
perdere, cur apricum
   oderit Campum patiens pulueris atque solis,
cur neque militares   5
   inter aequales equitet, Gallica nec lupatis
temperet ora frenis?
   cur timet flauum Tiberim tangere? cur oliuum
sanguine uiperino
   cautius uitat neque iam liuida gestat armis   10
bracchia saepe disco,
   saepe trans finem iaculo nobilis expedito?
quid latet, ut marinae
   filium dicunt Thetidis sub lacrimosa Troiae
funera, ne uirilis   15
   cultus in caedem et Lycias proriperet cateruas?

9

Vides ut alta stet niue candidum
Soracte nec iam sustineant onus
    siluae laborantes geluque
    flumina constiterint acuto?

dissolue frigus ligna super foco   5
large reponens atque benignius
    deprome quadrimum Sabina,
    o Thaliarche, merum diota.

permitte diuis cetera, qui simul
strauere uentos aequore feruido   10
    deproeliantes, nec cupressi
    nec ueteres agitantur orni.

quid sit futurum cras fuge quaerere et
quem Fors dierum cumque dabit lucro
    appone nec dulces amores   15
    sperne puer neque tu choreas,

donec uirenti canities abest
morosa. nunc et Campus et areae
    lenesque sub noctem susurri
    composita repetantur hora,   20

nunc et latentis proditor intimo
gratus puellae risus ab angulo
    pignusque dereptum lacertis
    aut digito male pertinaci.

10

Mercuri, facunde nepos Atlantis,
qui feros cultus hominum recentum
    uoce formasti catus et decorae
    more palaestrae,

te canam, magni Iouis et deorum   5
nuntium curuaeque lyrae parentem,

callidum quidquid placuit iocoso
    condere furto.

te, boues olim nisi reddidisses
per dolum amotas, puerum minaci   10
uoce dum terret, uiduus pharetra
    risit Apollo.

quin et Atridas duce te superbos
Ilio diues Priamus relicto
Thessalosque ignes et iniqua Troiae   15
    castra fefellit.

tu pias laetis animas reponis
sedibus uirgaque leuem coerces
aurea turbam, superis deorum
    gratus et imis.   20

11

Tu ne quaesieris, scire nefas, quem mihi, quem tibi
finem di dederint, Leuconoe, nec Babylonios
temptaris numeros. ut melius, quidquid erit, pati!
seu plures hiemes seu tribuit Iuppiter ultimam,
quae nunc oppositis debilitat pumicibus mare   5
Tyrrhenum, sapias, uina liques et spatio breui
spem longam reseces. dum loquimur, fugerit inuida
aetas: carpe diem, quam minimum credula postero.

12

Quem uirum aut heroa lyra uel acri
tibia sumes celebrare, Clio,
quem deum? cuius recinet iocosa
    nomen imago

aut in umbrosis Heliconis oris   5
aut super Pindo gelidoue in Haemo,
unde uocalem temere insecutae
    Orphea siluae,

arte materna rapidos morantem
fluminum lapsus celeresque uentos,   10
blandum et auritas fidibus canoris
    ducere quercus?

quid prius dicam solitis Parentis
laudibus, qui res hominum ac deorum,
qui mare ac terras uariisque mundum   15
    temperat horis?

unde nil maius generatur ipso
nec uiget quicquam simile aut secundum.
proximos illi tamen occupabit
    Pallas honores   20

proeliis audax. neque te silebo,
Liber, et saeuis inimica Virgo
beluis, nec te, metuende certa
    Phoebe sagitta.

dicam et Alciden puerosque Ledae,   25
hunc equis, illum superare pugnis
nobilem; quorum simul alba nautis
    stella refulsit,

defluit saxis agitatus umor,
concidunt uenti fugiuntque nubes   30
et minax, quod sic uoluere, ponto
    unda recumbit.

Romulum post hos prius an quietum
Pompili regnum memorem an superbos
Tarquini fasces, dubito, an Catonis   35
    nobile letum.

Regulum et Scauros animaeque magnae
prodigum Paulum superante Poeno
gratus insigni referam camena
    Fabriciumque.   40

hunc et incomptis Curium capillis
utilem bello tulit et Camillum
saeua Paupertas et auitus apto
    cum lare fundus.

crescit occulto uelut arbor aeuo   45
fama Marcellis; micat inter omnes
Iulium sidus uelut inter ignes
    luna minores.

gentis humanae pater atque custos,
orte Saturno, tibi cura magni   50
Caesaris fatis data: tu secundo
    Caesare regnes.

ille seu Parthos Latio imminentes
egerit iusto domitos triumpho
siue subiectos Orientis orae   55
    Seras et Indos,

te minor laetum reget aequus orbem:
tu graui curru quaties Olympum,
tu parum castis inimica mittes
    fulmina lucis.   60

13

Cum tu, Lydia, Telephi
    ceruicem roseam, cerea Telephi
laudas bracchia, uae, meum
    feruens difficili bile tumet iecur.
tunc nec mens mihi nec color   5
    certa sede manet, umor et in genas
furtim labitur, arguens
    quam lentis penitus macerer ignibus.
uror, seu tibi candidos
    turparunt umeros immodicae mero   10
rixae siue puer furens
    impressit memorem dente labris notam.
non, si me satis audias,

speres perpetuum dulcia barbare
laedentem oscula, quae Venus   15
  quinta parte sui nectaris imbuit.
    felices ter et amplius
      quos irrupta tenet copula nec malis
diuulsus querimoniis
  suprema citius soluet amor die.   20

14

O nauis, referent in mare te noui
fluctus. o quid agis? fortiter occupa
  portum! nonne uides ut
    nudum remigio latus

et malus celeri saucius Africo   5
antemnaeque gemant ac sine funibus
  uix durare carinae
    possint imperiosius

aequor? non tibi sunt integra lintea,
non di, quos iterum pressa uoces malo.   10
  quamuis Pontica pinus,
    siluae filia nobilis,

iactes et genus et nomen inutile,
nil pictis timidus nauita puppibus
  fidit. tu, nisi uentis   15
    debes ludibrium, caue.

nuper sollicitum quae mihi taedium,
nunc desiderium curaque non leuis,
  interfusa nitentes
    uites aequora Cycladas.   20

15

Pastor cum traheret per freta nauibus
Idaeis Helenen perfidus hospitam,
ingrato celeres obruit otio
  uentos ut caneret fera

Nereus fata. 'mala ducis aui domum   5
quam multo repetet Graecia milite
coniurata tuas rumpere nuptias
   et regnum Priami uetus.

heu heu, quantus equis, quantus adest uiris
sudor, quanta moues funera Dardanae   10
genti! iam galeam Pallas et aegida
   currusque et rabiem parat.

nequiquam Veneris praesidio ferox
pectes caesariem grataque feminis
imbelli cithara carmina diuides;   15
   nequiquam thalamo graues

hastas et calami spicula Cnosii
uitabis strepitumque et celerem sequi
Aiacem: tamen heu serus adulteros
   cultus puluere collines.   20

non Laertiaden, exitium tuae
genti, non Pylium Nestora respicis?
urgent impauidi te Salaminius
   Teucer, te Sthenelus sciens

pugnae, siue opus est imperitare equis,   25
non auriga piger. Merionen quoque
nosces. ecce furit te reperire atrox
   Tydides, melior patre,

quem tu, ceruus uti uallis in altera
uisum parte lupum graminis immemor,   30
sublimi fugies mollis anhelitu,
   non hoc pollicitus tuae.

iracunda diem proferet Ilio
matronisque Phrygum classis Achillei;
post certas hiemes uret Achaicus   35
   ignis Iliacas domos.'

16

O matre pulchra filia pulchrior,
quem criminosis cumque uoles modum
    pones iambis, siue flamma
        siue mari libet Hadriano.

non Dindymene, non adytis quatit   5
mentem sacerdotum incola Pythiis,
    non Liber aeque, non acuta
        sic geminant Corybantes aera,

tristes ut irae, quas neque Noricus
deterret ensis nec mare naufragum   10
    nec saeuus ignis nec tremendo
        Iuppiter ipse ruens tumultu.

fertur Prometheus addere principi
limo coactus particulam undique
    desectam et insani leonis   15
        uim stomacho apposuisse nostro.

irae Thyesten exitio graui
strauere et altis urbibus ultimae
    stetere causae cur perirent
        funditus imprimeretque muris   20

hostile aratrum exercitus insolens.
compesce mentem: me quoque pectoris
    temptauit in dulci iuuenta
        feruor et in celeres iambos

misit furentem. nunc ego mitibus   25
mutare quaero tristia, dum mihi
    fias recantatis amica
        opprobriis animumque reddas.

17

Velox amoenum saepe Lucretilem
mutat Lycaeo Faunus et igneam

defendit aestatem capellis
usque meis pluuiosque uentos.

impune tutum per nemus arbutos 5
quaerunt latentes et thyma deuiae
olentis uxores mariti
nec uirides metuunt colubras

nec Martiales haediliae lupos,
utcumque dulci, Tyndari, fistula 10
ualles et Vsticae cubantis
leuia personuere saxa.

di me tuentur, dis pietas mea
et musa cordi est. hic tibi copia
manabit ad plenum benigno 15
ruris honorum opulenta cornu;

hic in reducta ualle Caniculae
uitabis aestus et fide Teia
dices laborantes in uno
Penelopen uitreamque Circen; 20

hic innocentis pocula Lesbii
duces sub umbra nec Semeleius
cum Marte confundet Thyoneus
proelia nec metues proteruum

suspecta Cyrum, ne male dispari 25
incontinentes iniciat manus
et scindat haerentem coronam
crinibus immeritamque uestem.

18

Nullam, Vare, sacra uite prius seueris arborem
circa mite solum Tiburis et moenia Catili;
siccis omnia nam dura deus proposuit neque
mordaces aliter diffugiunt sollicitudines.
quis post uina grauem militiam aut pauperiem crepat? 5
quis non te potius, Bacche pater, teque, decens Venus?

ac ne quis modici transiliat munera Liberi,
Centaurea monet cum Lapithis rixa super mero
debellata, monet Sithoniis non leuis Euhius,
cum fas atque nefas exiguo fine libidinum   10
discernunt auidi. non ego te, candide Bassareu,
inuitum quatiam nec uariis obsita frondibus
sub diuum rapiam. saeua tene cum Berecyntio
cornu tympana, quae subsequitur caecus Amor sui
et tollens uacuum plus nimio Gloria uerticem   15
arcanique Fides prodiga, perlucidior uitro.

19

Mater saeua Cupidinum
   Thebanaeque iubet me Semelae puer
et lasciua Licentia
   finitis animum reddere amoribus.

urit me Glycerae nitor   5
   splendentis Pario marmore purius,
urit grata proteruitas
   et uultus nimium lubricus aspici.

in me tota ruens Venus
   Cyprum deseruit nec patitur Scythas   10
aut uersis animosum equis
   Parthum dicere nec quae nihil attinent.

hic uiuum mihi caespitem, hic
   uerbenas, pueri, ponite turaque
bimi cum patera meri: 15
   mactata ueniet lenior hostia.

20

Vile potabis modicis Sabinum
cantharis, Graeca quod ego ipse testa
conditum leui, datus in theatro
   cum tibi plausus,

clare, Maecenas, eques, ut paterni   5
fluminis ripae simul et iocosa
redderet laudes tibi Vaticani
    montis imago.

Caecubum et prelo domitam Caleno
tu bibes uuam: mea nec Falernae   10
temperant uites neque Formiani
    pocula colles.

21

Dianam tenerae dicite uirgines,
intonsum pueri dicite Cynthium
    Latonamque supremo
      dilectam penitus Ioui.

uos laetam fluuiis et nemorum coma   5
quaecumque aut gelido prominet Algido
    nigris aut Erymanthi
      siluis aut uiridis Gragi;

uos Tempe totidem tollite laudibus
natalemque, mares, Delon Apollinis   10
    insignemque pharetra
      fraternaque umerum lyra.

hic bellum lacrimosum, hic miseram famem
pestemque a populo et principe Caesare in
    Persas atque Britannos   15
      uestra motus aget prece.

22

Integer uitae scelerisque purus
non eget Mauris iaculis neque arcu
nec uenenatis grauida sagittis,
    Fusce, pharetra,

siue per Syrtes iter aestuosas   5
siue facturus per inhospitalem

Caucasum uel quae loca fabulosus
lambit Hydaspes.

namque me silua lupus in Sabina,
dum meam canto Lalagen et ultra   10
terminum curis uagor expeditis,
    fugit inermem;

quale portentum neque militaris
Daunias latis alit aesculetis
nec Iubae tellus generat, leonum   15
    arida nutrix.

pone me pigris ubi nulla campis
arbor aestiua recreatur aura,
quod latus mundi nebulae malusque
    Iuppiter urget;   20

pone sub curru nimium propinqui
solis in terra domibus negata:
dulce ridentem Lalagen amabo,
    dulce loquentem.

23

Vitas inuleo me similis, Chloe,
quaerenti pauidam montibus auiis
    matrem non sine uano
      aurarum et siluae metu.

nam seu mobilibus uepris inhorruit   5
ad uentum foliis seu uirides rubum
    dimouere lacertae,
      et corde et genibus tremit.

atqui non ego te tigris ut aspera
Gaetulusue leo frangere persequor: 10
    tandem desine matrem
      tempestiua sequi uiro.

24

Quis desiderio sit pudor aut modus
tam cari capitis? praecipe lugubres
cantus, Melpomene, cui liquidam pater
    uocem cum cithara dedit.

ergo Quintilium perpetuus sopor   5
urget: cui Pudor et Iustitiae soror
incorrupta Fides nudaque Veritas
    quando ullum inueniet parem?

multis ille bonis flebilis occidit,
nulli flebilior quam tibi, Vergili.   10
tu frustra pius, heu, non ita creditum
    poscis Quintilium deos.

quid si Threicio blandius Orpheo
auditam moderere arboribus fidem,
num uanae redeat sanguis imagini   15
    quam uirga semel horrida

non lenis precibus fata recludere
nigro compulerit Mercurius gregi?
durum: sed leuius fit patientia
    quidquid corrigere est nefas.   20

25

Parcius iunctas quatiunt fenestras
iactibus crebris iuuenes proterui
nec tibi somnos adimunt amatque
    ianua limen,

quae prius multum faciles mouebat   5
cardines. audis minus et minus iam:
'me tuo longas pereunte noctes,
    Lydia, dormis?'

inuicem moechos anus arrogantes
flebis in solo leuis angiportu,   10

Thracio bacchante magis sub inter-
   lunia uento,

cum tibi flagrans amor et libido,
quae solet matres furiare equorum,
saeuiet circa iecur ulcerosum   15
   non sine questu

laeta quod pubes hedera uirenti
gaudeat pulla magis atque myrto,
aridas frondes hiemis sodali
   dedicet Euro.   20

26

Musis amicus tristitiam et metus
tradam proteruis in mare Creticum
   portare uentis, quis sub Arcto
      rex gelidae metuatur orae,

quid Tiridaten terreat, unice   5
securus. o quae fontibus integris
   gaudes, apricos necte flores,
      necte meo Lamiae coronam,

Piplei dulcis. nil sine te mei
possunt honores: hunc fidibus nouis,   10
   hunc Lesbio sacrare plectro
      teque tuasque decet sorores.

27

Natis in usum laetitiae scyphis
pugnare Thracum est: tollite barbarum
   morem uerecundumque Bacchum
      sanguineis prohibete rixis.

uino et lucernis Medus acinaces   5
immane quantum discrepat: impium

lenite clamorem, sodales,
    et cubito remanete presso.

uultis seueri me quoque sumere
partem Falerni? dicat Opuntiae   10
    frater Megyllae, quo beatus
        uulnere, qua pereat sagitta.

cessat uoluntas? non alia bibam
mercede. quae te cumque domat Venus,
    non erubescendis adurit   15
        ignibus ingenuoque semper

amore peccas. quidquid habes, age,
depone tutis auribus. a miser,
    quanta laboras in Charybdi,
        digne puer meliore flamma!   20

quae saga, quis te soluere Thessalis
magus uenenis, quis poterit deus?
    uix illigatum te triformi
        Pegasus expediet Chimaera.

28

Te maris et terrae numeroque carentis harenae
    mensorem cohibent, Archyta,
pulueris exigui prope litus parua Matinum
    munera nec quicquam tibi prodest
aerias temptasse domos animoque rotundum   5
    percurrisse polum morituro.
occidit et Pelopis genitor, conuiua deorum,
    Tithonusque remotus in auras
et Iouis arcanis Minos admissus habentque
    Tartara Panthoiden iterum Orco   10
demissum, quamuis clipeo Troiana refixo
    tempora testatus nihil ultra
neruos atque cutem morti concesserat atrae,
    iudice te non sordidus auctor
naturae uerique. sed omnes una manet nox   15
    et calcanda semel uia leti.

dant alios Furiae toruo spectacula Marti,
   exitio est auidum mare nautis;
mixta senum ac iuuenum densentur funera, nullum
   saeua caput Proserpina fugit: 20
me quoque deuexi rabidus comes Orionis
   Illyricis Notus obruit undis.
at tu, nauta, uagae ne parce malignus harenae
   ossibus et capiti inhumato
particulam dare: sic quodcumque minabitur Eurus   25
   fluctibus Hesperiis Venusinae
plectantur siluae te sospite multaque merces
   unde potest tibi defluat aequo
ab Ioue Neptunoque sacri custode Tarenti.
   neglegis immeritis nocituram   30
postmodo te natis fraudem committere? fors et
   debita iura uicesque superbae
te maneant ipsum: precibus non linquar inultis
   teque piacula nulla resoluent.
quamquam festinas, non est mora longa; licebit   35
   iniecto ter puluere curras.

29

   Icci, beatis nunc Arabum inuides
   gazis et acrem militiam paras
      non ante deuictis Sabaeae
         regibus horribilique Medo

   nectis catenas? quae tibi uirginum   5
   sponso necato barbara seruiet,
      puer quis ex aula capillis
         ad cyathum statuetur unctis

   doctus sagittas tendere Sericas
   arcu paterno? quis neget arduis   10
      pronos relabi posse riuos
         montibus et Tiberim reuerti,

   cum tu coemptos undique nobilis
   libros Panaeti Socraticam et domum

mutare loricis Hiberis, 15
    pollicitus meliora, tendis?

30

O Venus, regina Cnidi Paphique,
sperne dilectam Cypron et uocantis
    ture te multo Glycerae decoram
      transfer in aedem.

feruidus tecum puer et solutis 5
Gratiae zonis properentque Nymphae
    et parum comis sine te Iuuentas
      Mercuriusque.

31

Quid dedicatum poscit Apollinem
uates? quid orat de patera nouum
    fundens liquorem? non opimae
      Sardiniae segetes feraces,

non aestuosae grata Calabriae 5
armenta, non aurum aut ebur Indicum,
    non rura quae Liris quieta
      mordet aqua taciturnus amnis.

premant Calena falce quibus dedit
fortuna uitem, diues et aureis 10
    mercator exsiccet culillis
      uina Syra reparata merce,

dis carus ipsis, quippe ter et quater
anno reuisens aequor Atlanticum
    impune. me pascunt oliuae, 15
      me cichorea leuesque maluae.

frui paratis et ualido mihi,
Latoe, dones et precor integra
    cum mente nec turpem senectam
      degere nec cithara carentem. 20

32

Poscimur: si quid uacui sub umbra
lusimus tecum quod et hunc in annum
uiuat et plures, age, dic Latinum,
    barbite, carmen,

Lesbio primum modulate ciui,   5
qui ferox bello tamen inter arma
siue iactatam religarat udo
    litore nauim,

Liberum et Musas Veneremque et illi
semper haerentem puerum canebat   10
et Lycum nigris oculis nigroque
    crine decorum.

o decus Phoebi et dapibus supremi
grata testudo Iouis, o laborum
dulce lenimen mihi cumque salue   15
    rite uocanti.

33

Albi, ne doleas plus nimio memor
immitis Glycerae neu miserabiles
decantes elegos, cur tibi iunior
    laesa praeniteat fide,

insignem tenui fronte Lycorida   5
Cyri torret amor, Cyrus in asperam
declinat Pholoen; sed prius Apulis
    iungentur capreae lupis

quam turpi Pholoe peccet adultero.
sic uisum Veneri, cui placet impares   10
formas atque animos sub iuga aenea
    saeuo mittere cum ioco.

ipsum me melior cum peteret Venus,
grata detinuit compede Myrtale

libertina, fretis acrior Hadriae 15
curuantis Calabros sinus.

34

Parcus deorum cultor et infrequens
insanientis dum sapientiae
consultus erro, nunc retrorsum
uela dare atque iterare cursus

cogor relictos: namque Diespiter, 5
igni corusco nubila diuidens
plerumque, per purum tonantes
egit equos uolucremque currum,

quo bruta tellus et uaga flumina,
quo Styx et inuisi horrida Taenari 10
sedes Atlanteusque finis
concutitur. ualet ima summis

mutare et insignem attenuat deus
obscura promens; hinc apicem rapax
Fortuna cum stridore acuto 15
sustulit, hic posuisse gaudet.

35

O diua, gratum quae regis Antium,
praesens uel imo tollere de gradu
mortale corpus uel superbos
uertere funeribus triumphos,

te pauper ambit sollicita prece 5
ruris colonus, te dominam aequoris
quicumque Bithyna lacessit
Carpathium pelagus carina;

te Dacus asper, te profugi Scythae,
urbesque gentesque et Latium ferox 10
regumque matres barbarorum et
purpurei metuunt tyranni,

iniurioso ne pede proruas
stantem columnam neu populus frequens
   ad arma, cessantes ad arma   15
      concitet imperiumque frangat;

te semper anteit saeua Necessitas,
clauos trabales et cuneos manu
   gestans aena, nec seuerus
      uncus abest liquidumque plumbum;   20

te Spes et albo rara Fides colit
uelata panno, nec comitem abnegat,
   utcumque mutata potentes
      ueste domos inimica linquis,

at uulgus infidum et meretrix retro   25
periura cedit, diffugiunt cadis
   cum faece siccatis amici,
      ferre iugum pariter dolosi:

serues iturum Caesarem in ultimos
orbis Britannos et iuuenum recens   30
   examen Eois timendum
      partibus Oceanoque rubro.

heu heu, cicatricum et sceleris pudet
fratrumque. quid nos dura refugimus
   aetas? quid intactum nefasti   35
      liquimus? unde manum iuuentus

metu deorum continuit? quibus
pepercit aris? o utinam noua
   incude diffingas retusum in
      Massagetas Arabasque ferrum!   40

36

Et ture et fidibus iuuat
   placare et uituli sanguine debito
custodes Numidae deos,
   qui nunc Hesperia sospes ab ultima

caris multa sodalibus, 5
  nulli plura tamen diuidit oscula
quam dulci Lamiae, memor
  actae non alio rege puertiae

mutataeque simul togae.
  Cressa ne careat pulchra dies nota 10
neu promptae modus amphorae
  neu morem in Salium sit requies pedum

neu multi Damalis meri
  Bassum Threicia uincat amystide
neu desint epulis rosae 15
  neu uiuax apium neu breue lilium.

omnes in Damalin putres
  deponent oculos nec Damalis nouo
diuelletur adultero
  lasciuis hederis ambitiosior. 20

37

Nunc est bibendum, nunc pede libero
pulsanda tellus, nunc Saliaribus
  ornare puluinar deorum
    tempus erat dapibus, sodales.

antehac nefas depromere Caecubum 5
cellis auitis, dum Capitolio
  regina dementes ruinas
    funus et imperio parabat

contaminato cum grege turpium
morbo uirorum, quidlibet impotens 10
  sperare fortunaque dulci
    ebria. sed minuit furorem

uix una sospes nauis ab ignibus
mentemque lymphatam Mareotico
  redegit in ueros timores 15
    Caesar ab Italia uolantem

remis adurgens, accipiter uelut
molles columbas aut leporem citus
   uenator in campis niualis
     Haemoniae, daret ut catenis   20

fatale monstrum. quae generosius
perire quaerens nec muliebriter
   expauit ensem nec latentes
     classe cita reparauit oras,

ausa et iacentem uisere regiam   25
uultu sereno, fortis et asperas
   tractare serpentes, ut atrum
     corpore combiberet uenenum,

deliberata morte ferocior,
saeuis Liburnis scilicet inuidens   30
   priuata deduci superbo
     non humilis mulier triumpho.

38

Persicos odi, puer, apparatus,
displicent nexae philyra coronae;
   mitte sectari, rosa quo locorum
     sera moretur.

simplici myrto nihil allabores   5
sedulus curo: neque te ministrum
   dedecet myrtus neque me sub arta
     uite bibentem.

COMMENTARY

NB Fragments of Greek lyric poetry are cited by volume and fragment number in the five-volume Loeb Library edition of Campbell, thus *GL*; his fragment numbers tally with Lobel–Page. Fragments of Greek elegiac and iambic poetry are cited by fragment number in the two Loeb Library editions of Gerber, thus *GEP* and *GIP*; his fragment numbers tally with West. Dates are 'before Christ' unless otherwise indicated or obviously not.

I

Metre: continuous asclepiads (see Introduction 7). Kenney 1983: 15 speculates on the possible reasons for this choice of metre, chiefly that it had perhaps never been used before by a Roman poet (though the related 'greater' asclepiad, used in *Carm.* 11 and 18, had appeared in Catullus). H. thus announced the novelty of his technique.

1–2 The ode opens with an address to Maecenas, and its closing couplet is also directed to him (ring-composition). H. thus in effect dedicates the whole three-book collection to him. This dedication is reinforced by a yet grander instance of ring-composition, for Maecenas is also the dedicatee of the penultimate poem in the collection, 3.29, H.'s greatest ode.

1 Maecenas: Gaius Maecenas (*OCD* 907–8) was one of Octavian's closest friends and advisers. His family originated in Arretium (mod. Arezzo), an Etruscan city. Without entering the senate or seeking magistracies, Maecenas wielded vast political influence. His considerable wealth, acquired from confiscated property, supported a luxurious life-style (cf. Seneca, *Epistulae* 114), generally downplayed by H. His lasting distinction is as a patron of the arts, chiefly poetry. Virgil, who dedicated the *Georgics* to him, introduced Horace to him in 38 (*S.* 1.6.54), and their subsequent friendship is charted in the first book of satires, the epodes, odes, and the first book of epistles. The degree of his influence upon the writers he befriended (these included as well Propertius and the tragic poet Varius) remains controversial: for discussion see Griffin 1984: 195, Gold 1987: 221–32, White 1993, and A. La Penna, art. 'Mecenate' in *EO* I 792–802.   **atauis edite regibus** 'descended from regal forefathers', but English cannot do justice to the remarkable Latin (which Virgil admired: see *Aen.* 7.474). The plural *ataui* (= *maiores*) is poetic (*OLD* 2). *editus* is a poetic synonym for *natus*, subsequently taken up in prose (*TLL* v 2.82.54); strictly speaking one is *editus* from one's mother, but the word is applied to either parent, or here remarkably to remoter ancestors (*TLL* v 2.84.31–2). *regibus* is an appositive noun treated attributively (= *regiis*) with *atauis*, poetic style (K–S I 232–3).

51

Maecenas deliberately remained an eques, so his poets proclaim the local distinction of his family, cf. 3.29.1 *Tyrrhena regum progenies* (the penultimate of the whole collection referred to above), and Prop. 3.9.1 *eques Etrusco de sanguine regum*. *rex* is equivalent to the Etruscan *lauchum*, Latinized as *lucumo*, the 'king' (or chief man) of the cities. Maecenas is reckoned on his mother's side to have been a Cilnius, another Arretine family, well connected in Etruria; in a familiar letter Augustus called him 'emerald of the Cilnii' (*Cilniorum smaragde*, reported by Macrobius, *Saturnalia* 2.4.12). It is now known from a sixteenth-century transcription of an Etruscan inscription that a Cilnius was indeed a *lucumo* (see Maggiani 1986: 176–7 and 187). The poets were not after all being extravagant (as claimed by N–H 1970: 4).

2 o et: the hiatus is regular after the interjection, cf. 35.38.   **praesidium . . . decus:** a common pairing, see *TLL* x 2.884.36–7; H. styles Pollio a *praesidium* at 2.1.13. *decus* is 'applied to a person who by his presence or in other ways confers distinction' (*OLD* 3), again of Maecenas at 2.17.4 *grande decus* and 3.16.20 *equitum decus*. *dulce* 'dear' (*OLD* 7), a colloquial term, exposes the personal affection, which is reinforced both by alliteration and by *meum*, that went with the social advantage H. gained from his friendship with Maecenas. 'To be known to be such a man's intimate, that was indeed worth boasting about', says Lendon 1997: 49, a claim confirmed by Cicero, *De amicitia* 70, where Laelius says that men who achieve pre-eminence elevate the status of their humble parents or less prominent friends.

3–34 The bulk of the ode now takes the form of a priamel, a focusing device consisting of two basic parts, the foil and the climax or cap. The foil enumerates or summarizes a range of options which then yield – with varying degrees of contrast or analogy – to a particular point of interest or importance, usually the writer's own, which caps the series. The priamel is found in early Greek poetry (Sappho and Pindar especially), and was considerably exploited by H.; it is also found in later poetry, for instance Shakespeare's Sonnet 91 'Some glory in their birth'. Here the foil consists of a catalogue of vocations or activities, presented in a pleasingly varied way: *sunt quos, hunc, illum, gaudentem, mercator, est qui, multos*. H. caps the foil with his own occupation (29–34), emphatically introduced with the anaphora of *me* (29, 30).

The list of vocations is not inert, rather it suggests different characters. The opening two, athlete (3–6) and politician (7–8), traditionally sought the highest honour (φιλοτιμία), whereas the owner of the granary (9–10) is a businessman whose aim is to acquire wealth (φιλοχρηματία). This trio clearly lives life in a conspicuous way, and the first two demonstrate success in their endeavours. The pair of the farmer (11–14) and the merchant (15–18) illustrate not so much a goal in life and its successful accomplishment, as the strength of a man's attachment to his occupation; they are moreover everyday types. The hedonist (19–22) returns us to an overall goal (φιληδονία), but not one out of the reach of an ordinary person.

The soldier (23–5) and the hunter (25–8) form a contrast with his self-indulgence, but keep within the everyday sphere.

3–6 H. draws his first candidate for supreme felicity from the Greek world, the charioteer successful at the chief of the panhellenic 'crown' games at Olympia. This choice hints at the mixing of Greek with Roman that will characterize the lyric poems.

3–4 sunt quos 'there are those whom . . .' = 'some' (*OLD sum* 6a).   **curriculo:** two interpretations are possible, either 'with his chariot' (*OLD* 5), or 'on the race-track'. The latter, however, might suggest the foot-race, whereas the former clearly points to the grandest competition, the four-horse chariot race.   **puluerem Olympicum | collegisse iuuat** 'it delights to raise a cloud of Olympic dust', cf. *S.* 1.4.31 *puluis collectus turbine.* The form of the adjective, *Olympicus*, is unusual, perhaps introduced into Latin by H.; the earlier form was *Olympius*, as at Plautus, *Stichus* 306 *ludos Olympios.* The simple infinitive (*collegisse*) as subject of *iuuat* is chiefly poetic, and frequent in H. (cf. 36.1–2, *TLL* VII 2.747.15–29). Its perfect tense, metrically handy, is also normal with an impersonal verb; in sense it is reckoned not to differ from the present, cf. *posuisse* 34.16n. and N–R on 3.18.15 *pepulisse.* The indicative *iuuat* instead of a consecutive subjunctive, which had become the norm in Caesar and Cicero in this sort of relative clause, retains the older, colloquial mood still found in some poets (H–S 558–9); cf. 19–21 *est qui . . . spernit*, 7.5.

4–5 meta . . . euitata = *euitatio metae*, a preferred Latin idiom, often identified as the *ab urbe condita* construction, explained at *NLS* §95: 'the noun together with the predicative participle forms an abstract noun-phrase wherein the leading idea is conveyed by the participle' (cf. Laughton 1964: 84–99, K–S I 766–8, H–S 393–4); in fact, the usage is wider, and an epithet can perform the same function as a participle (K–S I 770), cf. 3.29–30 *ignem . . . subductum*, 15.33–4 *iracunda . . . classis*, 36.9 *mutatae . . . togae*, 37.13 *sospes nauis.*
The racetrack at Rome (*circus*) was oblong in shape, and down its long axis ran a low stone wall (*spina*), at either end of which was a pier surmounted by three columns: this was the *meta*, turning-post, which the driver had to round with great care. See Humphrey 1986.

feruidis | . . . rotis: cf. Virg. *G.* 3.107 *uolat ui feruidus axis*; of course the wheels and axle of a racing chariot are literally hot.

5 palma: the earliest prize was a wreath of wild olive (κότινος). The palm was introduced in the Roman period (*RE* art. Phoinix, xx 401.17–26); it symbolized long-lasting fame (cf. Isidore, *Origines* 17.7.1 *est enim arbor insigne uictoriae . . . diuturnis uestita frondibus*, Ferber 2007: 148–50). For the notion cf. 4.2.17–18 *quos Elea domum reducit | palma caelestes.*

6 terrarum dominos: best taken as predicative with *euehit*: 'exalts (*OLD* 4b) them as lords of the earth', rather than with *deos*; the focus is on the new stature of the victor, not on the power of the gods, which anyway is not limited to the earth.   **ad deos:** the principle of ring-composition continues to operate at 30 *dis miscent superis*. 'Being conveyed to the gods/heaven/the stars' is a proverbial notion (Otto 1890: 62–3) for both a state of bliss and for the praise which secures it (so Nisbet on Cicero, *De domo sua* 75; cf. *Epist.* 1.17.34 *attingit solium Iouis et caelestia temptat*).

7–10 The construe of these lines has occasioned much debate, and emendation or varieties of punctuation have been proposed to put the apparent difficulty right, though such solutions have never secured wide editorial support. The problem is that, while both *hunc* 7 and *illum* 9 should be governed by *iuuat* 4, the intervening clause introduced by *metaque* 4 obscures the construction. This intervening clause can be taken as a parenthesis (as in Rudd's translation), though parenthetical clauses introduced by -*que* rarely disturb the syntax. For a possibly similar case cf. Manilius, *Astronomica* 4.551–2 *illum urbes et regna trement (nutuque regentur | unius) et caeli post terras iura manebunt*, with Housman's comment and addenda, and cf. H–S 473.

7–8 The identity of H.'s second candidate for felicity was uncertain even in antiquity. One scholiast, pseudo-Acro, reckoned he was drawn from Roman political life, the successful statesman who secured the important magistracies. This has long been the standard view (see further below). The other scholiast, Porphyrio, however, took him to be a popular individual, not necessarily a politician, greeted with applause in the theatre (see 20.3–4n.); N–H and Syndikus 2001: 28, n. 24, accept this interpretation. The difficulty with it is that the priamel as a whole lists occupations or at least life-styles, but the 'popular favourite' does not seem to qualify, nor is his popularity as enduring as that of the successful politician.

7 mobilium: voters are proverbially fickle (*OLD* 5, Otto 1890: 378), but they have so far agreed repeatedly to elect this man.   **Quiritium:** the word is chosen to designate the Roman people in their peacetime civic functions.

8 certat ... tollere: the scope of the complementary infinitive with verbs was much developed by the Augustans (see Wickham 1896: 406–7 for a list, and cf. *indocilis* 18n. for adjectives). It is found with *certo* from the time of Ennius (*TLL* III 896.51–74).   **tergeminis:** poetic diction. The word's meaning depends on how we understand *honoribus*. N–H take *honores* to be 'marks of esteem' (as at 28.10), specifically applause, and so *tergeminus* would mean 'thrice repeated, threefold'. *honores* is commonly taken however to mean 'public offices', the magistracies of the republic (so *OLD* 5, and Rudd), cf. *S.* 1.6.15–16 *populo, qui stultus honores | saepe dat indignis*, with specific reference to the three regular magistracies, quaestor (which admitted to the senate), praetor, and consul. Some believe that instead of quaestor the office of aedile is intended to be understood, but Sulla made the quaestorship obligatory, and the aedileship did not have to be held by patricians (see *OCD* art. *cursus honorum*). The case of *honoribus* could be either dative of goal (cf. *terris* 2.1n.) or instrumental ablative.

9 proprio . . . horreo: emphasis falls on *proprio*, which suggests the owners of the huge storehouses at Rome or Ostia, which were let for keeping the grain (among other commodities) needed to feed the metropolis. 'The granaries were privately owned and of great rental value . . . the most common pattern was for the merchant to hire space for his goods in a convenient warehouse' (Rickman 1980: 139–40). The Lollii (probably identical with or related to the dedicatees of 4.9 and *Epist.* 1.2 and 18) and Agrippa, the dedicatee of 1.6, owned important *horrea*; at 4.12.18 H. speaks of procuring a prestigious wine from the *horrea Sulpicia*. The usual interpretation, that H. had in mind a landowner on a grand scale, makes no essential difference between him and the farmer who follows.

10 Libycis . . . areis: the epithet provides colourful detail (cf. 13, 14, 15 below, and *passim*). H. may have in mind Cyrene and its fertile hinterland (see Rickman 1980: 108–12, especially 109), but *Libya* served as a general term for North Africa, the chief source of Rome's grain, cf. *S.* 2.3.87 *frumenti quantum metit Africa*. The *area* was a (usually) circular piece of ground carefully prepared for the threshing of the grain, which was beaten or otherwise abraded on its curved surface to release it from the straw and chaff. It was then tossed in the wind with shovels, so that the chaff was blown away (winnowing) and the remaining grain could be swept up (*uerritur*). For these tedious processes see the lucid account with illustrations by White 1970: 184–7.

11–14 A gliding transition moves us from the owner of a warehouse to the farmer.

11 gaudentem sets the tone: he rejoices in his work, and *patrios* explains why: the land belonged to his ancestors, cf. 12.43 *auitus* and *Epod.* 2.3 *paterna rura bobus exercet suis.* Not even an eastern kingdom will make him take up a different occupation, e.g., that of a trader. The construction with the infinitive, *findere*, is largely poetic syntax (8n., and cf. 34.16, with *TLL* vi 2.1704.60–1705.10). **sarculo** 'hoe', a basic tool. White 1967: 43–7 takes our passage to indicate that the land is hilly, and so cannot be turned with the plough.

12 Attalicis condicionibus: Attalus III, surnamed Philometor 'Motherloving', was king of Pergamon from 138 to 133. He was a sort of pre-echo of Nero, given up to art and luxury: he was credited with the invention of cloth inwoven with gold. On his death he left his kingdom to the Roman people (no one knows why: see C. Habicht, *CAH* viii 378). He thus became a byword for prodigality, cf. 2.18.5–6 *neque Attali | ignotus heres regiam occupaui*. For a possible sophisticated joke addressed to Maecenas see N–H on 2.18.6: the Attalid kingdom contained Lydia, homeland of the Etruscans.

13 demoueas, ut: the construction appears to be unique (*TLL* v 1.511.63–4), as if *demoueo* were a verb of persuading. **trabe:** poetic metonymy for 'ship' (*OLD* 4). *Cypria*, like *Myrtoum* (14), provides vividness; Cyprus had the timber to build ships (see Hill 1940: 1 172–3), and as an island it was a centre of maritime trade.

14 Myrtoum … mare: the southwestern part of the Aegean sea, which must have been well known to Roman traders and travellers. The origin of the name is uncertain (and was so in antiquity), but it probably derived from the small island of Myrtos at the extreme southern end of Euboea (*RE* xvi 1170.40–68).   **pauidus:** probably because the sea there was notorious for its storms, cf. 14.19–20, though sailors are commonly called 'fearful', as at 14.14 *timidus nauita*. *pauidus* and its noun *pauor* are slightly more poetic than their synonyms, *timidus* and *timor*; see the table in *TLL* x 1.813.47–63.   **secet:** used by poets to mean 'cleaving' a path through water or air (*OLD* 5), probably by analogy to τέμνειν.

15–18 By another gliding transition we move from the hint at the storms on the sea to the trader, fearful of just that. The farmer and the trader were two of the standard occupations regularly deployed by the poets; there is a full discussion by Smith on Tib. 1.9.7–10, pp. 362–3. Together they form a kind of polar expression or universalizing doublet (land and sea) to suggest that people everywhere are wedded to their chosen activities.

According to Vegetius, *Epitoma rei militaris* 4.39, the seas were closed to (military/government) shipping by the storms of winter from mid-November to mid-March (see Casson 1995: 270–2, and cf. the young man delayed abroad by winter winds at 4.5.9–12), though he acknowledged that merchants pushed their luck. The merchant here seems to be just such a risk-taker (NB *quassas* 18).

15 luctantem: here for the first time *luctor* governs the dative, *fluctibus*, a poetic construction (*TLL* vii 2.1734.78–1735.2), probably owed to the use of the dative in Greek with verbs of fighting or contention (see Mayer 1999: 167–8 for other instances in H.).   **Icariis** adds a picturesque detail and brings us into the part of the Aegean sea due east of the *Myrtoum mare*. It was named after Icarus, the son of Daedalus, who fell into its waters when his waxen wings melted in the heat of the sun (cf. 3.34–5, 4.2.1–4).   **Africum:** the villainous southwest wind, *creber procellis*, as Virgil described it at *Aen.* 1.85; cf. below 3.12, 14.5.

16 mercator: the trader undergoes danger to secure the wealth that will enable him to enjoy ease in retirement (cf. *S.* 1.1.31 *senes ut in otia tuta recedant*). *rates* 17 indicates trade on some scale, since he has at least two ships.

16–17 oppidi | … rura sui: his alternative to trading is to own land near his native town. The expression has been taken to indicate that ancient Italian farmers lived in an 'agro-town', and commuted to their fields. That situation however arose in the Middle Ages, and archaeological evidence demonstrates that the peasantry at any rate lived much closer to the land: see Garnsey 1979 = 1998, a reference owed to Dominic Rathbone. Our *mercator* if he was rich enough, could of course have lived in the town and left his estate in the hands of a *uilicus* 'bailiff', as did H. himself (see *Epist.* 1.14).   **laudat** suggests the ethical topic of discontent with one's occupation; it forms the theme of H.'s first satire, 1.1.3 *laudet diuersa sequentes* and 9 *agricolam laudat legum iurisque peritus*.

17 rates: poetic diction for 'ships' (*OLD* 2).

18 indocilis . . . pati: poetic syntax, the use of the infinitive with the adjective being a *pulcherrima figura*, according to the Latin grammarian Priscian (*GLK* iii 227.10). The range of the infinitive with adjectives, as with verbs (8n.), especially those implying capacity or skill, was much developed by Augustan poets, often in imitation of Greek (*NLS* §26, K–S i 684–6).   **pauperiem:** not always or exactly our 'poverty' (= *egestas, inopia*), but rather a relative term, the condition of not being rich (cf. 12.43 *Paupertas*). H. for instance said of himself at 2.18.10–11 *pauperemque diues | me petit*, but he still had a few slaves to wait upon his solitary table (*S.* 1.6.116 *cena ministratur pueris tribus*). The word is a poetic synonym of *paupertas*, and it enters the prose of the early empire (*TLL* x 1.850.64–6 and 852.63–73).

19–22 In contrast to the striving of the farmer and the merchant is the hedonist, whose life-style is generally taken to reflect that of H. as presented in many of the odes: nothing excessive, a refined enjoyment of the good things of life.

19–21 est qui . . . spernit: for the mood of the verb see *iuuat* 4n. *nec . . . spernit* is an understatement (litotes): he is very keen indeed to indulge himself. The high incidence of this figure throughout H.'s writing is characteristic of his urbane tone of voice.   **Massici:** understand *uini*. This choice wine came from the *mons Massicus* in northern Campania on the border of Latium; the *ager Falernus* lies to the south of this range. Massic wine aged well, for H. offers Messalla Corvinus the vintage of the year of his own birth at 3.21.1–8.

20 nec partem solido demere de die 'to take a slice out of the working day' (Rudd). The Romans observed set times for work and pleasure (Cicero, *Pro Murena* 74 *tempora uoluptatis laborisque dispertiunt*). To break ranks by starting one's drinking early was seen as taking time off the 'normal' (*solidus, OLD* 9c, and cf. 4.5.38–9 *integro . . . die*) working day, a sign of high living (see Fordyce on Catull. 47.6 *de die* and N–H on 2.7.6–7 *diem mero | fregi*). *pars* here, as at 2.17.5 *te meae . . . partem animae*, suggests a substantial part, hence Rudd's elegant colloquialism, 'slice'. This usage is accepted in *TLL* x 1.452.79–453.21, esp. 453.2–4 (following W. A. Camps, cited there); often *pars* without a term of specific quantity means 'half' (*OLD* 4b).   **demere:** for the infinitive with *spernit* see *tollere* 8n. For the combination of dissimilar elements, noun (*pocula*) + infinitive (*demere*), as objects of *spernit* see Bo Index 268–9; cf. 2.49–50.

21–2 nunc . . . nunc: this correspondence of temporal adverbs is poetic, until taken up by Livy (*OLD* 8). It is probably borrowed from Greek, νῦν μὲν . . . νῦν δέ.   **uiridi . . . sub arbuto** perhaps designedly evokes the pastoral ease of Virgil, *Ecl.* 7.46 *uos rara uiridis tegit arbutus umbra*. The tree, nowadays *arbutus unedo*, is the wild strawberry.   **membra . . . stratus** 'having stretched out (*OLD sterno* 5) his limbs'; commonly in poetry the perfect participle passive governs the accusative of words referring to parts of the body (*membra*), along Greek lines (*NLS* §19(ii), Bo Index 118, Courtney 2004), cf. 2.31 *umeros amictus*.

22 aquae lene caput sacrae: the placement of the epithets illustrates H.'s impressionistic word order. *lene* may be understood with *aquae* to suggest both the murmur of the water issuing from the ground (*OLD* 4), as well as its gentle movement (*OLD* 1). By the same token *sacrae* if understood with *caput* reminds us that it is particularly the source of a stream that is held sacred (cf. the sacrifice to the *fons Bandusiae*, 3.13). Plodding grammar finds here a highly artificial double displacement of the epithets = *lenis aquae caput sacrum* (so K–S 1 221). This displacement is sometimes given the name enallage, sometimes hypallage (the latter especially by ancient scholiasts).

23–8 The hedonist gives place to more energetic figures, the soldier and the huntsman. These activities were deemed complementary, as at *Epist.* 1.18.39–57; hunting kept a man fit for fighting.

23–4 lituo: by a sort of brachylogy, the omission of a word to be supplied in a different form (G–L §689), for *litui sonitu*. The *lituus* was a sort of curved bugle with a shrill note, whereas the *tuba* was straight and gave a low note. Their sound contrasts with that of the fountain in 22.

24–5 matribus | detestata: the past participle of the deponent is here passive, cf. 32.5 *modulate* (G–L §167 N2). The dative of agent, *matribus*, with the perfect passive is regular, cf. 21.4 *Ioui*, and 32.5 *ciui* (G–L §354; K–S 1 324–5). The advantage is economy: the poet does without a preposition (*a/ab*).

25 sub Ioue frigido: Jupiter was the Italian sky-god, and so by metonymy his name was used by the poets for the sky (*OLD Iuppiter* 2). *frigidus* hints both at the normal seasons for hunting, autumn and winter (cf. 37.19 *niualis*), and the usual times, night and early morning. But it also suggests the huntsman's enthusiasm for the chase: he endures the cold when he might be in bed with his young wife (*tenerae coniugis immemor*).

27 fidelibus: dogs are traditionally faithful, but the epithet has an everyday tone, unlike the elevated *fidus*; see Adams 1973: 139–40.

28 teretes ... plagas: *teres* 'fine' is used of any object with a smooth, rounded surface. Nets were hung in a curve to close off an area into which the game could be driven for the kill; a mettlesome brute might contrive to break through the barrier. H.'s word of choice for net is *plaga*, though he uses *retia* once (but *cassis* never); we must assume he is not making any known technical distinction as to function.　　　　**Marsus aper:** poets used the proper names of nations or tribes, and even of individuals (cf. *Dardanae* 15.10n.), adjectivally, rather than the adjectival forms in *–ius* or *–icus*, a point noted by Porphyrio on 4.6.12 *puluere Teucro: pro Teucrio puluere; ergo principali pro possessiuo nomine usus est* (see too Wackernagel 1928: 11 58–9 = 2009: 473–4, N–H on *Syra* 31.12, H–S 427). The Marsi lived in the mountains of central Italy, the modern Abruzzi, so the local colour of the epithet is appropriate. Boar was especially prized by the Romans as a food, particularly at grand dinner parties.

29–33 H. now puts the anticipated cap on the priamel by announcing his own vocation. The personal note is emphatically sounded with the anaphora of *me*, cf. 7.10, 31.15–16.

29 doctarum hederae praemia frontium 'the [crown of] ivies, [which is] the reward of poetic brows'. The word order is highly artificial (and so not found in the conversational satires): the appositional phrase sandwiches the referent word. The history of this stylistic feature is charted in H. by Solodow 1986: 129–40; to his examples may be added *Epist.* 1.18.104 *gelidus Digentia riuus. doctarum* is emphatic by position. This epithet is very much in fashion from the time of Catullus (see Fordyce on 35.16f.), as applied to poets. The σοφία of the older Greek poets could refer either to their 'wisdom' or to their 'skill'. The latter sense is common in Pindar, and favoured too by Callimachus, who asserted that poetic skill was to be judged by artistry (τέχνη; *Aetia* prologue fr. 1.17–18 Pfeiffer); in Latin this is *ars*. This aesthetic was summed up by his Roman followers in the word *doctus*. In addition to refined technique this 'learnedness' (the word is hard to translate) also entailed knowledge and exploitation of the literary tradition. The tradition is crucial for H. as the initiator of lyric verse in Rome.   **hederae:** Maas 1902: 526 observed that the plural of this word is the rule in poetry, wherever it produces the handier metrical form (here an anapaest); the nominative singular would only fit into verse with an elision (see further *TLL* VI 2.2588.9–11).

Ivy was connected with the cult of Bacchus because it was woven round the thyrsus, the staff carried by his attendants. Crowns of ivy, a plant deemed naturally cold, were reckoned a prophylactic against drunkenness (Isidore, *Origines* 17.9.23). H. thus here hints at the modestly sympotic character of much of the collection. Bacchus moreover inspired poets (see 3.25, and *Epist.* 2.2.78 *cliens Bacchi*) and his evergreen ivy suggests lasting renown (cf. *Epist.* 1.3.25 *prima feres hederae uictricis praemia*). There may even be a hierarchy of crowns: Bacchus' ivy and Venus' myrtle (38.5) seem appropriate to slight genres, but the demand for a crown of Delphic bay leaves at 3.30.15–16, the concluding poem of the collection, shows H.'s confidence in his achievement (so Plessis, followed by N–H). Cf. *TLL* VI 2589.58–2590.4. Finally, reference to crowns in Greek lyric often signalled the close of the poem, as here too (Rutherford 1997: 49–50); cf. the final poem, 38.

30 dis miscent superis: something more than *euehit ad deos* 6.

gelidum nemus: as H. will say at *Epist.* 2.2.77 *scriptorum chorus omnis amat nemus et fugit urbem*; the peace and coolness of the Bacchic grove better inspire the writer than the heated hurly-burly of the town.

31 Nympharumque leues cum Satyris chori: the usual attendants of Bacchus, cf. 2.19.3–4.

32 secernunt populo: cf. *Epist.* 2.2.77 (quoted in 30n.) and *AP* 298 *secreta petit loca, balnea uitat.* But there is probably also some sense of the poet as a being set apart, distinguished from the rest of men. That impression is presented pictorially by H.'s fanciful association with the Nymphs and Satyrs in 31. The whole picture indicates H.'s new attachment to the less realistic world of lyric poetry (as opposed to his earlier engagement with the more down-to-earth genres, satire and invective).   **si** adds an important condition, that the Muses must not withhold their support. There seems no special reason for naming specifically Euterpe and Polyhymnia, since at this time the Muses had not been assigned discrete provinces (N–H on 1.24.3). But the musical instruments are significant:

the *tibiae* 'reed-pipes' (a composite instrument, see *OLD* 1b) accompanied choral lyric, whereas the lyre was used by the solo-singer. Thus H. hints at his aspiration to compass both species of lyric.

34 Lesboum . . . barbiton: the epithet – unique in both Greek and Latin – probably alludes to Terpander of Lesbos, whom Pindar (fr. 125 Snell–Maehler) credited with the invention of the βάρβιτος, a kind of lyre (for other candidates see Maehler on Bacchylides, fr. 20B.1 Snell–Maehler). *Lesbous* is also programmatic, since H.'s models for lyric will turn out to be Sappho and Alcaeus, both also of Lesbos. (The use of a place-name to provide a generic marker may have been a device H. learned from Virgil, who similarly glanced at generic forebears in his bucolics (*Syracosio uersu*, 6.1) and *Georgics* (*Ascraeum carmen*, 2.176).)

barbitos is a loan-word, introduced into Latin by H. and taken up by subsequent poets (*TLL* II 1747.23–55); it is not a prose word, and even in contemporary Greek it was poetic diction (see West 1992: 59, n. 49). The programmatic scheme is kept up since the *barbitos* was associated with Dionysus and drinking parties; Aristotle, *Politics* 8.1341a39–1341b1, says that it was banned along with the *aulos* from education because it was designed to provide only pleasure, and not instruction. There is a fine red-figure winecooler depicting Alcaeus and Sappho each with a *barbitos* in the Munich Staatliche Antikensammlungen (upload.wikimedia.org/wikipedia/commons/7/7b/Alkaios_Sappho_Staatliche_Antikensammlungen_2416_full.jpg). For descriptions see Landels 1999: 66–7, Mathiesen 1999: 249–53 for discussion with illustrations, and Maas and Snyder 1989: 39, 113–28, especially 127 for its association with the Aeolic poets in H. (cf. 32.4 *barbite*).   **refugit tendere:** for the infinitive see 8n. and K–S 1 668 (where it is noted that *refugio*, unlike *fugio*, with an infinitive is poetic). Tightening the strings tunes them (*OLD tendo* 5b); the use of the simple form of the verb for the compounds (*intendo, contendo*) is a characteristic of poetic diction.

35–6 The priamel ended when H. announced his own activity, which, as he indicated, made him as happy as a man can be (as we should say, he is in heaven). But that leaves open a question: is he any good as a lyric poet? The question is not irrelevant because it was adroitly insinuated into the opening of the priamel, in which the first two examples (athlete, politician) were evidently successful. Thus H. can close the poem by returning to its addressee and putting the issue of his own success into the hands of his friend, Maecenas. If he will regard him as the equal of the lyric poets of Greece, then his happiness will be complete. This is a compliment to Maecenas' literary judgement, since classic status was normally conferred only gradually over time, when the favourable opinion of many readers could be taken as assurance of a writer's rank. Maecenas' taste, however, is so reliable that he can anticipate posterity. (Catullus had paid a similar compliment to Cornelius Nepos in his dedicatory poem.)

35 lyricis: in Greek the word first appears in the grammarian Dionysius Thrax (*c.* 170–*c.* 90), so it is of recent date to indicate the lyric poets (see Färber

1936: 17–16). When Cicero had used the word at *Orator* 183 he kept it in Greek (he used *melicus* without a problem at *De optimo genere oratorum* 1), so we may suppose that H. here gives it Roman citizenship.   **uatibus:** this much discussed word here suggests the antiquity and prestige of the classic poets of early Greece. Originally *uates* meant 'seer', but Virgil had used it in the *Eclogues* (7.28, 9.34, with Clausen's n. at 32–6) as a more dignified synonym of *poeta*; he went on to use it of himself at *Aen.* 7.41 (Horsfall's valuable n. ad loc. should be consulted for the large bibliography). H. clearly picked the word up from Virgil and regularly used *uates* both of himself (*Epod.* 16.66, *Carm.* 2.6.24 and 20.3, 4.3.14–15, 4.6.44, *Epist.* 1.7.11) and of other poets. Its tone is never uniform, however, and must be assessed within its context. For example, at *AP* 24 it has a decidedly ironic nuance, but at 400 it is manifestly dignified (see Brink ad locc., especially the extensive note on the latter, and cf. 31.2 below). If *uates* seemed to H. and his readers the 'traditional' native word for poet, then the grafting on to it of the loan-word *lyricus* is emblematic of H.'s own enterprise in the *Odes*; cf. 2.16.38 *Graiae … Camenae* and 4.3.23 *Romanae fidicen lyrae.*   **inseres:** Pfeiffer 1968: 206 proposed that H. was alluding to the Greek verb ἐγκρίνειν 'to admit/accept' someone into a group, more specifically a writer into the ranks of the classics (cf. *OLD insero²* 3c).

36 sublimi feriam sidera uertice: for the proverbial notion see *ad deos* 5n. and Hopkinson on Callimachus, *Hymn* 6.58. *sublimis* 'is a noble and antique word' (Brink on *AP* 165), suggesting both elation as well as elevation.

*

Structurally considered, this is an odd poem, since the priamel here does not serve as mere introduction to the leading theme, but constitutes the poem's substance (Kenney 1983:15–16). The function of this priamel must be determined, since both its foil and its climax or cap have been misinterpreted.

It needs to be seen at the outset that a priamel, taken as a whole, may be either neutral, in that no opinion or activity is privileged over any other, or argumentative, more or less, in that the final item or cap is set above some or all of the foil. Porphyrio regarded the present priamel as neutral: H. points out, he says, that *alium alio studio teneri*, implying that there is no depreciation of the other pursuits mentioned. An argumentative priamel is found in 31.3–16, where H. clearly rejects certain objects of desire.

Porphyrio's view of this first priamel long held the field. Musurillo 1962, however, maintained that this was imprecise, arguing that the catalogue of vocations was deployed to show that the poet's is the greatest of all (1962: 235). Two points: Musurillo did not demonstrate that H. found fault with the other activities listed, nor did he claim that the strategy of the priamel necessarily involves the privileging of the cap. N–H 1970: 1 developed Musurillo's position by insisting that the other occupations were described mostly in critical terms, so that H. could suggest that his own way of life is not only justifiable but superior. (When, however, they came to the farmer of lines 11–14 they reneged: 'a sympathetic sketch, drawn without satire'.) But neither did they claim that the priamel, as a form, was bound to be used argumentatively. Race 1982: 122–3 endorsed the view of Musurillo and N–H: 'Horace suggests by choice of word a flaw or limitation in each chosen endeavour', but he did not insist that the priamel in and of itself necessitated the rejection of the other activities. That extreme position was at last advanced by West 1995: 6: 'the expectation in the priamel is that the last item is preferred'. This claim can be rejected. Race 1982 amply demonstrated that many priamels are neutral. Here is an example in an earlier poem of H.'s, *S.* 2.1.24–8:

> quid faciam? saltat Milonius, ut semel icto
> accessit feruor capiti numerusque lucernis;
> Castor gaudet equis, ouo prognatus eodem
> pugnis; quot capitum uiuunt, totidem studiorum
> milia: me pedibus delectat claudere verba.

In this short, embedded priamel H. defended his activity as satiric poet by citing three pursuits: dancing, horse-racing, and boxing. Dancing he satirizes (cf. Cicero, *Pro Murena* 13 *nemo . . . saltat sobrius nisi insanit*), but racing and boxing, as activities enjoyed (*gaudet*) by gods, he simply notes. His point is that Castor and Pollux, as twins, might have been expected to have exactly the same tastes (cf. *Epist.* 1.10.3–5), and yet they do not. Moreover by illustrating activities among both men and gods H. suggests that his rule has universal application. The rule then follows: *quot capitum uiuunt, totidem studiorum | milia*, and he tacks on the activity he enjoys (*delectat*) as the cap of the priamel. No one suggests that *qua* capping item the poet possesses superior status to gods; Race 1982: 124 sees that the priamel gives emphasis by means of contrast. Writing poetry is what H. enjoys doing, and for a Roman it is probably preferable to the dancing of a drunkard, but not superior to what the gods like to do. The priamel here is largely neutral. It should then be accepted that in the first ode the priamel does not necessarily privilege the final item, the cap. Resolution of the issue may be sought by paying attention to the verbs H. deployed.

Just as in the satire, the ode too emphasizes the pleasure men take in their activities (the point was not lost on Schönberger 1966: 399–400), especially if they are successful at them. We first encounter *iuuat* 3, which applies to three vocations (athlete, politician, entrepreneur). That idea is picked up by *gaudentem* 11: the farmer rejoices even though his work is back-breaking. Finally, soldiers delight in their calling (*iuuant* 23), however hateful war is to mothers. H. was a realist and knew that there is no point in trying to argue men out of their pleasures (he tells the sad tale of such an attempt at *Epist.* 2.2.128–40). They know what they enjoy and, like the farmer in this poem, will not budge for any amount of money. The claims made for other activities will not faze them. Indeed, claims made for the superiority of poetry would fail to impress a Roman audience.

H.'s addressees are not only other poets, who might be sympathetic to such a claim; in the first book only Virgil, Albius, and Valgius are of the fraternity.

The rest, where we can identify them, are members of the political, social, and economic élite, men who had held the consulship (Sestius, Varus), earned triumphs (Agrippa, Plancus), or enjoyed political influence (Maecenas). Would such men pay serious attention to the claim that poetry was an activity superior to theirs? Would H. venture to make such a claim at the start of a collection that contained poems in praise of these men? Aristotle, in his *Nicomachean Ethics* 1147b30 and 1148a25–6, had listed victory, honour, and wealth as three indisputably 'natural' objects of desire; H. would be wasting his time in trying to subvert that commonly held view of them. So it might be prudent on balance to return to Porphyrio's view that the priamel here is largely neutral (cf. Syndikus 2001: 27–9 for a balanced discussion). That does not however mean that it is inert.

Kröhling 1935: 49 made the valuable point that H.'s own vocation, poetry, was still unusual for a Roman to adopt. By setting poetic composition on the same level with activities such as politics or military service, which his readers might be expected to approve of, H. implicitly staked a claim for the equal recognition of his own calling.

The priamel moreover is primarily a focusing device, and what we focus upon here is indeed H.'s devotion to his own calling, poetry (so Krasser 1995: 78–82). But this poem is also programmatic, and the cap announces something quite new in Rome's literary history, the engrafting of the Greek lyric tradition on to the stock of Roman poetry. H. will already have been known to readers as a satirist in the tradition of Lucilius and as an iambist in the tradition of Catullus and Bibaculus. By focusing on his activity as a poet H. is also able to announce a new direction: the grove, the chorus of Nymphs, Satyrs, the Muses, and the Lesbian lyre all together point away from the poetic genres which had occupied him hitherto and prepare the reader for a collection of lyric song where indeed the presence of Venus dancing beneath the spring moon with the Graces (4), or a visitation by Faunus (17), or the inspiration of the Muse (12) will not be found generically inappropriate.

2

Metre: sapphic (see Introduction 8)

1–12 Terrible weather conditions are a sign of divine displeasure.

1 terris: the dative of goal is poetic syntax (K–S I 320). Löfstedt 1942: I 180–7 observed that such datives are seldom purely local, but have a personal or personified reference; this is clearly true of *terris*, which includes the inhabitants of the land (cf. *NLS* §57).   **niuis:** snowfall at Rome was sufficiently uncommon to be taken for a prodigy.   **dirae** 'ill-omened', the language of augury, though poets apply it to anything 'dreadful'. H. here employs the distributional figure ἀπὸ κοινοῦ, which means 'in common', so that the epithet is to be understood equally with *niuis*. By means of this figure, which is mainly found in poetry (K–S I

54–5), single words or phrases are attached to more than one point of reference in the sentence. It is characteristic of the figure that the word or phrase to be taken 'in common' is usually in the second member and close to a conjunction. Here then the formula is characteristic: noun, conjunction + epithet, noun (Naylor 1922: xxii, §33, Bell 1923: 263–71, especially 268).

2 Pater commonly designates Jupiter even without any defining term (*OLD* 6b, cf. 3.29.44); it is here chosen out of respect: he acts as an angry father correcting a naughty child. Jupiter, as sky-god, controlled the weather (cf. 1.25). He has a role in the rest of the poem (19, 30).

2–3 rubente | dextera: Jupiter's hand is red-hot from his exercise. The expression is pretty clearly owed to Virg. *G.* 1.328–9 *corusca | dextra*, and indeed it serves as an intertext directing the reader to a poem, probably quite recently published when this ode was composed, that provided a number of motifs and reflections.   **sacras iaculatus arces:** *iaculor* is originally intransitive, and the thing or person aimed at is expressed by *in* + accusative. But poets made it transitive, on the model of βάλλειν, i.e., it was given two sorts of direct object, either the thing thrown or the person or thing aimed at. H. here follows Lucretius, *De rerum natura* 4.1053 in the latter construction, which is only found in poetry (*TLL* vii 1.74.7). *arces* is probably not the hills of Rome (despite *TLL* ii 742.16–17), since *sacras* suggests the presence of a temple. Commentators thus suppose it refers to the northern and southern crests of the Capitoline hill (cf. Ov. *Met.* 15.866), but Richardson 1992: 40 reckons the *arx* was the part outside the *area Capitolina* but within the fortifications, a view cautiously supported by Oakley on Livy 6.11.4. If he is correct, the plural here is poetic.

4, 5 terruit ... terruit: the anaphora is emotional, and joins the stanzas to one another; this sort of repetition is characteristic of lyric style (see Mastronarde on Euripides, *Medea* 99). By extending the sense of *terreo* to 'cause to fear', H. is the first to give it the construction of a verb of fearing, *ne* (K–S ii 253, H–S 534); this is taken up by later writers (*OLD* 2c cites Livy, to which add Tac. *Hist.* 2.63 *Sabinum Triaria ... terruit ne periculo principis famam clementiae affectaret*).   **gentes** 'mankind' (*OLD* 2b), i.e., not just Romans or Italians.

5–6 graue 'grievous' (*OLD* 10b).   **saeculum Pyrrhae:** Pyrrha and her husband Deucalion were the two mortals to survive a flood which destroyed the rest of mankind, more or less (the story is told by Ovid, *Met.* 1.313–415). The mythological element suits the lyric manner. *noua* ('unprecedented' *OLD* 2) *monstra* continues the language of augury.

7–12 This mythological elaboration, which illustrates the inversion of nature, has drawn critical fire since antiquity: Porphyrio remarked: *leuiter in re tam atroci et piscium et palumborum meminit, nisi quod hi excessus* ['digressions'] *lyricis concessi sunt.* (Similar criticism was levelled by Seneca in *Naturales Quaestiones* 3.27.13–14 at Ovid's description of the Flood in *Met.* 1.)

7 Proteus: the herdsman of Neptune/Poseidon's seals.

7–8 egit … uisere: poetic syntax: the infinitive, originally a dative, naturally expresses purpose or goal, chiefly with a verb of motion, cf. 23.10. This syntax is found in early Latin, and becomes elevated style thanks to Lucretius (G–L §421 n. 1(a), *NLS* §28, K–S 1 680–1, H–S 344–5).

9 piscium et summa genus haesit ulmo: Ovid appropriated the image for his own deluge, *Met.* 1.296 *hic summa piscem deprendit in ulmo. piscium genus* is an elevated expression (more so than simply saying *pisces*), taken over from Lucretius (e.g., 1.162) and Virgil. The conjunction *et* is postponed one place, as at 18 and 39 (cf. the list in Klingner's Index 337). This practice of postponing connectives was introduced into Latin by Catullus (though he did not postpone *et*, see Fordyce on 23.7), following his Greek models (e.g., Callimachus, *Aetia* 1, fr. 1.15 καί with Pfeiffer's annotation), and was much developed subsequently (Norden 1927: 402–4, Clausen's General Index to his edition of Virgil's *Eclogues*, s.v. postposition, Austin on Virg. *Aen.* 1.333, 4.33, 6.28, Marouzeau 1949a: 77–80). Postposition is not arbitrary but often provides emphasis for the word isolated from the rest of the sentence, here *piscium*, which is contrasted with *columbis* 10.   **summa … ulmo** 'in the tops of elm trees': the collective singular is normal in prose for the names of plants and trees, but the addition of an epithet is peculiar to poetry, cf. 5.1 *multa … rosa* (K–S 1 70).

11–12 superiecto pauidae natarunt | aequore dammae: a 'golden' pattern: epithets A and B are separated from their nouns a and b by the verb; see Naylor 1922: xiii–xv for discussion and list. The artistic arrangement has a mainly Hellenistic origin, see Hopkinson on Callimachus, *Hymn* 6.9, p. 88 n. 1. For *pauidae* see 1.14n. Deer are conventionally timid (cf. 23.2–3 *pauidam … matrem*, Virg. *Ecl.* 8.28 *timidi … dammae*), quite apart from their present predicament. *aequore* is largely poetic diction for 'the sea' (*OLD* 3).

13–20 The dreadful weather (1–4) prompted fears of a deluge on a mythical scale (5–12); by a gliding transition H. reports that there was indeed a flood, endangering (but not actually destroying) sacred buildings. The Tiber, before it was embanked in modern times, regularly flooded the low-lying parts of Rome; serious floods were regarded as portents (see Becher 1985).

Attempts are made to date the poem on the assumption that H. had a particular inundation in mind. This is misguided, since it is clear from our chief historical source for this period, Dio, that one Tiber flood was much like another: he records floods for 27 (52.20.1), 23 (53.33.5), 22 (54.1.1), and AD 15 (57.14.7) in similar terms, namely that the city was submerged and even navigable. The only exception is the flood of 23, when what he calls 'the wooden bridge' was swept away; this was the Pons Sublicius, and its destruction was always significant (see Richardson 1992: 299). If H. really had a particular flood in mind, he ought to have recorded in the poem some memorably striking detail which at least his earliest readers would have recognized as fixing events in a given year. This flood should be seen as generic (so Fraenkel 1957: 246 and now Becher 1985: 475 n. 33).

13 uidimus: H. associates his own experience with that of his readers, cf. *precamur* 30, *nostris* 47.   **flauum:** rivers are 'tawny' because of the sand and silt they carry, cf. Virg. *Aen.* 7.31 *multa flauus harena* of the Tiber (also 8.8 below and 2.3.18).

14 litore Etrusco: Porphyrio assumed the reference was to the Tiber's mouth, but nowadays the river-bank at the foot of the Janiculan Hill is preferred (for *litus* = *ripa* 'river-bank' see *OLD* 1c and *TLL* VII 2.1540.13–16). H.'s claim to autopsy better suits an event in Rome rather than down-river at Ostia.

15 ire deiectum: the supine in *–um* expresses purpose when used with a verb of motion; the addition of an accusative object is normal (G–L §435, H–S 381–2). This construction is not uncommon (14x) in the hexameter poems, where it may reflect conversational style, since it is often found in early comedy. On the other hand, its use is rare in elevated poetry (Austin on Virg. *Aen.* 2.786), and this is the sole example in lyric. Here the tone may be archaic, since the use of *ire* + supine to replace a simple verb is affected by historians (see Koestermann on Sallust, *Iugurtha* 31.27 *perditum eatis*).

15–16 monumenta regis | templaque Vestae: the first building is the *Regia*, the official headquarters of the *pontifex maximus* near the *Sacra Via*; across the street was the round *aedes Vestae* (Richardson 1992: 328–9 and 1992: 412–13). Both structures were thought to have been built by Numa Pompilius, the second king of Rome (cf. 12.33–4n.). The plurals are 'poetic', since only one structure is intended in each case.

17–18 Iliae dum se ... iactat ultorem 'whilst he boasted of himself (*OLD* 12b) as avenger for Ilia' (dative of advantage). *dum* regularly takes the present indicative (which is not 'historical') when it denotes a longer period during which the action of the main verb takes place; the indicative is retained even where the *dum*-clause depends on an infinitive (here *ire*); see *NLS* §221 and Roby §1663, and cf. 10.11 and 22.10. Ilia, a Vestal virgin, was the mother, by Mars (who raped her), of Romulus and Remus. She was ordered to be executed with them by drowning in the Anio (a tributary of the Tiber), or, as here, in Tiber himself, who made her his wife (see Skutsch on Ennius, *Annales* 1.xxxix for the divergent accounts).   **nimium querenti** 'loudly complaining'; *nimium* need not always convey the notion of excess, and the sense proposed here, 'greatly', is found in comedy (cf. *OLD nimium*[2] 2), so it may be a colloquial usage, or have sounded archaic by H.'s time (cf. *minus* 27). The burden of Ilia's complaint is debated. Some assume it was her unfair punishment, others the assassination of her descendant, the *pontifex maximus* Julius Caesar. Commager 1962: 180 reckoned that if the motive of her complaint were crucial it was up to H. to specify it. This is commendably brisk, but the issue really involves how we read a text. Up to now we have been told that one particular object of Tiber's onslaught is the temple of Vesta (16), and that suggests a grievance against the goddess, namely that she failed to look after her guiltless priestess (Clark 2010: 264–5). The first-time reader as yet has no idea that divine displeasure has anything to do with civil war or the assassination of Julius Caesar; these themes are played out later in the poem. So it is only on a 'second' reading that Ilia's complaint could be interpreted as having anything to do with Caesar. Such a reading may not be illegitimate, but it is far from 'innocent'.

18 ultorem strikes the keynote, cf. 44, 51.   **et:** postponed, 9n.

19 Ioue non probante: Jupiter wanted Rome terrorized, not destroyed (so Porphyrio). *non probante* is litotes, he disapproved. The reference to Jupiter at this point seems to effect ring-composition, by recalling that it was he who enabled the Tiber to flood in the first place (*Pater* 2). Thus the opening situation is brought to a close.

19–20 u- | xorius amnis: H. knew that the 'fourth' line of the sapphic stanza was really only a prolongation of the third, and so closely linked to it; hence the division of a single word over two lines is more apparent than metrically real. *uxorius* suggests a criticism, focalized (i.e., given a point of view internal to the narrative, see Fowler 2000: 40–63, with helpful definitions at 40–1) by Jupiter's disapproval. *amnis*, while not exclusively a poetic word, certainly belongs to a 'high' register (*TLL* I 1943.5).

21–4 Abruptly H. indicates that what the portents of bad weather and flood foretold was civil rather than foreign war. He casts this notion into the future: civil war is something posterity 'will hear of' (*audiet* 21, 23, an emphatic anaphora), in contrast to what 'we have seen' 13. The future tense here and the perfect at 13 open up a suggestive gap: what about the present? The next stanza will fill it.

21 ferrum 'the sword', by the figure metonymy (*OLD* 5). This metonomy is not exclusively poetic, but it is elevated. Plautus used it in Sosia's famous battle narrative, *Amphitryo* 232 *ferro ferit*; Caesar used it only once in direct speech, in a common alliterative phrase (*De bello Gallico* 5.30.3 *aut ferro aut fame*).

22 Persae: 'the Persians' of H.'s day were really the Parthians, here associated with their Persian ancestors; the word thus has poetic colour (*OLD Perses*[1] 1b; cf. *Medos* 51). They were *graues* 'formidable' (cf. 3.5.4 *grauibus . . . Persis, OLD* 14d) because their empire could be seen as Rome's rival in the eastern Mediterranean sphere. Recently both Crassus and Marcus Antonius had come to grief trying to subdue them. Augustus' policy towards them (and indeed towards other remote peoples) is matter for debate. Some argue for a 'reserved cordiality' towards Parthia, with reliance upon diplomacy, which indeed retrieved the military standards lost by Crassus at the battle of Carrhae in 53 (E. S. Gruen in *CAH* x 158–63, Syme 1991: 386, Campbell 1992: 220–8, especially 222 n. 1). Others – Wissemann 1982 and Brunt 1990: 456–64 – believe Augustus may well have intended to annex Parthia, if the opportunity arose. Contemporary poets certainly speak of an imminent war of reprisal against Parthia (e.g. 12.53–4, 29.1–5, 35.38–40, and cf. 21.15), and this presumably met with the approval of the *princeps*, whose public posture on the home front was one of aggressiveness towards a dangerous enemy. Is there any reason to suppose H. knew the true state of affairs?

melius perirent 'they had better perished', 'it would have been better that they had perished'; the adverb 'of judgement' qualifies the whole clause (K–S 1 795, H–S 827, Brink on *AP* 40 *potenter*, p. 125; cf. 3.15.8–9, 3.16.39–40). The imperfect subjunctive denotes unfulfilled past obligation (Handford 1947: 60–1).

24 rara iuuentus: the epithet underscores the effect of the civil wars on posterity. There were contemporary fears that the casualties had led to a reduced birth rate (see, e.g., Cicero, *Pro Marcello* 23, Dio 43.25); modern historians agree, e.g., Brunt 1971: 111.

25–30 The prodigies and their likely cause, civil war, must be dealt with, but how? The three questions form a clear crescendo of subject ideas: *populus – uirgines – Iuppiter*. All the interrogative pronouns are in different cases (polyptoton).

25 quem ... diuum: *diuum* is genitive plural, as at *diuum pater* 4.6.22 and *sacra diuum Serm.* 1.3.117 (N–W 1 175, and for the termination generally G–L §33R4). As such the genitive is partitive with the interrogative pronoun. Such a construction possibly either sounded archaic to a Roman ear (Plautus, *Asinaria* 716 *quem ... diuom*), or it might have been regarded as a grecism (so Servius on Virg. *Aen.* 6.341 *quis ... deorum*). At any rate, the expression is unusual and poetic (cf. 29.5–6).   **uocet** = *inuocet* 'are the people to invoke': the subjunctive is used in a question expressive of perplexity or helplessness (Handford 1947: 64). The simple verb form serves for the compound (H. never has *inuoco*), poetic usage for this verb (*OLD uoco* 1b).

25–6 ruentis | imperi rebus 'for the sake of the fortunes of their tottering power'. Norden 1939: 127–8 recognized in this expression a common dread of 'collapse', particularly of buildings, but also of the state as a whole and its power.

26 prece qua: the singular is found almost only in poetry (*TLL* x 2.1216.57–63 sets out the details).   **fatigent** 'are they to importune' (*OLD* 3b, common with the notion of prayer); for the subjunctive see *uocet* 25n.

27 uirgines sanctae: the Vestal virgins, who guarded the flame that burned perpetually on Rome's hearth in the *aedes Vestae* (16).   **minus audientem** 'who pays little heed to'. *minus* is colloquially used as a mild negative (*OLD* 4, Hofmann 1951: 146); *audio* in the sense 'heed' (*OLD* 10b) is especially appropriate for a god.

28 carmina 'ritual chants', the primary meaning, cf. *carmen Saliorum*.

29 scelus = *uitium* 23, and cf. *uitiis* 47. H. is unspecific about the nature of the crime: it may be civil war, or the assassination of Julius Caesar (suggested by 44), or the whole nexus of those events.

30–44 H. now lists some divine candidates who might shoulder the task of expiation. Apollo, Venus, and Mars were all guardians of Rome; Mercury is unexpected, and still not satisfactorily explained (see Miller 2009: 45–53 for general discussion and a fresh assault upon the problem). H. rings the changes, *uariatio*: Apollo is named, Venus appears under a cult title, and Mars is alluded to by his position as *auctor* of the Roman people. There is a similar invocation of a city's tutelary deities by the chorus in Aeschylus, *Septem* 91–149.

30 tandem uenias precamur 'come at last we pray'. *tandem* emphasizes *uenias* (*OLD* 2). The subjunctive alone (without *ut*) with *precor* is a poetic construction (*TLL* x 2.1157.52–62, where ambiguity is allowed for), cf. 3.7 and 31.18. It is a kind of parataxis (G–L §546.R2, K–S ii 229).

31 nube candentes umeros amictus: H. deploys Homer's description of a concealed or disguised god at *Il.* 5.186 νεφέληι εἰλυμένος ὤμους. The use of the descriptive participle evokes the hymnic style (Norden 1923: 166–8, especially 173); for the syntax of the accusative, which here reproduces Homer's, see 1.21–2n. and Courtney 2004: 427. *candentes* 'gleaming' translates the epithet φαίδιμος used of Odysseus' shoulder at *Od.* 11.128 (picked up by Sophocles, fr. 453 *TrGF*), and of Theseus' in Bacchylides 18.47. (Bell 1923: 315–16, following pseudo-Acro, takes it to be a case of hypallage for *nube candenti*.) Since the verb *amicio* means 'clothe', its sense here is metaphorical and poetic (*OLD* 2).

32 augur hints at why Apollo is the first to come to mind as an expiator: he can divine the cause of the gods' displeasure. The designation is poetic (cf. Virg. *Aen.* 4.376 and *TLL* ii 244.75–82 and 1367.27–30), and suggests the function of a Greek *mantis*, which Roman *augures* did not perform (cf. *CS* 61). Apollo is also appealed to because he drives away harm, cf. 21.14.

33 siue: here (and at 35 and 41) = *uel . . . si*; the disjunctive force of –*ue* does not apply to the three protases introduced by *si*, but to the apodoses, viz *uenias* (except 41), to be supplied from 30 (*OLD siue* 2, K–S ii 437). Translate: 'or you come, if . . .'. The usage recurs at 4.12, 6.19 (?), 15.25, 32.7 and indeed is common in poetry.

33–4 Venus was the mother of Aeneas and so interested both in Rome and in the Julian *gens*.

33 mauis: sc. *uenire*.   **Erycina** indicates Venus, by the figure antonomasia. She had a temple on Mt Eryx in western Sicily, and this cult was honoured in Rome with two temples, one dedicated on the Capitol in 215, the other in 181 (Richardson 1992: 408). *ridens* evokes her Greek epithet φιλομμειδής 'laughter-loving'; for the hymnic participle see *amictus* 31n.

34 quam: a relative clause which characterizes the divinity is common in prayers or hymns, see Norden 1923: 168–76, especially 173, and cf. 38 below, 10.2, 12.14–17.   **Iocus:** the literary personification is as old as Plautus, *Bacchides* 116 (in a list of other jolly 'divinities', cf. *TLL* vii 2.289.65–7). The personifying and divinizing of virtues, powers, and qualities was widespread in antiquity (Lind 1973–4, Morgan 2007: 311–13): literature, cult, and popular morality all endowed what society valued with divine origin or authority (philosophy sometimes opposed this practice). Roman poets, following Greek precedent, personified abstract notions, esp. as attendants upon gods (Feeney 1998: 87–92). No one showed the range and variety of H., according to L. Deubner, art. 'Personifikationen abstrakter Begriffe', Roscher iii 2105.36–51. Some of his personifications match those of Roman cult, but it seems unlikely this was by design.   **circum:** since there is normally a word-break after the fifth syllable of the sapphic hendecasyllable line, editors regard *circum* as a preposition in anastrophe (especially with the relative this is common, see *TLL* III 1115–20).

35 siue: see 33n.   **genus et nepotes:** this is probably an instance of hendiadys, 'the race of your descendants'. *nepotes* in this sense is poetic (*OLD* 3).

36 respicis 'show concern for' (*OLD* 8b especially of deities, and cf. Norden 1939: 147).   **auctor:** for Mars as the father (*OLD auctor* 15b) of Romulus and Remus see 17n. The word is not in the vocative, but is part of the predicate, 'you show concern as being our founder'.

37 satiate 'once you are glutted'. The participle is used predicatively (as in Greek), and so shares the jussive idea with *uenias* (again to be understood from line 30); see K–S I 255–6. H. hopes Mars, traditionally insatiable, will weary of the overlong 'game' of civil war and succour his people. Such a sentiment found a place in the ancient hymn (*axamenta*) of the *Fratres Aruales*: *satur fu, fere Mars* (line 3, see Norden 1939: 134). For the participial style of hymns and prayers see *amictus* 31n.   **ludo:** for warfare as a game from the gods' point of view cf. *spectacula* 28.17 and Bacchylides 17.57 ἀρηίων ἀθυρμάτων.

38–40 H. lists the aspects of warfare which delight Mars in an ascending tricolon; see Lindholm 1931: 163, 184, and cf. K–H on 21.1–4.

38 quem iuuat: for the relative clause see 34n. H. had a predilection for the singular number of the verb with a plurality of subject words, if the nearest was itself singular (G–L §285, K–S I 44, §13.1), a practice first enunciated by the English scholar Richard Bentley (1662–1742) in his note on 24.8.   **leues** 'smooth', from polishing (the first *e* is long).

39 acer 'fierce' (*OLD* 9); H. may be recalling Virg. *G.* 2.167 *genus acre uirum, Marsos*. For *acer in* . . . cf. 6.18 *in iuuenes* . . . *acrium* (*TLL* I 363.7–10 does not recognize these examples from H.).   **et:** postponed, see 9n.   **Marsi peditis:** cf. 1.28 *Marsus aper*. This tough mountain people, whose name suggests a connection with Mars, formed the backbone of the Roman army (rather like Scottish regiments in the British army), cf. 2.20.18 *Marsae cohortis*, 3.5.9, and see C. Letta, art. 'Marsi' in *EO* I 511–12 with ample bibliography. The second-century AD Greek historian of Rome Appian records a saying that the Romans had never gained a triumph over the Marsi or without them (*Bel. Ciu.* 1.46). *Marsi* is the emendation of the French scholar Tanaquil Faber (1615–72) for the transmitted *Mauri*; it is accepted by most editors, chiefly because the Mauretanians rode horses, they were not foot soldiers.   **cruentum** 'blood-stained'.

41–52 H. now turns to Mercury, disguised as a young man. Gradually the *iuuenis* takes on the features of Augustus, who is apparently on the path to apotheosis. Both parts of the concluding prayer (45–52), from *serus* to *tollat* and from *hic* to *Caesar*, form tricola of increasing length, the first of which overruns the bounds of its stanza. Prayer was a common closural device in Greek lyric (Rutherford 1997: 44–6).

41–3 siue mutata iuuenem figura | ales in terris imitaris almae | filius Maiae: *siue* should not be taken to mean *uel <uenias> si* as at 33 and

35 (though that is how Rudd translates); the construction here changes, and *siue* introduces a new condition, 'or if', of which the apodosis begins with *serus . . . redeas* 45, and continues to the end of the poem.

Popular religious belief in the Greek world occasionally detected gods in human form, cf. Acts 14.8–18, where the people of Lystra regarded Paul as Hermes/Mercury; in the Greek novel too the protagonists are sometimes taken for masquerading divinities (Chariton 1.1.16, 14.1; Xenophon 1.12.1; Heliodorus 1.2.1). But such a belief is unknown to the Romans, and more particularly, why H. chose Mercury as the god who assumed Augustus' form is unclear and much debated. White 1993: 178–80 provides a balanced account, and concludes that the equation between Mercury and Augustus was an off-the-cuff invention of H.'s, unrelated to popular or official encomium. Mercury was traditionally young, like Augustus, and he frequently mingled with mankind, to which he was particularly well disposed.

42 ales 'winged'. Mercury's *talaria* 'winged footwear' sped him on his way as messenger (cf. Virg. *Aen.* 4.239 *pedibus talaria nectit*, with Pease's extensive n.), and his *petasos* 'sun-hat' was also depicted as winged. Wings probably first appeared in the god's iconography, see *LIMC* v 2: 211, no. 123 for a winged sun-hat, and for winged boots 217, no. 203, 222, no. 262, and 227, no. 317 (especially fine wings on boots by the Cleophrades painter). Clear literary references in Greek, as opposed to Latin, to winged boots or feet are hard to find.

43 patiens uocari 'allowing yourself to be called' (hinting at the god's condescension). The infinitive with *patior* is complementary, and probably not a grecism (if it were, it would be unlikely to occur in a speech of Cicero's, see *De domo sua* 29 *sim passus a tali amicitia distrahi*). The predicate of the infinitive naturally has the same case as the subject, hence the nominative *ultor* (Roby xxii-xxiii and §1350, K–S I 702, *TLL* x 1.727.47–53).

44 Caesaris ultor: Romans were practical about revenge (a point many who deplore Aeneas' killing of Turnus at the end of the *Aeneid* tend to forget). Augustus made no bones about his pursuit of the assassins of Julius Caesar in his *Res gestae* 1.2 *qui parentem meum interfecerunt, eos in exilium expuli iudiciis legitimis ultus eorum facinus*, a passage which stresses the legality of the activity (cf. Dio 53.3.4). Moreover, after the battle of Philippi, in which he defeated Brutus and Cassius, he dedicated a temple to Mars Ultor (in due course the title was 'rebranded' as the vengeance taken upon the Parthians for the defeat of Crassus at Carrhae). Mercury is thus clearly being cast in Augustus' role.

45 serus in caelum redeas: an unexceptionable expression as applied to a god, Mercury, but since he is here identified with Augustus, H. insinuates artfully the notion that he too will return to his place of origin; cf. along with citations in N–H the interesting inscription dedicating a sacrarium to the *Lares Augusti*, *CIL* x 3757 = *ILS* 137 *caeloque repetes sedem*. The use of adjectival *serus* for an adverb (*sero*) is poetic, a grecism (=χρόνιος; K–S I 235–6), cf. 15.19 and *Epist.* 2.1.161; the word or its idea becomes common in imperial panegyric.

46 laetus 'propitiously', a word appropriate to a divinity (*OLD* 6, *TLL* VII 2.888.55–6). Adjectives of feeling too tend to supplant adverbs, in prose as well as verse (K–S 1 236–7); the positive adverb *laete* is however not much used.   **Quirini:** originally Quirinus was a separate divinity (Mankin on *Epode* 16.13), but his name was assigned (at an indeterminable date) to Romulus after his deification (Zetzel on Cicero, *De re publica* 2.20.3, and Myers on Ov. *Met.* 14.805–28, p. 202).

47–8 H. here evokes the myth of the maiden Astraea (equated with Justice), who, wearied by human wrongdoing, was wafted to heaven (Ov. *Met.* 1.149–50). *uitiis* picks up *uitio* 23.

47 iniquum 'angry at, hostile to'; the word is not uncommonly applied to gods (*TLL* VII 1.1640.43–62, *OLD* 5), cf. *penates . . . iniquos* 2.4.16, *Parcae . . . iniquae* 2.6.9, and *Vortumnis . . . iniquis Serm.* 2.7.14.

48 ocior 'swifter', i.e., than we could wish, since H. wants him to return *serus* 45. *ocior* is up-to-date poetic diction: the form is first found in the lyrics and in Virgil's *Aeneid* (*TLL* IX 2.413.27–9); the adverb, *ocius*, had already been long in use (it is first attested in Livius Andronicus). The *OLD* article on *ocior* obscures the history of the words; see rather *TLL* IX 2.414.19–25.

49–50 hic . . . hic: the adverbs, in an emphatic anaphora, contrast with *in caelum* 45.   **ames:** to be taken ἀπὸ κοινοῦ with *triumphos* and *dici* (cf. *dirae* III.); for different kinds of object word (noun, infinitive) with *ames* see *demere* 1.20n. The complementary infinitive (1.8n.) with *amo* is particularly common in H., who introduced it to Latin (K–S 1 674, *TLL* 1 1956.35–42). He borrowed the construction from Greek φιλεῖν, so this is a syntactical grecism.

50 pater: a term of respect (*OLD* 5b), appropriate both to mortals and divinities (cf. 2 above).   **princeps:** the word's first appearance applied to the emperor as a courtesy title (cf. 21.14, *TLL* X 2.1283.54–1284.3). H. must have been very quick on the uptake. It is the word Augustus later prefers to use of his position within the state in *Res gestae* 13, 30, and 32. Syme 1939: 311–12 was less than fair to the poet's feel for the emerging nomenclature.

51–2 neu sinas: the addition of a prohibition to a positive command by *neu* rather than *nec* is rare outside poetry (K–S 1 193), and Norden 1939: 130 demonstrated that it is peculiar to prayers, starting with the Arval hymn.   **Medos . . . inultos:** another allusion to the Parthians (cf. *Persae* 22n.), since the Medes of H.'s day were the people of the independent kingdom of Media Atropatene (mod. Azerbaijan), see Sherwin-White and Kuhrt 1993: 77–8; H. uses the romantic ethnology of poetry. *inultos* picks up the key theme of revenge (18, 44), and the need to take it upon the enemy which defeated Crassus and retained his standards. Thus H. suggests a new direction for vengeance, hinted at in 22.   **inultos te duce, Caesar:** Naylor 1922: xxx observed, with numerous further examples, the crescendo effect: 'The sentence is constructionally complete at *equitare*. All that follows is of added interest, i.e. " – unpunished – with you to lead – a Caesar!"' The ablative absolute *te duce* is identical with the subject of the sentence, a frequent 'violation' of the rule, here securing emphasis (G–L §410.3). *dux*, like *princeps*, was one of the vague appellations that Augustus favoured to describe his position (Syme 1939: 312).

*

The ode has a linear structure and is subdivided into two parts; the whole exhibits a typical progression from situation to response. The situation – terrible weather, floods, divine disfavour because of civil war – is set out in lines 1–24 and is articulated in groups of descending length: 3 (1–12) + 2 (13–20) + 1 (21–4). Lines 25–52 provide H.'s personal response to that situation: only divine aid can provide a remedy, but to whom should men turn? The two halves are linked by some common themes or language. The keynote of the poem is plainly vengeance (18, 44, 51), but proper measure is also in play (*satis* 2, *nimium* 17, *nimis* and *satiate* 37). Other key words are those suggesting fatherhood (3, 36, 50) and sonship (43), the latter perhaps emphasizing the duty of a son to avenge a father.

The questions in lines 25–30 are designedly unrealistic in terms of Roman religious practice, since the consuls and senate had traditional means of dealing with whatever they deemed to be *prodigia* (see *OCD* art. 'portents', p. 1228), especially floods, which were so frequent and might be seen either as warnings or as evidence of divine anger. Aldrete 2007: 91–165 describes the terrible effects of flooding, and at 219–21 he gives an account of the religious measures that could be taken to restore the *pax deorum*; see also Latte 1960: 203–4 for various remedies: sacrifices, *supplicatio*, or consultation of Sibylline books in really bad cases. The point is that the Romans did not share the Greek notion of pollution by crime or bloodshed, which required expiation (White 1993: 179). H. imaginatively exaggerates the situation and supplements traditional religious practices to make the reader feel that matters are too grave for human agency: only a god (but which one?) can put matters right.

Commager 1962: 175–94 argued that the theme is the poverty of a vengeance policy; what is needed is to unify and rebuild the community. This might be adjusted, and H. is to be seen as hinting a redirection of vengeful activity: there has been enough within Rome (floods, Caesar's assassins), and it is time to move outwards, against the Parthians.

White 1993: 180 and West 1995: 15 agree that H.'s strategy of praise here is improvisatory (for instance in the equation of Mercury and Augustus) and that he can be seen feeling his way to a personal grammar of panegyric, disconnected from more official expressions of homage.

Important for the last section of this poem is the finale of Virgil's first *Georgic*, with its sense of civil war as punishment (489), the appeal to Vesta (498), the notion of a saviour who is *iuuenis* (500) and who cares for earthly triumph (503–4), who will tarry on earth rather than return too soon to heaven. But the close of H.'s poem in its turn was exploited by Lucan for his *laudes Neronis* in *De bello ciuili* 1.33–66 (see Roche's commentary for a detailed analysis).

3

Metre: 'fourth' asclepiad (see Introduction 7–8)

1–8 H. prays to a ship to deliver his friend Virgil safely to his destination, Athens. For a similarly emotional address to the vessel which carries away someone dear to the speaker cf. Callimachus, fr. 400 Pfeiffer (two lines of an epigram).

1, 2 Sic 'on this condition'; *sic* commonly anticipates a condition for the fulfilment of a wish/vow/prayer (*OLD* 8d); that condition is expressed by an imperative or, as here, jussive subjunctive, *reddas* 7. For a, to us, more logical order cf. 28.25. The use of *sic*, rather than *ita*, is chiefly poetic, generated by metrical constraint (K–S I 191, H–S 331).   **diua potens Cypri** = Venus, by the figure antonomasia, cf. 19.10, 30.1–2, and 3.26.9 *o quae beatam, diua, tenes Cyprum*; her birth from the sea near Old Paphos gave her some control over it (cf. *NP* I 840). *diua/diuus* were not common synonyms for *dea/deus*. Cicero, who never used them in his correspondence, felt they conferred an archaic colour upon his 'laws', *De legibus* 2.19–22; by the same token they are found only once in a sacral formula in Livy, 7.26.4. Once too *diuus* appears at the end of the speech of Lepidus in Sallust, *Hist.* I, 55.27, and another historian, Sisenna used *diui* (fr. 123). Since *diua* and *diuus* are really only common in poetry, they may be deemed poetic diction, thanks to their archaic feel. *potens* is commonly combined with the genitive in poetry, as at 5.15, 6.10, 3.25.14, and *CS* I, to indicate the chief sphere of a divinity's influence (*TLL* x 2.285.33–64).

2 fratres Helenae = Castor and Pollux, by the figure antonomasia; they were protectors of sailors, cf. 3.29.64 *geminus ... Pollux*. For votive representations of them offered by rescued sailors see van Straten 1981: 96–7.   **lucida sidera:** either one or both of the brothers were believed to appear during a storm as a star, not to be confused with the constellation Gemini (cf. 12.28 *stella*, 4.8.31 *sidus*, *RE* art. 'Dioskuren. Retter zur See. Sterne' v 1096–7, and Bullock on Callimachus, *Hymn* 5.25 ἀστέρες). This was the atmospheric phenomenon now known as St Elmo's fire, a hot, ionized gas which forms during thunderstorms and glows around projecting objects, e.g., the masts or spars of sailing ships; the light's hue is blue to bluish-white (hence *lucida*, which is also used of the phenomenon by Cinna in his propempticon for Pollio, fr. 2 Courtney, and *alba* at 12.27). The 'star' appears after the most severe part of the storm is past, a relief to sailors: the worst was over, as H. describes at 12.29–32. Cf. Seneca, *Naturales Quaestiones* 1.1.13 *in magna tempestate apparere quasi* [NB] *stellae solent uelo insidentes; adiuuari se tunc periclitantes aestimant Pollucis et Castoris numine, causa autem melioris spei est quod iam apparet frangi tempestatem et desinere uentos*, and Pliny, *Nat. Hist.* 2.101 *exsistunt stellae et in mari. ... antemnis nauigantium aliisque nauium partibus ... insistunt ut uolucres*; Lucian, *Nauigium* 9, *Charidemus* 3. *lucidus* starts its life as a poetic word, though H.'s contemporary Vitruvius uses it in prose (*TLL* VII 2.1704.68–72).

3 uentorumque . . . pater = Aeolus, by the figure antonomasia. He was appointed 'steward' of the winds by Zeus (Hom. *Od.* 10.21). *pater* is used of one who is in charge of something, as at *S.* 2.8.7 *cenae pater* (*OLD* 4b).   **regat** 'guide your course' (*OLD* 4); for the singular see *iuuat* 2.38n.

4 obstrictis aliis 'all the rest being confined' (*OLD obstringo* 3, *alius* 6). Aeolus imprisoned the winds in a cave, cf. Virg. *Aen.* 1.52–4.   **Iapyga:** the termination is a Greek accusative singular of the third declension (G–L §65). In mythology, Iapyx settled in the 'heel' of Italy (to the Romans Calabria, to us Puglia), which was called Iapygia after him (Ov. *Met.* 15.703). A west-north-west wind blowing from there favoured ships sailing to Greece, so it was called after the territory *Iapyx* (3.27.20, *OLD* 3).

5–6 creditum | debes: the language is commercial in colour; cf. Statius' imitation, *Siluae* 3.2.6 *depositum* of a friend about to sail entrusted to Neptune.   **Vergilium:** P. Vergilius Maro was by this time Rome's most famous poet, thanks to his pastoral *Bucolica* (*Eclogues* to us) and didactic *Georgica*. Sometime in the early 30s he had befriended H., and in due course brought him to Maecenas' notice (*S.* 1.6.54–5). H.'s affection for him is warmly expressed at *S.* 1.5.41–2.   **finibus Atticis:** Attica is the territory in the south-east corner of mainland Greece, of which Athens is the chief city. Virgil presumably went there (if this poem records a real rather than an imaginary journey) for a holiday, or perhaps to study. Some interpreters, aware that Virgil did sail to Greece in 19, try to connect that visit to this poem, but there is no reason to suppose that when H. wrote it Virgil had any such intention, or if he did, that H. knew anything about it.

7 reddas . . . precor: 2.30n. *reddas incolumem* sustains the commercial imagery of the preceding lines; cf. Plautus, *Persa* 324 *omne argentum tibi hoc actutum incolume redigam.*

8 animae dimidium meae: cf. 2.17.5 *meae partem animae*, of Maecenas. Such expressions were proverbial (Otto 1890: 25–6), but H. reserves them for the people who matter to him.

9–24 The occasion of the poem, a prayer for the safe voyage of a friend, is now dropped, and H. launches asyndetically into reflections upon traditional themes, the hardihood of sailing and the transgression of natural limits. The section divides into two parts, the first of which concentrates on the first person to venture on the sea in a ship, the second on the crossing of natural boundaries, divinely set.

9–20 H. here dwells on the discoverer, πρῶτος εὑρετής, of sailing, a theme also for Propertius, 1.13–14 and Seneca, *Medea* 301–8 (a lyric which owes much to H.).

9–10 robur et aes triplex: proverbial (Otto 1890: 4), usually of the insensitive, but here of the imperturbable.   **erat:** for the singular see *iuuat* 2.38n.

10–11 fragilem truci | commisit pelago ratem: this 'golden' pattern (2.11–12n.) juxtaposes antithetic epithets. For *truci . . . pelago* cf. Catull. 63.16

truculenta ... pelagi and 64.179 *truculentum ... aequor. pelagus* is a loan-word from Greek, largely confined to poetry (*TLL* x 1.989.60–5), and by H. restricted to the *Odes*. Latin retains the neuter gender (G–L §34), cf. 35.8. For *ratem* see 1.17n.

12–13 Africum: 1.15n.   **decertantem Aquilonibus:** for the dative see *luctantem* 1.15n. *Aquilo* blows from the north-east, so the winds must meet head on. The plural of this, or of any, wind is largely poetic (*TLL* ii 376.13–20), though as usual it is taken up in the prose of the early principate.

14 Hyadas: poetic diction, a loan-word from Greek, for the native *Suculae*; the termination is also Greek, accusative plural of the third declension (G–L §65). The stars of the cluster Hyades, in the head of the constellation Taurus, are styled *tristes* 'gloomy' (cf. *OLD* 6, rather than 5b) because their morning setting in November heralds periods of rain (West on Hesiod, *Opera* 619ff.); Virgil called them 'rainy' *pluuiae, Aen.* 1.744, an etymological gloss.   **Noti:** another loan-word from Greek for the south wind, and hence poetic diction; its Latin name is *auster*.

15–16 quo non ... | maior: sc. *est.*   **arbiter Hadriae** 'governor' (*OLD* 3) 'of the Adriatic'. *Hadria*, borrowed from Greek, is a poetic word, first found in Catull. 36.15 (see Fordyce), for *Hadriaticum mare*, the sea which separates Italy from the modern Croatia, Albania, and north-western Greece. Elsewhere too H. says that the south wind lords it over this sea, *dux ... inquieti turbidus Hadriae*, 3.3.5. The poeticism is picked up by Tacitus, *Ann.* 15.34.1 *maris Hadriae traiectus.*

16 tollere: supply *siue* from the following *seu*. The usage, perhaps a grecism, starts in poetry and is then taken up in formal prose, e.g., by Tacitus (see K–S ii 436–7 for examples; *OLD siue* 4c is undernourished). It is important to distinguish this from *siue = uel si* (2.33n.), and from *siue* introducing a qualification (*OLD* 9).   **ponere** 'to lay', i.e., 'make calm', by ceasing to blow, cf. Virg. *Aen.* 5.763 *placidi strauerunt aequora uenti*; the sense is poetic (*OLD* 9), and seems original to H. This is probably an instance of the simple form of the verb preferred to its compound, *componere* (*tendere* 1.34n.).

17 gradum 'stride', i.e., vigorous approach, cf. 33. The word is often used of the steady onward pace of a marching army.

18–19 siccis oculis ... uidit: an example of double ἀπὸ κοινοῦ (cf. *dirae* 2.1n.), since *siccis oculis* goes with *uidit*, while the verb is to be supplied in 18. *siccis oculis* 'dry-eyed' implies unmoved. Bentley argued that weeping was no natural reaction to fear, and suggested *rectis* for *siccis*; he rather downplayed the context, which implies fear of death. Anyway, in Homer men do weep when they are afraid, e.g., the Greeks who reckon they will not be able to repel the Trojan attack upon the ships at *Il.* 13.88–9, the party sent to reconnoitre Circe's island at *Od.* 10.198–202 and 209, and the panic-stricken suitors at 20.349 (see Hainsworth on *Od.* 8.522 for the causes of weeping in Homer).   **monstra natantia:** whales and worse were among the stock terrors of the deep; cf. 3.27.26–7 *scatentem | beluis pontum*, 4.14.47 *beluosus oceanus* (the epithet there is unique).

19 et: for the connective at the end of the line see N–H 1970: xl (referring to 38 *infra*, 4.13.6, and cf. *in* at 21.14).

20 infames scopulos Acroceraunia: the apposition precedes its referent, an unusual arrangement, much liked by Ovid (for examples see Housman on Manilius, *Astronomica* 2.23). Acroceraunia may either be a mountainous promontory jutting far into the sea in northern Epirus, now called Kep i Gjuhëzës in Albania, or it may refer to the whole Ceraunian mountain range. Either way, it posed a threat to shipping, hence its bad name (*infames*).

21–4 It was a commonplace of ancient moralizing that seas (or rivers or chains of mountains) were natural or divinely sanctioned limits to human movement, which man impiously transgressed (see Smith on Tib. 1.3.37–40, pp. 246–7, and Wachsmuth 1967: 233–4).

21–2 deus ... | prudens: cf. 3.29.29 for similar divine providence. **abscidit** < *abscindo*, not *abscido*.

22 dissociabili 'sundering', both physically and morally: land and sea cannot be mixed, and men should not have meddled with the sea. The *–bilis* suffix is here instrumental (cf. Leumann 1963: 234), cf. *amabilis*, which can mean 'causing pleasure' (*OLD* 2) as well as 'lovable'. *dissociabilis* may be a coinage (H. offers a number with the *–bilis* suffix, see Bo Index 392).

24 non tangenda ... uada: touching what is forbidden is one form of sacrilege, cf. 35.35 *intactum*. The sea particularly was regarded as inappropriate for mankind, and so sailing was impious (see P. A. Gianfrotta, art. 'navigazione' in *EO* II 216–20); cf. 35.7–8. *uadum* properly means 'shallow water', but especially in the plural it is poetic diction for the waters of the sea, regardless of depth (*OLD* 4).   **rates:** 1.17n.

25–40 The poem now moves away from sailing, which evidently was just one example of human transgression. After stating a general truth about the whole human race (25–6), H. provides three mythological *exempla* to back it up; the *exempla* are related in decreasing length: Prometheus gets seven lines, Daedalus two, and Hercules one. The *exempla* are carefully chosen to cover land, sky, and underworld, and the individuals are identified by pleasingly varied means: *Iapeti genus, Daedalus, Herculeus labor*. But all three crumble upon analysis. H. is exemplifying the ruin wrought by the reckless daring of mankind (*gens humana*). But Prometheus was a god, and Daedalus' flight was successful up to a point (his son Icarus fell through his own folly, when against his father's advice he flew too close to the sun and so melted his waxen wings). Hercules did not choose to break into the Underworld, it was one of the labours imposed upon him; and he too was successful.

25 audax ... perpeti: H. is the first to attach the infinitive (1.18n.) to *audax* (a construction eased perhaps by the use of the infinitive with *audeo*); later poets follow him (*TLL* II 1248.47–52).

27 audax: repeated to effect transition to the *exempla*, and for emphasis.   **Iapeti genus** 'offspring of Iapetus' = Prometheus, by the figure antonomasia; for the highfalutin sense of *genus* here, a poetic loan-shift from γένος, see *OLD* 2, and cf. *Tantali genus* 2.18.38.

28 ignem: Hesiod twice told the tale of why Zeus withheld fire, which Prometheus stole and bestowed upon mankind, at *Theogonia* 562–9 and *Opera* 47–52. **fraude mala:** the expression evokes the Homeric κακὴ ἀπάτη (*Il.* 2.114). The epithet, not uncommon in poetry (*TLL* VI 1.1272.75–7), suggests the dire consequences of the deceit. **intulit** 'introduced' (*OLD infero* 6).

29–30 ignem ... subductum 'the theft of fire'; for the idiom, which is common after prepositions, see *meta euitata* 1.4–5n. The anaphora of *ignem* effects a link between the couplets. **aetheria:** a loan-word from Greek, and hence poetic diction (*TLL* I 1152.61).

30–1 macies ... cohors: in reprisal for the theft of fire, Zeus sent into the world of men a woman (possibly the first), called Pandora by Hesiod, *Opera* 81, who opened a jar and released, among other misfortunes, diseases (*Opera* 102–4). **noua febrium ... incubuit cohors:** see 2.5–6n. for *noua*. H.'s military metaphor is bold (*TLL* III 1552.10–12), and seems to develop the image initiated by Lucretius, 6.1143 *incubuit ... populo* (the plague at Athens). Both poets construe *incumbo* with a dative (here *terris*, cf. *OLD* 6), which, though found in prose (*Rhetorica ad Herennium* 1.18), is largely poetic syntax, recognized by Quintilian, *Institutio oratoria* 9.3.1, as a departure from the norm of preposition, *in* + accusative.

32–3 semotique ... tarda: before that final reprisal men had lived longer because free from sickness (Hesiod, *Opera* 90–2). *prius* is so placed as to modify both *semoti* and *tarda*, though an English translation must plump for one or the other. **leti:** poetic diction (*TLL* VII 1189.26–31), and so reserved for the lyrics; its sole appearance in the satires (2.6.95) characterizes the town mouse's pretentious turn of phrase. **corripuit gradum** 'stepped up her pace'. *corripio* can mean 'reduce' or 'diminish' something (*OLD* 8); applied to a stretch of road or ground it thus means 'render shorter', and so 'hasten over' (*OLD* 2). Here H. takes that sense a stage further, 'quicken the step'; he found an imitator in Statius, *Thebaid* 2.142–3.

34 expertus: sc. *est.* Daedalus was a famous craftsman, imprisoned by Minos on the island of Crete. To escape he flew away on wings made of wax and feathers. Ovid twice told the tale, at *Ars amatoria* 2.21–96 and *Met.* 8.183–259. **uacuum ... aera:** the phrase is owed to Virgil, *G.* 3.109, and ultimately derived from Pindar, *Olympian* 1.6. Since *aer* is a loan-word, the Greek termination, accusative singular of the third declension (G–L §65), is natural, but some Romans preferred the Latin form, *aerem* (*OLD* s.v. intro.).

36 perrupit: the long final vowel of the third person singular of the perfect is found in early Latin verse (G–L §131.4(b)6), but for H. it is an archaism, supported here by the ictus. **Acheronta** 'the Underworld' (*OLD* 2, and cf. 3.3.16), rather than specifically the river; the termination is the Greek accusative singular of the third declension (G–L §65). **Herculeus:** the epithet replaces a genitive, as at 4.17, 18.8, 34.11, a feature of poetic style. The labours of Hercules were proverbial, usually of toilsomeness, but here of striving (Otto 1890: 162). Twelve labours traditionally were imposed upon him by Eurystheus of Tiryns. The last was the fetching of Cerberus from the Underworld, Hades' guard-dog (he was later restored). This serves as an instance of the most daring form of transgression, when the living invade the realm of the dead.

37–40 H. draws the moral from his reflections upon mankind's unholy strivings: we act out of folly (*stultitia*), heaven punishes our crime (*scelus*).

37 ardui 'troublesome' (*OLD* 5); the genitive is partitive with *nil* (G–L §369). Since the basic meaning of *arduus* is 'steep' or 'towering', the word prepares for *caelum* in the next line.

38 caelum suggests the attack upon the Olympian gods by the Giants, who were defeated and imprisoned eternally. **petimus:** the first person plural is sympathetic, when the speaker associates himself with a deprecated action or attitude (Wackernagel 1926: 43 = 2009: 62–3); cf. 35.33, 36. **stultitia:** this word bulks large in the stoicizing *S.* 2.3, but its sense here is more general, 'human folly'.

40 iracunda ... fulmina: the epithet is transferred, *more poetico*, as at 12.59, for it is Jupiter who is angry. (Both odes end on this note.)

*

The structure of this poem is simple enough: a situation is described in the opening eight lines, and the rest of the poem is a response to that situation. H.'s concern for the safety of a cherished friend prompts gloomy reflections on the hardihood and impiety of seafaring (9–24). The ode thus begins, at any rate, as if it were a formal send-off, called a propempticon, a situation other poets developed, e.g. Cinna, mentioned in 2n., and Propertius 1.17 (Cairns 1972: 231–5). This character was recognized in the heading found in part of the MS tradition: *propemptice*. But after the opening prayer, combined with the critique of sailing and its inventor (for which see McKeown's introduction to Ov. *Am.* 2.11 and N–R on *Carm.* 3.27) the poem moves on to deplore mankind's audacious ambition in general (25–40). The original situation is thus gradually lost sight of amidst the moralizing diatribes (Syndikus 2001: 70). Similarly constructed is the eighteenth ode.

The tone of this ode however is harder to gauge. Wickham said, twice, that it is playful, but he did not illustrate wherein the 'play' is to be found. West 1995: 16–19 sees an element of fun, but regards the whole as severe, and yet rather inaccessible for the modern reader. Syndikus 2001: 70, n. 56 and Fitch 2006–07 agree with this assessment, discount the humour, and illustrate how easy it is for modern interpreters to dismiss the poem as a failure, largely because we do not share H.'s misgivings about man's ambitious nature. Perhaps the present state of the planet's ecology might induce some rethinking on that score.

It is important for an understanding of the ode to give due weight to the addressee, the ship. The poem is not addressed to Virgil; it is therefore not about him or about H.'s feeling for him, though that feeling is given warm expression at the close of the introductory section (7–8). Virgil's journey (real or imagined) is therefore not the theme, but only provides an occasion for larger moral reflections, rather like Milton's *Lycidas*, in which the death of a clergyman at sea serves as the springboard for serious reflections upon the state of the English church. Thus some of N–H's strictures 1970: 44–5 are groundless: this is not a poem of friendship, as they deem it, though friendship is an undeniable element.

Nor need the poem be understood allegorically. Nisbet 1995: 418–19, Syndikus 2001: 61, n. 13, Cucchiarelli 2005: 71, n. 122, and Fitch 2006-07 all crisply dismiss interpretations which find Virgil's voyage a metaphor for poetic daring, i.e. his composition of heroic epos. It is fairly observed that a poet's choice of genre or theme may prove to be a blind alley, but it is hardly a sin; the rhetoric would be excessive. The 'poetological' reading has nonetheless been reinvigorated by Harrison 2007a: 12–14 and Rumpf 2009, who also provides a thorough account of the problem of unity (2009: 292–6) and a helpful review of earlier 'poetological' strategies (2009: 296–300). But like their predecessors they fail to see that H.'s strictures would be 'over the top' if directed at poetic composition of any kind.

Traill 1982 suggested a political allegory in the final lines; West 1995: 17–18 accepted this with some adjustments. But they failed to recall that from line 25 on H. criticizes mankind as a whole, so that with *petimus* 38 he is not speaking of Romans in particular; the reference should still be to a general human failing. Nor is it clear how the reader is steered to take *scelus* 39 as alluding to civil war, and to see in Jupiter the figure of Augustus. Anyway, H. had dealt with the crime of civil war in the previous poem, and reversion to the theme in this one might be deemed inelegant.

That said, the prominent placement of this poem is significant. The two poems after the dedicatory ode are both on serious matters (however little they may meet with modern approval). The second ode concerns the state of Rome, the third focuses upon a more general issue of human psychology (reckless ambition) and morality (over-reaching 'natural' limits such as the sea or the sky). H. thus announces that his lyric output is not to be all wine and roses. They will however come with the next two poems.

4

Metre: see Introduction 8. The metrical scheme, unique in the collection, is well characterized by N–H 1970: 61: the lively long lines are pulled up by the slow iambics (there is only one initial short syllable, in line 2). The force of the ithyphallic in the iambic line is especially prominent in line 13.

1–12 The poem begins with a picture of spring as we see its effects around us on sea and land (a polar expression) (1–4). An imagined scene among divinities follows, which forms a polar unit with the first four lines: the activities of men and of gods (5–8). Then H. indicates what our response should be to the return of the cheerful season: the pleasures of a drinking-party (9–10) and thanksgiving to a god (11–12). Time is emphasized: *iam* (3, 5), and the anaphora of *nunc* (9, 11), and this note is sounded in the second half of the poem too: *iam* 'soon' (16), *nunc*, *mox* (20). Verbal echoes bind the parts together: *soluitur* (1) ∼ *solutae* (10), *decentes* (6) ∼ *decet* (9, 11).

1 Soluitur 'is thawing' (*OLD* 13b). The verb in initial position presents a vivid picture; Marouzeau 1938: 65 compared the similar opening of the later spring poem, 4.7.1, *diffugere niues, redeunt iam gramina campis*.   **acris:** the epithet was also used of winter by Ennius, *Annales* 420 Skutsch and Lucretius 6.373.   **uice** 'with the succession' (*OLD uicis* (genitive) 7), instrumental ablative; cf. 4.7.3 *mutat terra uices* (there are echoes aplenty of this poem in the rather grim later one, see the analysis in Thomas's commentary, pp. 174–5).   **ueris et Fauoni:** Roman spring began when the west wind blew again on 7 February, according to Columella, *De re rustica* 11.2.15 *Fauonii spirare incipiunt*, and this view was generally shared, e.g., by Varro, *Res rusticae* 1.28.1–2.

2 machinae: winches eased the passage of the ships over rollers (*OLD phalanga* b, and cf. *scutula*) and back into the water. Traditionally during the stormy winter months ships were beached (hence *siccas*), which also enabled them to be repaired (but see 1.15–18n.).

3, 5 iam: Catullus too had repeated this adverb, rather more urgently, in his spring poem, 46.1–2, and 7–8.

4 canis albicant pruinis: cf. Virg. *G.* 2.376 *frigora . . . cana concreta pruina*; the plural is poetic. *albico* is generally only found in poetry, e.g., the highly mannered *Attis* of Catullus (63.87), before the principate. The fifth-century writer Martianus Capella admired the 'elegant alternative' to *albeo* (*De nuptiis Philologiae et Mercurii*, 5.511 *satis crispa flexione*); it is the only passage of H. he quoted. The pleonasm of adjective and verb is not unusual, cf. Ov. *Met.* 3 515 *albentia tempora canis*.

5 Cytherea . . . Venus: she was in charge of the spring, especially the month of April, cf. Lucr. 5.737 *it uer et Venus*. The adjective *Cytherea*, found only here, is derived from the island in the Aegean, Cythera, one of Aphrodite's alleged birthplaces (for another cf. 30.1n.).   **choros ducit:** cf. *ducere . . . choros* 4.7.6.

6 iunctae . . . Nymphis Gratiae: they combine again at 30.6 and at 4.7.5. H. not surprisingly is the first to introduce to Rome the Graces, originally Greek deities, the Χάριτες; they appear frequently in his lyrics (3.21.22 in addition to the passages already cited).   **decentes** 'comely': *decens* is a coinage of H.'s, embraced by Ovid; it remained poetic diction until taken up by first-century prose writers. It will be echoed by *decet* in 9 and 11.

7 terram quatiunt pede: *quatio*, here used of dancing (cf. 4.1.27–8 *pede . . . quatient humum*, *OLD* 2b), is found chiefly in poetry before the prose

writers of the early principate (see Oakley on Livy 7.26.1).   **graues** perhaps
'oppressive' (*OLD* 6), because of the heat, or 'burdensome', referring to the weight
of the metal they work (*OLD* 10d). For the Cyclopes as smiths (rather than the
shepherds of the *Odyssey*) see Hesiod, *Theogonia* 140; Callimachus has them work-
ing for Vulcan (*Hymn* 3.46–50). They are forging thunderbolts for Jupiter, who
will need them in the stormy months ahead.

8 uisit 'goes and inspects' (*OLD* 2b) to ensure that they are ready for the
work ahead; the reading is defended by Bernays 2005; the variant *urit* cannot
mean 'fires up', 'makes blaze' (cf. *OLD* 2).   **officinas:** the workshops were
traditionally located either under Mt Etna on the east coast of Sicily, or under
the volcanic Lipari islands to the north.

9, 11 nunc decet … nunc … decet: repetition urges that appropriate
action is to be taken. This urgency is explained by the irruption of death into the
poem at 13 (Quinn 1980: 128).

9 uiridi … myrto: drinkers in antiquity wore a wreath (*corona*, 7.23, 17.27,
38.2) of flowers or leaves, either on the head or round the neck (or both!); see
Köchling 1914. Myrtle was one of the commonest materials for such crowns (cf.
38.5, 7; 2.7.23–5 *quis udo | deproperare apio coronas | curatue myrto?*); Cato the Elder
encouraged the suburban gardener to sow *coronamenta* 'flowers for crowns' of all
sorts, as well as *murtum coniugulum et album et nigrum*, presumably for the same pur-
pose (*De agri cultura* 8.2). Myrtle was moreover sacred to Venus (Plautus, *Vidularia*
17 *haec myrtus Veneris est*) and so appropriate to the symposium. Its astringent leaf
was also reckoned a prophylactic against the fumes of wine, according to the first-
century BC physician Philonides in his treatise on perfumes and wreaths, quoted
in extenso at Athenaeus, *Deipnosophistae* 15.675e.   **nitidum** 'glossy', because the
head was anointed with fragrant oil (= perfume, which was oil-based in anti-
quity); cf. 29.7–8 *capillis … unctis*, 3.19.25 *spissa te nitidum coma*, and *Epist.* 1.14.32
nitidi capilli.   **impedire:** poets gave the verb a weakened sense, *cingere*, as here
(*TLL* VII 1.531.30–3).

11 et 'too', 'also', 'likewise' (*OLD* 5).   **Fauno:** a native Italian divinity of
the wild woodlands, identified with the Greek Pan (see 17.2n., F. Trisoglio, art.
'Fauno' in *EO* II 374–5, and N–R's introduction to 3.18). His rural festival was
held in the winter (cf. 3.18.10 *cum tibi Nonae redeunt Decembres* = 5 December); his
urban festival on 13 February 'was not very successful' (Scullard 1981: 72). But *decet*
does not suggest an obligatory rite of the state religious calendar, so the sacrifice
here is presumably a private one, which is also suggested by its location in a
grove.   **lucis:** strictly speaking, 'sacred groves', a feature of Roman religion
and the haunt of Faunus (*TLL* VII 2.1751.52–1752.68 provides a vast collection of
references). *umbrosis* seems inappropriate to the time of year.

12 seu … siue 'either with a lamb, if he ask that, or with a kid, if he prefer
that'. *seu/siue* = *uel … si* (2.33n.). *agna* and *haedo* are instrumental ablatives,
a very rare construction with the normally transitive *immolare*. H. opted for a
construction which *facio* (in the sense 'sacrifice', *OLD* 24b), *sacrifico* and *supplico*

sometimes took (so Brink, *TLL* VII 1.489.54–60). Since sacrifice involves the death of the victim, there is an implicit transition to the next section of the poem.

13–20 In spite of the implied transition, the mood abruptly changes with the personification of Death and reflections upon mortality and loss. The Roman reader might have reflected that later in the month of February there was a series of important festivals in honour of dead ancestors (Scullard 1981: 69: 'a solemn mood must succeed the jollier festivals of mid-winter'). At last too an addressee for the ode is named (cf. 7.19).

13 pallida Mors: Quintilian, *Institutio oratoria* 8.6.27, recognized this expression as the kind of metonymy which indicates cause by effect, suited to poetry and oratory: *id quod efficit ex eo quod efficitur ostendimus* (cf. too *Rhetorica ad Herennium* 4.43). That death comes to one and all is of course proverbial (Otto 1890: 228), cf. 28.15, but for the polar concept 'rich and poor' cf. 2.14.11–12 *siue reges | siue inopes erimus coloni*. The personification of death is poetic (*TLL* VIII 1505.18–34). **aequo pulsat pede:** for Death's 'impartial' foot, contrasting with the foot of the dancers in 7, cf. in a similar context 2.18.32–4 *aequa tellus | pauperi recluditur | regumque pueris*. Impatient visitors kicked the door to rouse the doorkeeper (cf. Callimachus, *Hymn* 2.3, and Dover's uncertain comment on Aristophanes, *Clouds* 136). The alliteration of *p* gives an aural image. **paúperúm tabérnas:** Barr 1962: 10 drew attention to the way in which the trochaic rhythm represents 'the three dread knocks of the importunate spectre'. *tabernas* means 'huts' or 'cabins' (*OLD* 1), where the poor live; H. is not suggesting that Death catches up with them in the pub or shop where they work.

14 regumque turres: kings are a type of wealth (*OLD* 4, to which add Plautus, *Rudens* 931 *nauibus magnis mercaturam faciam: apud reges rex perhibebor*), and *rex* comes to mean simply 'a wealthy man' (Lejay on *S.* 1.2.86), especially when contrasted with the poor, as here and at 2.14.11–12 quoted above. Typically too they might construct towers in their gardens, as did Maecenas, cf. 3.29.10 *molem propinquam nubibus arduis*, and Caecina Tuscus, cf. Tacitus, *Historiae* 3.38.

o beate Sesti: *o* intensifies the appeal. *beate* picks up the implication of wealth in *regum*, a gliding transition. But since H. will go on to list the things Sestius cannot enjoy after death the word nudges him in the direction of an implicit moral, to make good use whilst he can of his riches ('you can't take it with you').

L. Sestius P. f. L. n. was born in about 73 (*OCD* 1396). He accompanied M. Iunius Brutus as his *quaestor* to the East after the assassination of Julius Caesar, and so it seems very likely, as Münzer suggested in *RE*[2] II 1885.56–9, that it was about that time he befriended H., who had joined Brutus' *cohors* as *tribunus militum* at Athens (cf. 2.7.1–2, where H. refers to that service). Sestius was amnestied after his proscription; he was appointed suffect consul, replacing Augustus in July 23 (Dio 53.32.3–4), the year of publication of the collection of three books of *Carmina*. His appointment will have been a signal from Augustus that, according to J. A. Crook in *CAH* x 85, it was 'business as usual' so far as the aristocracy were concerned: Augustus was no longer going to monopolize one of the consulships, as he had for eight years. The choice of a supporter of Brutus showed moreover that Augustus was prepared to forgive, forget, and reward former opponents (Professor Rathbone observes that if Sestius, for his part, had been an intransigent, he would never have accepted). The placing of this ode so prominently in the collection makes it 'political' in a way that its content would never suggest.

15 uitae summa breuis: proverbial (Otto 1890: 375).   **spem . . . longam:** cf. 11.7. This reflection has of course general application, but since the addressee Sestius was only to be consul for half a year there is a humorous irony to it.

16–17 iam te premet nox fabulaeque Manes | et domus exilis Plutonia: the sentence forms an ascending tricolon (2.38n.).   **iam** 'very soon now', a common sense, especially with the future (*TLL* VII 1.105.19–106.21), as at 2.5.10–11 *iam . . . distinguet*, 13 *iam te sequetur*, 15–16 *iam . . . petet* (*petit* in Rudd's Loeb must be a misprint, for he translates 'will rush').   **premet:** for the number see *iuuat* 2.38n. Death's constraint (for which cf. 2.14.9 *compescit*, 18.38 *coercet*) is in contrast with the loosening power of Spring.   **nox** 'death', a poetic metaphor (*OLD* 1g, a somewhat misleading account, since no epithet is required, as here and at 28.15).   **fabulae:** attributive (= *fabulosi* 'storied') with *Manes*, see *atauis . . . regibus* 1.1n. and H–S 159.

17 domus exilis: the expression, repeated at *Epist.* 1.6.45, becomes an oxymoron with the addition of *Plutonia*, for the Greek name of the god of the underworld, Pluto, was commonly associated with the word for wealth, πλοῦτος. *exilis* 'meagre' also contrasts with the wealth of Sestius (*beate* 14). *Plutonia* does not violate the classical practice of attaching only a single epithet to a noun since in effect it replaces a possessive genitive, *Plutonis* (see 3.36n.); the adjective is poetic diction.

simul: the conjunction (*OLD* 11), which H. uses in lyric and hexameter verse, but *simul ac* (*atque*) is found only in the hexameter poems.   **mearis** = *meaueris*, a syncopated future perfect. The verb is poetic diction, though it entered the prose of the early principate (*TLL* VIII 785.8–11).

18 regna uini sortiere talis: prolonged after-dinner drinking at the *comissatio* (= symposium) was regulated (up to a point) by the appointment of a president (called *magister* or *arbiter* or *potandi modimperator* by Varro *apud* Nonius Marcellus p. 142M) who imposed prescriptions (called *lex* by Catull. 27.3, Cic. *Verrines* 2.5.28, H. *S.* 2.6.69) for the proportion of wine to water. The appointment was left to chance, the throw of knucklebones (*tali*, as here, or dice (*tesserae*) (cf. 2.7.25–6 *quem Venus arbitrum | dicet bibendi?*, where *Venus* refers to the best throw, *OLD* 2b). H.'s phraseology appealed to Tacitus, cf. *Ann.* 13.15.2 *regnum lusu sortientium*.

19 Lycidan: the termination is a Greek accusative singular of the first declension (G–L §65). One aspect of the advanced hellenization of Roman élite society was the adoption of pederasty, or paedophilia as we would term it (there is no point in mincing words, since the boys were for preference prepubescent, hence *tenerum* here). They were of course pretty and generally Greek and usually slaves, so their compliance was assured; the social and literary background is described by Griffin 1994: 2, 16, 25–6, Williams 1999: 30–4, 37–8, and N–R's introduction to *Carm.* 3.20, pp. 239–40. (Homosexual relations with an under-age Roman boy of free birth, however, were deemed a *stuprum* by the *lex Iulia de adulteriis* and the severer *lex Scantinia*.)

19–20 quo calet ... tepebunt: *quo* is instrumental ablative, cf. 4.11.33 *non ... alia calebo femina*; but the use of a person as the instrument (rather than, say, *igne*) is poetic (H–S 133). Both verbs mean 'feel the warmth of love', and this metaphorical sense is first found in H.; *caleo* becomes popular with poets in this usage (*OLD* 6). *tepeo* is generally agreed to imply a lesser degree of erotic warmth than *caleo*, but opinion is divided as to the implication. Some reckon it indicates an early stage of affection (e.g., Knox on Ovid, *Heroides* 11.26), others (e.g., Woodman 1972: 775–6) that it suggests a loss of passion, a sense clearly found in two passages of Ovid (see *OLD* 3).   **uirgines:** Watson 1983: 127, 132–3 demonstrated that in poetry at any rate the word occasionally meant no more than 'young woman' in an erotic milieu, with suspension of the notions of respectability and unmarried status; cf. 6.17, 3.15.5.

*

The return of spring was a long-standing theme in Greek poetry. Alcaeus *GL* 1 286 typically refers (or so it seems) to the reopening of the seas, and we may compare that motif in the clutch of epigrams found at the start of the tenth book of the *Anthologia Palatina*. Alcaeus also regards the coming of spring as a good time for a drink, 1 367. H. combines these varied motifs here, but decorates the occasion with scenes of divine festivity or toil. Unexpected however is the irruption of Death upon the scene. Death will put an end, for mortals like Sestius at least, to the pleasures Spring renews. The message remains implicit, that the delights of drink and sex must not be deferred.

H. focuses at the end in a way characteristic of him (cf. the end of *Carm.* 3.20) on a peculiar detail, the delicate Lycidas. He is concerned less with sexual mores than with the lessons of time: Lycidas as a boy attracts young men, but he will age and become a young man himself, as such an object of interest to girls (again like Nearchus in *Carm.* 3.20). But the reader may be invited to reflect that time will age him yet more, and he may end up, like Lyce in *Carm.* 4.13, desired by no one. The lesson, which H. only hints at, is that we must take advantage of time while it is on our side (we note the insistent words for 'now' throughout the poem), and enjoy the pleasures it provides 'in due season'. The poem is thus ringed by thoughts of time's movement: winter is giving way to spring, Lycidas is growing older.

It was noted above that H. and Sestius had probably known each other for decades, which sufficiently accounts for the dedication of the poem. Altogether less clear until recently was the careful tailoring of this ode to its addressee. Will 1982, and especially 243 (helpfully paraphrased by West 1995: 21–2), demonstrated that much detail in the poem points to Sestius' business interests: he owned ships (*carinas* 2), which exported the products of his fired-brick and tile kilns (*officinas* 8), as well as wine amphorae. These manufactures were the source of his considerable wealth (*beate* 14). He may have lived in a turreted villa (*turres* 14) in the *ager Cosanus*.

5

Metre: 'third' asclepiad (see Introduction 7)

1–5 H. questions an attractive woman about her new admirer. His questions are not genuine: he is not interested in the lover's identity, but aims to suggest the girl's fickleness.

1 The verse is pictorial or 'iconic', i.e. the word placement pictures the scene (Highet 1957: 128): the girl is central, the slender boy hedges her in, and the pair is surrounded by many a rose; cf. 3.18.13 *inter audaces lupus errat agnos*, 27.51–2 *inter errem nuda leones* (with N–R).

multa ... in rosa 'on many a rose'; the rose is the flower of Venus, and so appropriate to the setting and the activity. For the collective singular see 2.9n. *ulmo*, and for the addition of an epithet in the singular indicating quantity, a licence freely developed in poetry, see the examples collected in K–S I 70 or H–S 161–2. (*OLD multus* 1c recognizes the usage but fails to cite Virg. *Ecl.* 1.33 *multa uictima*, apparently the earliest certain example; *TLL* VIII 1608.70–82, on the other hand, cites no examples from H.: cf. *multo ... milite* 15.6.) The precise sense of *in rosa* is debated (and H. may have intended ambiguity), but *multa* suggests that a couch is strewn with rose petals, rather than that the lad is wearing a large crown of roses. The Romans did indeed recline on roses: see Seneca, *Dialogi* 7.11.4 *aspice hos eosdem* [viz, *Nomentanum et Apicium*] *e suggestu rosae despectantes popinam suam*, where *suggestu* is the conjecture of the Dutch scholar Johann Friedrich Gronovius (1611–71), supported by appeal to Sen. *Epist.* 36.9 *in rosa iaceat*. As an alternative to strewing the couch, cushions might be stuffed with roses, cf. Cic. *Verr.* 5.27, *ut mos fuit Bithyniae regibus, lectica octaphoro ferebatur* [Verres], *in qua puluinus erat perlucidus Melitensis rosa fartus*. On the other hand, Cicero, *De finibus* 2.65 *potantem in rosa* and *Tusculanae Disputationes* 5.73 *an tu me in uiola putabas aut in rosa dicere?*, is clearly referring to crowns of roses; similarly Prop. 3.5.22 *caput in uerna semper habere rosa* (*OLD in* 36).   **gracilis ... puer:** the epithet enhances the delicate pathos of the noun, which suggests a very young male, a 'boy' out of his depth.

2 liquidis ... odoribus: poetic phraseology, owed perhaps to Virgil, *G.* 4.414 *liquidum ambrosiae diffundit odorem*. Unqualified, *odores* would normally have suggested plants burned for their fragrance, not perfume (= *unguentum*). The use of perfume by a male, frequently referred to by H. in his lyrics, is a hallmark of the life of luxury pursued by this *puer lepidus ac delicatus* (to paraphrase Cicero, *Catil.* 2.23); see Griffin 1994: 10–11.   **urget** 'embraces' (*OLD* 1).

3 antro 'grotto', a loan-word from Greek, ἄντρον, and so poetic diction (*TLL* II 191.37–8). Grottoes, a feature of Roman pleasure gardens (Farrar 1998: 61–2), could be either natural or artificial; they were cooled by water, and planted with moss. Seneca describes two such *speluncae* at the Baian villa of Vatia, *Epist.* 55.6. As H. sets the scene, luxury is the keynote, and the boy is out to impress.

4 flauam: a girl called Pyrrha (the Greek word from which it is derived means 'flame-coloured') would of course have blonde hair, which was esteemed in the Mediterranean world, as it still is with us. It was therefore characteristic of gods, heroes, and courtesans, such as Phyllis (2.4.14) and Chloe (3.9.19); see the exhaustive discussion by Pease on Virg. *Aen.* 4.590.   **religas:** for tying up the hair in a knot or bun, cf. 2.11.24 *comam religata nodo* (the text there is uncertain, but what H. described is not). Before the twentieth century women kept their hair long, and it was generally bound up into more or less elaborate coiffures.   **comam:** a loan-word from Greek, introduced into poetry by Ennius, *Annales* 349 Skutsch *comis passis*. It remained largely poetic diction (*TLL* III 1746.27–8), and H. excluded it from his hexameters.

5 simplex munditiis 'unadorned in your elegance'. The sentence seemed to end with the first stanza, but this run-over addendum encapsulates Pyrrha's allure: she has the art which conceals art, and hence appears *simplex* 'unadorned' (*OLD* 7), a word that perhaps also suggests, misleadingly, an ingenuous character (*OLD* 8). Both the noun *munditia* and its adjective *mundus*, of which H. is especially fond (see Mayer on *Epist.* 1.4.11 *mundus uictus*, and cf. *mundae ... cenae* 3.29.14–15) denote refinement, a mean between superfluity (like the boy's use of perfume) and deficiency. H.'s phrase generated something of a debate about cosmetics, see Gibson 2007: 34 (on Propertius 4.8.40 *munda sine arte*) and 94–6 (on Ovid and Tertullian).

5–12 H. reflects upon the boy's impending disillusion in a sentence of dazzling mastery. Characteristic are the appended adjectives or phrases (*insolens, credulus aurea, nescius aurae | fallacis*; Naylor 1922: xxx, §53), each of which exceeds its predecessor in length. Clauses and adjectives are joined by anaphora rather than conjunctions (*qui, qui; semper, semper*). Thus in the whole of this extended structure there is only one connective, *et* 6.

5 heu: H. sighs sympathetically over the trouble in store for the boy. Hofmann 1951: 14 observed that the word belongs to the high style of poetry (cf. *TLL* VI 2.2672.12–15).

5–6 fidem | mutatosque deos: *mutatos* is to be taken ἀπὸ κοινοῦ with *fidem* (cf. *dirae* 2.1n).   **flebit:** the transitive use of this verb is largely poetic (*TLL* VI 1.900.69, see the whole article).

6–7 aspera 'ruffled' (*OLD* 4c). For *aequora* cf. 2.11–12n.; the plural is poetic. H. introduces a common metaphor, woman as sea (cf. 33.15–16). As the

French scholar Dionysius Lambinus (1520–72) noted on 11–12, this metaphor is sustained through the rest of the poem. **nigris ... uentis:** ablative of instrument. Storm winds are coloured by the dark clouds they amass (Watson on *Epode* 10.5 *niger ... Eurus, OLD niger* 4a); contrast the 'white' clearing wind at 7.15–16.

8 emirabitur: apparently a coinage; the prefix intensifies (Roby §1950). *insolens* is a sort of appendix, explaining why he is so surprised now: lack of experience (*OLD* 1).

9 fruitur 'enjoy (sexually)' (add to both Adams 1982: 198 and *OLD* 4b). The verb also has a legal connotation appropriate to this context, implying use but not ownership (*OLD* 1). **credulus aurea:** juxtaposed epithets further characterize the boy's situation: he is heading for disaster. Pyrrha too is now characterized, but more suggestively: since gold is so precious, the epithet points to her radiant blonde beauty (*OLD* 5), a metaphor sustained by *nites* 13; but gold is also imperishable, unlike her affections.

10 semper ... semper: the anaphora perhaps parodies the boy's ardent yearning for the continuance of the relationship. **uacuam:** ambiguous, depending on the focalization: he wants her to be 'unattached' (*OLD* 9c), but she might see herself as 'fancy-free' (*OLD* 12a, and cf. 6.19). *uacuus* also has a legal overtone, 'unappropriated' (*OLD* 9a of land), which sits well with *fruitur* in the previous line. **amabilem:** Axelson 1945: 102–3 deemed the word 'unpoetic', because so few poets apart from H. himself used it. He ought however to have taken into account that poets using dactylic-based metres found most forms of adjectives ending in –*bilis* intractable where –*bilis* was attached to a long vowel of the stem. Perhaps too a better description of the tone is 'neutral', since the word was in everyday use.

11–12 sperat: supply for the sense *te fore*. **nescius aurae | fallacis:** yet a third appendix, emphasizing still the boy's inexperience. *aura*, which seems to pun on *aurea* 9 (Commager 1962: 66–7), is being used in two senses here. The first sustains the metaphor of a wind at sea (*OLD* 2; cf. Virg. *Aen.* 5.850 *fallacibus auris*); the second suggests an attractive 'emanation' (*OLD* 7), cf. the allure of Barine in 2.8.24 (with N–H's n.). *fallax* 'corrects' *simplex* 5 – the words are contrasted by Cicero, *De officiis* 1.63 *itaque uiros fortes et magnanimos eosdem bonos et simplices, ueritatis amicos minimeque fallaces esse uolumus* (with which cf. 3.57).

12–13 miseri, quibus | intemptata nites!: H. concludes his reflections upon Pyrrha's current affair with a generalized observation, hence the plural *miseri* 'pitiable'. *intemptata* first appears here, so it may be a coinage of H.'s, a calque upon ἀπείρατος (so K–H followed by *TLL* VII 1.2112.12–14); *OLD* puts it in section 1 'untried', but it might belong better in 1b (of territory, roads, etc.) 'not tried as a route' (here, obviously a metaphorical sense), since H. is comparing Pyrrha throughout to a sea on which a man ventures at his peril. **nites** 'your radiant beauty shines' (*OLD* 3b), of the 'glow' of youthful beauty (cf. 19.5 *nitor*, 33.4 *praeniteat*, and 2.8.6 *enitescis*). With respect to the metaphor of the sea it suggests light reflected from its calm, and thus inviting, surface (*OLD* 2, though no examples of the sea are quoted). Meleager has a similar conceit (*Anthologia Palatina* 5.156 = *HE* xxv 4130–1): the amorous Asclepias with shining eyes, like calm weather, coaxes men on to the sea of love (ἐρωτοπλοεῖν).

13–16 From the present we move back into the reminiscent past, and H.'s own experience of the girl (or one like her at any rate). He sailed that sea, and survived, just! The conclusion keeps up the metaphor of the girl as dangerous sea; her lovers are sailors, and they inevitably suffer shipwreck. If a man survived a real shipwreck, he would owe the god who saved him a thank-offering, and perhaps a record of the event. The latter took the form of a small depiction of the incident (*tabula uotiua*), to be hung on a wall in the god's shrine (*sacer paries*); we may still see such things in the Catholic churches of central Europe (and most affecting they can be). For such private vows see Ogilvie 1969: 38.

The composition of this final sentence merits careful analysis. To secure the personal ending (Ich-Schluß) the pronoun *me* is foregrounded; it is the subject of *suspendisse*. Four words then set the scene: a temple wall hung with a votive board. The verb *indicat* promises a revelation, but H. sustains the metaphor of the sea, rather than crudely saying, 'I survived being dumped by you.' What is revealed is the offering of the still drenched garments to the sea god. First come the epithets, *uuida* and *potenti*, and only in the last line the nouns which complete the sense of the whole.

13–14 tabula ... uotiua: the practice of dedicating a representation in repoussé metalwork or on painted pottery plaques or wooden panels (as here) or in sculptural reliefs was widespread in antiquity; they commemorated a variety of situations, not always calamitous (see Headlam on Herodas 4.19, van Straten (1981: 96–7 particularly for survivors of shipwreck)). Paintings were made by professionals, cf. *AP* 20–1 *si fractis enatat exspes | nauibus aere dato qui pingitur*.

14–16 uuida ... uestimenta: cf. Plautus, *Rudens* 573 *uestimentis uuidis* (the speaker Charmides has also survived shipwreck). *uuidus* is poetic diction, the everyday word being *umidus*.

15–16 suspendisse: this practice is also mentioned by Virg. *Aen.* 12.768–9 *seruati ex undis ... solebant ... uotas suspendere uestes*, and Diodorus in *Anthologia Palatina* 6.245 = *GP* iv 2118–23 (Diogenes dedicates his little cloak (λώπιον) to Cabirus). For the variety of votive offerings see Wachsmuth 1967: 133–42, esp. 140–1 n. 243 for clothing.   **potenti ... maris:** for the genitive and the aptness of *potens* see 3.1n.; cf. an inscription published in *L'Année épigraphique* 1955: 38, n. 119 *Neptuno <aq>uarum <po>tenti*. Brink 1969: 1 argued that this expression points exclusively to Neptune, and so he determined that the last word of the poem is *deo* (not *deae*, as conjectured by Zielinski and adopted by some editors, or at least mentioned in their apparatus criticus).

*

This is H.'s first poem dedicated to love in the collection, and it clearly hints at an unexpected erotic agenda in a lyric collection. The persona it presents is disabused and out of love, at any rate with Pyrrha. Her surface attractions are still undeniable, but the inexperienced will only be misled by them into baseless expectations of enduring affection. The implication is that the persona himself made the same mistake (perhaps not all that recently), but the reality is that he lived to tell the tale, and so to warn the unpractised. The focus on Pyrrha's victim, still a lad (*puer* 1), is also in effect programmatic, given the poem's placement in the book and collection, since more erotic poems will focus less on the speaker of the poem than on other people's affairs (e.g., 8, 27). The bad effects in their lives of strong feeling combined with inexperience will be an issue to explore. As West 1967: 103–4 urged, the setting and the persona's 'take' on the situation are entirely plausible in evoking a phase of erotic experience as it might be played out in the Rome of H.'s day.

The use of time once again deserves attention, since it helps to give the poem its structure. The boy's love affair is present (1–5), but its future can easily be predicted (5–8). We are brought back into the fool's paradise of the present (*nunc* 9), with his hopes for the future (*semper* 10). Lest the reader too heave sympathetic sighs (*heu* 5) for the disillusioned the observer reveals his own past experience (*suspendisse* 15) of such erotic storms: one has survived!

This poem, perfect of its kind, has had more of an effect upon readers than on scholars: Fraenkel 1957 ignored it entirely (as he ignored much of the love poetry); Nisbet 1999: 136–40 made it the foundation of valuable observations on H.'s art of word-placement. Storrs 1959 published less than half of the nearly five hundred versions of the poem he had collected over the years; Milton published his own version in 1645.

6

Metre: 'second' asclepiad (see Introduction 7), a stanzaic pattern found in Alcaeus *GL* 15.

1–4 A successful general is promised a panegyrical epos written by Varius.

1 Scriberis ... fortis 'you may well be written of as heroic' (*OLD* 15 *sub fine*: 'with predicate', as at *S.* 2.1.16 *iustum poteras et scribere fortem* (of Augustus), and cf. 14 below). There is nothing prosaic about the verb used of poetic composition: see Lejay on *S.* 1.4.12. The future tense in this context has a permissive or concessive aspect (K–S 1 144, H–S 311), since it prepares for the contrast between what Varius may undertake and what H. himself is equal to. But the prediction is more confident than if a concessive particle (*etsi*) were used, cf. N–R on 3.23.13 *tinguet*. Similar are *laudabunt* 7.1, *dicet* 7.9, and *bibes* 20.10.

Vario: ablative of agent without *ab* (with *alite* 2 in apposition). In his odes H. never uses the uneconomical ablative of agent with *ab*. Where he uses such an ablative without *ab*, the agent tends to be anonymous or of low status (a barber, slave boys, a crowd; see Bo Index 106, n. (***)). A named individual and a personal friend would be unusual, but is not clearly unacceptable. The dative of agent would be equally unusual, since in the lyrics it is elsewhere found only with a past participle passive (Richardson 1936: 118–20); it would also require the alteration of *alite* (2) into *aliti*; this has been proposed, but seems a drastic measure, since the text is not clearly faulty.

L. Varius Rufus was one of the most distinguished men of letters in H.'s day; indeed, he along with Virgil brought him to Maecenas' attention (*S*. 1.6.55). His own literary output was varied (see n. on 8 below), and H. had already praised his eminence as a writer of epic: *forte epos acer | ut nemo Varius ducit*, *S*. 1.10.43–4 (cf. *AP* 55 where he is paired with Virgil). See Wimmel 1983, *OCD* 1581, and P. V. Cova in *EO* I 926–9 for fuller information.

1–2 hostium | uictor: H. has not yet revealed the name of the dedicatee of his ode, but we must anticipate his revelation. M. Vipsanius Agrippa was one of Rome's most successful generals, though he refused three triumphs. *hostium* points to his defeat of foreigners, e.g., the Aquitani in 38, but his successes in civil war also might be indicated. This could be managed since Sextus Pompeius, thanks to his proscription in 43 (Dio 48.17.3, and see F. Miltner in *RE* xxi 2220.3–14), and Marcus Antonius (Suet. *Aug.* 17.2 *hosti iudicato*, and see C. Pelling in *CAH* x 54, n. 294 for the dating) were officially deemed to be enemies of the Roman state (for this sense of *hostis* see *OLD* 2b). Agrippa was with Octavian from the first, and along with Maecenas he was one of his most trusted advisers. He was consul three times, and it was his unprecedented aedileship of 33 which saw the beginning of the modernization of Rome: H. mentions his popularity (*S*. 2.3.185 *plausus*) and his *porticus* (*Epist.* 1.6.26); his building projects and schemes for the improvement of the infrastructure of Rome and her empire were on a colossal scale (we can still admire one of his aqueducts, the so-called Pont du Gard in southern France). See Roddaz 1984, *OCD* 1601–2, and P. Fedeli in *EO* I 620–3.

Maeonii carminis alite 'a bird of Homeric song', i.e., Varius can write epic. *Maeonii carminis* is genitive of description. Maeonia was a legendary name for Lydia, and the Lydian city of Smyrna was one of the places which claimed Homer as a native. H. seems to have been the first to deploy the geographical allusion in Latin (*OLD* 1b, 2, and cf. *Maeonius* ... *Homerus* 4.9.5–6). Poets had long been compared to birds for a variety of reasons: tunefulness (nightingales, swans), cacophony (crows, geese), or grandeur (eagles) (see Schwinge 1965: 438–40 for a crisp survey); H. will imagine himself transformed into a swan in 2.20.

3 qua ... cumque 'wherever'; Brink 1969: 1–2 followed the French scholar Marcus Antonius Muretus (1526–85) (*Variae Lectiones* IX 7) and Bentley in arguing that *qua ... cumque* should be preferred to the paradosis *quam rem cumque*, since 'whatever thing they did' must include failures or trivial matters along with successes. An original *qua* would easily be assimilated to agree with the following noun. The generalizing suffix *cumque* is separated by tmesis from the relative adverb (N–W II 489). The Swiss philologist Jakob Wackernagel (1853–1938) demonstrated that in some Indo-European languages unemphatic words (e.g., pronouns, particles) were treated as enclitic and tended to move to the second position in their sentences or cola, even if this entailed breaking up an integral word or phrase (many examples in prose and verse at K–S II 592–3); cf. 7.25 and 8.1–2. **nauibus aut equis:** a polar expression, referring to successes 'on sea and land', i.e., everywhere. Agrippa's sea victories were conspicuous, for he defeated the navy of Sextus Pompeius at Mylae and then at Naulochus in 36 (C. Pelling in *CAH* x 35) and commanded Octavian's fleet at Actium in 31. For the former victories he was awarded a naval crown, commemorated by Virgil, *Aen.* 8.684 *tempora nauali fulgent rostrata corona*.

4 miles: for the collective singular see *OLD* 1b, and cf. *multa . . . in rosa* 5.1n.

5–12 H. explains, with examples, that his talent is unequal to such heroic themes and would damage the reputation of anyone he undertook to praise along those lines.

5 nos: the plural of 'authorship' (H–S 19–20) is uncommon in H., who 'uses *nos* of himself as an author when he wishes to represent himself as a public character in whom folk generally are interested, or as a poet contrasting himself with other poets' (Hancock 1925: 48 and 53). **Agrippa:** the dedicatee is at last revealed. Agrippa may have repaid the compliment of this poem, for he was one of the *quindecemuiri sacris faciundis* who were in charge of the Secular Games of 17, for which a hymn, the *Carmen Saeculare*, was commissioned from H. **dicere** 'sing' (*OLD* 7b, cf. 32.3–4 for a related sense); the use conveys no prosaic overtone.

5–6 grauem | . . . stomachum 'fierce annoyance' (*OLD grauis* 15, *stomachus* 4, and cf. 16.16 for the seat of the emotion); *stomachus* seems much commoner in Latin in this sense than in Greek, from which the word is borrowed. H. clearly alludes to the first word and theme of Homer's *Iliad*, the intransigent μῆνις of Achilles. As ancient rhetoricians noted, H. by using an everyday word for μῆνις employed understatement; see, e.g., Charisius, *Ars Gramm. GLK* I 271 = 357Barwick on the figure *tapinosis: humiliter enim stomachum dixit pro ira*. The point is not to belittle Homer and his themes, but to show that H. really cannot himself rise to that stylistic height (Williams 1968: 758–60, West 1995: 29). **Pelidae** 'son of Peleus' (= Achilles), a patronymic, with the termination of a Latin first-declension genitive (G–L §65). The use of the patronymic was regarded as a figure, a sort of antonomasia (Quintilian, *Institutio oratoria* 8.6.29). **nescii** 'incapable of' with the infinitive *cedere* (1.18n.) is a poetic usage (*OLD* 3).

7 cursus . . . per mare: the ten-years' voyaging of Ulysses to his home Ithaca was the theme of Homer's *Odyssey*. **duplicis . . . Vlixei** 'two-faced (*OLD* 6b) Ulysses'; his lying is a prominent feature of Homer's tale, but he could also be painted in a more favourable light (cf. *Epist.* 1.217–26), see Stanford 1963.

duplex compromises the hero; in the opening line of the *Odyssey* he is called πολύτροπος 'versatile', a neutral word. *Vlixei* is quadrisyllabic here (cf. *Achillei* 15.34), but trisyllabic at *Ep.* 1.6.63; H. may have invented the *–ei* form of the genitive for its metrical convenience in his earlier epodes.

8 saeuam Pelopis domum: Pelops was the father of Atreus and Thyestes, brothers who fell out with tragic consequences (Atreus lured Thyestes into a feigned reconciliation, only to serve him up his sons for dinner). The theme was popular not so much in epic as on the stage; Sophocles and Euripides dramatized the myth in Athens, in Rome Ennius wrote a *Thyestes* and Accius an *Atreus*. H. is probably here alluding to Varius' own *Thyestes*, performed as part of the celebrations of Octavian's triumphs in 29. The play (now lost) was vastly admired and accorded classic status (Quintilian, *Institutio oratoria* 10.1.98, Tacitus, *Dialogus de oratoribus* 12.6).

9 tenues grandia '<we are too> lowly (*OLD* 10b) <for such> impressive themes'. Antithetical words are juxtaposed, cf. 13.14 *dulcia barbare*, 15.2 *perfidus hospitam*, 29.10 *arduis pronos*, 37.6 *Capitolio | regina*. They receive additional emphasis thanks to their being 'tacked on'. *tenues* agrees with *nos* 5, but *grandia* is in apposition to all the intervening object words (*haec, stomachum, cursus*, and *domum*), hence its neuter gender (G–L §286, H–S 435). Both words connote literary style. As Brink said on *Epist.* 2.1.224–5 *tenui* ['fine'] *deducta poemata | filo*, 'in an Augustan passage on poetry, [*tenuis*] would not be said without implied reference to Callimachus' λεπτός, λεπταλέος, cf. Pfeiffer on Callimachus fr. 1.24 Pf. Μοῦσαν ... λεπταλέην, and *OLD tenuis* 11, 12. As regards *grandis*, Cicero turned it into a term descriptive of the high style of oratory by a loan-shift from the Greek ἁδρός; both words mean 'full-grown' and in a literary context imply impressive theme, scale and diction (*TLL* vi 2.2179.64–5 and 2185.52–2186.26, *OLD* 6); see *De optimo genere oratorum* 2 *oratorum autem si quis ita numerat plura genera ut alios grandes aut graues aut copiosos, alios tenues aut subtiles aut breues ... putet*, Quintilian, *Institutio oratoria* 12.10.58. For *grandia* of epic and tragic themes and style see 2.1.11 *grande munus* (of Pollio's tragedies), *AP* 27 *professus grandia* and 80 *grandes coturni* (the tragic boot or buskin).   **pudor** 'diffidence' 'sense of inadequacy'; for this obstacle to composition it is crucial to compare *Epist.* 2.1.257–9. There H. is addressing Augustus and explaining why he cannot write him a panegyric, much as he would like to: *sed neque paruum | carmen maiestas recipit tua nec meus audet | rem temptare pudor quam uires ferre recusent*. H.'s favoured genres are slight in scale, and constitutionally he lacks the stamina for panegyrical epos. Hence his diffidence.

10 imbellis ... lyrae Musa potens: *imbellis* underscores H.'s unsuitability for martial epic. *lyra* is a loan-word from Greek and as such poetic diction (*TLL* vii 2.1948.79–84, with the table on p. 1949); for the genitive and the aptness of *potens* see 3.1n. The Muse's ban clinches the case, since higher themes of poetry will founder without her inspiration; H. evokes the ban Apollo placed on Tityrus (=Virgil) at *Buc.* 6.3–8, when he proposed to praise the martial achievements of Varus (so Cameron 1995: 464–5). Syndikus 2001: 94 noted that in the hexameter poems H. himself controls what he can or cannot write. **uetat:** for the singular see *iuuat* 2.38n.

11 laudes egregii Caesaris et tuas: H. neatly associates Agrippa with Augustus, thus praising the latter too but also magnifying Agrippa's importance. As a matter of historical fact Agrippa had been very careful to bolster Augustus' reputation, at the expense of his own. He had declined the first opportunity of a triumph because it would have shown up Octavian's lack of success, and he persisted in avoiding the limelight. H. was clearly aware that he should not wish to be singled out or distinguished from the *princeps* he served. The expression *egregii Caesaris* recurs at 3.25.4.

12 culpa ... ingeni 'by my defective talent' (*OLD culpa* 4). It is not that H. regarded his poetic talent as defective absolutely, but that it would prove defective if misapplied. There is no false modesty here. **deterere** 'impair' (*OLD* 4), a sense first found in H.

13-16 The function of this stanza in the economy of the argument is discussed in the end note. The focus is upon martial themes, drawn from the *Iliad*, and so it prepares for the complete contrast of the final stanza, in which H. describes themes congenial to his Muse.

13 tunica ... adamantina evokes the Homeric χαλκεοθώρηξ or χαλκοχίτων (not that these epithets are ever applied to Ares, who is simply χάλκεος 'brazen', as at *Il.* 5.704). Mars' cuirass (*OLD tunica* 1d) is here rather more exotic, made of impenetrable metal, *adamantinus* < *adamas*, a mythological substance (hence a poetic word), and suggests something extremely hard; the adjective was coined by H. The expression is picked up by a late translator (or scribe) of Irenaeus, *Aduersus haereses* 1.5.5 (not among Keller and Holder's *loci similes*), and by John Milton, *Paradise Lost* VI 542 'adamantine coat' (in a martial context).

14 scripserit 'could describe' (*OLD* 15 *sub fine* 'with personal object', and cf. 1 above); for the potential use of the aoristic perfect subjunctive in a question see Handford 1947: 97.

14-15 puluere Troico | nigrum: a realistic detail, cf. 2.1.21-2 *duces | non indecoro puluere sordidos* (*OLD puluis* 2b), not unknown to Homer (cf. *Il.* 21.541). **Merionen:** the termination is a Greek accusative singular of the first declension (G-L §65). West 1995: 30-1 makes the point that Meriones, while not a major figure in the *Iliad*, is on occasion associated with the superior Diomedes (see 15.26-8), and that might suggest the relationship between Agrippa and Octavian. **ope Palladis:** Pallas Athene assisted Diomedes in his attack upon Ares (*Il.* 5.793); a god's support enhances the hero's prestige.

16 Tydiden 'son of Tydeus' (= Diomedes), a patronymic with the termination of a Greek accusative singular of the first declension (G-L §65); cf. 5-6n. for the figure. **superis parem:** this expression picks up the charge of Ares, that in attacking gods Diomedes made himself 'equal to a god', δαίμονι ἶσος (*Il.* 5.884). *par* also suggests a 'match' for an opponent in a gladiatorial combat.

17–20 H. programmatically announces his proper sphere of activity.

17 nos ... nos: at 5 *nos* had introduced what H. could not manage. Here it introduces his strong suit, in a personal ending; anaphora emphasizes his chosen themes.

17–18 proelia uirginum ... acrium: ancient lovers, if literature reflects life, indulged in a good deal of rough stuff: torn hair and clothes (cf. 17.28), bruises, bites (cf. 13.12), and blows demonstrated passionate involvement (see Smith on Tib. 1.6.73–4, and cf. 1.10.53–66 or McKeown's introductory n. to Ovid, *Amores* 1.7, or Gibson on Ovid, *Ars amatoria* 3.565ff.). Such erotic brawling (*rixa*) was often compared to battle, and a metaphor of love as warfare was much elaborated; for *proelia* see *OLD* 3b, Spies 1930: 53, or Fantham 1972: 85–6. H. however deploys the metaphor here by way of contrast: he sings of battles indeed, but not those of serious warfare. For *uirginum* see 4.20n.

18 sectis ... unguibus: stylish girls keep their nails trimmed, but commentators and translators often divide in interpretation: are the nails trimmed to a point (so Ritter), or pared so as to do no real harm? The latter seems preferable, since H. is not describing Harpies. **in iuuenes:** to be taken with *acrium* as at 2.39–40 *acer ... in hostem*; this was the view of Porphyrio and of Bentley, not in his edition, but in a marginal note published in *Museum Criticum* 1 (1814) 194.

19 uacui 'unengaged', cf. 5.10. The standard interpretation and punctuation, with the comma after *uacui*, approved by Vahlen 1907: 1 327–8, is here accepted, since the claim in the final line only makes sense with *siue quid urimur*. Shackleton Bailey, following Brink 1969: 2, put the comma after *cantamus*; Rudd's text and translation are at odds with each other; see n. on 20. **siue quid urimur** 'or if I am afire with some (*quid*) love'. For *siue = uel ... si*, see 2.33, 35, 41n. *quid* is an internal accusative (G–L §333.1) with *uror*, a common metaphorical sense for the heat of erotic passion (*OLD* 6, Fantham 1972: 87–8, and cf. *urit* 19.5, 7). For a paradoxical conjunction of *uror* and *uacuus* cf. Ovid, *Amores* 1.1.26 *uror et in uacuo pectore regnat Amor* (with McKeown's n.).

20 non praeter solitum 'not contrary to my custom', i.e., 'habitually', or as Porphyrio says *ex consuetudine. praeter* is correctly glossed by *TLL* x 2.998.21: 'contra aequum, naturam, mores, consuetudinem etc.' *OLD praeter* puts our passage wrongly in §2 'surpassing, exceeding'; it belongs in §3 'out of line with'; by the same token *OLD solitus* 2b needs to recognize this sense. **leues** 'playful', in contrast with *grauem* 5, but also 'fickle' as a lover (*OLD leuis*¹ 15). In a literary context *leuis* marks a contrast between a 'light' genre and a 'serious' one, e.g. tragedy or epic; cf. 2.1.40 *leuiore plectro* in contrast with the solemnity of the Cean dirge of Simonides (see *OLD leuis*¹ 14, *TLL* VII 2.1212.57–8, part of an extensive collection of instances). As the last word of the poem it is emphatic and underscores H.'s sense of his own unfitness for epic composition. But in its immediate context, describing H.'s preferred themes and manner of dealing with them, it perhaps mounts something of a challenge to the currently fashionable intensity of love

elegy, as seen in Gallus (perhaps) and Propertius (his first book was probably
published in the early 20s).

*

This poem is usually described as a *recusatio*, a term first applied by Lucas
(1900: 319–33) to the *apologia* by means of which a poet declines a subject as being
beyond his powers, and in declining effectively does, at any rate in part, what he
declines. The term is however infelicitous (Brink on *Epist.* 2.1.257–9, pp. 257–9),
first and foremost because in classical Latin it does not mean 'refusal', but also
because it implies that there has been an actual invitation. Fedeli in *EO* ii 622
believes Agrippa asked H. to write an epic for him; White 1993: 140–1 speaks
more plausibly of a 'spontaneous disavowal'. The 'refusal' is no more than a ploy,
a stratagem for introducing the topic of praise. H. is aware that his own kind
of lyric will do less than justice to the merits of his subject (he will finally tackle
full-blown panegyric in his fourth book), so he here invents a situation in which
he refuses an imagined request or an implied expectation, pointing to a more
suitable candidate (that too is praise in its way). But of course he does praise his
subject after his own fashion, by indicating what he deserves, a proper panegyric
epos. Discussion of Augustan *recusationes* will be found in Hopkinson 1988: 98–
101, in Cameron 1995: 454–83, who for our poem (464–5) rightly stresses that it
advances no polemic against epic, unless H. was prepared to insult Varius as well
as Agrippa (Putnam 1995b: 53–9 supports a more negative interpretation), and
finally in Lyne 1995: 31–9 (cf. 75–8 for his account of this poem).

The layout of this ode is problematic, especially the function of the fourth
stanza (13–16) in the overall economy of the argument. Its role was apparently
first questioned by the Dutch scholar, P. Hofman Peerlkamp (1786–1865), who
characteristically deleted it; he secured the support of the German scholar Moriz
Haupt (1808–74), among others. Its logic indeed seems flawed, if it is assumed
that the poem has a strictly linear structure. H. said at the outset that Varius
had Homeric qualities. But the question in 13–16, 'Who could worthily com-
pose martial epic?', seems to demand the answer, 'No one', or at any rate, 'No
one but Homer', which seems to undermine the claim made for Varius. But is
the poem's structure linear?

At this point we must raise another issue, the theme of the poem. There
is an undeniable panegyric element, but the point of the poem is rather H.'s
poetic capabilities and themes (so Syndikus 2001: 87). *nos* 5 introduces an eight-
line sentence that indicates what he cannot manage with any hope of success.
That pronoun is picked up and emphasized by repetition in 17, where he gives a
positive account of his poetic themes. The core of the poem is thus programmatic,
not panegyrical, and the programme is enunciated first in negative and then in
positive terms: 'I cannot write martial epic, the battles I sing are lovers'.' If this
analysis is correct, then the first, panegyrical stanza is purely introductory; it
might be called a foil or even be reformulated as a priamel: 'Let others compose
epic, my themes are slighter.' Once H. is launched upon the central theme,

what he cannot and can do, the first stanza is forgotten, since it has done its job in providing background for H.'s programmatic statement. The fourth stanza thus becomes less problematic, once it is read not as reverting to the topic of the priamel (Hofman Peerlkamp's criticism), but as a part of H.'s programmatic statement. Its function is in fact not dissimilar to that of the opening stanza (as N–H recognize), in that it too serves as a foil, here to the closing positive announcement of the sort of theme H. finds congenial. Putting this all together, a paraphrase of the layout would run as follows: 'Others may write heroic epic, Varius for instance (1–4), I cannot manage such themes (5–9) and would make a hash of the undertaking (9–12). Epic is very difficult to bring off (13–16), so I devote my skill to singing of erotic battles.'

On this analysis, the problematic fourth stanza deploys the traditional 'affected modesty topos' (see Curtius 1953: 83–5), as was recognized by Vahlen 1907: 1 329–31, who argued that H.'s basic idea here was 'qui digne scripserim ego?', but that he cast it into a general form to make a greater impact. Wickham seems to feel the same when he says that '*Quis* ... ?' (13) = 'How few can!' (though the Latin does not quite mean that). Syndikus 2001: 88, n. 8 takes a similar line. When we consider too the content of this stanza, which, unlike the second, concentrates on martial themes drawn from the *Iliad*, we see how it prepares for the complete contrast of the final stanza, in which H. describes themes congenial to his Muse.

The modesty of the fourth stanza, as indeed of other parts of the poem, also calls for comment. N–H twice speak of H.'s ironic pretence in this ode: 'ironic pretence of incapacity' on *nos* 5, and 'ironic pretence of triviality' on *leues* 20. This is misleading. In the first place, H. subscribes to an accepted hierarchy of literary genres, in which lyric and love poetry came well below epic and tragedy (see Brink on *Epist.* 2.1.250–9, pp. 253–4). The Greek lyric poet Ibycus, *GL* III 282, had long before H. renounced as too much above him the martial themes of Homeric epic in favour of his own lyric concern, the beauty of Polycrates. Secondly, as regards his own literary capacity and inclination, in *AP* 38–40 H. explicitly advised writers to ensure that they chose genres for which they had an aptitude. (To cite the wisdom of the turf: there are horses for courses.) To be sure H. knew that a good lyric was better than an indifferent epic, but in this poem he speaks the literal truth; he was not cut out for that sort of writing.

7

Metre: dactylic hexameter + dactylic tetrameter, a scheme found only once in Greek, see Page 1942: 408. See Introduction 9.

1–14 Others may praise the beautiful and storied cities of Asia and Greece (1–9), which do not impress H. as much as the attractions of Tibur (10–14). The poem opens with a priamel (Race 1982: 126–8) in which there is an element of literary criticism (see on *carmine perpetuo* 6). Since an ode usually has an addressee, however, and no-one has been addressed in these opening lines, the reader might wonder what this is all leading up to.

1 Laudabunt alii 'others may praise'; for the concessive future see *scriberis* 6.1n. Encomia of cities were common in verse and in prose, and rhetoricians, e.g. Menander the Rhetor, Treatise 1 346–66 (pp. 33–71 in the edn. of Russell – Wilson), suggested appropriate topics. H. glances at climate (*claram* 1), site (*bimaris* 2), built environment (*moenia* 3), patron deity (*Baccho* and *Apolline* 3, *Palladis* 5, *Iunonis* 8), local products (*oliuam* 7, *equis* 9, *pomaria* 14), prosperity (*ditis* 9, *opimae* 11), and the character of the inhabitants (*patiens* 10). He does not, however, mention one item characteristic of the praise of cities, viz the founder. He saves that for the *exemplum* drawn from the story of Teucer, who founded Salamis in Crete, an *exemplum* that is relevant to his addressee.   **claram Rhodon:** the termination is a Greek accusative singular of the second declension (G–L §65). Rhodes here is the federal city of the eponymous island. *claram* suggests two senses, 'renowned' (cf. Catull. 4.8 *Rhodumque nobilem*) and 'bright', since the island had a famous cult of the sun, owed to its brilliant climate (cf. Lucan 8.247–8 *claramque* | ... *sole Rhodon*).   **aut ... aut ... ue ... uel ... uel ... aut:** the variety is peculiar to poetic style (Austin on Virg. *Aen.* 2.7, citing *TLL* II 1570.72–1571.20).   **Mytilenen:** the termination is a Greek accusative singular of the first declension (G–L §65). Mytilene, the chief city of the island of Lesbos, was praised by Cicero, *De lege agraria* 2.40 *urbs et natura ac situ et discriptione* ['arrangement'] *aedificiorum in primis nobilis.* See Labarre 1996, and *NP* VIII 650–3. H. joins Rhodes and Mytilene as attractive to visitors at *Epist.* 1.11.17.

2 Epheson: for the termination see *Rhodon* above, 1. H. had presumably visited the city when he was *tribunus militum* in the retinue of Brutus (cf. *S.* 1.7.18–19 *Bruto praetore tenente* | *ditem Asiam*). The beauty of its ruins (excavated mainly by the Austrian Archaeological Institute) still attracts large numbers of tourists. See *NP* III 1078–85.

2–3 bimaris ... Corinthi | moenia: Corinth, situated southwest of the Isthmus which joins the Peloponnese to mainland Greece, owed its prosperity to its command of two harbours, one (Cenchreae) on the Saronic gulf, the other (Lechaeum) on the gulf of Corinth. Hence the poetic epithet *bimaris*, a coinage of H.'s, taken up by later poets. The walls of ancient cities were often included by encomiasts among their praiseworthy features; anyone who has seen the fine fourth-century ashlar of the fortifications of Messene will understand why. But contemporary Corinth, which had been re-established as a Roman *colonia* in 44, may not have had walls of any pretension.   **Baccho Thebas:** understand *insignes* ἀπὸ κοινοῦ from line 4 (cf. *dirae* 2.1n.). Thebes was the birthplace of Bacchus.   **Delphos:** Delphi was the site of one of Apollo's most famous oracular shrines, hence *Apolline ... insignes*, which also applies ἀπὸ κοινοῦ to *Tempe*.

4 Thessala: see *Marsus* 1.28n.; prose preferred *Thessalicus*, cf. Livy 33.35.7 *ad Tempe Thessalica.*   **Tempe:** the form is a Greek neuter plural. Tempe is a wooded valley through which flows the Peneus, the river in which Apollo purified himself after slaying the snake Pytho at Delphi. There he plucked the local laurel to form a crown (laurel = δάφνη, and Daphne was the daughter of the river Peneus). See Aelian, *Varia historia* 3.1.

5 unum opus 'sole task', as at Cicero, *De oratore* 2.162 *uno opere*. H. implies a degree of monotony (so Cameron 1995: 345).   **est:** for the mood see *iuuat* 1.4n.   **intactae Palladis urbem** = Athens, by the figure antonomasia, of which Athena/Minerva was the patron divinity. She is called *intacta*, 'virginal', literally 'untouched', because she was ever a virgin; this sense is poetic (*TLL* VII 1.2068.66–72). For Pallas see on 12.19–20.

6 perpetuo: as a literary term, largely neutral (*TLL* X 1.1643.57–74). Cicero had used it to distinguish continuous history from monographs (*Ad familiares* 5.12.2) and Varro to define *poesis*, continuous epic like the *Iliad* or *Annales* of Ennius (*Menippeae* 398). But H. is generally reckoned to import a hint of criticism, for Callimachus in the prologue to his *Aetia* fr. 1.3 Pfeiffer had alleged that his critics faulted him for failing to produce 'one continuous song', ἓν ἄεισμα διηνεκές. Ovid picked up H.'s expression at *Met.* 1.4, where *perpetuus* also has temporal sense and indicates that the poem spans the ages from creation to the poet's own time.   **et** at line end effects enjambement.

7 undique 'from every source', i.e., literary, historical, and mythological; similar is *undique desectam*, 16.14–15.   **praeponere** 'place on the front' (the purely local sense is actually quite rare, *TLL* X 2.773.41–2).   **oliuam:** a poetic word, here in the sense of 'olive leaves' (*OLD* 2b; cf. 8.8); the everyday word *olea* appears only outside lyric in H. The choice of plant is pointed, since Minerva gave the olive to Attica as a gift.

8 plurimus 'very many a one', but *TLL* VIII 1610.67–8 wonders if this really is a collective use without a noun, deeming the matter unexplained. Housman observed on Lucan 3.707, *multus … moriens*, that *moriens* is as much a noun as *aeger* in Juv. 3.232 *plurimus … aeger*, and so neither had any bearing on this passage, an opinion N–H did not recall. H.'s usage remains unique.   **in Iunonis honorem:** Juno/Hera was the patron divinity of Argos, where her temple, the Argive Heraion, was built on an impressive scale (cf. Pausanias 2.17.1). At Hom. *Il.* 4.51–2 Hera says that three cities are dearest to her, Argos, Sparta, and Mycenae.

9 aptum … equis: the periphrasis evokes the Homeric compound ἱππόβοτος 'grazed by horses', *Il.* 2.287; H. recycles the expression at *Epist.* 1.7.41 *non est aptus equis Ithace locus*. *Argos*, neuter singular, is poetic diction, borrowed directly from the Greek; in the less elevated style of the hexameter poems H. thrice uses the regular Latin plural, *Argis* (locative).   **dicet:** for the future see *laudabunt* 1n.   **dites … Mycenas** recalls the Homeric πολύχρυσος 'rich in gold', *Il.* 11.46 (see Finglass on Sophocles, *Electra* 9); cf. *Priapea* 75.1–2 *sacratast |*

Iunoni . . . Mycena ditis. dites, < *dis*, whilst not exactly poetic diction, is a choicer word than *diues*, as appears from the table of usage in *TLL* v 1.1588.10–45.

10 me: for the cap of the priamel see 1.29–36n. It would be usual at this point to turn to the things that the writer admires, but H. employs a favoured strategy, now handily known as the *schema Horatianum* (Schmidt 2002: 356–7), whereby he continues the foil of the priamel, mentioning here further items that do not much attract him, before homing in on his preferences. Cf. *Epist.* 1.4.8–11 (with Mayer's n.).   **patiens Lacedaemon** 'hardy Sparta'; endurance of suffering and privation was at the heart of the Spartan ethos, cf. Nepos, *Alcibiades* 11.4 *Lacedaemonios quorum moribus summa uirtus in patientia ponebatur.* H. here adopts the Greek termination of the third declension nominative; the Latin form was *Lacedaemo*.

11 Larisae: in H.'s day the administrative centre of Roman Thessaly. *opimae* renders Homer's ἐριβῶλαξ 'loamy', *Il.* 2.841; modern Larisa is still surrounded by a rich agricultural plain. Time however has not been kind to the ancient remains, see *NP* vi 1152–4. There may be a reason for rounding off the list of Greek cities with references to Sparta and Larisa; the former is at the southern end of the Peloponnese, the latter up in the north of Greece proper (Macedonia was always separate), so the two sum up the whole of Greece and dismiss it (but not with contempt).   **percussit** 'has impressed' (*OLD* 8).

12–14 H. now sets against the best Greece had to offer his preferred Italian locality. It matches, indeed trumps, its foreign rivals because of divine presence (*Albunea*), dramatic scenery (*praeceps*), heroic foundation (*Tiburnus*), and useful produce (*pomaria*).

12 domus Albuneae resonantis: Albunea was a prophetic nymph or sibyl, referred to by Varro (*Res diuinae* fr. 56a Cardauns = Lactantius, *Diuinae institutiones* 1.6.12); she is not to be confused with Virgil's Albunea: see Horsfall on Virg. *Aen.* 7.81–106, pp. 96–7, and Giuliani 1970: 24–5. *resonantis* is transferred to her by the figure hypallage; strictly speaking it is her *domus* which 'echoes'.

13 praeceps 'cascading'. The river Anio (mod. Aniene) falls about 130 metres in two drops (but the present falls are not exactly where they were in H.'s day).   **Tiburni lucus:** traditionally Tiburnus was one of three Argive brothers who founded Tibur (mod. Tivoli). (For a different brother see 18.2n.; 2.6.5 *Tibur Argeo positum colono* is ambiguous.) The grove suggests a hero-cult and is referred to by Pliny, *Naturalis historia* 16.237: *apud eos* [i.e., *Tiburtes*] *extant ilices tres etiam Tiburno conditore eorum uetustiores, apud quas inauguratus traditur.* See Giuliani 1970: 8–11 for the varied foundation myths.

13–14 uda | mobilibus pomaria riuis: the homely charm of suburban apple-orchards contrasts with the splendour of Greece's fabled cities. *udus* is a poetic epithet, taken up in early imperial prose. Since *riuis* is taken to mean 'irrigation channels' (*OLD* 2), *mobilibus* probably refers to the shifting of the watercourses now one way, now another (cf. *OLD* 3), rather than to the swift flow of the water (an interpretation sometimes adopted, e.g. *OLD* 2 and Rudd's 'hurrying'). Tibur in fact had an elaborate irrigation system, thanks to the river Anio: see Evans 1993.

15–21 H. now turns to his addressee, the link between them, their shared love of Tibur, only emerging at the end of the section.

15–17 Weather conditions provide a moral lesson, as at 9.9–12, 2.9.1–8: the south wind clears the skies, and it brings rain (Virg. *G.* 1.462 *umidus*, Ov. *Met.* 1.66 *pluuius*), but not continuous(ly).

15 For the 'golden' pattern see 2.11–12n.

15–16 albus 'clear' (*OLD* 3b), juxtaposed for contrast with *obscuro*, indicates the result of the blowing of the south wind, *Notus* (for which see 3.14n.); cf. *alba ... stella* 12.27, *albus ... Iapyx* 3.27.19–20, and similarly Virg. *G.* 1.460 *claro ... aquilone* (where Servius compared our passage). The epithet also suggests that H. had in mind the clearing wind called by the Greeks the 'white south wind' (λευκόνοτος). **parturit:** since storms and their clouds could be described metaphorically as 'pregnant' (cf. *OLD grauidus* 2), it is no great step to extend the metaphor to a rain-bringing wind. Still, the usage is exceptional (*TLL* x 1.535.12–13), not least because this verb, unlike *pario*, is originally intransitive (*TLL* x 1.532.10–11).

17 perpetuos: emphatically placed and predicative. Bentley, followed by Brink 1969: 2, detected an illogicality: 'quid enim tantopere notandum, quod *perpetuos* imbres non parturiret?' (His positioning of the negative is to be noted.) He favoured the equally well attested *perpetuo*: '*Saepe*, inquit, Auster serenum facit, neque *perpetuo* parturit imbres.' (His placement of the adverb is pointed.) They failed to see that the negative goes as well with the epithet as with the adverb: *Auster non-perpetuos imbres parturit*, the south wind brings rain but not continuous(ly). Thus either reading is logical, and here *perpetuos* is preferred on the principle of *uariatio*.

sapiens 'be sensible' (*OLD sapio* 6); this form is to be taken as the participle (not the adjective), used politely instead of an imperative. Like *sapias* 11.6, H. appeals to common sense, not philosophical wisdom. **finire memento** 'be sure to (*OLD memini* 4a) set limits to' (*OLD* 4, not 7 'put an end to', cf. Housman on Manilius, *Astronomica* 5.328 *finem*), more urbane than a direct injunction.

18 Commentators divide between those who take 'life's sorrowful troubles' to be unspecific (in effect, man's usual lot) and those who detect a veiled allusion to the past the addressee had to live down: he had allowed the proscription of his brother, L. Plotius Plancus (Velleius Paterculus, 2.67.3, claims he actually engineered his inclusion on the list), and he had betrayed the contents of the will of M. Antonius to Octavian (Plutarch, *Antonius* 58.4).

19 molli 'smooth, mellow' (*OLD* 8), probably borrowed from Virgil, *G.* 1.341 *mollissima uina* (the epithet is not common of wine: *TLL* viii 1380.43–5). *merum* is strictly speaking an adjective with the noun *uinum* in ellipse, but in general it is found alone, used substantively; it is favoured by poets (*TLL* viii 848.65–6, Plautus, Lucilius, Virgil, and Horace), perhaps because of its handy iambic shape. **Plance:** L. Munatius Plancus was a *nouus homo* (*cos.* 42), who had served under Julius Caesar. He had supported M. Antonius, before a timely switch in 32 to Octavian, for whom he proposed the name 'Augustus' (*OCD* 1000, Watkins 1997, and M. Malavolta, art. 'Planco' in *EO* I 858). The embedding of his name between *molli* and *mero* is an iconic way of binding him to the advice H. gives: he is to be closely associated with mellow wine (cf. *dulci, Tyndari, fistula* 17.10n.).

fulgentia will find a contrast in *umbra* 21.

20 tenebit: Page, in his introductory discussion of the poem, urged that the future contains an implicit invitation or encouragement to return to Tibur.

21 Tiburis ... tui: the scholiasts say Plancus was born there, and a republican inscription from Tibur names a Munatius as a local magistrate (*ILS* 6231); Syme 1979: 585 confirms his 'citizenship' of the town.

21–32 H. now offers his addressee a mythological *exemplum* to reinforce his own advice, a strategy he had also employed at *Epode* 13.11–18, Chiron's prophecy and advice to Achilles (it is usual for the mythical narrative to include speech). The strategy is also found in Alcaeus *GL* I 38A, in which Melanippus is urged to drink, and is told the story of Sisyphus (though that story has nothing to do with drinking). H. was also following Greek precedent in using the speech within the myth to close his poem, cf. for example Bacchylides, *GL* IV 15 (Rutherford 1997: 53–5).

Teucer was a son of Telamon and the Trojan princess Hesione. After the Trojan war his father refused to let him return to Salamis (the island in the Saronic gulf) because of his failure to avenge the death of his half-brother, Ajax (Velleius Paterculus 1.1 *non receptus a patre Telamone ob segnitiam non uindicatae fratris iniuriae*; but there are variant accounts). Teucer thus had to seek another home, on the island of Cyprus, which he named Salamis. His fate is mentioned by Dido at *Aen.* 1.619 *finibus expulsum patriis, noua regna petentem*, and it was the subject of a famous play of Pacuvius, probably based on one by Sophocles. Plancus had two points of contact with Teucer: he did not (or perhaps could not) protect his brother L. Plotius Plancus from proscription, and he was a founder of cities, viz Lugudunum (mod. Lyons), and Raurica (mod. Augst, of which there are fine remains east of Basle); he commemorated this in his epitaph, E–J 187 = Braund 352.

21 Salamina: the termination is accusative singular of the Greek third declension (G–L §65, and see Remark 3).

22–3 tamen: despite the grim prospect of exile he 'nonetheless' managed to cheer himself and his companions with drink.   **uda Lyaeo | tempora:** Porphyrio took the epithet as transferred: *ipse udus*. His temples were not literally 'moist' with wine; the epithet implies 'drunk' (add to *OLD* 1c); cf. Tib. 1.2.3 *multo percussum tempora Baccho. Lyaeus,* 'the loosener', was a cult title of Dionysus but meant by metonymy 'wine', as at *Epod.* 9.38 *curam ... dulci Lyaeo soluere* (where *soluere* is an etymological pun; see Mankin ad loc. for fuller details).   **tempora ... uinxisse:** cf. 4.1.32 *uincire tempora. populeus* is a poetic adjective, coined for metrical convenience by Ennius, *Annales* 588 Skutsch, to replace *pop-ulnus/populneus*. The poplar was sacred to Hercules (Gow on Theocritus 2.121 and Fordyce on Virg. *Aen.* 8.276–7), so by tying on a crown made of its leaves (4.9n.), Teucer puts himself under the care of the hero (so Kiessling, followed by Köchling 1914: 15). Hercules was a traveller (cf. *uagus* 3.3.9), and so an appropriate guardian of Teucer. He was also the chief divinity worshipped at Tibur. **fertur** indicates that a traditional tale is being told, like that of Prometheus (16.13) or Regulus (3.5.41); cf. *dicunt* 8.14, *narratur* 3.21.11, and φαῖσι 'they say' in Sappho, *GL* 1 166, and Alcaeus, *GL* 1 343. Such appeals to tradition became something of a mannerism in Roman poetry (see Fordyce on Catullus 64.1 *dicuntur*). But that does not rule out poetic invention, and H. may well be making up this particular situation (so Fehling 1989: 158 n. 158, 161) so as to provide the advice with a suitable mouthpiece.

24 tristes recalls *tristitiam* 18.   **affatus** 'addressing'; the perfect participle of a deponent is often used with present sense: (K–S 1 759–60). *affor* appears first in the tragedian Accius and is common in the *Aeneid* and *Metamorphoses*: it is high style, solemn and weighty. Here the note is one of consolation (*TLL* 1 1245.43–6, 1246.50–7).

25–32 The speech of Teucer evokes past (*promisit, passi*) and future (*feret, ibimus, iterabimus*) in order to focus upon the immediate present: *nunc* 31.

25 quo nos cumque: for the tmesis and position of *nos* see *qua rem cumque* 6.3n.   **feret ... fortuna:** a modern scholar might regard this as an instance of *figura etymologica*, since *fortuna* like *fors* derives from *fero*, though unlike *fors* (see *TLL* VI 1.1128.37–47), *fortuna* is rarely if indeed ever again found with the radical verb. The difficulty however is that there is no evidence that a Roman made the connection between the nouns and the verb. Skutsch on Ennius, *Annales* 186 Sk. was therefore right to suggest the figure was used unconsciously. **melior** 'more gracious, kindly' (*OLD bonus* 4b), in contrast with *peiora* 30 (now past).

27 nil: here to be taken with adverbial force (*OLD nihil* 11), cf. 26.9.   **Teucro duce** = *me duce*. The use by a speaker of his own name instead of a personal pronoun is emotional, and the tone depends on the context: here heroic self-confidence. See Norden or Austin on Virg. *Aen.* 6.510, Mayer on Lucan 8.80.   **auspice Phoebo** 'with Apollo to support us' (*OLD auspex* 3); cf. Statius, *Siluae* 2.2.39 *auspice Phoebo* and 3.5.74–5 *auspice condita Phoebo | tecta*. *Phoebo* is Bentley's correction of the paradosis, *Teucro*. Many editors accept the paradosis because they believe it evokes the technical expression *ductu et auspicio* (see Ogilvie on Livy 3.1.4). But there are two objections to this. First, *auspex* is never used of the general who had the *auspicia*. Secondly, if Teucer by some stretch of the imagination could serve as *auspex*, 'the one who gets omens from the flight of birds' (*OLD* 1), then Apollo is redundant, and *enim* 28 is left with no clear function. *enim* only has explanatory force if Teucer has mentioned Apollo, and explains his role. The confusion of proper names may seem implausible,

but a number of the manifest errors in the tradition were generated in this way,
e.g., *Mauri/Marsi peditis* 1.2.39, *Euro/Hebro* 1.25.20, *Apuliae* 3.4.10 (no convincing
emendation yet made).

28–9 The oracle of Apollo (who was often associated with the foundation
of new towns or colonies) is also referred to by Teucer himself in Euripides,
Helen 148–50.   **certus** as first word of its line makes a neat contrast with the
first word of the subsequent line *ambiguam* (Collinge 1961: 4).   **ambiguam**
'indeterminate' (*OLD* 6); the newly founded Salamis will cause confusion, since
the name might refer to the island in the Saronic gulf or the new town in
Cyprus.   **tellure:** as a synonym for *terra*, poetic diction; *tellus*, though archaic,
is not found in Sallust, Livy (except referring to the goddess), or Tacitus, and it
was particularly used of the earth as a divinity (a temple was dedicated to her in
268).   **Salamina:** see 21n.

30–1 o . . . peioraque passi: chronological considerations make it pretty
certain that Virgil was indebted to this passage at *Aen.* 1.199 *o passi grauiora*. Both
poets however owed something to Hom. *Od.* 20.18 'endure, my heart, you have
borne something even more horrible' (a line H. had already appropriated at
S. 2.5.20–1). *peiora* contrasts with *melior* 25 (what lies ahead).   **mecum:** the
sharing of dangers strikes an heroic note (N–H on 2.7.1).

31 uino recalls *mero* 19.   **pellite curas:** one of the functions of wine, cf.
Epist. 1.15.19 [*uinum*] *curas abigat. curae* are the μέριμναι or μελεδῶναι found in
Greek symposiastic poetry, again banished or scattered by drink (*Cypria* fr. 13,
Theognis *GEP* 883).

32 ingens: a high-style word (*TLL* VII 1.1536.17–20, 22–4), much used by Vir-
gil. It often conveys a sense of awesome size or extent; Caesar for instance used it
thrice: to describe the huge islands in the lower Rhine (*Bellum Gallicum* 4.10.4), the
vast forest of the Ardennes (*B.G.* 5.3.3), and bulky Germans (*B.G.* 1.39.1).   **iter-
abimus** 'cross again' (*OLD* 6d); the verb is poetic (*TLL* VII 2.547.51–3, and see
550.53–5). For *aequor* see 2.11–12n. Presumably they had just returned from Troy,
only to be banished.

*

'This ode largely resists analysis', said Collinge 1961: 18–19, and Moles 2002:
88 concurred that it is one of the most problematic of the odes. Its structure
clearly gave trouble even in antiquity, and Porphyrio argued against dividing it
into two after line 14.

The poem has three clearly marked-off parts. In the first, 1–14, Tibur is given
pride of place by means of a priamel (which hardly disparages the towns that
H. rejects, since many of them enjoyed divine favour). The second part, 15–21,
deploys a meteorological analogy with which to advise Plancus to put an end to
sorrow with drink. The third part, 21–32, backs up that advice with a mythological
exemplum. The first and second parts are linked by references to Tibur, which H.
and Plancus both like equally. The second and third parts are linked by the

sorrow (*tristitiam* 18, *tristes* 24) that wine (*mero* 19, *Lyaeo* 22, *uino* 31) dispels. But the links do not seem to bind the themes together. The opening section privileges what is near and known to the remote, however glamorous. The second and third sections however presuppose indifference to place; what matters in them is the ability to banish care with drink, a sympotic motif appropriate to lyric. Syndikus 2001: 97–9 and 104 makes a brave effort to show how these parts work together, if not logically, then psychologically. He usefully draws attention to the similar argument in *Epist.* 1.11; there indifference to place is urged because it will not free us of our cares in the way that *ratio* and *prudentia* can (wine is not the answer in that moralizing epistle!).

As problematic as the structure is the purpose of this complex poem; interpretations are very various, and Moles 2002: 88–91 provides a balanced account of his immediate predecessors' views, many of which he repudiates. His main argument (helpfully summarized at 2002: 90–1) is that the poem is indeed focused on praise of Plancus, who, like Sestius of the fourth ode (2002: 105), had been 'rehabilitated' under Augustus – he was to be censor in 22. Moles particularly argues for the relevance to Plancus of the Teucer myth (he is not alone in that). N–H on the other hand, 1970: 93, urged that too close a parallel between them should not be sought, a warning reiterated by Hubbard 1973: 20: 'we know too much about Plancus and most of what we know is not relevant'.

That warning deserves attention. We know a lot about Plancus thanks to the ancient historical and anecdotal record, much of which postdates the ode (its date of composition is far from clear, perhaps by design). It is worth asking therefore how much H. or his readers might have known of the man, apart from rumour and speculation. There were as yet no histories of the whole triumviral period down to Actium, so some of the pieces of detailed information which interpreters, e.g. Tatum 2005, bring to bear upon this poem may actually have been unknown to H. For instance, the tradition, clearly hostile to Plancus, which we find in the Tiberian historian Velleius Paterculus, may only have emerged well after Plancus' death (Moles 2002: 92 with n. 48 reckons it must go back to the 20s, without evidence for the claim). We are also told that Pollio was writing invectives against Plancus, but we do not know when he did so or indeed that they were ever published. We also know, as H. almost certainly cannot have, that Cicero, in a letter written to Plancus in December of 44 (*Ad familiares* 10.3.3 = SB 355), had said that there was a time when men thought Plancus something of a trimmer (*nimis seruire temporibus*). This general opinion is sometimes cited, but what Cicero goes on to say is equally interesting: *quod ego quoque existimarem, te si ea quae patiebare probare etiam arbitrarer. ea quae patiebare* 'the things you put up with' looks like a pre-echo of *patiens* 10 and *passi* 30 in this poem. The political confusion of the civil wars and the triumviral period compelled many men to 'put up with' actions, even their own, of which they did not approve in order to survive and prosper.

8

Metre: greater sapphic (see Introduction 8)

1–16 H. questions Lydia about her boyfriend Sybaris because their love-affair distracts him from his usual pursuits. At first, his questions are indirect, and they form a tricolon crescendo (provided we read subjunctives in lines 6 and 7, indeed the period thus formed is a good reason for so doing). All begin with an insistent *cur*. At 8 he moves to direct questions, repeating the insistent *cur*. The final question (13–16) moves us into the realm of myth.

1–2 per omnes | te deos: the placement of enclitic *te* within the supplication formula exemplifies Wackernagel's law (6.3n.). By H.'s day, perhaps even earlier, such word order was archaic, rather than idiomatic (see Jocelyn on Ennius, *Achilles* 3–4 J., H–S 398); it is preserved mainly in poetry (K–S I 584 exclude classical prose, but it is found in a speech in Livy, 23.9.2; cf. the passages cited in *TLL* x 1.1157.65–1158.32).

2–3 amando | perdere: the enjambement produces a surprise oxymoron, 'love the destroyer'.

4 oderit 'shuns' as at 38.1, and 3.1.1 *odi profanum uulgus* (Fordyce on Catull. 68.12 gives a good account).   **Campum:** the Campus Martius was a popular gathering place, especially for exercise, see *S.* 1.6.126, 2.6.49 (for H.'s activities there), and *AP* 161–2 *imberbis iuuenis ... gaudet equis canibusque et aprici gramine Campi*. A young man who lost interest in joining his friends there might be prey to love, cf. Prop. 2.16.34.   **patiens pulueris atque solis:** a concessive idea, 'though able to endure', should be understood with the participle. Tacitus picked up the phraseology at *Hist.* 2.99.1 *impatiens solis pulueris tempestatum* to describe the demoralized troops of Vitellius.

5–6 militares | inter aequales 'along with his soldierly companions'.

6–7 Gallica ... ora 'the mouth of a Gallic [horse]'; the epithet is in effect boldly transferred by the figure hypallage from a noun that has been suppressed (Bell 1923: 329). *Gallica* suggests a cavalry mount, since the Gauls served as cavalry, not infantry; it is not a horse for show. *ora* is poetic plural, since Sybaris is riding one horse, not driving a chariot.   **nec:** postponed (2.9n.). Norden 1927: 404 lists examples, starting with Catullus, and noted that there are no instances in the *Sermones*, and only one in the *Epistles* (1.18.37) so this hyperbaton seems characteristic of high style.   **lupatis ... frenis:** bits furnished with jagged teeth, to abrade the animal's mouth (for illustrations see Hyland 2003: 70–1).   **temperet** 'controls' (*OLD* 8).

8 flauum: see 2.13n. For swimming in the Tiber after exercise see Vegetius, *Epitome rei militaris* 1.3.4 *sudorem cursu et campestri exercitio collectum natans iuuentus abluebat in Tiberi* (also 1.10.3). Griffin 1994: 89 notes the erotic overtones of all H.'s references to the practice (e.g., 3.7.27–8 *nec quisquam citus aeque | Tusco denatat alueo*, 3.12.7 *simul unctos Tiberinis umeros lauit in undis*). Romans, unlike Greeks, were keen to acquire the skill (see Auberger 1996: 56–8, who refers to Suet. *Aug.* 44).

oliuum 'exercise', by metonymy: athletes applied olive-oil to their limbs before and after training (see Golden 2004: 113–14). The word is poetic diction (*TLL* IX 2.567.81–3) for the everyday *oleum*, which H. only uses outside lyric (cf. *oliua* 7.7n.).

9–10 sanguine uiperino | cautius uitat: proverbial (Seneca the Elder, *Controuersiae* 7.6.20, [Theophrastus], *Characteres* 1.7, Otto 1890: 25) and colloquial, cf. *Epist.* 1.17.30 *cane peius et angui uitabit.*

10–11 gestat ... bracchia 'does he no longer have arms'; this use of *gesto* with parts of the body as direct object is uncommon (*OLD* 5a, *TLL* VI 2.1965.52–60), and may be modelled on the commoner use of *gero* (*OLD* 3, *TLL* VI 2.1932.9–28).

11–12 saepe disco, | saepe trans finem iaculo nobilis expedito 'he who often gained renown for hurling the discus or the javelin beyond the mark'.   **disco:** either understand *misso*, from *expedito*, or take the latter as a sort of zeugma. The construction is like that of *meta euitata* 1.4–5n., and the ablative is causal. For the discus see Golden 2004: 54–5.   **trans finem:** this expression shows that H. did not have in mind aiming at a mark or butt, the sort of contest described by Silius Italicus, *Punica* 16.557–74. More commonly in antiquity both the discus and the javelin were thrown for distance, as in modern athletics. In such competitions the contestants placed markers – Homer called them σήματα at *Od.* 8.192–3 – where their own discus or javelin fell. Sybaris usually throws beyond the furthest such mark set by other competitors. There are fine illustrations of the practice in Miller 2004: 60–3, 68–73.   **iaculo:** for the javelin see Golden 2004: 91.   **nobilis** 'renowned' (*OLD* 2c w. ablative expressing cause of fame); cf. 12.27.   **expedito** 'released' (*OLD expedio* 2c), but Hiltbrunner in *TLL* v 2.1605.61–3 rightly regards the usage as rather bold (*audacius*) and cites no precise parallels. The basic sense of the verb is 'disentangle, free up', and that is not inappropriate to casting a javelin. To fly true, it must rotate about its axis, like a bullet; the rifling of a gun-barrel puts spin on a bullet, the javelin was given spin as it was released from a thong (*amentum*) wrapped round its middle and held by two finger tips (illustrations in Miller 2004: 68–73).

13–16 H. closes by comparing Sybaris to Achilles in a highly allusive reference to the attempt of his mother Thetis to prevent his going to fight at Troy: she dressed him as a girl and hid him among the daughters of King Lycomedes of Scyros. H. gives the story a slight twist, however, in suggesting that Achilles, like Sybaris, shirked his proper activities because he was unwilling to be parted from the king's daughter, Deidamia. For ending with a brief mythological *exemplum* or comparison see Rutherford 1997: 53–5 and Fain 2007, esp. 320. Catullus too ended poems with comparisons, e.g., 11.22–4, 25.22–3, 65.19–24, though not mythological.

13–15 marinae: Thetis was a sea-nymph.   **filium ... Thetidis =** Achilles, by antonomasia. The elevated phrase 'son of marine Thetis' (which

H. recycled at 4.6.6) may be borrowed from a Greek source, since it is found in Pindar, *Paean* 6.84, and Euripides, *Andromache* 108 (the epithet is varied). **dicunt:** cf. *fertur* 7.23n. Supply as infinitive *latuissse*. **sub** 'just before' (*OLD* 23). **funera** 'the destruction' (*OLD* 8b); the phrase *funera Troiae* is also found in Lucretius, *De rerum natura* 5.326, and in both cases the plural is poetic.

16 in caedem et Lycias ... cateruas: the combination of a concrete noun (*cateruas*) with an abstract (*caedem*) is known as syllepsis, not zeugma; it is characteristic of the high style, as can be seen from the discussion of Leo 1878: 1 197–200 (add Catull. 44.15 *et me recuraui otioque et urtica*), so there is no need to doubt its aptness at 3.5.10–11 *anciliorum et nominis et togae | oblitus*. The Lycians were allied to the Trojans.

*

H.'s love poetry has one oddly dominant feature: much of it is concerned with the love affairs of others. We have seen this already in the fifth poem, and it will crop up again in the twenty-seventh (cf. too 2.5 and 12, 3.7, 12, and 20, and see Cairns 1977).

The addressee, Lydia, is rather like Pyrrha of the fifth ode, in that her boyfriend is really no match for her. But why are the questions, to which of course H. knows the answers, addressed to her? One reason might be that this amused address implies criticism of the boyfriend Sybaris, whose name suggests his new addiction to the self-indulgence associated with the inhabitants of that south Italian town, the Sybarites. Sybaris is the first of a number of athletes in H.'s poetry (cf. Enipeus of 3.7.25–8 and Hebrus of 3.12.7–9); athletics had for some time been a standard leisure activity at Rome of the better sort of young man. (The assumption that Augustus encouraged such training is speculative.) As many have observed, Sybaris finds himself in the position of Plautus' Philolaches in the *Mostellaria*, who bewails that love has driven out all thought of manly exercise (142–53). Philolaches blames himself for the situation. If H. questioned Sybaris himself, the implied blame would be tactless. Hence the indirection of questioning the girl, who could not care less anyway, another source of the poem's humour. The gentle criticism is of a piece with H.'s persona in the odes: love is something to be taken in moderation, and Sybaris' infatuation is a form of excess, which has diverted him from activities at which he excelled. He is in some measure failing himself (cf. the crisp critique of Iccius at 29.16 *pollicitus meliora*). The humorous 'undercover signals' in H.'s treatment of contemporary erotics are assessed by Connor 1987: 61–4. There may however be a further hint about the young man in the closing mythological *exemplum*: is it possible that Sybaris like Achilles will revert to type? Just as the hero in the end went to war, so Sybaris may recover from his erotic daze (so Quinn and Syndikus 2001: 111; cf. Rutherford 1997: 54–5 for a similarly allusive use of myth at the close of Pindar's ninth Olympian ode).

9

Metre: alcaic (see Introduction 8)

1–8 H. addresses an as yet unnamed companion, drawing his attention to the winter weather in an elaborate tricolon sentence. (Some treat the sentence as a question; Rudd has it both ways.) He then offers his companion, who is now named, specific advice for dealing with the wintry conditions.

The opening of the poem, which is the first to use the alcaic metre, is a reworking of a song by Alcaeus, *GL* 1 338:

> ὔει μὲν ὁ Ζεῦς, ἐκ δ᾽ ὀράνω μέγας
> χείμων, πεπάγαισιν δ᾽ ὑδάτων ῥόαι . . .
>   ἔνθεν
> κάββαλλε τὸν χείμων᾽, ἐπὶ μὲν τίθεις   5
> πῦρ, ἐν δὲ κέρναις οἶνον ἀφειδέως
> μέλιχρον, αὐτὰρ ἀμφὶ κόρσαι
> μόλθακον ἀμφι<βάλων> γνόφαλλον

'Zeus sends rain, there's a great storm from heaven, streams of waters are frozen . . . thence . . . Down with the storm! Stoke up the fire, mix in the honeysweet wine unsparingly, and put a soft pillow round your brow.' (Campbell, adapted.) H., like Catullus in his famous adaptation of an ode of Sappho's (*Carm.* 51), compresses by omission of some details (e.g., the soft pillow). Similar is the opening of *Epode* 13: bad weather outside encourages drinking within doors.

1–4 Vides . . . acuto?: a direct simple question without an interrogative particle is lively and conversational; it can express a variety of emotions, cf. 25.7–8, 29.1–5 (G–L §453, K–S II 501–3).   **ut** 'how' (*OLD* 2b).   **stet** 'stands proud' (*OLD* 4).

1–2 niue candidum: the phrase recurs at 3.25.10.   **Soracte:** a conspicuous mountain north of Rome, isolated from the main Sabine range by the Tiber. The name provides local colour.

3–4 For the image cf. Ovid, *Ex Ponto* 2.2.94 *unda . . . uincta gelu.*   **laborantes:** cf. *querqueta Gargani laborant* 2.9.7 (with wind).   **constiterint** 'are congealed' (*OLD consisto* 1b).   **acuto:** we speak of cold as sharp, but the adjective seems to be poetic usage in Latin (*OLD* 6b, *TLL* I 466.65–6), perhaps a loan-shift from Greek, see LSJ s.v. ὀξύς II 1.

5 dissolue: the verb forms a gliding transition by contrast with *constiterint*.   **super foco:** prose used the accusative (which was feasible here), poets favoured the local ablative, cf. 12.6, 18.8 (K–S I 572). Roman domestic heating was surprisingly primitive, and H.'s 'hearth' was probably an oblong metal brazier, with handles, similar to that illustrated in Adam 1999: 264.

6 large . . . benignius: Alcaeus used only the one adverb, ἀφειδέως 'unsparingly', so H. here enhances the sense of abundance (rather as Catullus in

Carm. 51 enhanced the first line of Sappho's poem which served as his model). The comparative *benignius* implies more generously 'than usual'.   **reponens** 'setting down' (*OLD* 8).

7 deprome: the *vox propria* for bringing food and drink out of store for consumption (cf. 37.5).   **quadrimum:** four-year-old wine perhaps counted as mature, though not to the taste of connoisseurs (Gow on Theocritus 7.147).   **Sabina:** more local colour (absent apparently from Alcaeus). Sabine wine was not among the best, though clearly acceptable (cf. 20.1).

8 Thaliarche: a Greek name, meaning 'master of the festivity'.   **diota** 'jar': the word is not found elsewhere in Latin. It is borrowed from the Greek (H.'s loan is now acknowledged in the Revised Supplement of LSJ); δίωτος 'two-eared' was applied to vessels with two handles on the flanks, here presumably the amphora. For the shape see Edmunds 1992: 32 n. 19: *CIL* xv 2, Pl. II. Since the wine had been transferred from the larger *dolium* to this smaller vessel, it will have benefited from 'bottle-age'.

9–18 H. now offers more general advice to his companion, which is prompted by their situation and suited to his friend's age. The advice in lines 13–18 is cast in a tricolon crescendo.

9 permitte diuis cetera: such advice is typical at a drinking party, cf. *Epode* 13.7 *cetera mitte loqui*. We can control the moment, and should concentrate on that, leaving what is beyond our control – the weather, tomorrow – to higher powers to sort out.

9–12 qui simul 'for the moment they ...', an instance of 'free relative connection' (*NLS* §230.6, Bolkestein 1996). The relative pronoun closely connects two independent clauses, the second of which here gives a reason for the first (so Nauck). This sort of connection is either awkward or impossible to render into modern vernaculars, which prefer a pronoun with the appropriate conjunctions (G–L §610, cf. K–S II 319); similar is 12.27 *quorum simul* 'the moment their ...'. What further complicates the idiom here for a modern reader is that the role of the connecting relative pronoun is confined to the subordinate clause (*simul*), and abandoned in the main clause (H–S 568–9, esp. 570). An example of this from Plautus, *Rudens* 435 *at ego basilicus sum: quem nisi oras* ('so unless you beseech me'), *guttam non feres*, suggests that the Roman would not have found the idiom particularly formal or literary.

The sentence as a whole is another instance of the *schema Horatianum* (Schmidt 2002: 356), in that it omits description of the state of the sea after the storm is calmed, and moves instead on to the land, where the trees are no longer whipped about. Thus H. combines artistically land and sea (a polar expression), and takes us back to the *siluae* of the opening stanza.

10–11 strauere: this archaic form of the third person plural perfect indicative active is much preferred by poets to the form in *–erunt*, which is only found twice in H.'s lyrics (see Klingner Index 335).   **aequore:** 2.11–12n.; the ablative is local.   **feruido** 'boiling', i.e., not hot but foaming, cf. Virg. *Aen.* 7.24; the usage seems to be poetic (*OLD* 4).   **deproeliantes** 'fighting it out'; *deproelior* is presumably a coinage of H.'s and only found here; cf. *depropero* 2.7.24, *denato* 3.7.28, and *delitigo AP* 94.

12 ueteres … orni: the epithet, which should be taken ἀπὸ κοινοῦ with *cupressi* (cf. *dirae* 2.1n.), suggests that the trees have survived storms aplenty. On the other hand, *antiquam … ornum* at Virg. *Aen.* 2.626 and *annosam … ornum* at 10.766 point to a topos, the aged tree (Pease on *Aen.* 4.441 *annoso … robore quercum*). *orni* are the manna ash, *fraxinus ornus.*

13 cras 'tomorrow' in a non-literal, poetic sense = in the future (*OLD* b).   **fuge quaerere** 'avoid asking'. The polite form of negative command in Latin (*noli* + infinitive) was clumsy, and H. has it only in his more colloquial *Epistles*, 1.16.69 and 18.28. Poets devised periphrases with verbs whose basic sense implied avoidance or cessation, e.g., *mitte* 38.3n. (G–L §271.2, n. 2). This use of *fugio* (*OLD* 11b) may be a grecism, cf. Euripides, *Troades* 891 for φεῦγε + infinitive; Lucr. 1.1052 *illud … longe fuge credere* seems to be the first instance (*TLL* VI 1.1491.64–73 collects examples, but not all are of the imperative). For the idea cf. 11.1 *ne quaesieris.*   **et:** see N–H p. xli for enjambement of first and second lines of the alcaic stanza in this way.

14 quem … cumque: for the tmesis see 6.3n., though here the intervening words are not unemphatic. *dierum* is a partitive genitive, and its use with the adjective *quicumque* is poetic style, cf. 10.19, 29.5.

14–15 lucro | appone 'reckon it pure gain' (*OLD lucrum* 1c, *appono* 8), literally 'set it down to profit'. This is clearly a book-keeping metaphor, but H. has elegantly varied the standard expression, *in lucro ponere.*

15–16 nec … | sperne: the addition of a negated imperative to a positive by *nec* is commonest in poetry (K–S I 204).

16 puer 'young as you are'; not vocative, but to be understood as predicative to the subject.   **tu:** emphatic (cf.11.1), the advice is *ad hominem.*   **choreas:** a loan-word from Greek, so poetic diction. Except for ritual dances, e.g., of the Salian priests (36.12n., 37.1–2), the frostier Romans took a dim view of dancing, particularly by professional *saltatores* and their amateur imitators (Warnecke, art. 'Tanzkunst', *RE*² IV 2247.20–38 collects evidence, to which should be added H. himself, 3.6.21–2 *motus doceri gaudet Ionicos | matura uirgo*), but it is clear that some enjoyed dancing at private functions at any rate, cf. 36.12.

17 donec 'as long as' (*OLD* 4). This sense is first found in Lucretius and adopted by H. (also at 3.9.1); historians take it up.   **uirenti:** understand *tibi*, dative of advantage with *abest*. H. seems to be the first to use the word in this metaphorical sense; cf. 4.13.6–8 *ille* [Cupido] *uirentis et | doctae psallere Chiae | pulchris excubat in genis.* (*uiridis* is found even earlier with this sense.)   **canities** contrasts with *uirenti*, and picks up *candidum* 1. The word is largely poetic (*TLL* III 260.2–3) and is here for the first time used by metonymy to mean 'old age'. *morosa* too is used by metonymy, 4.13n.

18–24 H. concludes with advice that develops the idea of *dulces amores* in a vividly Roman setting. The sentence, extending over two stanzas, is divided into two halves and articulated by anaphora of *nunc et* (18, 21), which emphasizes the time for action. The spatial movement narrows, from the open Campus Martius and the piazzas, down to the shelter of an *angulus* and a girl's finger.

18 Campus: 8.4n.   **areae** 'open spaces', not specifically 'exercise ground' (so *OLD* 1d).

19 lenes . . . susurri: for the whisperings of lovers cf. Prop. 1.11.13 *quam uacet alterius blandos audire susurros*, the *lenia uerba* of Tib. 1.8.2, the ὀαρισμοί of the Greeks (cf. Theocritus 27 entitled Ὀαριστύς).   **sub:** for the sense see 8.14n., i.e., at dusk.

20 composita 'arranged' (*OLD* 9).   **repetantur:** with extraordinary economy the verb has different senses with the different subjects (syllepsis). With *Campus* and *area* it means 'return to' (*OLD* 1), with *susurri* 'resort again to (an activity)' (*OLD* 3), with *risus* perhaps 'recover' (*OLD* 5b), and with *pignus* 'claim' (*OLD* 8).

21 nunc et: see *nunc et* 4.11n.

21–2 The organization of the words provides an object lesson in the flexibility of an inflected language. *latentis*, *proditor*, *intimo*, and *gratus* are all adjectival in function, and so keep the reader in suspense. The subsequent nouns, which follow the order of the first three qualifiers, then resolve the meaning. (For the adjectival use of nouns in *–tor* see H–S 157.)

22 puellae: Pasquali 1920: 84 says she cannot be 'una comune meretrice'. Why not? Or rather, why assume she is 'comune'?

23 pignus: a bracelet or ring taken from the girl to guarantee that she will meet Thaliarchus again (if she is to recover it).   **lacertis:** since the bracelet is taken from only one arm, this is a poetic plural, chosen to avoid one more final *o*.

24 male 'hardly', a colloquial negative, which found its way into high style (Virgil, *Aeneid* narrative, Tacitus; *OLD* 6); as Hofmann 1951: 145 says, she is 'not really' hanging on to the bangle. Contrast the usage of *male* at 17.25.   **pertinaci** 'tenacious', in fact a rare sense (the word usually means 'obstinate, stubborn', cf. *OLD* 1 and *TLL* x 1.1794.13–20); H. 'restored' the original meaning (cf. 36.20).

*

Formally considered, the ode is a characteristic example of 'situation and response': the situation, winter weather, is sketched in the first stanza, and the rest of the poem offers advice on what to do in such circumstances. At first the advice is in keeping with the cold weather, and injunctions to stoke up the fire (*dissolue* 5) and get out the drink (*deprome* 7) are obviously appropriate. But then the advice drifts into something more general: *permitte* 9, *fuge* 13 and *appone* 15 have no clear bearing on the particular situation sketched in the first stanza. The weather conditions too as described in the third stanza illustrate a general law, not an unexpected change of season (West 1995: 42). The final prohibition, *nec ... sperne* 15–16, focuses specifically on the addressee and has nothing at all to do with the weather. Indeed everything from that point concerns the addressee, and winter is forgotten. This has seemed to some to involve 'topic drift': we start in the winter, but apparently end in a more clement season. Such an interpretation mistakes the anaphoric force of the adverb *nunc* at 18 and 21, which does not refer to the immediately present time of speaking, but to the addressee's time of life, specified by *puer* 16: 'now, while you are young' (so West 1995: 43 and Syndikus 2001: 114; Mitscherlich 1800: 110 had glossed 'dum per aetatem licet').

It is possible to read the opening stanza symbolically, as proposed by Wilkinson 1968: 130–1, and now accepted even by the palinodic Nisbet 1995: 414–16 (but not by Pöschl 1991: 33). The opening stanza, read metaphorically, suggests the miseries of old age. This is picked up in 17 where *uirenti*, itself obviously metaphorical, and *canities* (an echo of *candidum* 1) are tellingly juxtaposed. This interpretation pulls the poem back together into an integrated whole. There is no topic drift because H. was never just referring to the look of the landscape in winter (memorable though his picture is); the winter scene has a pathos, especially *nec iam sustineant onus | siluae laborantes*, that points to metaphor. So there are after all two situations and two appropriate responses. Winter can be dealt with by warmth and wine; the prospective miseries of old age must urge us to make the most of what Leopardi called the 'età piú bella', our springtime youth.

Recently, the view that Thaliarchus is H.'s boyfriend has gained currency (Edmunds 1992: 54–9, West 1995: 43–4, Holzberg 2009: 120). It is a harmless enough reading, and it is fair to note that H. admits his attraction to Lyciscus (*Epode* 11.24), Gyges (2.5.20), and Ligurinus (4.1.33–40) – though the only ode addressed to a boyfriend is in the last book, 4.10, to Ligurinus. But this interpretation derives its plausibility from a strict temporal denotation of the word *puer* 16, i.e., someone younger than about sixteen, e.g., Ligurinus (4.10.7). But elsewhere H. designates young men (*iuuenes*) as *puer*, e.g., Lydia's lover Telephus (13.11), the unnamed 'brother of Opuntian Megylla' (27.20), and Lollius Maximus (*Epist.* 1.2.68). The word *puer* of itself therefore does not guarantee that Thaliarchus is still the socially acceptable age for a paederastic affair. For a general account of this issue see A. Perutelli, art. 'omosessualità' in *EO* II 589–91.

Leigh Fermor 1977: 74 relates movingly how a bond was forged between him and the German general he had abducted on Crete in the Second World War when they chanced to reveal to each other a knowledge of this well-loved ode. Its closing scene in the back alleys of Rome was re-evoked by N. Hawthorne in Ch. 17 of *The Marble Faun*:

> Some youths and maidens were running merry races across the open space, and playing at hide and seek a little way within the duskiness of the ground tier of arches, whence now and then you could hear the half-shriek, half-laugh of a frolicsome girl, whom the shadow had betrayed into a young man's arms.

10

Metre: sapphic (see Introduction 8)

1–8 H. addresses the god Mercury in a hymn of praise (*te canam* 5) which initially focuses upon the god's civilizing traits (hence his appeal to H.). There is no prayer. Typical hymnic elements are the references to the god's ancestry (*nepos Atlantis*, 1; Norden 1923: 148), and to his qualities (*facunde* 1), his beneficial *inuenta* (2–4, *lyrae parentem* 6), and functions (*deorum nuntium* 5–6).

1 facunde = λόγιος 'eloquent' (though that epithet of Hermes only occurs in later Greek). Mercury's rational and civilized character is emphasized; he also needed the ability to persuade in his role as messenger, cf., e.g., *Homeric Hymn* 2.335, where he has to persuade Hades to give up Persephone.   **nepos Atlantis:** his mother was Maia (2.43), daughter of Atlas (his father was Jupiter). Ovid borrowed this phrase at *Fasti* 5.663, and indeed picked up a number of other details from this ode.

2 qui: for the relative clause in a hymn see 2.34n.   **feros cultus hominum recentum:** at *S.* 1.3.100 H. described early man as a *mutum et turpe pecus*. Mercury's gifts of speech and graceful exercise civilized him in mind and body. *cultus* 'way of life' (*OLD* 8) is a poetic plural.   **recentum:** this form of the genitive plural, instead of *–ium*, is archaic but maintained in poetry for metrical reasons (*OLD* offers further exx.), especially for participles, cf. *fugientum* 3.18.1, Catull. 34.12 *sonantum*.

3 uoce 'language' (*OLD* 9) picks up *facunde*: the artful use of speech is the cornerstone of civilization, cf. Ov. *Fasti* 4.668 *quo didicit culte lingua docente loqui*.   **catus** 'canny'; an archaic (N–R on 3.12.10–11) rather than 'unpoetical' word (N–H ad loc.), perhaps revived by H. (Brink on *Epist.* 2.2.39). Though the adverb *cate* (a form that would not scan at this place in the line) was used by Cicero in his adaptation of Aratus' *Phaenomena* (550 (304)), H. prefers the predicate adjective (2.45, 46nn.).

3–4 decorae | more palaestrae 'the institution of the attractive wrestling-place'. *decorae* is used by the figure metonomy described at *pallida* 4.13n.: exercise makes the athletes' bodies 'graceful' (so *TLL* v 1.214.5–9, and cf. x 1.98.50–3); *decorus* in this sense is largely a high-style usage (cf. *OLD* 1). Mercury was also associated with gymnastics generally and games, cf. Ov. *Fasti* 4.667 *nitida ... laete palaestra*. *more* suggests that Mercury further civilized mankind by imposing rules on their competitive activities, so that boxing and wrestling were no longer brawls. Mercury's civilizing gifts of speech and athletic training are also combined in an early imperial inscription on a statue base, *CIL* vi 520 = *CLE* 1528B2 *sermonem docui mortales atque palaestram*.

5 canam: the future is typical of Greek hymns and encomia (Norden 1923:153, Willcock on Pindar, *Olympian* 11.11–15, p. 58): the poet fulfils an intention by announcing it, e.g., *Homeric Hymn* 6.1–2 'I shall sing of lovely Aphrodite ...'. Some linguists call this a 'performative' utterance, in that it carries out what it proposes.

6 nuntium: Mercury's most characteristic activity, from the *Odyssey* on. **curuaeque lyrae parentem:** for *lyra* see 6.10n. Since its sound box was originally a tortoise-shell, *curua* describes it precisely (cf. 3.28.11 and Ov. *Fasti* 5.54, 415). The sense of *parens* is here extended to mean an inventor (*TLL* x 1.362.36–7). The story of how Mercury, on the day of his birth, turned the tortoise into a singer is related in the *Homeric Hymn*, 4.24–61.

7–8 callidum ... condere: H. is the first to attach the infinitive (1.18n.) to *callidus*, syntax perhaps eased by the use of *calleo* with the infinitive (though that too is poetic syntax). Later poets follow H. (*TLL* III 172.20–1). *condere* 'to hide' (*OLD* 5) prepares enigmatically for the story alluded to in the following stanza.   **iocoso ... furto:** Mercury was a thief, but his dodges amused, cf. 12 *risit*.

9–16 Hymns commonly referred to notable exploits. H. offers two, in sharp contrast: the first concerns a senior god, Apollo, the second a tragic mortal, Priam; the first is amusing, the second solemn.

9–12 Mercury's theft of Apollo's cattle on the day of his birth is related in the *Homeric Hymn*, 4.68–403 (it is the chief incident of the poem). The stanza exemplifies H.'s command of the periodic style. Reorganized, the thought would run: 'olim Apollo, dum te puerum terret minaci uoce nisi boues per dolum amotas reddidisses, uiduus pharetra risit.' The initially po-faced tone (*minaci, terret*) dissolves finally in laughter (*risit*).

9–10 te picks up anaphorically *te* at 5, and is in turn picked up at 13 (Norden 1923: 143–63, especially 153), cf. 35.5n.   **olim:** the 'once-upon-a-time' of our fairy tales, cf. *S.* 2.6.79 (the country and the town mouse), *Epist.* 1.1.73 (the vixen and the lion).   **boues ... per dolum amotas:** he made the cattle stolen from Apollo walk backward into the cave where he hid them at Pylos, whilst he wore special sandals (*Homeric Hymn*, 4.76–86).   **nisi reddidisses:** represents in reported speech, implied by *uoce* 11, the opening words of Apollo's very threat: *nisi reddideris*. The pluperfect subjunctive is correct sequence after *terret*, which is an historic present. *amotas* is a legalism (*OLD* 2).

11 dum terret: see 2.17n.   **uiduus** 'deprived of', with an ablative of separation, is poetic usage (*OLD* 4), perhaps a loan-shift from the Greek use of χῆρος (Cicero is the first to use the word in this sense in a translation from Aeschylus, but the Greek original is lacking). In the *Homeric Hymn*, 4.514–15, Apollo only expresses a fear that the child will filch his lyre and bow, but Alcaeus, according to Porphyrio, invented the actual theft.   **pharetra:** a loan-word from the Greek, it is found largely in poetry and most infrequently in prose (*TLL* x 1.2009.9–11; for the *e*, long by position, see Courtney 2003: 130: it preserves its natural short quantity at 2.16.6 *pharetra decori*). But it might not be exactly poetic diction: since the Roman army did not fight with bows and arrows, prose writers had little cause to mention quivers.

13–14 The second exploit is drawn from the last book of the *Iliad*, when Hermes is sent to help Priam ransom Hector's body from Achilles.

13 quin et 'and furthermore' (*OLD quin* 3b); this is the poetic version of *quin etiam*, and marks the transition to a higher theme.   **duce te:** see *te* 9n. Mercury appeared to Priam in the guise (more deception) of a young prince (*Il.* 24.347–8), one of Achilles' attendants, who would see him safely into the Greek camp.

14 Ilio ... relicto: leaving the protection of the city exposed Priam to danger.   **diues:** Priam was of course 'rich' as a king, but *diues* hints at the ransom he was bringing Achilles.

15 ignes: the watch fires of the camp guards. They are called *Thessalos* because Achilles and his followers, the Myrmidons, came from Phthia in Thessaly, cf. 2.4.10 *Thessalo uictore*.   **Troiae:** dative with *iniqua*.

17–20 The solemnity of the incident sketched in the previous stanza prepares for the serious close, a reference to Mercury's role as conductor of the dead to the Underworld, ψυχοπομπός. He performs this function in the opening lines of the last book of the *Odyssey*.

17 tu: see *te* 9n.   **animas** 'spirits' of the dead, a largely poetic sense, as Servius noted on Virg. *Aen.* 4.242: *animas pro 'umbras' secundum poeticum morem*; see *TLL* II 72.44–72.   **reponis** 'duly install' (Rudd), a sense related to the common notion of laying to rest (*OLD* 10b). He settles the souls of the good in Elysium, here referred to as *laetis ... sedibus*; H. focuses on the agreeable aspect of the job. The picture is less attractive at 24.15–18.

18–19 uirgaque ... aurea = his epithet χρυσόρραπις in Hom. *Od.* 5.87; whatever the gods use is golden. This wand may be distinct from his herald's staff, the *caduceus* (see Pease on Virg. *Aen.* 4.242).   **leuem** 'insubstantial' (*OLD* 7), especially of the spirits of the dead.

19–20 superis deorum | gratus et imis: a 'polar expression' divides all the gods into those above and those below. *deorum* is a partitive genitive attached to an adjective in the positive degree, a mannered construction found in poets (e.g. 4.6.31 *uirginum primae*, *S.* 2.2.6 *alios ... dierum festos*) and historians. This poetic periphrasis has the effect of making the idea expressed by *superis* and *imis* stand out with a quasi-substantival force, and so is slightly stronger than *dis superis et imis*; once again cf. Ov. *Fasti* 5.665 *superis imisque deorum*. *imus* is largely a poetic word, with the exception of some common adverbial expressions, e.g., *ad imum*, *ab imo* (*TLL* VII 2.1395.77–1396.41).

*

Porphyrio says this hymn was modelled on Alcaeus' hymn to Hermes, the second poem in the first book of the Alexandrian edition of his lyrics (Page 1955: 252–8). Its first stanza alone is preserved, *GL* I 308 (with full testimonia), and indeed its metre is the sapphic. There is also a fragmentary summary of the contents of the hymn, *GL* I 306C(a), from which it is deduced that H.'s third stanza, relating the theft of Apollo's bow as well as that of the cattle, is owed to Alcaeus' hymn (Apollo's threats are referred to in lines 15–16). H.'s treatment is seen to be altogether denser, with numerous themes crisply touched upon, rather than one narrated in detail. It is noteworthy too that the themes and qualities chosen by H. all belong to the Hellenic Hermes – the commercial aspects of the Roman Mercury are ignored.

The question of religious sentiment in literary hymns is bound to arise, and so it should be understood that even the so-called Homeric hymns, as well as those of Alcaeus, were entertainments, not cult-hymns. The tradition of composing hymns in this way was continued by Callimachus (among others), and, predictably, there is considerable debate about his 'sincerity'. Hopkinson 1984: 12–13 draws attention to the coexistence in later literary hymns of intellect and (the effect) of emotion, producing 'a sophisticated dissonance'. There is probably just such a dissonance in the last stanza of this poem: no one seriously maintains that H. believed in a blissful afterlife. But the concept was an attractive part of poetic tradition, and that could be feelingly evoked. Feeney 1998: 40–4, discussing 'Hymns in Books', usefully compares non-religious settings of the Roman Catholic Mass, perhaps in particular that for the dead, the so-called 'Requiem'. Such settings are a sort of dialogue with tradition, in which the expression of a religious feeling or of a personal conviction is not the aim of the exercise. And yet the exercise is not merely formal or formulaic.

11

Metre: 'fifth' or greater asclepiad (see Introduction 7–8). There are word breaks after the sixth and tenth syllables, and one of the features of the phraseology of this poem is the care shown in lodging important words or phrases in that central choriamb, e.g., *scire nefas* (a sharp parenthetic remark), *Leuconoe* (the addressee), *ut melius* (an exclamation), *uina liques* (a symbolic injunction to enjoy life), *dum loquimur* (West 1995: 52–3). It is useful to contrast H.'s practice in the eighteenth poem, which makes little use of the ring-fenced central choriamb.

1–3 Leuconoe's expectations are projected well into the future, concerning which she consults astrologers. H. forbids this on practical grounds and urges endurance of whatever befalls.

1–3 Tu: emphatic: whatever others may do, she should not have recourse to astrology.   **ne quaesieris ... nec ... temptaris:** the perfect subjunctive in prohibitions is an old construction, common in Cicero's letters but uncommon in poetry (only here and at 18.1 in the lyrics; Handford 1947: 48). H. thus adopts a conversational tone (cf. *S.* 2.2.16 *ne biberis*, 2.3.220 *ne dixeris*, *Epist.* 1.6.40 *ne fueris hic tu*). Continuation of the prohibition by *nec*, rather than *neu*, found at 36.10–16, is largely poetic (K–S I 194, H–S 338).   **scire nefas:** understand *est*. The parenthesis is conversational in tone. H. is not questioning the morality of astrology as a whole, but of 'horoscopic' astrology, which aimed to establish an individual's longevity; cf. *ultra fas* at 3.29.31–2 in a similar context (Dicks 1963: 72–3).   **quem mihi, quem tibi:** her concern for H.'s longevity suggests an erotic bond between them.   **finem** 'end of life', a pregnant sense (*OLD*

10). **Babylonios | ... numeros:** a reference to astrology, 'the art of converting astronomical data [= *numeri, OLD* 2c] into predictions of outcomes [= *finem*] in human affairs' (*OCD* art. 'astrology'). It originated in Babylon, then came to Egypt and the Greek East, whence it made its way to Rome. It was becoming increasingly fashionable in Rome during H.'s lifetime; Maecenas seems to have been a devotee (cf. 2.17). See Griffin 1994: 5, n. 29, Bakhouche 2002.

3 ut 'how much ... !', exclamatory (*OLD* 2); supply *est. ut* so used is rare with a comparative, *quanto* or *quam* being preferred.

4–8 H. began with prohibitions but moves now to positive advice (paraenesis). However much time we are allotted for life, we should put narrow bounds to our hopes and make the most of the present. The first piece of advice is cast into a tricolon crescendo. The three verbs are in the jussive subjunctive, a colloquial usage at home in poetry where advice is being given (Handford 1947: 43).

4–6 seu ... Tyrrhenum: editors divide over the question of the apodosis with which this protasis belongs. Some regard *ut melius ... pati* as the apodosis, but the exclamation has more force without the straggling tail of a conditional protasis, which is also felt to produce an unacceptable rhythm by ending the sentence after the third syllable of the line. The protasis works much better with the three jussives in 6–7. The proper response to the storm raging outside is a glass of wine with a friend indoors (cf. 9.6–8), and the advice to restrict hope suits the uncertainty of how much time we have to dispose of.

4 hiemes: by the figure synecdoche *hiems* 'winter' stands for a year, an example of poetic diction (cf. 15.35, *TLL* VI 2.2778.74–5).   **tribuit Iuppiter:** picks up *di dederint* 2, and that suggests that *tribuit* is perfect. *ultimam* stands as a predicate with *hanc*, to be understood from *hiemes*, which serves as antecedent for *quae*.

5 quae nunc: the relative clause and the adverb suddenly provide a *mise-en-scène* for the poem. It is winter outside (as in 9). The scene is further developed: H. and Leuconoe are near the coast (her place, perhaps) on a stormy day. The three quadrisyllabic words seem to represent the pounding of the sea (Wilkinson 1968: 142).

6 sapias 'be sensible' or, more tactfully, 'take my advice' (Rudd, *OLD* 6), cf. *sapiens* 7.17.   **uina:** poetic plural (K–S I 77), deployed only where metrically helpful; H. uses the normal singular wherever it fits. The scene is further developed, along lines similar to those of the ninth ode: H. and Leuconoe should make the best of their confinement with a soothing drink.   **liques:** wine had to be strained (*OLD* 2) to remove impurities (pips, stalks, sediment).

6–7 spatio breui 'within a narrow compass'; the ablative is apparently instrumental, though it appears to be local in English translation.   **spem longam:** cf. 4.15, where there is also a contrast to *breui*.   **reseces** 'cut back, prune' forms a gliding transition to *carpe* 8.

7 dum loquimur: H. and Leuconoe have been using up valuable time in discussing the impropriety of astrology and the wisdom of enjoying oneself: it

is time to get down to business! Ovid echoes H. at *Amores* 1.11.15 *dum loquor,
hora fugit*; cf. Petronius, *Satyricon* 99.3 *dum loqueris, leuis pruina dilabitur.*   **fugerit**
'it will be gone', a proverbial notion (Otto 1890: 112). The independent future
perfect, again largely conversational (G–L §244, n. 1, K–S 1 147–8), gives an air of
positiveness.   **inuida** 'grudging', because personified time's (*aetas*) hasty flight
shortens the scope for pleasure.

8 carpe 'pluck' or even 'harvest' (West), with a view to enjoyment. *carpo* is
here boldly metaphorical with *diem* (*OLD* 2), a usage recalling Pindar's metaphor-
ical use of δρέπω 'cull, pluck', e.g., *Pyth.* 6.48 ἥβαν δρέπων, 'culling youth'
(a poem also laid under contribution in 3.30.1–5, which recalls 7–14); it also
seems to echo Epicurus' use of a similar sounding verb, καρπίζω, when he
said that the wise man 'enjoys' not the longest but the most agreeable time
(*Epist. ad Menoeceum* 3. 126). Otto 1890: 342 lists other injunctions to make use of
time, but Görler 1995: 53–5 (with bibliography) stresses that H.'s formulation is
essentially unique, hence its memorability.   **credula postero:** understand
diei from *diem*. The construction of *credulus* with the dative, clearly owed to the
verbal character of the adjective, is only found in poetry before Tacitus (*TLL*
IV 1152.33–42).

*

H. insists that the future was invented to spoil the present. His famous injunction
carpe diem 'is by no means ... the advice of a sensualist playboy; ... it is an
invitation to conversion', claims Hadot 1995: 224. He goes on to specify that H.
invites us to be aware of the immense vanity of our desires, of the imminence of
death, and of the unique quality of the present instant. The value H. insistently
set upon the present moment is to be situated within the philosophical traditions
of the Stoics and above all the Epicureans; both sects privileged the present over
the irretrievable past and the uncontrollable future. Both Stoics and Epicureans
urged a radical revision of the value we attach to time, especially to the future.
Our hopes for the future can be a curse, and so their teaching privileged the
present, to the detriment of the future. The Epicurean's goal, pleasure, could
only exist in the present moment, and a life lived in the present (along Epicurean
lines, to be sure) was relaxed and serene. It is clearly this view of the value of
the present which H. indelibly inscribes into this poem. Leuconoe is making
the capital error of projecting her concerns into the future, and H. sets about
converting her, not just to stop her conjectures about what the future holds for
him and for her (as lovers, presumably), but to get her to conform her way of
life to a new sense of the supreme value of the present. H. has already given
similar advice to Thaliarchus at 9.13–15, where the notion was also advanced
that additions to the present moment are pure gain, all the more welcome for
being unexpected, as he will say in a later *Epistle*, 1.4.15. The mind happy with
the present should shun concern with anything in the future (2.16.25–6). It is a
constantly varied but consistent theme.

12

Metre: sapphic (see Introduction 8)

1–12 H. proposes to sing in praise of men, heroes, and gods, and casts about for individuals to honour.

1–3 Quem uirum aut heroa ... quem deum?: H. evokes the opening of Pindar's second Olympian ode: τίνα θεόν, τίν' ἥρωα, τίνα δ' ἄνδρα κελαδή-σομεν, but he reverses the order in a rhetorical *gradatio*. Similar citations from Greek models, which serve as mottoes, are used at 18.1, 37.1 (see A. Cavarzere, art. 'motto iniziale' in *EO* II 706–10). For another relevant Pindaric parallel see 45n. **heroa:** the termination is the accusative singular of the Greek third declension (G–L §65). **lyra:** 6.10n.; here it suggests the solo singer. **acri | tibia** 'shrill pipe', the instrument (in Greek, aulos) which accompanied choral song; for illustrations and description see Landels 1999: 24–46. Quintilian, *Institutio oratoria* 8.2.9, cited this expression for its application to the noun of exactly the right epithet, *le mot juste*. **sumes** 'will you undertake' (*OLD* 15); for the infinitive *celebrare* see 1.18n., and cf. *Epist.* 1.3.7 *scribere sumit*. The future *sumes* is found in part of the tradition, but most editors prefer the present *sumis*. Willis 1972: 168–9 however noted that in general scribes are twice as likely to turn a future into a present as *vice versa*, and here the future is appropriately encomiastic (10.5n.). **Clio:** her name, Κλειώ, is derived from the Greek word for renown (κλέος), so she is an appropriate Muse to invoke for encomium; her identification with historiography probably postdates H.

3–4 iocosa ... imago: the same phraseology at 20.6–8, with the same notion of redoubling praise. *imago* was the current word for echo (*OLD* 3b); that Greek word entered the language only after H.'s time.

5–6 H. lists possible locations in storied Greece where the Muse's song may be heard. Such lists of alternatives featured in hymns and prayers because the supplicant had to be as comprehensive as possible when addressing a divinity (see Bulloch on Callimachus, *Hymn* 5.60–5, with n. 2 or Kenney on Apuleius, *Metamorphoses* 6.4.1), cf. 21.6–8.

5 Heliconis oris: Helicon is a mountain in Boeotia, where the Muses appeared to Hesiod (cf. *Theogonia* 22–34). *ora* means 'region, district' (*OLD* 3), as at 55 below and 26.4. **Pindo:** Pindus, however, a range dividing Thessaly from Epirus, had no traditional association with the Muses (despite the claims of our dictionaries); Virgil had mentioned it at *Ecl.* 10.11, and H. may have derived it from him. For *super* see 9.5n. **gelido ... Haemo:** Haemus, the Balkan range, was associated with Orpheus' place of origin, Thrace (24.13); again, it seems that Virgil may have been H.'s source, cf. *G.* 2.488 *gelidis conuallibus Haemi*. *gelido* should be applied ἀπὸ κοινοῦ to *Pindo*, cf. Seneca, *Medea* 384 *Pindi niualis uertice* and *dirae* 2.1n.

7–12 Encomiastic poets often promoted their own activity by stressing the power or durability of song. H. follows suit pictorially by dwelling on the singer's control of motion: what naturally moves (rivers, winds) he stops, he animates what naturally stands still (trees). As in the similar mythological elaboration of 2.9–12, there is an element of humour in the description (e.g., *temere, auritas* (perhaps)).

7 unde: H. imitates the strategy of Pindar, who used the relative ὅθεν, e.g., at *Olympian* 1.8, to elaborate his thought.   **uocalem:** H. gives the adjective a special sense, 'with a fine voice', that is taken up by subsequent poets (*OLD* 2).   **temere** 'blindly' (so *OLD* 1), but 'readily' (*OLD* 4) is an attractive alternative, though there are very few examples of this sense without a negative.   **insecutae:** understand *sunt*.

8–10 Orphea: the termination is the accusative singular of the Greek third declension, though Latin shortened the final *a* (G–L §65).   **materna:** Orpheus' mother was usually reckoned to be the Muse Calliope (his father was Apollo).   **rapidos morantem | fluminum lapsus:** cf. 3.11.14 *riuos celeres morari* (of a lyre's power). The plural *lapsus* avoids syntactical confusion and a succession of four words ending in *m*.

11–12 blandum ... ducere: H. is the first to attach an infinitive (1.18n.) to *blandus*; Statius picks up the syntax (*TLL* II 2037.50–5). For this charm of Orpheus cf. 24.13–14, esp. *blandius*.   **et** 'even' (*OLD* 6), so Rudd. Some commentators and translators take *et* to be a postponed connective (2.9n.), while others regard it as an adverbial use, with the sense noted at 4.11. Both seem weak, since making trees uproot themselves to follow Orpheus is more incredible than slowing down rivers. With the sense 'even' *et* is still adverbial; the usage is poetic, and seems to be a loan-shift from the adverbial use of καί. More examples are collected by Hofmann in *TLL* v 2.908.22–38 (where Virg. *Ecl.* 10.76 however seems misplaced). The issue resurfaces at 28.7, and 37.25, 26.   **auritas:** modern readers not unnaturally find the epithet amusing, but that a Roman reader's funny-bone was tickled is less clear. Porphyrio, for instance, did not say the expression was *ioculariter dictum*, but *audenter dictum*, a bold stroke; cf. Manilius, *Astronomica* 5.327 *siluis addidit aures* and Sidonius Apollinaris, *Carm.* 2.72 *compulit auritas ad plectrum currere siluas* (both of Orpheus).   **fidibus canoris:** apparently borrowed from H. by Virgil at *Aen.* 6.120 (both are referring to Orpheus).

13–24 Reversing the initial order *uir-heros-deus*, H.'s encomium begins with the gods, Jupiter naturally coming first (13–18). Then follow Pallas (19–21), Bacchus (21–2), Diana (22–3), and finally Apollo (23–4). They are chosen as children of Jupiter (the idea is set in motion by *generatur* 17).

13 dicam 'sing of' (*OLD* 7b), cf. 25. For the 'encomiastic future', found also at 19, 21, 25, and 39, see 10.5n.   **solitis ... laudibus** 'customary praises'; *solitis* suggests that H. is well aware of the tradition of beginning songs with a reference to Zeus/Jupiter (Otto 1890: 178–9).   **Parentis** = Jupiter. H. seems to have been the first to give this word the usage commonly accorded to *Pater* (2.2n.); it remained poetic diction (*TLL* x 1.363.36–47).

14–17 qui ... qui ... unde: for relative clauses, here forming a list, in a hymn see 2.34n.

14 hominum ac deorum: a universalizing doublet, since men and gods comprise all higher life.

15–16 mundum 'sky' (*OLD* 1), Jupiter's particular care (2.2n.). **temperat** 'regulates, maintains in a state of balance', cf. 3.4.45 *qui terram inertem, qui mare temperat* (*OLD* 9). **horis** 'seasons' (*OLD* 6); the normal meaning of the Latin word is 'hour', but by a loan-shift (though *hora* is already a loan-word!) H. is the first to 'restore' to it a sense of the Greek ὥρα; everyday Latin used *tempus* (*TLL* VI 3.2964.6–7).

17 unde = *a quo* (*OLD* 8), an archaic use of the adverb instead of a relative (found also at 28.28), characteristic of high style (Virgil was keen on it: see Austin on *Aen.* 1.6).

18 secundum 'close' (*OLD* 10c).

19–20 proximos … | … honores: for the special status of Pallas as daughter of Jupiter/Zeus born directly from his head, see the references collected by Bullock on Callimachus, *Hymn* 5.132–3. **occupabit:** the French scholar Robertus Stephanus (= Robert Etienne, 1503–59) corrected the spelling of the paradosis, *occupauit*, since H.'s song ought to be cast in the 'encomiastic' future (13n. *dicam*; see Brink 1969:2). **Pallas:** a poetic sobriquet (not a cult name) in Greek of Athena (= Minerva), points to the goddess's martial aspect (Hesiod, *Theogonia* 926 'the mistress who delights in clamour, wars, and battles'); one derivation of the epithet was from the verb πάλλειν, 'to shake', e.g., a spear (see Roscher III 1335), and she was commonly depicted with helmet and spear.

21 proeliis audax: to be taken with *Pallas*. The ablative with *audax* is poetic syntax, taken up by first-century AD prose writers (*TLL* II 1248.40–7). Some (e.g., N–H on 2.19.8) take the expression with *Liber*, in which case the connective *neque* is postponed. To this it may be objected that wherever else H. postpones *neque* he does not produce ambiguous government of the words (for examples see Klingner's Index, p. 337).

neque te silebo: understatement (1.19–21n.) is commonly combined with an apostrophe in panegyric, cf. 4.10.30–1 *neque ego te … silebo* (see Harrison on Virg. *Aen.* 10.185–6). For the tense see 10.5n. This transitive use of *sileo* (*OLD* 3b) is poetic, and then taken up in early imperial prose.

22 Liber: an Italic divinity of vegetation identified with Dionysus. **Virgo:** Diana (cf. *OLD* 3a), here in her capacity as huntress.

23 metuende: cf. 2.19.8 *graui metuende thyrso*; the vocative gerundive is characteristic of high style (cf. *Epist.* 1.1.1 *dicende*).

25–32 H. now moves to heroes, i.e., sons of divinities but born of mortals, who secured divine status for themselves as benefactors of mankind. Their status is indicated by reference to their mortal line, grandfather and mother respectively. Both Hercules and the Dioscuri had temples and cults in Rome.

25 dicam: see 13n. for the sense and the tense. The word is repeated here to announce the shift from gods to heroes. **et:** 4.11n. **Alciden** = Hercules, whose 'paternal' grandfather was Alceus; this may therefore be called a quasi-patronymic, found almost only in the poets. For the termination see 6.16n. **pueros** = *filios*; Porphyrio noted that this was a loan-shift from the Greek, as did Servius on Virg. *Aen.* 4.94 (παῖς means 'son' or 'daughter' as well as 'child'). The usage is largely confined to poetry (*OLD* 2 cites a number of Horatian examples, e.g. 19.2). The sons of Leda (by Jupiter), Castor and Pollux, are meant, by the figure antonomasia.

26–7 hunc . . . illum: the former is Castor, the latter Pollux, cf. *S.* 2.1.26–7 *Castor gaudet equis, ouo prognatus eodem | pugnis.* **superare . . . nobilem:** the phrase is to be taken ἀπὸ κοινοῦ with *hunc* (cf. *dirae* 2.1n.). H. seems to be the first to attach the infinitive (1.18n.) to *nobilis* (cf. 8.11–12n.); he is followed by Silius Italicus, *Punica* 11.74. **pugnis** < *pugnus*, not *pugna*. He was a boxer.

27–32 quorum simul: for the syntax of the relative cf. 9.9n. *qui simul.* H. says nothing of Hercules as benefactor but instead dwells upon the saving powers of the Dioscuri, perhaps because they were believed to be still operative at sea (cf. 3.2), whereas Hercules' services were over and done with.

27–8 alba 'bright', with an implication, as at 7.15 (where see n.), that it clears away the storm. *stella* refers to St Elmo's fire, see *lucida sidera* 3.2n.

28–30 refulsit . . . defluit . . . concidunt . . . fugiunt: the verbs are carefully placed to show the immediacy of the effects of the star's appearance.

31 sic uoluere: the will of the gods is traditionally effected easily and promptly. For the form of the perfect see 9.10n. **ponto:** a loan-word from Greek and as such poetic diction, confined by H. to the *Odes*; it is discussed by Skutsch on Ennius, *Annales* 217.

33–48 post hos marks the transition from Greek heroes to men, and the men are exclusively Romans. Romulus arguably bridges the two categories, since as founder of Rome he was obviously a native benefactor, and so secured divine honours as Quirinus (see 2.46n.). This is seen most clearly at 3.3.9–16, where a list of already deified benefactors comprises Pollux, Hercules, Bacchus, and finally Romulus-Quirinus.

33–6 The sentence construes thus: *dubito <utrum> memorem Romulum an regnum an fasces an letum.* The omission of *utrum* is not unusual (K–S II 525). *dubito* seems to be placed so as to make a sharp break between the three early kings and a recent hero of the Roman Republic.

33–4 quietum | Pompili regnum: the second king of Rome was the Sabine Numa Pompilius (*OCD* 1217–18). Unlike the martial reign of Romulus, his was traditionally characterized by peace, hence *quietum*; cf. Cicero, *De republica* 2.26.1 *amorem eis [= Romanis] otii et pacis iniecit.* He was credited with Rome's legal and religious constitution (Cicero, *De republica* 2.26–7, Livy 1.19).

34–5 superbos | Tarquini fasces: the fasces were bundles of rods tied with a red thong around an axe, the head of which projected from them. These bundles were originally carried in front of the king by lictors, and during the Republic in front of superior magistrates. They symbolized judicial power and punishment; indeed the rods were actually used for chastisement. *superbos* really belongs in sense, by the figure hypallage (1.22n.), with the name of Rome's last king, Tarquinius, surnamed the proud (Livy 1.49, *OCD* 1475). He is placed in H.'s list because, for all his hated pride, he had worked to make Rome great, both by territorial conquest and by his grand building works, such as the temple of Jupiter on the Capitoline, the largest temple in Italy.

35–6 Catonis | nobile letum: an unexpected (and in the view of some editors, unacceptable) jump from Rome's legendary past to H.'s own day. M. Porcius Cato committed suicide after the battle of Thapsus in North Africa in 46 rather than live under the tyranny of Julius Caesar. He thus became a controversial exemplar of Roman *uirtus*, but not so controversial that his memory lay under a cloud in the Augustan period; he probably figured prominently in Pollio's history of the period, cf. 2.1.24 (*OCD* 1225–6, Syme 1979: I 210). For *letum* see 3.32–3n.

37–44 In the previous stanza H. took a snapshot of the span of Roman history from its very origins to his own day. Now he fleshes out the picture with exemplary Romans, concluding the section with a moral observation: poverty and agriculture were the foundation of their greatness.

37 Regulum: M. Atilius Regulus, so ran one tradition, was allowed to return on parole to Rome by his Carthaginian captors in about 250 to negotiate an exchange of prisoners (*OCD* 207). Instead he successfully urged the senate to reject the deal; but he kept his word and returned to a horrible death in Carthage. He thus became an *exemplum* of loyalty and courage, frequently cited by Cicero (see Dyck on *De officiis* 3.97–115). H. dedicates a grand ode to his speech in the senate, 3.5, and the historicity of the tale is carefully assessed by N–R, pp. 80–1.   **Scauros:** the use of the plural may be generic, 'a Scaurus' (K–S I 72, and cf. 86–7), chosen to avoid yet another accusative singular ending in *–um*, or H. may have had in mind more than one distinguished Scaurus. M. Aemilius Scaurus rose from poverty to the consulship in 115; he then became censor in 109 and finally *princeps senatus* (*OCD* 22). He was regularly praised by Cicero (though not by Sallust, *Iugurtha* 15.4) and entered the Roman exemplary mainstream; Valerius Maximus styled him *lumen ac decus patriae* and recorded how his son, repudiated by him for cowardice in battle, committed suicide (5.8.4). N–H suggest M. Aurelius Scaurus, consul 108, who, after his capture, was killed by a Cimbrian for saying that the Romans would never be beaten.

38 The line is notable for its use of alliteration.

prodigum 'lavish', is here first given a positive sense; H.'s lead is taken up by a number of poets (*TLL* x 2.1613.3–20).   **Paulum:** L. Aemilius Paulus, consul in 219 and 216, fell on the field of Cannae fighting Hannibal (*OCD* 21). H. describes him as *animae prodigum* because he preferred death amid his slaughtered soldiers to the offer of a horse to carry him away from the battle (Livy 22.49.6–13). Since his name might suggest the adjective *paulus* there is probably a pointed verbal play with *magnae* 37 (so Buecheler 1915–30: II 318–19).   **Poeno** = Hannibal, by the figure antonomasia, though it is possible that by the figure synecdoche this is a collective singular referring to the Carthaginians as a whole (cf. *Parthum* 19.12n.).

39 gratus may be taken adverbially, 'gratefully' (so Rudd). As a Roman, H. owes these national figures thanks for their services to the community and for the good example they set; he renders his thanks by praising them in song (*camena*).   **insigni:** this, like the word before it, suggests reciprocity: H.'s song acquires renown because of the renowned figures it celebrates. Many take the word as active or 'causative', 'that bestows renown' (Rudd). There is, however, no example of such a usage (cf. *TLL* VII 1.1904.58), and in fact it would not have been true: these figures were famous already, and would continue to be so in lists of exemplary Romans, even without H.'s poem.   **referam:** for the encomiastic future see 10.5n.   **camena:** originally the Roman equivalent of the Muse, and like the Greek Μοῦσα, the word came to be used, by the figure metonymy, for 'song'. Here it has patriotic force, appropriate to the context.

40 Fabriciumque: C. Fabricius Luscinus (consul in 282 and 278, censor in 275) was a byword for honesty and frugality; he not only refused gifts from Rome's enemies and handed over a would-be assassin to his intended victim, Pyrrhus, he also demoted a senator for possession of more than ten pounds' weight of silver (Livy, *periocha* 14, *OCD* 585). Like Regulus, he was also frequently cited by Cicero (see Dyck on *De officiis* 3.86). For a single word as 'fourth' line of a sapphic stanza cf. 30.8 *Mercuriusque*.

41 incomptis Curium capillis: Manius Curius Dentatus was four times consul and in 272 censor; he was a successful general who triumphed over the Samnites in 290 and saw off the king of Epirus, Pyrrhus, at Beneventum in 275 (*OCD* 414). His traditionally austere lifestyle was illustrated by the story that the Samnite ambassadors, who had come to bribe him, found him cooking a turnip for his dinner (Pliny the Elder, *Naturalis historia* 19.87). *incomptis ... capillis* is a descriptive ablative (G–L §400, *NLS* §83). The plural may be regarded as largely poetic, since the singular of this everyday word was standard (*TLL* III 314.71), and here the singular could easily have been used. The Romans were aware that barbers were unknown until imported from Sicily in about 300 (Varro, *Res rusticae* 2.11.10), so it was assumed that all traditional figures were shaggy-headed (cf. *intonsi Catonis* 2.15.11). Family busts presumably confirmed this assumption. By way of contrast cf. *pectes* 15.14.

42 utilem bello: to be taken with all three direct objects in this sentence. H. emphasizes the benefits conferred on Rome by her soldiers.   **Camillum:** M. Furius Camillus, censor in 403, conquered Veii in 396, and was regarded as Rome's second founder (Livy 5.49.7 *conditor alter urbis*); much that is said of him in the historical tradition is propagandistic invention (*OCD* 615–16). His simple way of life was proverbial (Otto 1890: 68, e.g., Cicero, *Pro Caelio* 39).

43 saeua 'harsh' (*OLD* 6), cf. 35.17.   **Paupertas:** here clearly personified with *tulit* 42, she is a mother of soldiers; for the meaning cf. *pauperiem* 1.18n. The link between modest means and soldiery was a moral commonplace at Rome;

wealth and luxury clearly sapped the fighting spirit. (On the other hand, it was less often openly acknowledged that poor men joined the army less for patriotic reasons than with a view to enrichment from spoils, cf. 29.1–2.) At 3.1.1 H. urges the tough young soldier to learn *angustam amice pauperiem pati*.

43–4 auitus ... | ... fundus: that farmboys made good soldiers was a related commonplace of Greek and Roman moral thought, most trenchantly expressed in the speech Virgil put into the mouth of Numanus Remulus at *Aen.* 9.603–13 (cf. 3.6.37–8 *rusticorum mascula militum | proles*, Cato, *De agri cultura, praef.* 4 *ex agricolis et uiri fortissimi et milites strenuissimi gignuntur*, Xenophon, *Oeconomicus* 5.14–16). For *auitus* 'ancestral' see *patrios* 1.11n.   **apto | cum lare** 'with a dwelling to match'. H. naturally assumed that Roman farms of old were small; Cincinnatus and Regulus owned only seven 'acres' (Valerius Maximus 4.4.6–7). Some editors however reckon that a word is needed which sustains the notion of modest circumstances, and adopt the conjecture *arto* printed in the Milan edition of 1477 (cf. *paruo sub lare* 3.29.14), an alteration endorsed by Brink 1969: 2–3.

45–8 This stanza forms a sort of coda and moves from the past (*tulit*) to the present (*crescit, micat*), which allows H. to praise Augustus as chief representative of the Julian family.

45 crescit ... aeuo: H. here appropriates an image from Pindar, *Nemean* 8.40 'excellence grows as a tree shoots up with refreshing dew', reminding us of the poem's Pindaric character. H. seems to be tactfully passing over the family's years of obscurity before its recent prominence. *occulto* means *occulte procedens* according to Porphyrio, so the expression is condensed (cf. *TLL* IX 2.366.77–80). *aeuum* is an old word, uncommon outside poetry (Kempf's *TLL* articles on *aeuum* and its near-synonym *aetas* do not clarify usage): whereas *aetas* was always in general use, Plautus has *aeuum* once, Terence not at all; Ennius has it in his epic and tragedies, as does Pacuvius; Cato and Caesar never used it, Cicero kept it out of speeches and letters; it appears twice in Sallust, in Livy thrice. Clearly it was not an everyday word.

46 Marcellis: the tradition uniformly offers the genitive singular, *Marcelli*, which most plausibly refers to M. Claudius Marcellus, five times consul in the late third century, winner of the *spolia opima*, and conqueror of Syracuse in 212 (*OCD* 340–1). It is however not obvious why he is so conspicuously linked with the *Iulium sidus* (Augustus), or how his fame grows over time. The answer seems to be that after the deaths of his distinguished son and grandson, the family was politically eclipsed until three members held the consulship between 51 and 49. Moreover, Augustus' sister Octavia had married the consul of 50, C. Claudius Marcellus (*OCD* 340), and their son M. Claudius Marcellus married Augustus' daughter Julia in 25; he was an aedile in 23 (*OCD* 341). So the family of the Claudii Marcelli was definitely in the ascendant. This suggests, however, that it is no longer a matter of one man's fame, but of a whole family's. Hofman Peerlkamp therefore emended *Marcelli* to *Marcellis* (dative plural, of advantage), a proposal favoured by some (e.g., Shackleton Bailey, Williams 1968: 271; *contra* Brown 1991:

338–9). Given the dynastic bond which the stanza seems to hint at and celebrate, reference to a single Marcellus is after all unlikely, and the emendation to the dative plural is here accepted.

46–8 inter omnes: the end of a list is often signalled by a comprehensive term like *omnis* (see Mayer on Lucan 8.734 *totus*). **Iulium sidus:** 'star' in an encomiastic sense (*OLD* 3c; found also in Greek), and here applied to Augustus, or perhaps more generally to the Julian gens, of which he was currently the outstanding member (Brown 1991: 336–7). The expression however evokes Virgil's *Caesaris astrum* (*Ecl.* 9.47), the comet of 44, which was taken as proof that Julius Caesar was now a god (*OLD* 4, and see Ramsey 2006: 106–25). In fact, Augustus, once he advertised himself as restorer of the Republic in the 20s, was at pains to dissociate himself from Julius, its destroyer (see Syme 1979: I 213–14). **inter ignes | luna minores:** another encomiastic commonplace derived from Greek models, e.g., Bacchylides 9.27–9 'for he was conspicuous among pentathletes, as the bright moon outshines the light of the stars'; cf. *Epod.* 15.1–2 *fulgebat Luna . . . | inter minora sidera*. Lucretius provides a fine example, in his praise of Epicurus, 3.1043–4, *qui genus humanum ingenio superauit, et omnes | restinxit, stellas exortus ut aetherius sol*.

49–60 By a gliding transition the poem turns back in conclusion to Jupiter, whose functions are now combined with those of Caesar (= Augustus), hinted at in the reference to the *Iulium sidus* (47). This combination is remarkable in its break with Republican political tradition and the advertisement of the sort of theory of kingship devised in the Hellenistic Greek East, where rulers were thought to be the viceroys of Zeus (Fears 1977: 125–9). That notion is adumbrated in lines 49–52, where the interlaced words *tibi . . . Caesaris . . . tu . . . Caesare* emphasize the point. H. goes on to define their respective spheres of activity: the king rules the earth (*orbem* 57), Jupiter the sky (*Olympum* 58). The king is depicted as a warrior, but both he and Jupiter have a concern for justice and morality (*aequus* 57 and lines 59–60). There is a helpful discussion of this concept and its reception at Rome by Cairns 1989: 21–5, with the bibliography for our passage cited in n. 95.

50 orte 'born of' (*OLD orior* 7). **Saturno:** Saturnus was the Roman equivalent of Kronos, father of Zeus. For similarly highfalutin forms of address see Tarrant on Seneca, *Agamemnon* 234. **cura** 'charge of' (*OLD* 7, and cf. §9), a word suggestive of Rome's administrative system.

51 fatis: with a word H. elides the battle of Philippi, the second Triumvirate, the war against Antony, and all the manoeuvring that helped Octavian up the greasy pole. It was, claims the encomiast, fate that put him into Jupiter's care. With *data* understand *est*.

51–2 secundo | Caesare: the ablative absol., though grammatically subordinate, contains the leading idea of the sentence: 'may Caesar hold second place in your kingdom'. *Caesare* picks up *Caesaris* for emphasis, by the figure polyptoton. Some find this expression a contradiction of what was said at 18, but H. makes it plain with *te minor* 57 that Augustus is still very much Jupiter's subordinate. The idea here is that rulers are god's representatives on earth, vicegerents.

53 Parthos Latio imminentes: for *Parthos* see 2.22n. To say that they posed a threat to Latium, the territory around Rome, was an exaggeration typical of encomium.

54 iusto 'well-earned' (*OLD* 2b), i.e., fulfilling the prerequisites (for which see Beard 2007: 187–218); see Fletcher *apud* Woodman on Velleius Paterculus 2.47.1 for the expression. Some years after publication of this ode, on recovery of the lost standards from Parthia, Augustus allowed a triumphal arch to be constructed (Richardson 1992: 23), though his 'victory' was diplomatic, not military.

55–6 The vision of territorial empire widens to the east of Parthia, to take in India and China, thus evoking the achievement of Alexander the Great. **subiectos Orientis orae** 'adjacent to the region of the rising sun'; see *OLD subiectus*[1] and *oris* 5n.   **Seras et Indos:** *Seras* is a Greek third declension accusative plural in form, hence the short quantity of the final syllable (G–L §66.4). They are the Chinese, first mentioned by Virgil at *G.* 2.121; see Poinssotte 1979. Less fabulous were the Indians, who did indeed send an embassy to Rome (Aug., *Res gestae* 31.1), a fact later hymned by H. *CS* 55–6. But that they were really the objects of conquest is an encomiastic fantasy (cf. *Persae* 2.22n., Syme 1991: 385, N–R on 3.29.27–8).

57 te minor: a crucial consideration, reiterated at 3.6.5 *dis te minorem quod geris imperas* (of the Romans generally).   **laetum:** for this cliché of panegyric cf. Virg. *G.* 4.560–1 *uictor . . . uolentes | per populos dat iura* (Octavian is the *uictor*).   **aequus** 'fair' (*OLD* 6c); as usual poetry prefers an adjective to an adverb, 'fairly'.   **orbem** 'the world' (*OLD* 12b, *TLL* IX 2.915.7–12), without the defining genitives *terrarum* or *terrae* is poetic diction, cf. 35.30.

58 quaties: 4.7n.   **Olympum** 'the heavens', rather than the mountain where the gods were believed to dwell (cf. *OLD* 1b).

59–60 parum = *non*, a colloquial softening of the negative adverb (*OLD* 3b).   **inimica . . . fulmina:** cf. 3.40n.   **lucis:** for the dative of goal see *terris* 2.1n. Sacred groves (4.11n.) were polluted by unsanctioned entry or the cutting of their trees, among other faults; since the violation might not be noticed, Jupiter had to launch into them a lightening bolt to indicate the need for expiation, e.g., by sacrifice of a pig.

*

Encomium, or praise of an individual, had long been a fundamental function of Greek poetry, and in due course it came to feature in Roman literary culture as well. Cicero, for instance, had partly based his defence of the Greek poet, Archias, who claimed the Roman citizenship, upon his services in praising eminent Romans, such as Marius, Lucullus, and Cicero himself (cf. *Pro Archia* 19–21, 28). We also know of Latin epics composed to celebrate the achievements of contemporary generals (see Courtney 2003: 199–200). Clearly by the late Republic the poetry of praise was an established feature of literary culture, and one of the attractions of lyric for H. was presumably the scope it offered him to try his hand at panegyric. We have already seen, in the sixth ode, how he praised Agrippa by indirection, claiming (entirely plausibly) an inability to compose the sort of epic that would do Agrippa's achievements justice. Here at last he ventures upon encomium in the high lyric style.

That style is chiefly represented (for us) by Pindar, and H. ensures by means of an opening motto derived from Pindar that the reader appreciates the manner which is to be adopted in the present poem (Race 2010: 156–62). This nod in Pindar's direction has however been taken too much to heart by some critics, who have tried to demonstrate a triadic structure, analogous to Pindar's strophe-antistrophe-epode, for the poem as a whole. The tide seems to have turned at last, and such attempts are rightly seen as misguided (Syndikus 2001: 137, Brown 1991: 327–8). The motto serves only to indicate the tradition within which the poem ranges itself; it is not a structural clue. Nonetheless, that Pindar remains a significant presence throughout the ode has been argued by Hardie 2003 (he provides as well an overview of the debate about H.'s debt to Pindar).

N–H 1970: 145 faulted the structure for its lack of unity. But this criticism fails to recognize that everything down to line 46 is foil, a sort of priamel, leading up to the cap, Augustus, who is then closely linked with Jupiter in the concluding prayer (51–2) and described as a successful general. Such preambular lists, though admittedly not on this scale, are to be found in Pindar (see Willcock 1995: 62, on *Isthmian* 7, with further examples).

The opening motto proposes a trio of praiseworthy beings: man, hero, god. Instead of answering the initial question in the same order H. sets about his praise chiastically, listing gods (13–24), Greek mythological heroes (25–32), and finally Roman men (32–48). The concluding three stanzas combine the last man referred to (*Iulium sidus* = Augustus) with the first god praised, Jupiter; the link with the opening salvo is strengthened by allusion to his paternity (*Parentis* 13, *pater* 49). Brown 1991: 328–30 argues persuasively that lines 33–6, where praiseworthy men are first introduced, serve as an introduction, and that Romulus and Cato are chosen to represent the span of Rome's history from its foundation to the collapse of the Republic. The 'sketchy and impressionistic' list which then follows in lines 37–46 focuses on those who played important roles in military crises, sometimes involving their own self-sacrifice (Brown 1991: 334–40). Augustus, who is the cap of the priamel, is plainly regarded as worthy to be ranked among the great Romans of the past whose names appear in the immediately preceding list.

The conclusion of the poem focuses on the relation between Jupiter and Augustus: both are rulers (*regnes* 52, *reget* 57). The three final stanzas are organized with particular care. In the first Jupiter dominates, and Caesar is subordinate. The second focuses exclusively on the martial prowess of Caesar. But as the sentence begun in that stanza moves to its main verb in the first line of the last stanza, Jupiter is reintroduced (*te* 57), so that the final stanza once again associates the leader with the divinity.

H. here expects his readers to be informed about the contemporary theory of kingship. Kings, or rather, rulers, are under Jupiter's immediate care, and may even be seen as his appointees or viceroys. Obviously, such a proposition had to be advanced tactfully, given the Roman antipathy to the word 'king'. It is thus significant that H. first presents Augustus as a triumphant general (53–6), so that what he will rule in fairness is not said to be Rome, but the world (*orbem* 57). This tactfully leaves aside his constitutional position in the city; he is seen more traditionally as one who will enlarge the empire, so a patriotic note is loudly sounded.

13

Metre: 'fourth' asclepiad (see Introduction 7–8)

1–12 H. describes to Lydia the physical symptoms of the emotions he feels when she praises her new boyfriend Telephus or when he sees the traces of their lively love-making on her body. Such detailed lists in erotic contexts start with Sappho, *GL* I 31, imitated by Catullus 51 (both poems well known to H., see 22.23–4n.).

1 tu emphasizes Lydia, and will prove to be in contrast with *meum* 3. The juxtaposition of the proper names, *Lydia Telephi*, is obviously telling, but to the ancient reader of an unpunctuated text it might at first blush, and before the proper syntax of *Telephi* was apparent, have suggested the attachment of a man's name in the genitive to a woman's to indicate her belonging to him in some way (e.g., as wife), cf. Ovid, *Heroides* 7.193 *Elissa Sychaei*, Lucan 2. 343–4 *Catonis Marcia* (K–S I 414).

1–2 Telephi ... Telephi: a disparaging parody of Lydia's own repetition of her boyfriend's name.   **ceruicem:** H. consistently uses the singular, which is poetic diction (*TLL* III 946.8–14), even when there is no metrical need to do so, as here.   **roseam:** as *OLD* 2c observes, the adjective implies youth, but jealous H. may be hinting at effeminacy.   **cerea** 'waxen' with reference presumably to colour (so *TLL* III 861.84, first thus in H.), though smoothness may also be implied (again, effeminate traits).

3 uae 'alas' (*OLD* 1). The tone of the interjection is hard to pin down. In comedy, and presumably colloquially, it was regularly equipped with a dative of the person concerned. The absolute usage is found in higher poetry, e.g., Catull. 64.195 (*misera* should not be taken with *uae*) and the examples in *OLD* 1b.

4 H. describes his jealous anger in seemingly plain language. Ancient writers associated the liver (ἧπαρ, *iecur*) with a range of emotions; such association is found mainly in the poets of both languages, so this seems to be poetic rather than scientific physiology.

5–8 From the symptoms of jealousy, H. turns to those of love, a topos of erotic writing (see Kenney on Apuleius, *Metamorphoses* 5.25.5). The language is straightforward and unadorned, like the feelings.

5 color: the lover's complexion shifts between pallor and flushes (cf. Apollonius Rhodius, *Argonautica* 3.297–8 of Medea). More graphically, Sappho said that she had turned paler than grass, *GL* i 31.14–15.

6 manet: the singular is more in line with H.'s practice than the plural *manent*, which is also transmitted (2.38n., Brink 1982: 33). Bentley and K–S i 46–7 point out that with such connectives or disjunctives the number of the verb as a rule follows the nearest subject word. The plural was presumably introduced to 'mend' the metre, but the lengthening of –*et*'s quantity is normal (N–H p. xxxix, and on 2.13.16 *timet*).

umor: tears again are typical of the lover, cf. 4.1.33–4 *cur | manat rara meas lacrima per genas?*, and for the phraseology *CIL* 6.25617.7 = *CLE* 965.5 *quicumque tuis umor labetur ocellis* (this inscription dates to AD 10).   **et:** postponed (2.9n.).

7 arguens 'betraying' (Rudd), found in a similar context at *Epod.* 11.10.

8 quam 'how' could be taken equally well with either *lentis* or *penitus* 'deeply'.   **macerer** 'I am being tormented' (*OLD* 4); the colloquial metaphor, here erotic, is discussed by Fantham 1972: 59, n. 9; cf. *Epode* 14.15–16 *me ... Phryne macerat*. The word's original culinary sense, 'steep', is clearly lost sight of, cf. *Ciris* 244 *amor noto te macerat igne*.   **ignibus:** for the common erotic metaphor see *OLD* 9 and Fantham 1972: 87; cf. 27.15–16. Ovid adopted the phrase *lentis ignibus* at *Ars amatoria* 3.573. The word effects a gliding transition to *uror*.

9 uror: not here of erotic passion (for which see 6.19n.); H. returns to his jealousy (see Fantham 1972: 87).

9–10 candidos ... umeros: entirely appropriate to a girl.

10–11 turparunt: *turpo* is found chiefly in poetry.   **mero:** instrumental ablative with *immodicae*. *merum* 'unmixed wine' is deliberately chosen to suggest the boy's brutish behaviour; drunkenness made him overstep the limit of acceptable erotic behaviour, and he bruised Lydia (for *merum* and *rixa* cf. 18.8).   **rixae** might suggest serious quarrels (cf. 17.26, Yardley 1976), but Telephus is not depicted as jealous; more likely it means erotic tussles, as at Catull. 66.13 and Prop. 2.15.4 (cf. 6.17–18n.).

11–12 furens 'passionate'; a poetic sense, common in Virgil, when used metaphorically of passionate love (*TLL* vi 1.1627.28–42).   **impressit ... notam:** examples of this kind of erotic kiss were collected by Sittl 1890: 42, n. 5 and W. Kroll, art. 'Kuß', *RE* Supplementband v 513.7–8; cf. Catull. 8.18 *cui labella mordebis?*   **memorem** 'preserving the memory (of something)', here 'telltale' (West, Rudd); the active sense, first found in H. and picked up by later poets, is unusual (*TLL* viii 661.48–59).

13–16 H. winds up his description of his feelings with a warning to Lydia.

13–14 non ... speres 'you mustn't expect'; the subjunctive is potential, verging with the negative on a jussive. With *speres* supply *fore* as the dependent infinitive, and some such notion as *amantem* as its subject, with which *perpetuum* agrees as complement.   **si me ... audias** 'if you'd heed me' (*OLD* 11); 'sic saepissime in enuntiatione condicionali', says *TLL* ii 1288.31–2 of this colloquial expression.

14 perpetuum 'lasting', an unusual sense applied to a person (*TLL* x 1.1641.47–55) but natural enough in an erotic context (cf. Catull. 109.2). **dulcia barbare:** juxtaposition heightens antithesis.

15 oscula: Lydia's lips, not their kisses. *osculum* is the diminutive of *os, oris* 'mouth', but it had come to have for its everyday meaning 'kiss'. Poets however were inclined to rekindle the radical meaning of the word, see *OLD* 2, and cf. *TLL* ix 2.1109.32–4.

16 quinta parte: Lydia's kisses are very special indeed, but what exactly is meant by specifying 'with a / the fifth part' of Venus' nectar is much debated (and it was pretty clearly misunderstood by Porphyrio, who took kissing to be one of the five stages of lovemaking). N–H (followed in *TLL* x 1.469.11–29) argue that since Venus' nectar is bound to be extremely sweet, a fifth part will still be very sweet; they rightly scout the notion of 'quintessence' because it is anachronistic, dating as it does to the Middle Ages. Why however H. specified a fifth is not explained, though the phrase itself is not unusual (*OLD quintus*¹ 2).

17–20 H.'s advice is concluded with a generalized counter-example of the felicity which attends a calmer, indeed virtually marital, relationship, the sort which, by implication, he, an older man, would provide. The strategy is similar to the appeal made to Tyndaris in 17 (see Gibson on Ovid, *Ars amatoria* 3.565ff. for H.'s persona of mature lover).

17 felices ter 'thrice blessed'. The adverb intensifies the adjective, and the expression looks like a loan-shift from τρίσμακαρ; cf. Ov. *Met.* 8.51 *o ego ter felix.*

18 irrupta: only found here, it is presumably a coinage of H.'s. **copula:** the metaphorical sense is milder than *catena*, and was used by Nepos of the devoted bond of friendship, *Atticus* 5.4. **nec:** here does double duty, and negates both *diuulsus* and *soluet* (Mayer 2001: 66).

20 suprema ... citius die 'before the final (*OLD* 4b) day' (Rudd), i.e., of death.

*

The poem invites some reconstruction of its imagined background. H. and Lydia have split up, and she now has an attractive young lover, Telephus. She flaunts her satisfaction, and H. discovers to his surprise that he is after all still attracted to the girl and wants her back. So – and here the poem begins – he makes an emotional appeal, rare in his lyric, and at the close hints at an erotic ideal of untroubled companionship. All along he is striving to detach the lovely Lydia (he praises her features with a purpose) from the thuggish Telephus, and yet it is clear from the opening lines that she is besotted with him, despite (or perhaps even because of) his rough treatment of her. H. does not seem to realize that Telephus has won the battle before the poem has begun (so Sutherland 2005: 72–3). All H. can do therefore is emphasize the boy's violence and describe his own reaction to it; he warns Lydia that such passion is not the foundation of the long-term relationship she seems to want.

The final four lines have given interpreters the greatest headache, since their detached, almost solemn tone seems out of keeping with the rest of the poem, and even somewhat at odds with H.'s normal erotic ethos, since he is not as a rule interested in enduring affairs. The movement of the poem, it should be remembered, owes something to its models, Sappho, *GL* 1 31 and Catullus 51 (an adaptation of Sappho's poem). Both devote the bulk of their poems to physical descriptions of their incapacity in the presence of the beloved, and both conclude with a considered reaction to or reflection upon that condition. Sappho says 'but all can be endured', and Catullus ascribes his erotic plight to his *otium*. H.'s shift of tone from the emotional to the reflective is indebted to theirs. But there is a capital difference: Sappho (apparently) and Catullus (manifestly) address themselves, whereas H.'s calm remarks are probably still directed at the original addressee, Lydia. Why?

Segal 1973 and Maurach 1992 helpfully review the aporia of interpreters of this final stanza and indicate, in very different ways, paths to a clearer understanding of what H. may be up to here. Segal cogently stresses the persuasive function of the poem; building on that we should see the final lines too as primarily part of H.'s strategy for luring Lydia from Telephus (a strategy not dissimilar to that in 17). H. starts with a description of the violence of his own feelings to convince her of his continuing commitment. He moves then to a sober warning (13–16), suggestive of concern. He concludes with a generalized statement of an erotic ideal, which he implies Lydia would enjoy by sticking with him. The solemn, romantic tone he adopts is part of the rhetoric of erotic persuasion, at least as directed primarily at Lydia. But the poem, like almost all the lyrics, has two addressees, Lydia and the implied reader. To the latter, the final lines may prove to be humorous, for the implied reader has an advantage over Lydia in knowing rather more about H. as lover. She may be impressed by the ideal he implicitly offers her, but the reader is amused at what is after all a seduction ploy.

14

Metre: 'third' asclepiad (see Introduction 7)

1–3 H. passionately urges a ship that is about to be carried back out to sea to make an effort to reach port. H., unlike his apparent model, Alcaeus, *GL* 1 6.8 ἐς δ' ἔχυρον λίμενα δρόμ[ωμεν 'let us race into a secure harbour', is not on board the vessel, so he does not appeal to any companions.

1, 2 O: the repeated interjection betrays depth of feeling.   **referent:** the idea of the prefix is picked up by *iterum* 10.   **noui | fluctus:** cf. Alcaeus, *GL* 1 6.1–2 τόδ' αὖτε κῦμα τὼ προτέρω †νέμωτ† | στείχει 'this wave in turn comes (?like) the previous one'.   **quid agis** 'what are you up to?', a colloquial expression, here with an overtone of anxiety (*OLD ago* 27b).   **occupa** 'make for' a destination (*OLD* 6b). The implication is that the ship must do so 'before it is too late' (cf. *OLD* 11, 12).

3–10 H. draws the vessel's attention to its unseaworthy condition after storms. Similar is a list in Alcaeus, *GL* 1 208.7–9 πὲρ μὲν γὰρ ἄντλος ἰστοπέδαν ἔχει, | λαῖφος δὲ πὰν ζάδηλον ἤδη, | καὶ λάκιδες μέγαλαι κὰτ αὖτο, | χάλαισι δ' ἄγκυ<ρ>αι, τὰ δ' ὀήϊα … 'the bilge-water covers the mastbox; all the sail lets the light through now, and there are great tears in it; the anchors are slackening; the rudders …'. But again, Alcaeus is on shipboard, H. is not, nor is his list addressed to the ship. H.'s style is different too: his description flows over the boundaries of the lines.

3–9 Views about the run of this sentence vary, but Quinn's explanation is the most satisfactory. It is formed of three clauses of increasing length, a tricolon crescendo. (Contrast Alcaeus' first three end-stopped lines.) The first clause ends with *latus* 4, and we need to understand *sit* as its verb. The reason is twofold. First, the flank stripped of oars is something that can actually be seen (*uides*), and secondly that is the crucial point: the vessel now lacks a degree of manoeuvrability; 'groaning' is not an issue. The second clause, *et … gemant*, naturally combines the mast and the yardarms attached to it; *uides* loses some of its denotation of sight and here connotes perception generally (Rudd translates 'notice', cf. *OLD* 9b). The final clause, *ac … aequor*, presents the worst case: the vessel is likely to break up; again *uides* means 'notice'.

3–4 ut at line end hurries the reader on.   **nudum** 'deprived of' with an ablative of separation is poetic syntax (*OLD* 10b).

5 saucius Africo: the instrumental ablative with the adjective is poetic syntax. For *Africus* see 3.12n.

6 gemant: since moaning is not something inanimate objects do, the usage is classed as poetic by *TLL* vi 2.1762.45–77.

sine funibus: ships, both merchant and naval, were often 'undergirded' with stout cables to secure the hull, but H. seems to have in mind, as did Alcaeus, *GL* 1 6.7 φαρξώμεθ' ὡς ὤκιστα [τοίχοις] 'let us strengthen [the ship's sides] as quickly as possible', the process known as 'frapping', passing cables under the keel in bad weather to further reinforce the hull. Casson 1995: 91–2 explains and describes the varied procedures (the process is clearly older than he allows).

7–9 durare 'endure' (*OLD* 6); usually in this sense the verb is intransitive (*OLD* 5), but poets made it transitive.   **carinae:** poetic plural, since a ship has only one keel.   **imperiosius | aequor** 'the too overbearing sea'. The enjambement suggests the sea's unusual force, enhanced by the comparative. For *aequor* see 2.11–12n.

9–10 non … non: anaphora emphasizes the ship's destitution.   **lintea** = *uela*, poetic diction for 'sails' (*TLL* vii 2.1467.24–39).   **di:** the ship's guardian divinities, *tutelae*, whose images were prominently placed on the stern (see Casson 1995: 346–7 for discussion and illustration). Violent storms could wrench off these attachments.

10 uoces: 2.25n. The subjunctive is final/purpose in a relative clause.

11–16 The ship's claims to consideration do not inspire confidence: take care! The sentence as a whole is another example of the *schema Horatianum* (7.10n., Schmidt 2002: 359–60): the vessel actually boasts of three features in none of which the sailor puts any trust; the three are distributed, two (*genus* and *nomen*) appearing in the concessive clause and one (the painted stern) in the main clause.

11 Pontica pinus: the territory of Pontus, which became a Roman province in 63, stretched along the southern shore of the Black Sea. Its pine forests provided timber for shipbuilding, e.g., the yacht praised by Catullus (4).

12 nobilis: take with *siluae*.

13 iactes: the personification of ships was as common in antiquity as nowadays. Catullus' yacht was equally boastful of her ancestry (4.15–16).   **inutile:** to be taken with both *genus* and *nomen* ἀπὸ κοινοῦ (cf. *dirae* 2.1n.).

14 nil: adverbial, 7.27n.   **pictis ... puppibus:** for painting ships see Casson 1995: 211–12, who notes that the encaustic (i.e., wax-based) paints were not purely decorative but protected the wood. H. has in mind the more elaborate images that might be represented. *puppibus* refers only to the stern of the ship addressed, so this plural is poetic.   **nauita:** archaic and poetic for everyday *nauta* (*OLD* s.v.). H. confines the word to his lyrics (including the *Epodes*).

15–16 nisi uentis | debes ludibrium 'unless you deserve the winds' mockery'. H. experimentally treats *debeo* metaphorically, like the verb ὀφλισκάνω, which means 'incur' a penalty (as a legal term), but it also has an extended usage with undesirable objects like laughter (see Mastronarde on Euripides, *Medea* 404).

17–20 H.'s own (*mihi*) emotional concern is now highlighted: *taedium, desiderium*, and *cura* all have affectionate overtones. He advises the ship to avoid treacherous waters.

17–18 nuper ... nunc: the adverbs compensate for the unusual ellipse of verbs in the relative clause, viz *eras* with *taedium*, *es* with *cura*. The temporal contrast seems pointed, without providing clues as to the likely date of the poem's composition.

18 desiderium, though it has an erotic sense (*OLD* 2), is surprisingly not found in elegy of the beloved.   **cura** 'object of concern' (*OLD* 8) may also have an erotic colour, in an appropriate context (*TLL* IV 1475.42–60). The words are not strongly marked generically.   **non leuis:** understatement, see 1.19–21n. and cf. 18.9.

19–20 The word order produces the golden pattern.

interfusa 'flowing between'. The word appears to be a Virgilian coinage. It is poetic diction until the prose of the early principate. H. was the first to use it with an accusative object (for intransitive verbs made transitive by the prefix cf. K–S I 268).   **nitentes:** cf. *fulgentes ... Cycladas* 3.28.14; H. imagines the gleaming marble of one of the islands, Paros.

20 uites: jussive subjunctive (11.6n.).   **aequora:** 5.7n.   **Cycladas:** for the termination see *Seras* 12.56n. The islands in the Aegean were so called because they surround Delos in a circle, κύκλος. Livy said that the area was *uentosissima* (36.43.1).

*

What is this poem about? Few believe that H. is concerned for a real ship; if he were, the situation would be hard to envisage, and the language of 17–18 would be weird. Most therefore feel the poem is an extended metaphor, i.e., an allegory. Now the capital problem with allegory as a mode of reading and interpretation is that it often appears arbitrary; there seem to be no firm controls upon the decoding of the metaphors. This poem itself for instance was variously interpreted in antiquity, though the substratum of all the interpretations was political. Porphyrio took the ship to represent the party of M. Brutus, under whom H. had served at Philippi; pseudo-Acro took it to be the party of Sextus Pompeius. Pseudo-Acro also reported that some took the ship to stand for the state, *res publica*, and such an interpretation was sketched by Quintilian, *Institutio oratoria* 8.6.44: *allegoria ... aliud uerbis, aliud sensu ostendit ... plerumque continuatis tralationibus* ['extended metaphors'], *ut* 'O nauis, referent in mare te noui fluctus: o quid agis? fortiter occupa portum!', *totusque ille Horati locus, quo nauem pro re publica, fluctus et tempestates pro bellis ciuilibus, portum pro pace atque concordia dicit.* A strong support for a political reading was the long-established tradition of encoding a ship as a symbol either of the state (see, e.g., Hutchinson on Aeschylus, *Septem* 62–4 (795–6), Collard on Euripides, *Supplices* 267–9a, Ferber 2007: 193–5) or of some group within the larger community. Such for instance was the particular character of the allegory in the poetry of Alcaeus, esp. *GL* 1 6 and 208, who applied it specifically to his own party (see Cucchiarelli 2004 and 2005). It is above all H.'s indebtedness to Alcaeus which encouraged a belief in antiquity that the ship in this poem represented either a political group or the whole *res publica Romana*. The latter interpretation remains the standard (see most recently Clay 2010: 139–40), despite revisionist interpretations, e.g. Kruschwitz 2007.

The specific parties proposed by the scholiasts, however, do not recommend themselves, since the defeat of Brutus and of Pompeius in the civil wars render *nunc* 18 and the advice in 19–20 outdated and hollow. A concerned appeal to the whole community of Romans is altogether more timely, just because it does not have to be pinned down to any particular occasion or individual. Moreover H.'s claim in 17–18 to have recovered a devoted concern that had been lost makes sense as applied to the welfare of the state or community. He had supported the losing side at Philippi and might well have decided thereafter to keep aloof from public adventures. Such for instance was the reaction of the equestrian C. Matius to the assassination of Julius Caesar; with the death of the man to whom he had devoted his energies he saw every reason to retire to Rhodes and live a quiet life (see Cicero, *Ad familiares* 11.28). H. might well have felt something similar after Philippi. But once in the circle of Maecenas, his concern for the *res publica* might indeed have been recovered. That is a not implausible reading of the poem's close.

When might such a concern have developed in H.? This is not easy to say, and commentators differ among themselves. N–H 1970: 181 could see no reason for H. to be so desponding in the late 30s just before Actium, yet Syndikus 2001: 165–6 feels that this is exactly the period in which H. is most likely to have felt such anxiety. *Non liquet.*

Allegory allowed H. to suggest this change of attitude by way of traditional imagery, the endangered ship of state – perhaps Americans will think of Whitman's lament for the assassinated President Lincoln, 'O captain, my captain'. Hubbard 1973: 13–17 offers an especially attractive reading. She notes that H. is alone, whereas his model Alcaeus is implicitly part of a group; she draws attention to the refinement of H.'s vocabulary and concept in a word like *taedium* (it is impossible to imagine his model speaking thus).

But since allegory is, as noted above, slippery to decode, it comes as no surprise that the ship has been interpreted as a real ship or as H. himself or as a woman or as poetry. Joceyln 1982, Nisbet 1995: 416–18, and Syndikus 2001: 162, n. 13 between them record and dismiss most of these readings: they favour a political ship. Knorr 2006 brings the bibliography up to date, before reviving an erotic reading.

One final observation: this is the first poem in the collection to describe a change of heart, and that situation will recur in an erotic context (*Carm.* 17) and a philosophical one (*Carm.* 34); 3.9 and 14 turn on a similar point.

15

Metre: 'second' asclepiad (see Introduction 7)

1–5 A narrative introduction sets the scene in mythical times.

1–2 Pastor = Paris, by the figure antonomasia (*OLD* 1b). Hecuba had dreamt whilst she was pregnant with Paris that she would bear a firebrand; this was interpreted as a sign that the child would bring destruction to his city, so he was given to a shepherd to expose on Mt Ida near Troy. Typically in such tales, the shepherd instead brought the boy up as his own, so Paris took to the shepherd's life until he was recognized as Priam's son.   **traheret:** suggests an illegal act (*OLD* 5), though Helen went voluntarily.   **freta** 'the sea', a sense chiefly poetic, especially in the plural (*OLD* 3).   **nauibus | Idaeis:** the timber for the shipbuilding was traditionally cut on Mt Ida (cf. Euripides, *Hecuba* 631–4). That there was a fleet is mentioned by Hector in *Il.* 3.46.   **Helenen:** the termination is accusative singular of the Greek first declension (G–L §65).   **perfidus hospitam:** juxtaposition enhances contrast. This particular juxtaposition suggests the Greek compound word ξειναπάτης 'host-cheater' applied to Paris by Alcaeus, *GL* 1 283.3, and Ibycus, *GL* 111 282(a).10. The most outrageous aspect of the abduction of Helen was that Paris trampled underfoot the bond of guest-friendship, a point emphasized by Menelaus at *Il.* 3.353–4. *perfidus,* owing to its delayed position, should not be taken as an epithet with *pastor*, but as an independent idea, 'the faithless fellow'.

3–4 ingrato celeres obruit otio | uentos: the words are arranged to form a 'golden' pattern. *ingrato* is an instance of focalization, as the ancient commentators saw: Paris resents the delay; Porphyrio however assumed that the winds were annoyed, *quia feroces sunt et semper saeuire cupiunt*. Pseudo-Acro hedges: it is either the winds or Paris. **obruit:** the subject is Nereus, whose name is delayed by its placement in the dependent final clause.

4 caneret 'foretell' (*OLD* 8); since prophecies were in verse they could be sung. **fera** 'cruel' (*OLD* 6).

5 Nereus fata: the name of the speaker and the nature of his utterance are emphatically delayed till the end of the sentence, which is also the beginning of a new stanza. Nereus was a sea god, the son of Pontus, father of Thetis and so grandfather of Achilles; his truthfulness is attested by Hesiod, *Theogonia* 233–6. For his prophetic powers see West on Hes. *Theog.* 233 ἀψευδέα.

5–8 Nereus' prophecy begins abruptly without any polite address, and its first word, *mala*, sets the tone.

5 ducis: *duco*, esp. with *domum*, strongly suggests marriage, but in comedy the same expression could be used of taking home a prostitute (*OLD* 5b); supply *eam* as object and as antecedent for *quam*. **aui** 'portent' (*OLD* 3b). Nereus talks like a Roman, since official diviners, *augures* (see the *OCD* article), used the signs provided chiefly by birds (*auis, ales*) to determine whether an undertaking should proceed. Cicero says in *De diuinatione* 1.28 that the presence of *auspices* was in his time largely confined to weddings, so *auis* is particularly appropriate to this context, cf. *nuptias* 8 (despite Fordyce's scepticism at Catull. 61.20). For similar phraseology cf. 3.3.61 *alite lugubri*, Epode 10.1 *mala soluta nauis exit alite*.

6 multo . . . milite: for the collective singular see *miles* 6.4n.; the ablative is instrumental.

7 coniurata . . . rumpere: the infinitive with *coniuro* is characteristic of high style (Sallust, *Catilina* 52.24, Virg. *G.* 1.280). There are two oaths that H. might have in mind here. An oath was exacted by Helen's father Tyndareus from her many suitors to defend the man chosen by him to become her husband; the A scholium on Hom. *Il.* 2.339 συνθεσίαι τε καὶ ὅρκια believes that oath is referred to there and claims the story was related by Stesichorus, *GL* III 190. Subsequently, an oath was sworn at Aulis by the assembled Greek army, which promised never to return until Troy was taken (cf. Pease on Virg. *Aen.* 4.426 *Aulide*). Since this is a prophecy, it seems more likely that the latter oath, which had not yet been taken, is the one referred to. But it is certainly possible that both oaths are meant. *rumpere* with *nuptias* means 'cut short' (*OLD* 9), cf. *Aen.* 4.292 *tantos rumpi non speret amores*; it must be given a more generalized sense, 'destroy', with *regnum* 8.

8 regnum: the scope of the future disaster is widened to include all of Troy (cf. *genti* 11 and 22, and 33–6), cf. Hector's reproach to Paris at *Il.* 3.50 'a great bane to your father, your city, and all your people'. *uetus* is emphatically positioned for pathos; cf. Virg. *Aen.* 2.363 *urbs antiqua ruit* (of Troy).

9–12 Nereus interjects a pathetic vision of events, a narrative technique known as diatyposis or hypotyposis: see Quintilian, *Institutio oratoria* 9.2.40. The French commentator Dionysius Lambinus (1520–72) noted this shift.

9–10 heu heu: the gemination emphasizes distress and sympathy; for *heu* see 5.5n. **quantus ... , quantus ... , quanta:** emphatic anaphora marks Nereus' impassioned speech, cf. *nequiquam* 13, 16, *non* 21, 22, *te* 23, 24. This sentence forms a tricolon crescendo. **sudor:** war is hard work, so fighters sweat, especially in ancient battles which were usually fought in the summer; cf. *Il.* 2.390 ἱδρώσει δέ τευ ἵππος ἐύξοον ἅρμα τιταίνων 'and your horse will sweat as it pulls along the polished chariot', and *Epode* 10.15 *o quantus instat nauitis sudor tuis*.

quanta ... funera 'how many [heroic] deaths'. Poets allowed the use of *quantus* in the plural where prose used *quot* (Fordyce on Virg. *Aen.* 8.537 *quantae ... caedes*), but here there is also a sense of quality or degree, not just number. For *funus* 'death' see *OLD* 3. **moues** 'you are stirring up/initiating' (*OLD* 17). **Dardanae:** Dardanus was an ancestor of Priam. For the adjectival use of the proper name (here of an individual rather than a people) see *Marsus* 1.28n. and cf. *Romulae genti* 4.5.1 (the proper adjective is *Dardanius*).

11–12 The vision ends emphatically with the arming of a divinity, Pallas (12.20–1n.), an inveterate enemy of Troy, because, like Juno, she had been slighted by Paris when he adjudged Venus the fairest goddess. Polysyndeton – *et . . . -que . . . et* – underscores her eagerness for battle. For the syllepsis (*galeam, aegida, currus + rabiem*) see 8.16n.

11 aegida: the termination is the accusative singular of the Greek third declension (G–L §65). The *aegis* was a goat-skin worn by Pallas (and some other gods) either as a mantle or a kind of breastplate (Kirk on Hom. *Il.* 2.446–51, p. 162).

12 currusque: poetic plural (*TLL* IV 1519.84–1520.4; the singular was possible here); this particular usage may be influenced by the plural ἅρματα.

13–20 Nereus returns to prophetic mode, by a gliding transition from one goddess, Pallas, to another, Venus. H. alludes to a similar sentiment at *Il.* 3.54–5, where Hector upbraids Paris, saying that his lyre and hair and looks will be of no real use to him once he has fallen in the dust.

13 praesidio: causal ablative with *ferox* 'arrogant' (*OLD* 4). Paris was under Venus' protection once he awarded her the prize for beauty.

14 caesariem: poetic diction (*TLL* III 108.15–18). Male grooming was a minefield at Rome, since one needed to be tidy without seeming effeminate or Greek (which came to the same thing). Ovid set out the ideal agenda in *Ars amatoria* 1.513–24 (Hollis's introductory n. provides the context). The old Roman style was shaggy (cf. *incomptis* 12.41n.), but in H.'s day gentlemen kept their hair short (as we see in the idealized portraits of Augustus), so combing would have been unfussy. What is in mind here is the elaborate care long, and probably perfumed, hair required; cf. the *comptos . . . crines* of Paris that caught Helen's eye at 4.9.13–14 and the *pexo capillo* of Catiline's crew (Cicero, *In Catilinam* 2.22 with Dyck's n.).

14–15 grata . . . feminis . . . carmina: a deliberate evocation of the contrasting theme of Achilles' song in *Il.* 9.189, κλέα ἀνδρῶν 'the famous deeds of men'. **imbelli:** cf. 6.10.   **cithara:** a loan-word from Greek and as such largely poetic.   **diuides** 'you will articulate', a singular expression, much discussed. *TLL* v 1.1609.31–3 quotes Porphyrio's gloss *dispones*, but helpfully suggests, following Nauck–Hoppe, a pun derived from the Greek verb μελίζειν. The point would be that the Greek word for lyric song, *melos*, also means a limb. Cf. Marius Victorinus, *Ars Gramm.* 1.13, *GLK* vi 54.13–16: *nec immerito apud quosdam haec communiter mele appellantur quae nos carmina interpretamur et membra quia mele Graeci diuisas membrorum uocet partes.* A similar notion may lie behind Jerome, *Epist.* 60.4.2 *stridorem suum in dulce crucis fregerunt melos*: a wail is an 'inarticulate' sound, but if 'broken/divided' into discrete parts or limbs it becomes song.

16 thalamo 'in your bed-chamber' (*OLD* 2), a loan-word from Greek and poetic diction. The local ablative without *in* of a noun without an epithet is noteworthy and usually poetic (K–S ii 353–4; Lejay collects Horatian examples at *S.* 1.5.87 *oppidulo*). H. has in mind the scene in *Il.* 3, especially 380–1, when Venus snatched Paris from the battlefield and transported him to his bedroom with Helen.

16–17 graues | hastas = Homer's ἔγχος βριθύ, *Il.* 5.746.   **calami** 'arrow'; weirdly misplaced in *OLD calamus* 1b 'reed', when it should be under 6. This sense is exclusively poetic, because the word is borrowed from the Greek, though κάλαμος is not much used to mean arrow. It is remarkable how Latin extended the meaning of some loan words; *gyrus* is a classic example, and cf. *stomachus* 6.6n.   **spicula:** the final *a* remains short before the two consonants of the following word, see Raven 1965: 25 (*Cnosius* is a 'Greek derivative').   **Cnosii:** archery was long associated with the island of Crete, of which Cnossos was one of the chief cities, so poets commonly decorated words for bow, arrow, and the quiver with epithets referring to Crete (see Williams on Callimachus, *Hymn* 2.33 Λύκτιον). The reference to arrows is slightly odd, since the bow is rarely used as a weapon in the *Iliad* (it was a dubiously heroic weapon), but it has a point in Paris' case; cf. 20n.

18–19 celerem sequi: H. likes *celer* with an infinitive (1.18n.): cf. 3.12.11, 4.6.39–40, and *Epist.* 1.20.25; the syntagm is borrowed from Greek, ταχύς + infinitive (H–S 351). His lead is followed in the mannered prose of the elder Pliny, *Nat. hist.* 16.186 and 35.194.   **Aiacem:** the son of Oileus was the swift runner, cf. *Il.* 2.527 (for Ajax, son of Telamon, see 7.21–32n.).

19–20 tamen . . . serus: elliptical: 'though too late [to be of much use to Troy], you will nonetheless . . .'; for the word order see Munro on Lucr.

3.553 (where this line is adduced) and Housman on Lucan 1.333. For *serus* see 2.45n. **adulteros:** hypallage (1.22n.). **cultus** 'finery' (*OLD cultus²* 6, and cf. 4.9.15 again of Paris' fine clothing); the plural is poetic. There is a commonly accepted variant, *crines*, which would pick up by contrast *caesariem* 13; fouling the hair in the dust is a standard motif, cf. Pindar, *Nemean* 1.68 (in the prophecy of Tiresias), Virg. *Aen.* 12.98. But that is not in H.'s manner: he is more likely to add a new idea rather than repeat one. The death of Paris at the hands of Philoctetes, who used the bow of Hercules, was related in Lesches' *Little Iliad* and presumably in Sophocles' *Philoctetes in Troy*.

21–6 Another passage of vivid imagination of the scene (cf. 9–12n.).

21–2 non ... respicis? 'don't you see?', an indignant question (*OLD non* 4, cf. K–S II 503), as at 3.20.1 *non uides* (a surprised question). **Laertiaden:** 'son of Laertes' (= Ulysses), a patronymic; for the termination see 6.16n., and for the figure 6.5–6n. **exitium tuae | genti:** an allusion to one of his *ruses de guerre*, either the Trojan horse or the theft of the Palladium (or both). The metonomy of *exitium* is poetic usage, perhaps founded on the Greek use of ὄλεθρος, for which see LSJ s.v. II; the more usual predicate dative *exitio* is found at 28.18. The dative of disadvantage *genti* with a noun instead of the objective genitive is also poetic; cf. Plautus, *Bacchides* 1054 *sciui ego iam dudum fore me exitium Pergamo*, Ennius, *Alexander* 61 Jocelyn, *eum* [Paris] *esse exitium Troiae, pestem Pergamo*. The dative may have been generated by analogy to its use with the adjective, cf. 16.17 *ira exitiosa hominibus*, and it makes an effective echo with line 11; textually considered the genitive is the obvious reading and the more likely to replace the mannered dative.

22 Nestora: accusative singular termination of the Greek third declension (G–L §65; Cicero used *Nestorem* in prose). He came from Pylos in the western Peloponnese.

23–4 urgent ... te ... te: repetition emphasizes the sole object of their pursuit.

24 Teucer: 7.21n.

24–5 Sthenelus sciens | pugnae: Sthenelus was the charioteer of Diomedes and would find a place in the Trojan horse. A present participle, regarded as adjectival, normally governs an objective genitive (G–L §375); cf. *citharae sciens* 3.9.10, *rixarum metuens* 3.19.16 (3.24.22). It is therefore surprising that Quintilian, *Institutio oratoria* 9.3.10, regarded this phrase as 'figured', i.e., a departure from the norm: *iunguntur interim schemata: 'Sthenelus sciens pugnae'; est enim 'scitus pugnandi'* (presumably he took the use of *pugna* = 'fighting' to be a metonymy). The expression reproduces Hom. *Il.* 5.608 εἰδότε χάρμης, and so appropriately evokes epic.

25 siue = *uel ... si* (2.33, 35, 41n.). **imperitare:** an elevated word found in epic and history.

26 non ... piger: litotes (1.19–21n.).

26–36 Prophecy (*nosces*) and imagination (*ecce*) merge into a picture of the ultimate fate of Paris (*fugies* 31), and of Troy (*proferet* 33, *uret* 35).

Lowrie's own view, 1997: 127, is that the poem is 'about' poetry, and she tries to demonstrate this by drawing attention to what she feels are its links with poems in its immediate vicinity.

The theoretical battle lines were clearly demarcated by Archibald MacLeish in his 'Ars Poetica' of 1926: 'a poem should not mean | but be'. Some readers of this poem are content that it should exist, others insist that it must signify. There is no resolution.

16

Metre: alcaic (see Introduction 8)

1–4 H. assures an unnamed young woman that it rests with her to put an end to his vituperative attacks, by the destruction of his verses. The first line is conciliatory, designed to flatter and appease.

2 quem ... cumque: for the tmesis see 6.3n.

3–4 pones: the future guarantees her ability to effect what H. implicitly invites her to do (cf. 20.1 *potabis*). **iambis** 'invectives' (*OLD* 2b), like H.'s epodes, so called because the iambus was the commonest measure employed in their composition, though they did not have to be exclusively in the iambic metre. **flamma | ... mari:** instrumental ablatives. H. substitutes for the colourless idea 'water' the sea, and a whole one to boot; Syndikus 2001: 180 rightly finds the exaggeration amusing. Both fire and water are good means for destroying poems, since fire burns papyrus, and water washes away ink; cf. Tib. 1.9.49–50 with the further references in Smith's n.

5–12 H. now grandiloquently denounces the power of anger, which is compared to demonic possession (5–8), and its strength is such that no other force can quench it (9–12). The halves of this complex idea are evenly balanced: four examples of ecstatic disturbance are matched by four ineffective deterrents, the last of which, Jupiter himself, is the most impressive. But whose anger is at issue: the outraged girl's or the lampooner's? Arguably, it is both.

5–9 The sentence is constructed by use of ἀπὸ κοινοῦ: the predicate (*quatit mentem*) appears in the second colon, and the adverb *aeque* is reserved to the third. But the run of the whole sentence is perplexed by the addition of the fourth colon (7–8). The leading idea is that gods of ecstasy do not unbalance the minds of their priests or devotees as much as (*aeque ... ut*) anger upsets the minds <of men generally>. The Corybantes however are the disturbed ones, not the disturbers (see below). The only way to bring the fourth *exemplum* into line with what precedes would be to take it to mean something like 'not in the same way does the repeated sharp clash of bronze cymbals disturb the Corybantes', but that is not what the Latin says.

5–6 Dindymene = Cybele, the *Magna Mater*, worshipped on Mount Dindymon in Phrygia. Her priests were the emasculated Galli (cf. Catull. 63). The adjective is used as a noun by Callimachus, *Epigram* 40.2 Pfeiffer Δινδυμήνης.

3.553 (where this line is adduced) and Housman on Lucan 1.333. For *serus* see
2.45n.   **adulteros:** hypallage (1.22n.).   **cultus** 'finery' (*OLD cultus²* 6, and
cf. 4.9.15 again of Paris' fine clothing); the plural is poetic. There is a commonly
accepted variant, *crines*, which would pick up by contrast *caesariem* 13; fouling the
hair in the dust is a standard motif, cf. Pindar, *Nemean* 1.68 (in the prophecy of
Tiresias), Virg. *Aen.* 12.98. But that is not in H.'s manner: he is more likely to add
a new idea rather than repeat one. The death of Paris at the hands of Philoctetes,
who used the bow of Hercules, was related in Lesches' *Little Iliad* and presumably
in Sophocles' *Philoctetes in Troy*.

   21–6 Another passage of vivid imagination of the scene (cf. 9–12n.).

   21–2 non ... respicis? 'don't you see?, an indignant question (*OLD non* 4,
cf. K–S II 503), as at 3.20.1 *non uides* (a surprised question).   **Laertiaden:** 'son
of Laertes' (= Ulysses), a patronymic; for the termination see 6.16n., and for the
figure 6.5–6n.   **exitium tuae | genti:** an allusion to one of his *ruses de guerre*,
either the Trojan horse or the theft of the Palladium (or both). The metonomy of
exitium is poetic usage, perhaps founded on the Greek use of ὄλεθρος, for which
see LSJ s.v. II; the more usual predicate dative *exitio* is found at 28.18. The dative
of disadvantage *genti* with a noun instead of the objective genitive is also poetic; cf.
Plautus, *Bacchides* 1054 *sciui ego iam dudum fore me exitium Pergamo*, Ennius, *Alexander*
61 Jocelyn, *eum* [Paris] *esse exitium Troiae, pestem Pergamo*. The dative may have been
generated by analogy to its use with the adjective, cf. 16.17 *ira exitiosa hominibus*,
and it makes an effective echo with line 11; textually considered the genitive is
the obvious reading and the more likely to replace the mannered dative.

   22 Nestora: accusative singular termination of the Greek third declension
(G–L §65; Cicero used *Nestorem* in prose). He came from Pylos in the western
Peloponnese.

   23–4 urgent ... te ... te: repetition emphasizes the sole object of their
pursuit.

   24 Teucer: 7.21n.

   24–5 Sthenelus sciens | pugnae: Sthenelus was the charioteer of
Diomedes and would find a place in the Trojan horse. A present participle,
regarded as adjectival, normally governs an objective genitive (G–L §375); cf.
citharae sciens 3.9.10, *rixarum metuens* 3.19.16 (3.24.22). It is therefore surprising that
Quintilian, *Institutio oratoria* 9.3.10, regarded this phrase as 'figured', i.e., a depar-
ture from the norm: *iunguntur interim schemata: 'Sthenelus sciens pugnae'; est enim 'scitus
pugnandi'* (presumably he took the use of *pugna* = 'fighting' to be a metonymy).
The expression reproduces Hom. *Il.* 5.608 εἰδότε χάρμης, and so appropriately
evokes epic.

   25 siue = *uel* ... *si* (2.33, 35, 41n.).   **imperitare:** an elevated word found
in epic and history.

   26 non ... piger: litotes (1.19–21n.).

   26–36 Prophecy (*nosces*) and imagination (*ecce*) merge into a picture of the
ultimate fate of Paris (*fugies* 31), and of Troy (*proferet* 33, *uret* 35).

26–7 Merionen ... nosces: an adaptation of Hector's remark about Achilles at Hom. *Il.* 18.269–70 'one will well recognize him'. For the termination of the proper name see 6.15n.

27 ecce: Dionisotti 2007 describes the varied ways in which Virgil first exploited this colloquial interjection in epic; she observes, 2007: 87, that it can highlight the final item of a list, which may be its particular function here. She notes too, 2007: 91, that this is its only occurrence in H.'s lyrics, perhaps therefore an appreciation in a poem on the boundary between lyric and epic of his friend's innovative epic style. For *ecce furit* cf. *Aen.* 8.228 *ecce furens.* **furit ... reperire:** the infinitive (1.18n.) is first found here with *furo* (*TLL* vi 1.1626.20–1).

28 Tydides: see 6.16n. **melior patre:** repudiates Agamemnon's criticism at *Il.* 4.399–400, by accepting the claim of Sthenelus, that the sons were superior to their fathers (*Il.* 4.405).

30 uisum ... lupum: Ovid picked up the expression at *Ars amatoria* 1.118 *uisos ... lupos* (a debt not noticed by Keller–Holder).

31 sublimi ... anhelitu 'with shallow panting'. *sublimis* (*OLD* 3d) is H.'s unique loan-shift from a Greek medical term, μετέωρος, and it suggests that the breath is only 'high up' in the lungs. **mollis** 'cowardly' (*OLD* 13).

32 non hoc: litotes. Nereus knows the past as well as the future. H. expects us to recall Helen's reproach to Paris at *Il.* 3.430–1: 'You used to boast that you excelled warlike Menelaus in the strength of your hands and your spear'. Ovid followed suit at *Heroides* 16.357–8. **tuae** 'your girlfriend' (*OLD* 2d, and cf. 25.7 *me tuo*). Nereus parodies the sort of affectionate language lovers use, cf. Terence, *Adelphoe* 289 *mea tu*. It is a very effective close to the part of the prophecy that concerns Paris alone.

33–6 Nereus, now finished with Paris, concludes his prophecy with a hint at the time-scale of the doom of Troy: protracted but inevitable. The two sentences are set paratactically beside each other, but the first is logically concessive.

33–4 iracunda ... | ... classis Achillei 'the anger of Achilles' contingent', a construction explained at 1.4–5n.; the epithet really belongs to Achilles (hypallage), in allusion to his μῆνις, the first word of the *Iliad*. *classis* could mean 'fleet', since all the Greeks had sailed to Troy, but West and Rudd take it to mean 'forces', an archaism found perhaps in Virg. *Aen.* 7.716 but misunderstood by Livy 4.34.6 (see Ogilvie ad loc.). *Achillei* is quadrisyllabic, see *Vlixei* 6.7n. **diem proferet** 'will postpone (*OLD* 10) the day (of doom)'. The expression has overtones of Roman business and legal life (see *TLL* v 1.1051.22–5), though *dies* in this context, as also at Seneca, *Hercules furens* 190, suggests the final day (so *OLD* 8).

34 matronis strikes a note of ironic pathos, ironic because Paris' adultery causes the deaths in battle of the husbands of respectable women, pathetic because their widows will become slaves.

35–6 post ... domos: this sentence stands in adversative asyndeton to the preceding; Rudd naturally translates, 'yet, after ... '. **hiemes:** see 11.4n.

There is a sharp contrast with *uret*.   **Achaicus** 'Greek' (especially as opposed to the Trojans, rather than strictly 'Achaean', cf. *OLD* 2), a poetic usage.

36 ignis Iliacas: this, the transmitted reading, produces an unusual glyconic 'base' in H., a trochee instead of a spondee. Textual critics secure the normal spondee by emending *Iliacas*, but they do not explain why any need was felt so to gloss an allegedly original *Pergameas* or *Dardanias* or *barbaricas*. Others defend the paradosis by pointing to Homer's metrical practice, which generally indicated an initial digamma for *Ilios*; they allege that H. may be imitating that practice (but did he really know about the digamma in Homer?), so that *ignis* can scan as a normal spondaic 'base' for the glyconic.

*

There is nothing like this poem in the rest of the collection. It has no addressee, neither is it a case of self-address. After a brief setting of the scene, it is entirely taken up with the speech of a mythological figure. Porphyrio says that the poem is an imitation of the choral lyric poet, Bacchylides, and he refers specifically to a prophecy by Cassandra in a now very fragmentary dithyramb, *GL* IV 23. Freestanding mythological narratives were also composed by early Greek monodists. Two songs of Alcaeus, *GL* I 42 and 283, which relate the infatuation of Helen for Paris and its impact upon the Trojans, seem to lie behind this one. (For the moralizing via myth of Alcaeus see Page 1955: 278, 280 and Bowra 1961: 168–70.) In both poems the tone is strongly critical of Helen (and in 42 she is compared unfavourably to Thetis). H. seems to be aligning himself with this tradition, with the focus here shifted to Paris: that he will despite Nereus' warning nonetheless proceed on his way to Troy with Helen condemns him.

What, it is of course nowadays asked, is the poem 'about', what does it 'mean'? Some, like Fraenkel 1957: 189, with n.1, will be content to see the poem as an experiment pure and simple, something H. never repeated. Along with Saintsbury 1923: 257 n.1 they may thus choose to enjoy the poem for its 'wonderfully scenic character'.

The majority will more probably agree with Lowrie 1997: 130 that 'we' feel a need for a poem to signify. The problem with our poem however is that it offers little by way of internal clues to its interpretation (Lowrie 1997: 127), beyond the implicit moral condemnation of the adulterous couple. The highway to interpretation has long been allegorical: behind Paris and Helen lurk Antony and Cleopatra. This interpretation both Fraenkel and Lowrie repudiate, in their different ways, as do Syndikus 2001: 173 and Cucchiarelli 2005: 47–53. A further reason for rejecting this attempt to give the poem contemporary colour is that the presumed equivalence is faulty. Nereus warns Paris (who is the focus of the poem) that the abduction of Helen will not be the ruin of himself alone, but also of his whole people. Now Antony was ruined by his love for Cleopatra, but it was Cleopatra who brought ruin upon her own kingdom, which after her death became an imperial province of the Roman empire. The equation is too imperfect to be plausible.

Lowrie's own view, 1997: 127, is that the poem is 'about' poetry, and she tries to demonstrate this by drawing attention to what she feels are its links with poems in its immediate vicinity.

The theoretical battle lines were clearly demarcated by Archibald MacLeish in his 'Ars Poetica' of 1926: 'a poem should not mean | but be'. Some readers of this poem are content that it should exist, others insist that it must signify. There is no resolution.

16

Metre: alcaic (see Introduction 8)

1–4 H. assures an unnamed young woman that it rests with her to put an end to his vituperative attacks, by the destruction of his verses. The first line is conciliatory, designed to flatter and appease.

2 quem ... cumque: for the tmesis see 6.3n.

3–4 pones: the future guarantees her ability to effect what H. implicitly invites her to do (cf. 20.1 *potabis*).   **iambis** 'invectives' (*OLD* 2b), like H.'s epodes, so called because the iambus was the commonest measure employed in their composition, though they did not have to be exclusively in the iambic metre.   **flamma | ... mari:** instrumental ablatives. H. substitutes for the colourless idea 'water' the sea, and a whole one to boot; Syndikus 2001: 180 rightly finds the exaggeration amusing. Both fire and water are good means for destroying poems, since fire burns papyrus, and water washes away ink; cf. Tib. 1.9.49–50 with the further references in Smith's n.

5–12 H. now grandiloquently denounces the power of anger, which is compared to demonic possession (5–8), and its strength is such that no other force can quench it (9–12). The halves of this complex idea are evenly balanced: four examples of ecstatic disturbance are matched by four ineffective deterrents, the last of which, Jupiter himself, is the most impressive. But whose anger is at issue: the outraged girl's or the lampooner's? Arguably, it is both.

5–9 The sentence is constructed by use of ἀπὸ κοινοῦ: the predicate (*quatit mentem*) appears in the second colon, and the adverb *aeque* is reserved for the third. But the run of the whole sentence is perplexed by the addition of the fourth colon (7–8). The leading idea is that gods of ecstasy do not unbalance the minds of their priests or devotees as much as (*aeque ... ut*) anger upsets the minds <of men generally>. The Corybantes however are the disturbed ones, not the disturbers (see below). The only way to bring the fourth *exemplum* into line with what precedes would be to take it to mean something like 'not in the same way does the repeated sharp clash of bronze cymbals disturb the Corybantes', but that is not what the Latin says.

5–6 Dindymene = Cybele, the *Magna Mater*, worshipped on Mount Dindymon in Phrygia. Her priests were the emasculated Galli (cf. Catull. 63). The adjective is used as a noun by Callimachus, *Epigram* 40.2 Pfeiffer Δινδυμήνης.

adytis . . . Pythiis: for the local ablative without *in* cf. *thalamo* 15.16. *ady-tum* is a Greek loan-word and as such poetic diction (the plural also seems to be poetic). The old name for Delphi was Pytho, whence the epithet, *Pythiis*. *Pythiis* is the conjecture of the Irish philologist, Arthur Palmer (1841–97), for the transmitted *Pythius*; it is discussed, but not accepted, by N–H and accepted by Shackleton Bailey and Rudd. It is the shrine, not its resident, which wants the epithet.   **quatit** 'unbalances' (*OLD* 4), and cf. 4.7n.   **incola** = Apollo, by the figure antonomasia (cf. *pastor* 15.1). The incoherent babbling of his priestess at Delphi had to be interpreted so as to provide a prophecy.

7 Liber: 12.22n.; his followers (not strictly priests) were Maenads or bacchants. Thyiades might be better, as they were an elected band, not casual. See N–R introduction to 3.25.

8 geminant . . . aera 'clash the cymbals'. The use of *gemino* is unusual (*TLL* VI 2.1739.1–3), an extension of its meaning 'join closely' (cf. *OLD* 4c). *aera* is a poetic synecdoche, since the cymbals are made of bronze (first in Lucr. 2.637, cf. *OLD* 6, *TLL* I 1073.58–64; Greek did not use χαλκός in the same way, oddly enough).   **Corybantes:** the short *e* of the final syllable replicates its Greek value (G–L §66.4). The Corybantes were mythical ministers of Cybele, but H. was not alone in identifying them with the Curetes, mythical ministers of Rhea and guardians of the baby Zeus on Crete; cf. Dodds on Euripides, *Bacchae* 120–34, p. 84. N–H try to urge that they do produce madness in others, but the evidence assembled by Mayor on Juvenal 5.25 *de conuiua Corybanta uidebis* – a guest whose brain is addled by inferior wine – is against this interpretation.

9 irae: Latin idiom employs the plural of abstract nouns to suggest repetition: 'angry outbursts' (N–W I 636–7, Löfstedt 1942: 34 quotes Plautus, *Miles gloriosus* 583 *irae leniunt*).

9–11 For equally ineffectual deterrents cf. *S.* 1.1.38–9 *cum te neque feruidus aestus | demoueat lucro neque hiems ignis mare ferrum.* H.'s lyric style is decorated, the satiric austere.

9–10 Noricus . . . ensis: the same phrase is found at *Epode* 17.71. Noricum, in H.'s day a kingdom allied to Rome in the easternmost Alps (the province of Carinthia in modern Austria), was an important source of iron (*OCD* 1048–9, Healey 1978: 64; cf. 29.15). *ensis* is poetic diction; H. uses the everyday *gladius* only at *S.* 2.3.276.

10 naufragum: H. seems to be the first to give the word causal sense 'shipwrecking', which is taken up by other poets (*OLD* 2).

11 tremendo: poetic diction (*OLD* s.v.).

12 Iuppiter . . . ruens: H. has a thunderstorm in mind, during which the sky (*sub Ioue* 1.25n.) seems to collapse (*OLD ruo* 6b, a poetic usage).

13–16 An aetiological myth accounts for the presence of anger in our human make-up. There is no precise model for this version. Maecenas wrote a work entitled *Prometheus* according to Seneca, *Epist.* 19.9; it is lost and cannot be dated, but it is always possible that H. flatteringly lifted the account from that work. On the other hand, it is just as likely to be an *ad hoc* invention of his own. This version of the myth assumes that man was created last, and so had to be equipped with qualities extracted from the animals. Mankind is thus a 'cocktail' of all the qualities which individually characterize particular animals.

13 fertur: 7.23n.   **Prometheus** took a hand in the creation of mankind according to Protagoras' myth in Plato, *Protagoras* 320d–321; see Mayor on Juvenal 14.35 *meliore luto finxit praecordia Titan*.

13–14 principi 'original' (*OLD princeps*[1] 4).   **limo:** 'earth' in some form or other (dust, mud, clay) was commonly felt to be the main material out of which mankind was fashioned.   **coactus:** best taken as a participle, not as an infinitive (with *esse* to be understood) co-ordinate with *apposuisse*. He was compelled because he had no other raw materials left over and had to equip mankind with what could be amputated from (*desectam*) other sources (*undique*), i.e., animals.

15 et = *etiam* 'as well', 4.11n.

15–16 leonis | uim: the lion is the very type of anger, see Lucr. 3.294–8, especially *uis ... uiolenta leonum*.

16 stomacho: the seat of the emotion of anger (6.6n.).

17–21 After the parable H. provides two *exempla* of the disastrous effects of anger, one on an individual, the other on entire communities. A similar train of thought is found in Catull. 51.13–16 *otium, Catulle, tibi molestum est* ... , | *otium* ... *beatas | perdidit urbes*.

17 irae: 9n. The repetition links the stanzas.   **Thyesten:** for the termination see 6.15n. No extant version of the myth supports H.'s claim exactly. Thyestes seduced Aerope, the wife of his brother Atreus, who therefore drove him from Mycenae. Anger thus seems more appropriate to the outraged husband, who got his revenge by serving up Thyestes' sons to him at a feast.   **graui** 'terrible' (*OLD* 10b).

18 strauere 'have laid low' (*OLD sterno* 7, and for the form of the perfect see 9.10n.); in this sense largely poetic diction (and common in Virgil, though found in Livy too). The poetic tone is enhanced by the use of an inanimate subject.   **urbibus:** cf. 4.15.19–20 *ira quae procudit enses | et miseras inimicat urbes*. Cities were described as *altae* either because of the height of their walls and buildings (*OLD* 1, citing Virg. *G.* 1.485) or because they were sited on hills (*OLD* 3a); either way the epithet also suggests their pride. The dative indicates 'disadvantage'.   **ultimae** 'earliest', i.e., primary, original (*OLD* 3). With *causae* 19 it is a predicate nominative with *stetere*.

19 stetere 'have been fixed' (*OLD sto* 19, and for the form of the perfect see 9.10n.); cf. Virg. *Aen.* 7.553 *stant belli causae*.

21 hostile aratrum: just as a plough was used to trace out the boundaries of a new town, so the site of a destroyed town was ploughed over to return the land to agricultural use, cf. Manilius, *Astronomica* 4.555–8 *urbibus augebit terras iunctisque iuuencis | moenia succinctus curuo describet aratro, | aut sternet positas urbes inque arua reducet*

| *oppida et in domibus maturas reddet aristas.* The elision of *–um* produces the regular word-break after the fifth syllable of the alcaic hendecasyllable.

22–8 H. now offers the addressee the advice that was withheld at the outset and closes by presenting himself as a model to follow for change of heart.

22 compesce mentem 'control (*OLD* 5b) your emotions' (*OLD* 6; Rudd). The verb, first found in Plautus but seemingly avoided by prose writers until the early principate, is poetic diction (Quintilian foisted it into Cicero's speech *Pro Rabirio perduellionis reo* 18). *mentem* picks up the same word in line 6.

me quoque: the sharp advice is promptly followed up by a mitigating admission that H. too was subject to strong feeling, but that he has had a change of heart. This provides the poem with its personal conclusion (cf. 28.21, though there the speaker is not H.).

22–4 pectoris | ... feruor 'hot temper' (*OLD feruor* 4). The expression is not metaphorical, but reflects the current medical view that heated blood accounts for anger; cf. Cicero, *De oratore* 1.220 *quid esset iracundia, feruorne mentis* ... ?

23 temptauit 'afflicted' (*OLD* 10).   **dulci iuuenta:** *iuuenta* is a largely poetic synonym for *iuuentas/iuuentus* (*TLL* vii 2.740.68). The phrase *dulcis iuuenta* is also to be found in Maecenas, *Symposium*, quoted by Servius *auctus* on Virg., *Aen.* 8.310: *idem umor ... dulcis iuuentae reducit bona.* It would be interesting to be able to establish priority and the likely direction of borrowing. Maecenas' dialogue ought to have been written before the death of Virgil in 19, since he along with H. was among the interlocutors. It was suggested above (13–16n.) that H. might have borrowed from Maecenas, but here the use of the poetic noun suggests the reverse.

24 celeres: the iambus, closely related to the rhythm of normal speech, was reckoned a 'swift' measure, cf. Brink on *AP* 252 *pes citus.*

25 nunc contrasts with *iuuenta* 23, since the persona H. presents in his lyric is uniformly that of a man of mature years (as in fact H. was) who has put hot-headed youth behind him.

26 mutare here means 'to give up x (accusative) in exchange for y (instrumental ablative)' (*OLD* 3b, and contast 17.2); the infinitive with *quaero* is poetic syntax, as at 37.22. *tristia* picks up *tristes* 9.

27 recantatis 'retracted'. This is the first appearance of the word in Latin, and it is presumably H.'s coinage, a calque upon παλινῳιδέω. Plato relates in the *Phaedrus* 243a that the lyric poet Stesichorus had slandered Helen in a poem, for which she (by this time a divinity) struck him blind; he composed new poems (*GL* iii 192 and 193) retracting the aspersions, for which he recovered his sight. For fuller discussion see Allan 2008: 18–22.   **amica** 'friend' (Rudd) or 'girlfriend' (*OLD* 2)?

28 animum 'affection' (*OLD* 9c: 'feelings towards others'). For the phrase cf. 19.4.

*

The situation sketched in this ode has proven singularly difficult to extrapolate. N–H 1970: 202–3 offered a 'brief consideration of the movement of the poem', designed to undermine its misinterpretation as a palinode, i.e., the retraction or recantation (cf. *recantatis* . . . | *opprobriis* 27–8) of libellous comment. Their outline is attractive, but, as West 1995: 78 pointed out, it nonetheless does not smooth away all problems. A woman is angry with offending lampoons, presumably H.'s own. (Similar is the situation in Catullus 36.) But when were they supposedly written? Usually H. refers to published works, but the lampoons referred to here are not among the *Epodes* (though interpreters look there for clues). If they were, the woman could hardly put an end to published work by destroying a single copy of it (though the ghost of Cynthia, in Prop. 4.7.77–8, orders him to burn the poetry he wrote, and published, about her). Moreover, the claim at the end of the poem that his lampoons were composed in his youth suggests he had finished both with that genre and with the attitude of mind which deployed it, whereas the opening stanza only makes sense if he is still turning them out at a time when maturer counsels prevail. (Such new lampoons, however, would at least not be published, so the advice to destroy them would make sense.) Finally, the mother's presence is unexplained, unless we are to imagine that the alleged lampoon had insulted the mother for good measure.

The tone of the sermon on anger (5–22) is universally seen to be ironic and amused, but that does not mean that the underlying sentiment is to be discounted. H. has turned his back on the excessive emotions of youth (cf. the criticism of Telephus in 13 and the description of his own changed persona at 3.14.25–8), now under control after the lapse of time.

17

Metre: alcaic (see Introduction 8)

1–12 H. announces that the herd of goats on his country estate is under the protection of Faunus. Only at 10 does an addressee, Tyndaris, appear, and her name is delayed for a reason.

1 Velox: Ovid picked up the epithet at *Fasti* 2.285–6 *ipse deus uelox discurrere gaudet in altis | montibus.*   **amoenum . . . Lucretilem:** a hill near H.'s estate in the Sabine country, not now identifiable (*EO* I 558); for the region see Bradshaw 1989: 160–86. The epithet praises the locality. H.'s poetry is shot through with references to the parts of Italy he knew and loved; the visit of a divinity adds prestige to the landscape.

2 mutat 'takes x (accusative) in exchange for y (ablative)' (*OLD* 2, and contrast the usage in 16.26).   **Lycaeo Faunus:** Pan (identified with Italian Faunus, 4.11n.) dwelt on Mount Lycaeus in Arcadia. As a guardian of flocks he was welcome on H.'s estate. Divine protection of the estate and its owner is something claimed in the imaginative odes, but not in the realistic satires or epistles. Faunus saved H. from the fall of a potentially lethal tree trunk (2.17.28), and is accorded a hymn, 3.18.

3–4 capellis: dative of advantage with *defendit* (K–S I 313–14), as in Virg. *Ecl.* 7.43 *solstitium pecori defendite* (which may here be recalled in a pastoral scene); with this verb the syntax is poetic (*TLL* V 1.294.74–81).   **usque** 'invariably' (*OLD* 5b).

5 impune tutum: the juxtaposition strikes a keynote of the poem, safety and security. Quite why, the reader cannot yet know.   **arbutos:** 1.21n.

6 thyma: poetic plural, cf. *Epist.* 1.3.21 *quae circumuolitas agilis thyma?*

7 olentis: difficult to translate adequately. Porphyrio said it meant 'stinking' (*foetent*, and cf. *putidus* as applied to Maevius at *Epode* 10.1), but that it is gentler, thanks to the figure litotes, 'understatement'. That is fair: *oleo* means 'give off a smell', good or bad depending on context. The non-committal word is appropriate to lyric style, and the reader is left to understand that the smell is disagreeable.   **uxores:** used of an animal, the word is assumed to be humorous, though Porphyrio described it as 'charmingly applied' *uenuste*; this is apparently the only time it is so used.   **mariti:** *maritus*, on the other hand, is used even by agricultural writers to mean 'mate' (*OLD maritus²* 2). Martial picked up H.'s phrase at *Apophoreta* 14.141.1 *olentis barba mariti*.

8 colubras: poetic diction in the main for everyday *serpens* (*TLL* III 1727.39–43).

9 Martiales ... lupos: the wolf is the familiar of Mars, cf. Virg. *Aen.* 9.566 *Martius ... lupus.*   **haediliae** 'female kids' (a rare word).

10 utcumque 'whenever'; H. seems to be the first to give the word a temporal force, cf. 35.23, 2.17.11, 3.4.29, and 4.4.35.   **dulci, Tyndari, fistula:** the addressee is finally named (the form of her name is the vocative of the Greek third declension, see G–L §65 s.v. Paris). H. delayed to do so until he came to mention something that would specially appeal to her, music, for she too is a musician. For this reason too her name is embedded between *dulci* and *fistula* (Fraenkel 1957: 206, La Penna 1989: 335–53, Nisbet 1999: 140); for similar word order cf. 7.19 *molli, Plance, mero* and 3.29.3 *cum flore, Maecenas, rosarum.* What seemed to be nothing but praise of the landscape may now be turned to some other purpose related to the interests of the addressee. The pipe, *fistula*, was Pan's instrument of choice (Faunus strictly speaking was no musician); for illustration and description see Landels 1999: 69–71. H. artfully leaves it open whether the pipe is being played by the god or by some shepherd.

11 Vsticae cubantis: even H.'s ancient commentators were not sure about Ustica: was it a hill or a valley (cf. *EO* I 558 for the uncertainty)? A hill seems more likely, because of the *saxa* 12 and the desirable contrast with *ualles*. That has a bearing on the meaning of *cubans*, not taken into account by *OLD cubans* 2b. If Ustica was a hill, then it means 'sloping'; if a valley, then 'low-lying'. Either way the sense will be unique and imaginative.   **personuere:** for the form of the perfect see 9.10n.

13–14 The divine protection described in the first dozen lines is now extended to the poet himself (and H. dons the persona of the poet). **di ... dis:** the anaphora is emphatic. H. often draws attention to his sense of being divinely protected, from his childhood (3.4.17–18) to adulthood, when he survived a number of near-fatal incidents (Philippi 2.7.13–14, the fall of a tree 2.13 and 2.17.27–30, shipwreck 3.4.28). These are all more serious than being saved by Apollo from a pest in *S.* 1.9.78. See Krasser 1995.   **tuentur:** picks up *tutum* 5, and rounds off this part of the poem.   **musa:** his poetry too gives H. a special claim upon divine care (cf. Tibullus 2.5.113 *diuum seruat tutela poetas*), a notion stretching back to the miraculous preservation of singers and poets like Arion (Herodotus 1.23) and Simonides (Cic. *De orat.* 2.352–3).   **cordi est** 'is dear to' (*OLD cor* 5b). This expression, in which *cordi* is a final dative, was used with reference to the gods in earlier Latin (Ellis on Catull. 44.3) and is still so used in Livy (Ogilvie on 1.39.4), though its range was extended. For the number of the verb see 2.38n.

14–28 Having stressed the safety of his domain, H. turns to invite Tyndaris – *tibi* 14 points the change of direction – to join him there. The musical attractions have already been suggested, but the close of the poem, starting from *nec* (22), also indicates why she might welcome retreat from the city.   **hic (14) ... hic (17) ... hic (21):** anaphora drives home the many inducements the locality has to offer the visitor, and structurally it articulates a tricolon crescendo. *tibi* 14 is frequent in invitations, e.g. 3.29.1 (Maecenas), *Epist.* 1.5.7 (Torquatus).

14–16 H. first stresses abundance (*copia*, also at *CS* 60 in connection with the horn of plenty) of good things to eat (he postpones drink, for a reason). The abundance of the language here is an example of 'stylistic enactment'; Commager 1962: 351 recognized this without using the term, defined by Hornblower 2008: 36 as the device by which the words chosen literally represent and suggest ('enact') what is being described.

15 ad plenum 'to the full' (*OLD plenus* 16a), an adverbial phrase borrowed, it seems, from Virgil, *G.* 2.244.

15–16 benigno | ruris honorum ... cornu 'her horn, generously bestowing the countryside's glories'; for the genitive cf. *S.* 2.3.3 *uini somnique benignus*. But K–S 1 441, H–S 77, and, more hesitantly, *OLD opulentus* 3b and *TLL* IX 2.839.37–8 take the genitive with *opulenta*, likewise an adjective connoting fullness. *honores* 'glories' (*OLD* 6b) is found again in an agricultural context at *S.* 2.5.13 *quoscumque feret cultus tibi fundus honores*.   **cornu:** H. is keen on the image of the horn of plenty: *CS* 59–60, *Epist.* 1.12.28 (cf. Otto 1890: 94).

17–18 Caniculae | uitabis aestus: H.'s promise is guaranteed by the protection of Faunus, cf. 2–3. *Canicula* 'the dog-star', in the constellation Canis Major, was called in Greek Sirius. It is the brightest star in the night sky, and its 'rising' in late July heralds the summer's hottest days (*aestus*, for this sense of the plural see Löfstedt 1942: 134–5). Hence a further inducement to leave sweltering Rome for the cool of the Sabine hills.

18 fide Teia: *fide* is a poetic singular (*TLL* VI 1.692.59–76, and cf. 24.14), since the plural is the common number in prose, and indeed generally in H., cf. 12.11. *Teia* alludes to the sixth-century lyric poet Anacreon, who was born in the Ionian city of Teos, cf. *Epod.* 14.10 *Anacreonta Teium*. The themes of his poetry were largely erotic; Tyndaris' musical skill and her chosen repertoire indicate that she is a cultivated prostitute.

19 dices 'you will sing of' (6.5n.).   **laborantes** 'distressed' (*OLD* 6), by love as the context shows, as at 27.19. *in* 'in respect of' denotes the point of reference with a word expressive of emotion (*OLD* 41f); *uno* 'one and the same [man]' (*OLD* 3), viz Ulysses (Odysseus).

20 Penelopen … Circen: for the terminations see 6.15n. Penelope was the wife to whom Ulysses so longed to return that he even relinquished the favours of a goddess, Circe. But H.'s memory seems to have played him false here. For when Ulysses told Circe that he wanted to return home, she made no difficulties (*Od.* 10.489) because she was not in love with him; it was the sea-nymph Calypso who resented having to let him go (*Od.* 5.116–44).   **uitream:** the epithet was obscure to H.'s Roman commentators, but picked up by Statius, *Siluae* 1.3.85. Though her mother was a daughter of Oceanus, Circe, unlike Calypso, was not a sea-nymph, so colour ('glass-green') may not be the point (unless H. has indeed confused the two goddesses). Perhaps he had in mind the cloudy glow of Roman glass, as pseudo-Acro suggested: *lucentem nitore*. The word remains as mysterious as the woman.

21–8 The final sentence fills the last two stanzas with a grand tricolon crescendo period.

21 innocentis … Lesbii: sc. *uini* (cf. 20.1). H. at last comes to the wine. He leaves it for the prominent closing place in his list of allurements because it will remind Tyndaris that it was drink that fuelled the assault upon her by her lover Cyrus. H. implies that no such rough stuff will befall her *in reducta ualle* 17, since the wine he offers was noted for not going to the head (it was also much esteemed according to the elder Pliny, *Nat. hist.* 14.73, cf. *Epode* 9.34). Its name perhaps suggests too his own literary taste for the poetry of Alcaeus.

22 duces 'you will drink' (*OLD* 25b), a sense chiefly found in poetry (or prose under its influence); cf. 4.12.14 *pressum Calibus ducere Liberum*.

22–3 Semeleius … Thyoneus: i.e., Bacchus, the son of Jupiter and Semele, who was also called Thyone.   **confundet … proelia:** a unique phrase (*OLD confundo* 3c), which has eluded the *TLL* at x 2.1655.40–70. There were many expressions for beginning battle, *proelium committere* being the chief of them (*OLD committo* 8, cf. 4.14.14–15 *graue proelium | commisit*). Poets followed Lucretius in deploying *proelium miscere* as a more vivid expression for the confusion of battle (*OLD misceo* 13b, and cf. §§3b and 4b). H.'s variant on that is more graphic still, and the whole expression gives the quarrels of lovers a mock-epic character.

24 nec metues: Tyndaris will be as carefree as the goats (*nec . . . metuunt* 8).

25–6 Cyrum, ne . . . iniciat: the subject of the verb in the subordinate clause of fearing is 'anticipated' as the object of *metues*; this is called prolepsis (K–S II 578–81, H–S 471–2), cf. Plautus, *Menaechmi* 861 *ego illum metuo . . . ne quid male faxit mihi*, Terence, *Eunuchus* 610–11 *metuo fratrem | ne intus sit*, and 35.9–13 (*TLL* VIII 905.62–6). The usage seems to be colloquial in origin.

25–8 ne . . . uestem: for lovers' brawls see 6.17–18n.

25 male dispari 'no match', physically. *male* is a colloquial intensive (Hofmann 1951: 74, *OLD* 10), usually applied to a word with an 'unpleasant' sense. Here, however, it helps define a neutral term: *dispar*, unlike *impar* 'inferior', usually indicates mere difference (at 4.11.31 *disparem uites* the context shows that it means 'superior person'). Similarly, at *S.* 1.3.45 *male* with *paruus* indicates that the child referred to is 'stunted'. Contrast *male* at 9.24.

26 incontinentes . . . manus: the epithet is transferred by the figure hypallage from Cyrus, who lacks self-restraint; cf. 4.8.19 *auidas manus . . . heredis* (where Bentley toyed with reading *auidi*).

27 coronam: 4.9n. The pattern described on *dirae* 2.1n. suggests that *immeritam* 28 is to be applied ἀπὸ κοινοῦ to *coronam*.

28 crinibus: a largely poetic word, not used by H. in his hexameters.   **uestem:** tearing another's clothes inflicts shame, cf. Gibson on Ovid, *Ars amatoria* 3.569 for further examples.

*

The structure of the poem is made up of two parts (though the border may be drawn at slightly different points: Syndikus 2001: 189, n. 32 assesses the views). The first part (here taken to run to the middle of 14) is descriptive, the second (from the middle of 14 to the end) is implicitly an invitation to Tyndaris to enjoy with H. the place described in the opening. The two halves are linked by common elements: absence of fear (*nec . . . metuunt* 8 – *nec metues* 24), avoidance of heat (*igneam | defendit aestatem* 2–3 – *Caniculae | uitabis aestus* 17–18), Mars (9–23), and music (Faunus' *fistula* 10 – Tyndaris' lyre 18).

   The first, descriptive half is a rhapsody upon the Sabine landscape in which H. owned an estate (see S. Quilici Gigli, art. 'la villa in Sabina, la dimora a Tivoli' in *EO* I 253–8). This estate is described in more down-to-earth, though no less affectionate terms in H.'s hexameter poems; here it is clearly transposed into an idealized landscape, more fruitful perhaps than in reality, a place divinely protected and conducive to song. Such praise, however heartfelt, is rhetorically directed however. The ode has an addressee, and the praise of the landscape which she is about to be invited to share with the poet is designed as an inducement: all the estate's special qualities will appeal to her, especially given her erotic difficulties with a jealous thug. By contrast H. claims 'là, tout n'est qu'ordre et beauté, | luxe, calme et volupté' (Baudelaire, *Les fleurs du mal*, 'L'invitation au voyage' – also an invitation to a girl to join the poet).

The movement of the poem is typical: the opening is in stark contrast with the close, and the rustic idyll which Tyndaris is invited to share is set against the urban symposium she has presumably had quite enough of (the contrast by way of foil did not escape Campbell 1924: 227). This antithetical movement recalls the situation in the thirteenth ode: the girl (Lydia there) was keen on a passionate boy, but H. felt he offered something less hurtful and more stable. The theme is varied and elevated here with the notion of divine presence and protection. Some see in this contrast a jibe at the erotic code of contemporary elegy. That may be so, but H. always presents himself in his lyrics as older than the protagonists of elegiac affairs, and his manner suits his time of life; when he was young, it was different.

Putnam 1994: 357–8, n. 1 gives a helpfully crisp résumé of current interpretations, the more aggressive of which he politely repudiates; Griffin 1994: 20 offers reflections on Tyndaris' name and what it suggests.

18

Metre: 'fifth' or greater asclepiad (see Introduction 7–8)

1–6 H. advises Varus to plant a vineyard on his estate, since wine banishes cares.

1 A motto drawn from Alcaeus, *GL* 1 342 μηδ' ἓν ἄλλο φυτεύσῃς πρότερον δένδριον ἀμπέλω. The source of the quotation, Athenaeus, claims that it is a piece of general advice (*Deipnosophistae* 10.430C). If that is true, H.'s is more particular, being addressed to Varus and specifying a locality for the vineyard (2). **Vare:** unidentifiable. Some MS superscriptions – but not the scholiasts – identified him with the Quintilius whose death is mourned in 24, but there is no sound reason for supposing that that Quintilius bore the cognomen Varus (though it is a known cognomen in that *gens*). H.'s friend Pompeius (2.7) is given the cognomen Varus in the MSS superscriptions and by pseudo-Acro, and the name Varus occurs in *Epod.* 5.73. N–H argue for the distinguished jurist Alfenus Varus (assuming however that the Alfenus of Catull. 30 is also the Varus of Catull. 10 and 22). **sacra:** not found in Alcaeus, the epithet puts the vine in a different light, as something belonging to a god, and it prepares us for the religious turn which the poem takes in the second half (West 1995: 91). H. may have appropriated the expression from Ennius' tragedy *Athamas*, 121 Jocelyn *uitis inuentor sacrae*, part of a messenger's description of a Bacchic orgy. **prius** 'for preference' (*OLD* 2). **seueris** 'plant'. For the perfect subjunctive (here of *sero*) in a prohibition see *ne quaesieris* 11.1n. **arborem:** *uites iure apud priscos magnitudine quoque inter arbores numerabantur*: the Elder Pliny, *Nat. hist.* 14.9. In ancient Italy (and in modern, until fairly recently) vines were trained up elm trees (cf. 2.15.4–5), and so rose to a considerable height. The sort of close-cropped short vine we see nowadays is owed to French viticulture.

2 circa 'in the vicinity of', with locative force (*OLD* 4, and Rogers on Frontinus, *De aquaeductu* 71.1).   **mite** 'kindly' (*OLD* 7b), a reference to the mild climate and fertility of the soil, cf. 4.3.10 *Tibur . . . fertile.*   **Catili:** one of the traditional founders of Tibur (cf. 7.13 for another, Tiburnus), Catillus was variously identified (and his name was variously spelled): see Horsfall on Virg. *Aen.* 7.670–7 and 672.

3 siccis 'the sober' (*OLD* 7).   **nam:** the particle is postponed (2.9n.). But usually it is only delayed by one word; it is much rarer in the third place (Norden 1927: 403, Klingner Index 338).   **dura:** take as a predicate with *omnia.*   **proposuit** 'has appointed' (*OLD* 8).   **neque:** as last word in the line it effects a close enjambement with the following line.

4 mordaces 'gnawing', an unusual metaphorical sense, owed to H. (*OLD* 3b); cf. 2.11.18 *curas edaces.*   **aliter:** there is an ellipse of the full thought, 'nor otherwise than by taking a drink of wine'.

5 post uina i.e. 'after <drinking> wine', a common sort of ellipse, illustrated by Langen on Valerius Flaccus, *Argonautica* 1.139 *post pocula.* For *uina* see 11.6n.   **grauem militiam** 'the hardship of campaigning'; the epithet is in an emphatic position (Naylor) and applies ἀπὸ κοινοῦ to *pauperiem.*   **crepat** 'harps on' (*OLD* 4). H. is surprisingly fond of this verb, which moreover he uses as a transitive verb of speaking, virtually alone in classical Latin (the only example before him is Plautus, fr. inc. 162 *neque leges crepo*).

6 The question requires a verb, which clearly cannot be *crepat*; by the figure zeugma a verb of related sense, e.g., *dicit*, or even of opposite sense, e.g., *laudat*, can be supplied; cf. K–S II 565–6, Kenney on Lucr. 3.614, where a verb of opposite sense is to be supplied, and Jacobson 1987: 526. For the sentiment cf. *Epist.* 1.5.17–18.

pater: the honorific appellation, common with the names of gods (*OLD* 6), reinforces the idea of *sacra* 1.   **decens:** 'graceful' is the main notion, but given the moralizing thrust of the ode 'appropriate' may also be understood (see 4.6n.).

7–11 Mythological *exempla* warn against the misuse of a divine gift.

7 ac ne quis 'and yet to prevent someone from . . .'. *ac* has a slight adversative sense (*OLD* 7), and *ne* introduces an elliptical or parenthetic final clause, which gives the poet's motive for citing the subsequent example (*OLD* 13, G–L §545 R3, K–S II 233–4, H–S 535); such clauses usually come first in their sentence; cf. *ne doleas* 33.1n.   **modici** 'restrained' (*OLD* 8), cf. *uerecundum* 27.3; it is emphatic by position (cf. 20.1).   **transiliat** 'use to excess'; the basic idea is 'overstepping' a limit (*OLD* 7), implied by *modici.* For *Liberi* see 12.22n.

8–9 Centaurea: an Horatian coinage; the epithet replaces a genitive (here causal: they started the brawl), see 3.36n. The Centaurs were guests at the wedding of the King of the Lapithae, Pirithous; one of them, Eurytion, tried to rape the bride, Hippodame. The use of the Centaurs as a warning about the dangers of wine goes back to Homer's *Odyssey*, 21.295–304. They figured in the metopes of the

Athenian Parthenon, and Ovid will tell the story at *Met.* 12.210–576.   **monet**
... | ... **monet:** anaphora emphasizes the warnings.   **super mero:** for
the local ablative see 9.5n., for *merum* 13.10n.   **Sithoniis:** strictly a Thracian
tribe, but the word is poetic geography and diction for 'Thracian' generally.
H. refers to the deplorable drinking-habits of Thracians, for which see Nepos,
Alcibiades 11.4 *Thracas, homines uinolentos*, and cf. 27.1–2 and 36.14.   **non leuis:**
for the understatement see 1.19–21n., and cf. 14.18. *Euhius* was a cult-title of Bac-
chus/Liber, deliberately chosen here to suggest the dangerously ecstatic power
of wine.

10–11 cum fas atque nefas exiguo fine libidinum | discernunt auidi
'when in their eagerness for sex (*OLD libido* 3b) they draw too fine a line (*OLD
finis* 6c) between right and wrong' (Rudd, adapted). *libidinum* should be taken with
auidi (*OLD* 5, rather than 6). H. hints at some sort of incest, perhaps like the freak
version of the tale of Sithon and his daughter Pallene as narrated by Nonnus,
Dionysiaca 48.90–237 (though his passion was not drink-induced). Ash notes that
Tacitus seems to have had this passage in mind at *Hist.* 2.56.1 *in omne fas nefasque
auidi.*

11–16 H. focuses upon himself at the close: he will not offend the god by
impiety (11–13), and he asks the god not to afflict him with the ill effects of the
misuse of wine (13–16).

11 candide 'fair' (*OLD* 5b), a common epithet of Bacchus.   **Bassareu:**
another, rarer cult title, referring to the Thracian bacchants, who wore fox-skin
(βασσάρα). The termination is of a Greek vocative, see G–L §65, s.v. *Orpheus.*

12 inuitum 'against your will' is predicative with *te* 11.   **quatiam:** H.
seems to have in mind the thyrsus, a ritual staff 'shaken' by Bacchic devotees,
which could be identified with the god himself. Cf. 4.7n.   **obsita:** the neuter
plural is deliberately vague. The 'things covered' are the god's *orgia* 'mystic
emblems', which were usually kept in a box (*cista*) under leaves, presumably of
ivy and the vine.

13 sub diuum 'out into the open'. The accusative is obviously necessary with
the idea of motion inherent in *rapiam*, but it alters a standard expression, *sub diuo*
(found at 2.3.23 and 3.2.5), and so may have sounded slightly unusual (it occurs
nowhere else in the classical language).

tene 'check, restrain' (*OLD* 19); for a similar deprecation addressed to Liber
cf. *parce* 2.19.7.   **Berecyntio:** the epithet strictly speaking designates Cybele,
but the pipe and tambourine were musical instruments characteristic of ecstatic
cults generally (cf. Catull. 64.261–3).

14–15 For the personifications see 2.34n.

14 caecus Amor sui: cf. Sen. *Epist.* 109.16 *amor sui excaecat.*

15 tollens ... uerticem: cf. 3.16.19 *tollere uerticem*; the act implies pride.
uacuum in the vicinity of *Gloria* suggests κενοδοξία 'vainglory'.   **plus nimio**
'far too much', *nimio* being ablative of measure of difference with a comparative
(G–L §403, *OLD nimio*). The expression is colloquial, but the word order is

singular: the Roman in the street usually said '*nimio plus*', as we learn from Plautus, who as a rule puts the adverb before the comparative (see Lodge 1933: II 170, K–S I 402).

16 Fides 'Loyalty' in an 'antiphrastic' sense, meaning really 'Disloyalty', according to Fraenkel in *TLL* VI 1.681.78–682.4. He included this passage among others which illustrate an aspect of loyalty much esteemed by the Romans, namely the ability to keep a secret (cf. *OLD fides*[1] 8b), which this *fides* does not manage, at any rate when weakened by wine. Drink loosens the tongue, a danger against which H. will warn Lollius at *Epist.* 1.18.38 *commissumque teges et uino tortus et ira* (cf. *S.* 1.4.84–5 *commissa tacere | qui nequit*).   **perlucidior uitro** 'as clear as glass'. The use of the comparative ablative is often no more than a compendious form of simple comparison; *niue candidior* means 'snow-white'. See Fordyce on Catull. 35.16–17 *Sapphica puella | musa doctior* and especially Brink on *Epist.* 2.2.83; cf. 19.6. Löfstedt 1942: 316–17 noted the high incidence of this ablative in H.'s poetry, especially his lyrics, which he attributed, p. 318, following K–H's n. here, to the influence of his Greek models. The construction also has the virtue of economy as against the use of *quam*. *perlucidus* is here metaphorical, a usage not exclusive to poetry (*TLL* X 1.1520.32). For a close on a comparative cf. 36.20 and 3.6.48 *progeniem uitiosiorem*. In the major asclepiad there is normally a caesura after the second choriamb; to secure this the prefix *per* is regarded as detachable.

*

The poem, structurally similar to the third, is made up of three parts: advice to Varus (1–6), a general warning against misuse of wine embodied in mythological *exempla* (7–11), and finally H.'s own resolution regarding the wine-god, with his hope for reciprocal restraint on the god's part. The addressee fades from sight after the fourth line, since Varus is unlikely to have been in the financial straits referred to in the fifth (*pauperiem*). By the sixth line there is an entirely new addressee, Bacchus, who dominates the rest of the poem. Thus the end of the poem is a long way from its starting-place, rather like the third ode. That said, H. had early on introduced with *sacra* a sense that wine is something more than a mundane beverage and must be treated with respect.

The style of the first section is largely straightforward, but it changes radically in the middle section (Mitscherlich 1800: 194): the repetition of *monet* stresses the urgency of H.'s warning examples, and the ending of sentences in mid-line (11, 13) suggests his own agitation. We are swept from the reassuring suburb of Tibur to the barbaric Sithonians (goodness knows exactly what they got up to!). The strangeness continues in the perplexed closing section, with its cult names and places, its bewildering music.

Quinn found the poem curious, unusual, and perhaps experimental: all entirely fair. N–H's general assessment, 1970: 228–9, is equally alert (and not unlike Mitscherlich's), save for one point: Pöschl 1986 and West 1995: 89–91 place more weight on the references to decency (6) and restraint (7), and Pöschl dwells on the drink-induced moral failings listed at the close. The poem's implicit message might well be endorsed by a society appalled at the binge-drinking of its young.

19

Metre: 'fourth' asclepiad (see Introduction 7–8)

1–4 H. is dismayed to find himself in love once more. This was a commonplace of Greek erotic lyric, and recurs as a theme in 4.1.

1 Mater ... Cupidinum = Venus, by the figure antonomasia. The plural *Cupidines* is first found in Catull. 3.1 (see Fordyce's n.). The line is recycled at 4.1.5, in a similar context.

2 Thebanae: Semele was the daughter of Cadmus, the founder of Thebes. **iubet:** for the singular see *iuuat* 2.38n. Passion is an imperative. **Semelae puer** = Bacchus, by the figure antonomasia. For Semele see 17.22, and for *puer* 12.25n. Drink of course makes us amorous, and the reference to Bacchus suggests that H. has just seen the girl at a symposium.

3 Licentia 'Wantonness', a literary personification (*OLD* 2c); see 2.34n.

4 finitis ... amoribus: the expression is probably general: H. thought he was finished with love affairs but has learned his mistake. Some however take it to be specific, e.g. 'to a love that was over' (Rudd), in other words this is not the first time H. has fallen for the girl. **animum reddere:** cf. 16.29.

5–8 He identifies the object of his passion, Glycera, and lists her physical attractions.

5, 7 urit: 6.19n. Anaphora emphasizes the powerful effect of her charms. **nitor:** cf. *nites* 5.12–13n. (*OLD* 2b).

6 The phraseology of this line is appropriated by Seneca, *Phaedra* 797 *lucebit Pario marmore clarior* (of Hippolytus).

Pario marmore: Virgil was the first Roman to refer to the highly prized white marble from the Cycladic island of Paros (*G.* 3.34 *Parii lapides*). For comparisons to this marble in erotic contexts see Page on Rufinus, *Epigram* X 2 (= *Anthologia Palatina* 5.28.2). **purius:** for the sense of the comparative see 18.16n.

7 proteruitas: the girl is 'forward' in her sexuality, something of a role-reversal, but hardly unwelcome to H., cf. 2.5.15–16 *iam proterua | fronte petet Lalage maritum*.

8 lubricus aspici 'unsettling to behold' (Rudd), an arresting phrase: the primary sense here of *lubricus* is 'smooth, polished' (so *OLD* 2d, and cf. Martial 9.56.11 *uultu lubricus*, of a beardless boy), but active too is a secondary sense, 'hazardous' (*OLD* 4). H. alone joins the infinitive (1.18n.), here passive (H–S 351), to *lubricus*.

9–12 The effect of this passion is loss of interest in the composition of epic poetry.

9 tota: Venus is entirely involved in her attack on H. (*OLD* 4).   **ruens** by its similar sound evokes what Phaedra said at Euripides, *Hippolytus* 443 Κύπρις … ἦν πολλὴ ῥυῆι 'if the Cyprian comes in full flood' (the verb is ῥέω).   **10 Cyprum:** 3.1n., and cf. 30.2n.   **Scythas:** the Scythians were a nomadic people, inhabiting the plains north and north-east of the Black Sea. Augustus recorded that an embassy of theirs had sought Rome's friendship (*Res gestae* 31.2), probably in 25, so it was possible for H. to regard them as a subject people, cf. *CS* 55 *iam Scythae responsa petunt*.

11 uersis … equis: an allusion to the tactic of eastern mounted archers, who feigned retreat but could swivel round and fire a devastating shot at the pursuing enemy.

12 Parthum: for the Parthians see *Persae*, 2.22n. The singular is used collectively by the figure synecdoche to refer to the people generally, especially in military contexts (K–S 1 67–8).   **dicere:** 6.5n.   **quae nihil attinent** 'irrelevancies' with regard to H.'s current infatuation (*OLD attineo* 7, *nihil* 11b adverbial). The expression is colloquial and casts the epic themes into a more realistic perspective.

13–16 All H. can do is try to mitigate the onset of love by sacrifice, so he orders his slaves to make preparations. We again encounter the *schema Horatianum* (7.10n., Schmidt 2002: 360), since H.'s basic idea is that he will sacrifice wine, incense, and an animal to Venus, but he reserves the victim for a new statement.

13 hic … hic: anaphora generates urgency, enhanced by placement of the second adverb at the line's end, which effects enjambement.   **mihi:** the so-called ethic dative, expressing someone's interest in the action (*OLD ego* c; *NLS* §66); cf. 32.15. Translation is often difficult (Rudd does not try here); 'for me' (West), or even 'please', are possible.   **caespitem:** simple turf served as a makeshift altar (*OLD* 3b); *uiuum* indicates that the grass is still fresh (N–R on 3.8.3–4).

14 uerbenas 'greenery'; no particular plant is meant, since the word embraces a variety of flowery or leafy plants used in religious rites; cf. 4.11.6–7 *ara castis | uincta uerbenis*.   **pueri** 'slave-boys' (*OLD* 5).   **turaque:** incense was first brought to Greece by Phoenician traders, and its earliest use was in the cult of Aphrodite, herself a Semitic god (Burkert 1985: 62, and cf. Sappho, *GL* 1 2.3–4 'altars smoking with incense'); it was later used in religious cults generally. The plural is poetic, though it can refer to individual grains of incense.

15 patera: the shallow dish held by the sacrificer.   **meri:** only unmixed wine was suitable for sacrifice.

16 lenior 'more gentle' (*OLD* 5), esp. of gods, cf. 3.18.3 (Faunus), *S.* 2.7.93, Ov. *Am.* 2.13.21 (Ilithyia); for the adjective preferred to an adverb see 2.45n.

*

The structure of the poem is straightforward: an unexpected situation, the return of love, is described in a series of statements, which seem to be 'internal', in that there is no addressee (1–12). When H. has decided how to handle the situation, addressees appear: the slave-boys (14). His orders to them conclude the poem (13–16). The agents of the return of love are all divinities (1–4), and the object of love is clearly physically attractive (5–8). (Sutherland 2003 offers a feminist reading, in which due weight is not given to *grata* 7; Glycera's brazenness could not be so described if H. felt threatened by it.) The effect of this passion (9–12) rounds off the description of the poet's situation: he cannot tackle serious poetic themes. He can however try to mitigate the onslaught, and the poem closes with the measures he takes to do so. This ending is unexpected, since usually the lover appeases Venus with a view to securing the affection of the beloved. H. characteristically wants something rather different, a less consuming passion (Syndikus 2001: 207).

N–H rather downplayed the tone of the poem, which is better caught by Burck 1966: 175–88, who emphasized H.'s more serious attitude to love here. For instance, Venus is a more impressive figure than Cupid as generator of passion, and she is described as *saeua*, hardly a bantering epithet; she issues a command (*iubet* 2). She attacks moreover 'con tutta forza', *tota ruens*. But as N–H did fairly remark, H. is no obstinate Hippolytus, and he decides on a policy of appeasement; he does not repudiate emotion but aims to soften its impact. More might be made of that policy.

H. seems to be subverting not so much the myths of tragedy as the contemporary attitude to love found in the elegists. Could one imagine Propertius for instance adopting a policy of appeasement? His very first elegy suggests an entirely different reaction to finding himself in love's grip: Love has trodden Propertius' head beneath his feet, he now lives recklessly and can think up no stratagems to make his life easier (cf. also 2.15.29–30). H. on the other hand is clearly not without resource, because he regards love as powerful but not overmastering. Its effect can be mitigated (*ueniet lenior*). This attitude is of a piece with the doctrine he will later enunciate in *Epist.* 1.1.19 *mihi res, non me rebus subiungere conor* (Propertius clearly took the opposite view, that he must bend to circumstances). Of course, it has also to be borne in mind that the persona H. presents in his lyrics is that of an older man, who might indeed be expected to have profited from experience in these matters.

20

Metre: sapphic (see Introduction 8)

1–8 H. promises Maecenas a wine that will be local but distinctive. This may be taken either as an invitation (the usual interpretation) or as a response to a self-invitation by Maecenas.

1 Vile ... Sabinum: sc. *uinum* (cf. 17.21). It becomes clear that the wine was produced on H.'s own estate, which however did not much favour the vine, cf. *Epist.* 1.14.23 *angulus iste feret piper et tus ocius uua*, hence *uile*. (H. nowhere expressly says that the estate was a gift from Maecenas, though this has often been assumed since antiquity. If the assumption is correct, then the wine produced on the estate will be offered as a mark of gratitude.)   **potabis:** *poto*, unlike *bibo*, implies excess, as, e.g., at Sallust, *Catilina* 11.6 *ibi* [in Asia] *primum insueuit exercitus populi Romani potare.* The future serves either as an invitation or a promise.   **modicis** 'ordinary' (*OLD* 5), refers to quality not size (cf. *Epist.* 1.5.2 *modica . . . patella*), since the cantharus was in fact large. H.'s point is that he cannot provide silver or crystal vessels even for distinguished guests.

2 Graeca: continuing the emphasis on his own modest arrangements H. here uses the everyday epithet *Graecus* instead of its elevated synonym *Graius* (found, e.g., at 2.16.38 *spiritum Graiae tenuem Camenae*); see further Austin on Virg. *Aen.* 2.148 for the distinction, especially in prose. The point of recycling the Greek wine jar (*testa*) was thought by Porphyrio to be the addition of superior flavour (as whisky is stored in recycled sherry casks), but N–H argued that, since Greek wine had an admixture of salt water, the jar, impregnated with salt, would help to preserve a wine with less staying-power. The two explanations are however hardly inconsistent.   **ego ipse:** emphatic, to point up the private act in commemoration of a public occasion.

3 conditum leui, i.e. *condidi et leui*, ' I bottled and sealed' (*leui* is the perfect of *lino*). The form of the expression exemplifies a crisp idiom in which the action of one verb is expressed participially as the object of another, as at Virg. *Aen.* 6.8 *inuentaque flumina monstrat.*

Wine was fermented in a vat (*dolium*) and then drawn off (*diffundo*, cf. *Epist.* 1.5.4 *uina . . . diffusa*) into more convenient jars (cf. *diota* 9.8, *amphora* 3.8.11, *cadus* 3.29.2, *lagoena Serm.* 2.8.41), which were sealed with a smear of pitch over the cork stopper (*corticem astrictum pice* 3.8.10). The vintage year was recorded either by incision into the earthenware or by a tag (*pittacium*) with the name(s) of the consul(s) inscribed on it (cf. *Epist.* 1.5.4 *iterum Tauro*). Again, H. personalizes the occasion by recording (mentally) a different event.

3 datus: understand *est.*   **in theatro:** built by Pompey in the Campus Martius (and so near the Tiber) and dedicated in 55 (Richardson 1992: 383–5, Sear 2006: 57–61).

4 plausus: a form of acclamation (ἐπισημασίαι) welcome to public figures in the ancient world, cf. Cicero, *Ad Atticum* 1.16.11 *itaque et ludis et gladiatoribus mirandas* ἐπισημασίας *sine ulla pastoricia fistula* ['hissing'] *auferebamus* and *Pro Sest.* 115–18. H. had referred to the *plausus* accorded Agrippa for his aedileship, *S.* 2.3.185, and again to an acclamation for Maecenas at 2.17.22–7. For the alleged occasion see the endnote.

5 clare . . . eques: Maecenas apparently took some pride in not seeking entry into the senatorial class, and his poets therefore harp upon his distinction within his own station, cf. 3.16.20 *equitum decus* and especially Prop. 3.9.1–2 *Maecenas, eques Etrusco de sanguine regum | intra fortunam qui cupis esse tuam.* Since the point is that Maecenas was a cut above other knights, H. probably wrote here *clare* rather than the only authoritatively transmitted reading, *care*, for he will be stressing his friend's standing, rather than his own (or popular) feeling for him (the words are confused again at 3.14.7, where editors tend to prefer *cari* to *clari*). For the mannered word order see 1.29n.

5–6 paterni | fluminis ripae: the Tiber rises in the Appenines to the northeast of Arezzo, Maecenas' *patria* (see *Maecenas* 1.1n.). *ripae*, nominative case, is a poetic plural.

6–8 Cf. 12.3–4n.   **redderet:** for the singular see *iuuat* 2.38n.

7–8 Vaticani | montis: the Janiculan ridge, across the Tiber and opposite the Campus Martius; what we nowadays know as the Vatican hill came to be distinguished from it in Christian times (Richardson 1992: 405).

9–12 In contrast to the humble Sabine which H. offers, he now lists four esteemed native wines, the names referring to them all prominently placed at the beginnings or ends of lines. He might have said, simply, that all four were readily available to Maecenas, but not to himself. But he more artistically deploys the *schema Horatianum* (7.10n., Schmidt 2002: 360): he grants Maecenas only two and denies himself two more. Yet more artistically still, he never repeats the way in which he identifies the four wines.

9 Caecubum: understand *uinum*. This was among the finest of south Latian wines, which Maecenas naturally had a store of (cf. *Epod.* 1–4, especially *repostum Caecubum*); cf. 37.5, a special celebration. Tchernia 1986: 34 observes that H. never serves such a fine wine himself. The vineyards had decayed by the time of the elder Pliny (*Nat. hist.* 14.61).   **prelo ... Caleno:** cf. 31.9 and 4.12.14 (quoted on 17.22 above) for the locality, Cales (mod. Calvi Risorta, see *EO* 1 427), in Campania. The elder Pliny put its wine into the third rank (*Nat. hist.* 14.65). The *prelum* (< *premo*) was the press-beam of the wine-press; there is a sketch of one with its parts named in White 1984: 31, and there are good illustrations, especially of a modern working model, in Tchernia 1999: 48–107.   **domitam** 'subdued', i.e., 'pressed', but the more energetic verb is poetic usage (cf. *OLD domo* 5).

10 tu bibes 'you may drink'; for the concessive/permissive aspect of the future see *scriberis* 6.1n. Some find this usage uncomfortable after *potabis* 1, and Shackleton Bailey therefore prints Keller's emendation *bibas. tu* here contrasts with *mea*, as at 2.12.9–14 *tu* [also Maecenas] ... *dices* [also concessive] ... *me*.

10–12 mea: contrasts with *tu* and focuses the conclusion upon H. himself ('Ich-Schluß').   **Falernae | ... uites:** the *ager Falernus* is also in Campania and produced a wine Pliny put into the second class (*Nat. hist.* 14.62).   **temperant ... pocula** 'mix my drinks'. The vines and hills provide the wine that is mixed in the cups. *tempero* means 'blend' (*OLD* 6), since water was added to wine to dilute its strength and thus prolong conviviality. *pocula* is here used by a (largely poetic) metonymy to mean the drink in the cups (*OLD* 2, cf. *Epode* 17.80 *desiderique temperare pocula*).   **Formiani | ... colles:** the hills of Formiae are in southern Latium. H. also refers to this wine, again as one he does not serve, at 3.16.34 *Laestrygonia Bacchus in amphora*.

*

If one assumes that this poem represents an invitation, it had at least one antecedent in Latin, Catullus 13, *cenabis bene, mi Fabulle*. We find there the same use of the future of invitation, and the notion that the guest is rather better off than the host (Fabullus is invited to bring the dinner!). But the host nonetheless has something special up his sleeve for the guest. This fruitful tradition of poetic invitations is illustrated by Williams 1968: 103–31, especially 129 for our poem, but Edmunds 1982 refines the approach, arguing for its Roman origin.

The elaboration of the poem's art compensates for the unpretending wine. H. has little control over its quality but maximum control over his own creation.

Some interpretations hinge upon the occasion of the acclamation in the theatre. It should be premised that H. has nothing at all to say about the reason for the crowd's applause, and that if the reason were important he could easily have given it. Undeterred from asking inappropriate questions which can only be answered with extraneous information, some identify the occasion with Maecenas' recovery from illness, and they point to an acclamation recorded at 2.17.22–6. But Mitscherlich 1800: 210 pointed out that Maecenas could easily have received an ovation in the theatre on more than one occasion. Even in the later poem illness is not specified as the threat to Maecenas' life; it is to the scholiasts we owe that information, which may have been guesswork. (A larger question is whether H. really expected his readers – readers a century on or in remote Spain – to know any of this.) This poem should be interpreted only in the light of what it tells us, namely that H. put up the wine he now offers his friend on an occasion of the public expression of esteem. H. thus commemorates the personal and private act which complemented the public one. There may too be a contrast between the ephemeral nature of the acclamation and the somewhat more enduring quality of the wine. But what really lasts is the poem, and it eternizes the short-lived acclamation and the wine and the friendship.

Nisbet 1995: 419–21 argues against an allegorical interpretation of Commager 1962: 326 (the wine = the poem), among others.

21

Metre: 'third' asclepiad (see Introduction 7)

1–4 H. invites young girls and boys to sing in praise of Diana, Apollo, and their mother Latona. Cult statues of these three divinities were set up by Augustus in the newly dedicated temple of Apollo Palatinus (cf. 31 below, and see Zanker 1988: 85–9, Richardson 1992: 14, and Galinsky 1996: 216).

1 Dianam: hymns usually begin with the name of the god to be celebrated (cf. Catull. 34.1 *Dianae sumus in fide*). Diana was a native Italian divinity, assimilated to the Greek Artemis. The first syllable retains its original long quantity, perhaps an archaic effect.   **tenerae ... uirgines:** so too at 4.1.26 *cum* *teneris uirginibus.*   **dicite** 'sing of' (6.5n.). The opening command to the choir is a standard feature of cult-hymns, and of parodies of them (see Bullock on Callimachus, *Hymn* 5.1–32, p. 109, and Hopkinson on Callimachus, *Hymn* 6.1 ἐπιφθέγξασθε 'sing the refrain').

2 intonsum ... Cynthium = Apollo, by the figure antonomasia; he is here identified by the name of a hill, Cynthus, on the island of Delos, his birthplace (10 below). The epithet replicates ἀκερσεκόμης (*Il.* 20.39); it indicates Apollo's eternal youthfulness, since Greek boys first cut their hair on attaining manhood. Roman boys on the other hand seem to have kept their hair trimmed (on the so-called Ara Pacis Augustae only the very little boy clinging to Agrippa has uncut ringlets), so it is not likely that the epithet hints at the *pueri*.

3–4 supremo | ... Ioui = 32.13–14; the epithet is especially used of Jupiter (*OLD* 7). For the dative of agent see *matribus* 1.24n.   **penitus** 'deeply' (*OLD penitus*[1] 3); the point is that Latona was one of Zeus's wives, not the victim of a casual rape (cf. Hesiod, *Theogonia* 918–20, where she comes in the list just before Hera).

5–12 H. gives the girls and then the boys their proper themes.

5 uos: supply *dicite* from the preceding stanza.   **laetam fluuiis et nemorum coma:** for Diana's woodland haunts cf. 3.22.2 *custos nemorum, CS* 1 *siluarum potens*, and Catull. 34.9–12 *domina ut fores | siluarumque uirentium ... amniumque sonantum* (all of Diana). *nemorum* suggests her cult title *Nemorensis*. For *nemorum coma* cf. 4.3.11. *coma* is a loan-word (5.4n.), and one of its capital advantages was that it brought with it a metaphorical sense, 'leafage', unknown to the native Latin words for hair: see LSJ s.v. κόμη II and *OLD* 3.

6 quaecumque introduces a list of sites favoured by the goddess (see 12.5–6n.). None is known for cult (though at *CS* 69 cult is certainly hinted at), but H. has chosen well-wooded mountains, suitable for hunting.   **gelido:** the etymological play on the proper name – Algidus suggests *algor* 'chill' – is not uncharacteristic of learned poetry; cf. 3.23.9 *niuali ... Algido*. O'Hara 1996: 64–5 labels this the 'single-adjective gloss'. The identity and location of this mountain remain matter for speculation (see M. P. Muzzioli, art. 'Algido' in *EO* 1 492b), but it seems to be southeast of Rome in the area of Tusculum. What matters is that H. blends local Italian with mythical or remote geography.

7–8 nigris aut Erymanthi | siluis: Erymanthus is a mountain-chain in the Peloponnese straddling Arcadia, Elis, and Achaea. Roman readers knew it from Homer, *Od.* 6.103, where it is designated as a favoured hunting ground of Artemis; for its dark woods cf. 4.12.11–12 *nigri | colles Arcadiae* (they please Pan).   **aut:** postponed (2.9n.); Norden 1927: 404 lists examples.

8 Gragi: a mountain in Lycia, west of the river Xanthus. Euripides described it as 'full of wild beasts' (ἔνθηρος, fr. 669.2 Kannicht, from the *Sthenoboea*).

9 Tempe: see 7.4n. The alliteration in this line is remarkable.

10 natalemque ... Delon Apollinis 'Delos, the birthplace of Apollo'; for the substantive *natalis* see *OLD natalis*[2] 4, and for the termination of *Delon* see *Rhodon* 7.1n. Delos, an island of the Cyclades group in the Aegean Sea, was famous for its cult of Apollo and Artemis/Diana.

11–12 insignemque pharetra | fraternaque umerum lyra: the word order suggests a sort of double ἀπὸ κοινοῦ, whereby *umerum* must be supplied in the first colon and *insignem* in the second. The quiver and the lyre, Apollo's constant attributes (Williams on Callimachus, *Hymn* 2.19), are symbolic of his activities in war and peace. For *pharetra* see 10.11n.; both ablatives are instrumental. For Apollo's shoulder as a theme of the boys' song cf. 3.28.9–10 *cantabimus . . . Nereidum comas.*

12 fraternaque . . . lyra: Mercury was the half-brother of Apollo, son of Jupiter and Maia (2.43). He gave him the lyre (10.6) to appease him for the theft of his cattle (10.9–10n.). The lyre is one of Apollo's standard emblems (cf. *TLL* VII 2.1949.76–80). For the loan-word see 6.10n. **-que** 'or' links alternative possibilities which cannot simultaneously be true (*OLD* 7).

13–16 The final stanza focuses upon Apollo's support, since he was Augustus' patron divinity (31.1–2n.) as well as an averter of evil (cf. 2.30–2). It was a widespread conviction that evil did not simply evaporate, it had to be diverted somewhere, upon someone or something else, goats, for instance (Callimachus, *Aetia* 75.12–13 Pfeiffer), or swine (Matthew 8: 30–2) or an enemy, whether personal or public (cf. 3.27.21–4, and Catull. 44.18–20). This practice is nowadays called ἀποπομπή (see *NP* 1 896 for a brief discussion and bibliography, Weinreich 1968: 17–21, Fraenkel 1957: 410–11 on 4.1, Ogilvie 1969: 33; scholars will note that *auersio* is not correct Latin for this kind of diversionary tactic). Versnel 1976: 389–93 and 1981: 17–21 has discussed the concept in Rome; all of his examples are drawn from literature, especially poetry, and he offers no evidence of such prayers in the official cult of the Roman religion. H.'s assurance that the misfortunes will fall on Parthians or Britons (peoples at either extremity of the empire) arises therefore from an entirely private or imaginative impulse.

Some reckon the reference to dearth and plague is specific, since plague afflicted Rome in 23 (so Dio 53.33.4–5). H. however is unlikely to have knocked off the poem in the light of current events; dearth and plague were recurrent and related scourges in antiquity, and he need not have had any particular occasion in mind (so K–H, and cf. Norden 1939: 202).

13 hic . . . hic: anaphora of the demonstrative is characteristic of hymns and prayers (Norden 1923: 163–6; cf. 10.9n. for the second person). **bellum lacrimosum** = πόλεμον δακρυόεντα Hom. *Il.* 5.737.

14 pestemque 'plague', a choice synonym of *pestilentia* (for usage see *TLL* x 1.1927.44–51). Apollo as a god of healing (*medicus*) had received a temple in 431 for driving plague from Rome two years earlier (Livy 4.25.3 and 29.7); in 208 the *ludi Apollinares* were permanently instituted as a result of plague. See Scullard 1981: 159–60, 164. **principe:** 2.50n. **in:** the preposition, only found here as last word of its line (N–H 1970: xl), effects enjambement.

15 Persas: 2.22n. For a similar curse, cf. Ovid, *Ars amatoria* 3.248 *inque nurus Parthas dedecus illud eat.* **Britannos:** the Britons are here regarded as an enemy upon whom misfortune deserved to fall; cf. 35.29–30n.

16 uestra ... prece: the possessive pronoun is emphatically positioned to suggest the efficacy of the prayer of innocent youngsters; for the singular see 2.26n.

*

The poem evokes the tradition of choral hymn, but obviously it is not itself a hymn (Norden 1939: 201; Quinn and Miller 2009: 265–9 are somewhat casual in observing distinctions). H. instead takes upon himself the role of 'master of ceremonies', a persona found in the hymns of Callimachus. He thus works by indirection. Unlike Catullus in his poem 34, H. does not impersonate the choruses, nor does he pray in his own person for the welfare of Rome (that might seem presumptuous). Rather he acts as a sort of adviser to the young, helping them to frame their song. He is confident that their prayer will be heard.

The first stanza proposes three themes (Diana, Apollo, Latona) to two choirs of children. The girls are to address Diana, the boys Apollo, and perhaps both groups will sing of Latona (who is after this point forgotten). H. then gives the girls more detailed matter in the second stanza, and in the third to the boys. Their song was to be dedicated to Apollo, who becomes the sole focus of the final stanza, appropriately, given the nature of the prayer.

Catullus had ended his choral lyric with a prayer for the Roman people, but without any specific enterprise in view. H.'s implied prayer has a more immediate and patriotic ring to it, since the Britons and Parthians were, in theory at any rate, troublesome enemies marked down for defeat (Williams 1968: 155–6). Feeney 1998: 43 rightly regards the whole poem as 'saturated with context' in a way that Catullus' was not.

N–H take it amiss that H. has nothing here to say about the senate, but why should he have? Even in *CS* the only reference to the senate is in line 17, where the context is focused upon the recent marriage legislation.

22

Metre: sapphic (see Introduction 8)

1–8 H. informs his friend, Fuscus 4, that the upright man has no need of defensive weapons, however forbidding the country he intends to cross.

1 Integer uitae 'a man of unblemished life' (*OLD integer* 13), cf. 3.2.30 and *S.* 2.1.5; the addition of a genitive of respect or reference is poetic syntax (cf. *S.* 2.3.65 *integer mentis*, and *TLL* VII 1.2079.43–9); see generally G–L §374 N. 6, *NLS* §73(6). For an illuminating discussion of this thoroughly Roman moral quality, *integritas*, see Kaster 2005: 134–48, especially 139.

This opening may be a motto drawn from Alcaeus, *GL* I 130B, if the recon-
struction ἄγνος τοῖς βιότοις 'pure with regard to way of life' is accepted and it
is agreed to be the first line of a poem: see Hutchinson 2001: 205–6. There are
possibly further thematic links. Alcaeus is reluctantly in exile in what he calls
'the back of beyond', whereas H. as usual is happy to be at his villa. Alcaeus
may refer in line 10 to 'wolf-thickets', and a wolf has a walk-on part in H.'s
poem.

sceleris: this genitive too is unusual. It can be explained as another genitive
of respect ('pure with regard to wrong-doing'), but the idea of separation in
purus (free from something besmirching) is related to that of want or lack, which
the genitive naturally conveys (K–S I 441–2, H–S 107); we find the ablative of
separation, normal for conversation, with *purus* at *S.* 2.3.213 *purum ... uitio ...
cor.* As Brink says on *AP* 212 *liberque laborum,* 'H. liked experimenting with this
type of construction'. Here at the beginning of the poem the mannered syntax is
grandiloquent and enhanced by the chiastic word order.

3–4 grauida: poetic for *plena* (*OLD* 2). For *pharetra* see 10.11n.   **Fusce:**
Aristius Fuscus was one of H.'s intimates. He played a trick on the poet, described
at *S.* 1.9.61–74, and he is included in a list of H.'s preferred readers at *S.* 1.10.83;
he also received an epistle, 1.10. The scholiasts further identify him variously as
a dramatist and a grammarian.

5–7 siue ... siue ... uel: the use of *uel* for the final alternative is poetic
(K–S II 436). Marouzeau 1949b: 214 drew attention to the careful placement of
the epithets at the end of three successive lines, enhancing the exotic character
of the places named.

5–6 iter ... facturus: both are to be taken ἀπὸ κοινοῦ (cf. *dirae* 2.1n.),
and *est* is to be understood.   **Syrtes:** two bodies of dangerously shallow water
off the coast of North Africa between Carthage and Cyrene, but H. and Virgil
(colluding?) use the word to refer to the adjacent desert territory (cf. *OLD* s.v. c).
aestuosas is appropriate either to the 'sweltering' desert or to the 'seething' tides
of the shallows, which were notorious.

7 quae loca = *per loca quae,* but the antecedent has been drawn into the
relative clause, for economy's sake.

7–8 fabulosus | ... Hydaspes: *fabulosus* is first found here, so perhaps
a coinage. The Hydaspes (mod. Jelum) is a river in Kashmir; Virgil brought
its name to Latin poetry at *G.* 4.211, though he styled it *Medus.* The river was
'storied' thanks especially to the battle fought there by Alexander the Great
against the elephants of Porus, cf. Quintus Curtius, *Historiae Alexandri Magni* 8.13–
14.   **lambit** 'laps'; H. is the first to use *lambo* metaphorically of a river (*TLL*
VII 2.900.55–72) with the sense of *alluo*; cf. *mordet* 31.8.

9–16 The opening had no clear reference to H., who now explains (*namque*)
that a local (*silua ... in Sabina* 9) encounter with a wolf proves the opening
maxim: for all its vast size, it ran away from him, though he had no weapon (*fugit
inermem* 12). For the tradition of deploying such paradigms see Fraenkel 1957:
185–6.

9 me silua lupus: the basic elements of the incident are economically listed. Each element will then be developed, especially the scary wolf. **Sabina** contrasts with the exotic localities of 5–8. That wolves were found there is clear from 17.9.

10 canto 'sing of' (*OLD* 1c), cf. *S.* 1.5.15–16 *absentem ... cantat amicam | ... nauta*. For the present tense with *dum* see 2.17n. **Lalagen:** for the termination see *Helenen* 15.2n. H. begins to correct the lofty moralism of the opening stanzas, since he does not claim that it was his spotless character which saved him from the wolf. Rather he insinuates the commonplace of the protected lover, who is by definition pure of heart and under Venus' care, not that H. mentions specifically divine protection (see Smith on Tib. 1.2.27–8, McKeown on Ovid, *Amores* 1.6.9–14).

10–11 ultra | terminum: the preposition at line's end effects enjambement. *terminum* is 'the boundary-stone' of his estate. After the far-flung places of the opening stanza, there is an amusing bathos to the homely locality. **expeditis** 'cleared up' (*OLD* 3). The less well attested reading *expeditus* 'released from' (*OLD* 2b) is attractive, but it may be owed to Porphyrio, who explains the phraseology thus: *curis autem expeditis pro 'ipse curis expeditus, id est securus'*. In effect he regards it as a transferred epithet (cf. *TLL* v 2.1619.42–5). For the singer's freedom from care cf. 26.1–7.

12 inermem: prominently placed, the word underscores the claim of the opening stanza, *non eget*. Next to *fugit*, it creates a slight oxymoron, best rendered by a concessive idea: 'though I had no weapons', 'unarmed as I was'.

13–16 H. describes the wolf in the grandiloquent language of the opening stanzas.

13 quale portentum: construe as *tale portentum* (nominative in apposition to *lupus*) *quale*. The word is often used of 'prodigious' animals (*OLD* 2), and if a wolf entered the city of Rome, then it was literally a portent. **militaris** contrasts with *inermem* 12; the Apulian had a reputation as a fighter (cf. *S.* 2.1.34–9).

14 Daunias 'the land of Daunus', a coinage, and only found here; it is formed like a Greek proper adjective in the nominative singular. Daunus was a legendary king of northern Apulia, and poets deployed his name variously to designate the territory or its people. **alit:** for Apulia as the home of wolves see 33.7–8.

15 Iubae tellus = Mauretania or Numidia, by the figure antonomasia; for *tellus* see 7.29n. Juba II was restored to his paternal kingdom of Numidia by Octavian in 30; in 25 he received in exchange for it the two provinces of Mauretania. He wrote on a number of learned topics, and some stories found in other sources about lions may derive from his book on Africa; since his name means 'mane' in Latin there may even be an amusing pun here.

16 arida nutrix: an oxymoron, since a 'wet' nurse provided the baby with her milk.

17–24 H. returns to the opening theme of journeys in dangerous or disagreeable places. The two stanzas, joined by the impressive anaphora of *pone*, present opposite types of landscape, first the misty north, then the sultry south.

17, 21 pone: the imperative serves as a lively replacement for the protasis of a conditional sentence (G–L §593.4).   **pigris ... campis:** an unusual expression (*OLD piger* 1b, *TLL* x 1.2110.44–5), suggesting that the land is 'idle' because uncultivated; the ablative is local.

19–20 quod latus: construe similarly to *quale portentum* 14; *latus* is in apposition to the *ubi* clause. *latus* 'quarter' (*OLD latus²* 7) reflects the ancient view of the earth as flat, with sides or flanks.   **nebulae:** poetic plural, as at 3.3.56.   **malus ... | Iuppiter:** we too speak of 'bad' weather; cf. *sub Ioue* 1.25n.   **urget:** for the singular see 2.38n.

21–2 sub curru ... | solis: the sun's chariot is a common poetic image (*OLD currus* 1e).

23–4 dulce ridentem ... dulce loquentem: the accusative of a neuter adjective (usually singular, but sometimes plural) used adverbially starts its career in poetry (Catullus and Lucretius), and historians adopt it; it should probably be regarded as a grecism (G–L §333 R6, Roby §1096, H–S 40). Müller 1908: 77–84 provides numerous examples, but for H. specifically see F. Muecke, art. 'lingua e stile' in *EO* II 764a; he even employs it in his hexameters, e.g. *S.* 1.3.26 *cernis acutum* (cf. Mayer on *Epist.* 1.7.27). The anaphora of *dulce* is emphatic: Lalage's every utterance is charming.

dulce ridentem evokes Catullus, 51.5, itself a compressed appropriation of Sappho, *GL* 131.3–5 ἆδυ φωνείσας ... καὶ γελαίσας ἰμέροεν 'sweetly speaking and charmingly laughing'. But H. goes back to the original as well for a term Catullus had elided: *dulce loquentem* renders Sappho's 'sweetly speaking', ἆδυ φωνείσας. This is an example of 'double allusion' to be added to those discussed by McKeown 1987: 37–45. *loquentem* also puns on the girl's name (Lalage means 'chatterbox').

                                    *

Despite the possible motto derived from Alcaeus, the poem as a whole has no obvious model in Greek lyric, indeed it is hard to imagine one. The manner of proceeding is striking: why not address the poem to Lalage herself? H. seems to have preferred indirection because he could not have indulged his humour – and his chosen addressee, Fuscus, liked a joke, see *S.* 1.9.60–74 – if he had spoken to the girl herself about the experience. As for the alleged experience, the scholiasts were aware that the encounter with the wolf might be amusing rather than true: *dubitandum tamen utrum ioculariter an uere dicantur* (so pseudo-Acro). For the humour in this poem see Collinge 1961: 80, n. 2 (who anticipates Cowan 2006 as regards *Iubae ... leonum*) and Connor 1987: 31–6. Whilst the humour of the poem is nowadays more generally recognized, it is interesting to note that the Christian polemist (he had been a pagan), Lactantius, *Diuinae Institutiones* 5.17.18, took the doctrine of the opening stanza to be serious (but that is often the way when quotations are wrenched from their context).

The structure is simple (despite Collinge 1961: 80–1). H. opens with a premiss or claim about the immunity of the good man (1–8). That claim he substantiates by a personal experience, which is introduced logically (*namque* 9) and described

(9–16); much of the description is dedicated to exaggerating the fearsomeness of the wolf (with geographical details to maintain the motif of the opening). The poem ends with an expression of H.'s literally unbounded devotion to Lalage – the geographical details revert to the opening second stanza. Both Quinn and Tarrant 1995: 36–7 note the lightheartedly warped logic of the conclusion: H. ought to say that wherever he finds himself, his virtue will keep him safe, but his 'sweetly foolish infatuation' attributes his safety to his tuneful love of Lalage.

Joking and irony apart, the poem nonetheless insinuates a guiding principle of H.'s self-presentation or persona: the poet, the darling of the Muses, is a being set apart, and one manifestation of his self-sufficiency is his general cheerfulness, an immunity from cares, cf. the opening vaunt of 26 *Musis amicus*. This point is made by Campbell 1924: 197–8, 'Horace rides a freelance in the spiritual world' (he then quotes the last two stanzas of this poem). These claims are not to be taken as conventional commonplaces.

23

Metre: 'third' asclepiad (see Introduction 7)

1–4 H. compares Chloe, who avoids his erotic advances, to a skittish fawn whose fears are groundless.

1 inuleo 'fawn', like deer, conventionally timid. Anacreon had used just such a simile, *GL* II 408 ἀγανῶς οἷά τε νεβρὸν νεοθηλέα | γαλαθηνὸν ὅς τ' ἐν ὕληι κεροέσσης | ἀπολειφθεὶς ἀπὸ μητρὸς ἐπτοήθη 'gently, like a new-born suckling fawn, which is frightened, left in the woods away from its horned mother'. The context is uncertain; Campbell suggests that the poem began 'I draw near you gently, as though you were ... a fawn' and an erotic application of the simile seems likely in the light of the same strategy in II 417. **similis** does not usually introduce a simile, but poets occasionally gave it this function (*OLD* 2). **Chloe:** a speaking name, for in Greek it means 'green shoot'. This provides the theme for the poem, the girl's tender age.

2–3 pauidam ... | matrem: 2.11–12n.

3 non sine: cf. 25.16 (*OLD sine* 1e); this urbane understatement (*litotes*) is characteristic of the lyrics (10x).

4 siluae scans as trisyllabic (also at *Epod.* 13.2), a metrical feature known as diaeresis, the splitting of one syllable into two.

5–8 H. elaborately explains (*nam ...*) why the fawn's fear is *uano* 'empty' 3. The rustling leaves and lizards in bushes pick up the notions of *aurarum* and *siluae* respectively.

5 uepris 'thorn bush'; the singular is poetic, for the word usually appears in the plural (later prose writers under the influence of poetry adopt the singular). *uepris* is the correction of Gogavius. The transmitted reading in this and in the next line is *ueris ... aduentus* 'the arrival of spring'. That reading was explained by Porphyrio as an elaborate instance of hypallage: 'ueris aduentu folia inhorruerunt', an explanation hesitantly approved at *TLL* VII 1.1601.13–16; the reading is defended by Renehan 1988: 320–4 (Rudd accepts it too). But Gow, following Bentley, objected that (*a*) the approach of spring does not cause leaves to rustle so suddenly that a fawn would be frightened and (*b*) that the approach of spring and the movement of lizards are absurd alternatives. A thorn bush, with its moving leafage, can easily be agitated by the wind.

6 ad uentum: this is the correction of the French humanist M. A. Muretus (1526–85) for the transmitted *aduentus*. *ad* 'at, by' (*OLD* 33b) indicates response to a physical stimulus, cf. Virg. *G.* 3.134 *ad Zephyrum paleae iactantur*.

7 dimouere: for the form of the perfect see 9.10n. **lacertae:** some interpreters fancy that H. intended this word to be understood metaphorically, like the Greek σαύρα, to mean 'penis', thus activating Chloe's real fear. There is however no evidence that the word was ever so used, see Adams 1982: 30, 216.

9–12 One simile begets another: H. however is not like a predatory big cat, and anyway it is time for Chloe to act her age. H.'s simile may owe something to Theognis, *GEP* 949–50 νεβρὸν ὑπὲξ ἐλάφοιο λέων ὣς ἀλκὶ πεποιθὼς | ποσσὶ καταμάρψας αἵματος οὐκ ἔπιον 'like a lion trusting in its might, I snatched a fawn from the doe with my claws, and did not drink its blood'; though the context is uncertain, it may be erotic. On the other hand, the debt may be to a lyric (now fragmentary) by Cydias, *GL* III 714, preserved in Plato's *Charmides* 155d: a man who encounters a handsome youth is warned to take care μὴ κατέναντα λέοντος | νεβρὸς ἐλθὼν μοῖραν αἱρεῖσθαι κρεῶν 'in case, a fawn against a lion, you be seized as his portion of flesh' – here a youthful beloved poses the danger to the older lover.

9 atqui 'and yet': one of H.'s favourite adversatives, especially placed emphatically at the beginning of a stanza, cf. its tremendous effect at 3.5.49 *atqui sciebat*. **ego te** forms the loaded antithesis to *uitas ... me* 1. **aspera** 'fierce' is commonly used of animals (*OLD* 9b), e.g., a lion (3.2.10–11), or snakes (37.26).

10 Gaetulusue: cf. 3.20.2 *Gaetula ... leaena*. Gaetulia was a region in northwest Africa, and the epithet became conventional in poetry for particularly savage lions. **frangere** 'to crunch (with the teeth)' (*OLD* 2c is less satisfactory than either L–S s.v. I, which compares Statius, *Thebaid* 11.28 *armenti reges magno leo fregit hiatu*, or *TLL* VI 1.1244.1–11). *frangere* is certainly drastic and might be explained as focalization: this is how Chloe views H.'s intentions, though he tactfully keeps silent on the subject. The infinitive, expressing purpose (2.7–8n.), appears to be unique with *persequor*, though it goes unnoticed in *TLL* x 1.1689.57–8.

11 tandem expresses impatience, 'come now' (Rudd); the phrase *tandem desine* is found at 2.9.17, where N–H remark upon the similar movement of the two poems. **matrem:** the echo of *matrem* 3 effects ring-composition. The emphasis thus secured for the word may convey a subliminal message: Chloe, like the fawn, has a mother, i.e., a girl who matured into a woman and duly mated with a man to produce a child.

12 tempestiua: cf. the more self-aware Rhode at 3.19.27, who pursues the handsome Telephus. This word justifies H.'s wooing of the girl: she is the right age now for a man/husband (*uiro*); cf. Virg. *Aen.* 7.53 *iam matura uiro* (Lavinia), and contrast 3.11.11–12 *adhuc proteruo | cruda marito.* Chloe is presumably in her late teens (see Shaw 1987: 43).

*

This is a cool seduction ode, ably discussed by Fredricksmeyer 1993/94, who scouts some darker (mis)interpretations; Edmunds 2010: 353–8 offers some brief readings illustrative of various kinds of reception. The poem is elaborated with contrasting animal similes – 'you are like a fawn, but I am no tiger', which impart to the poem an Anacreontic ethos. Time, with the changes it brings, is central to H.'s thinking about human experience. In the adaptation of the Anacreontic simile it is crucial that H. drop the notion that the fawn is 'new born'. His fawn is old enough to look for its mother in the pathless mountains. Just as there are right times of the day and year for particular activities, so too are there stages in our own lives that are appropriate for certain types of behaviour (cf. the advice to Thaliarchus in 9), a notion perhaps reinforced for a Roman male by specified ages at which one entered public life, served in the army, secured public office, or joined the senate. Not to observe the proprieties of age is a mistake which may prove silly or serious. We may contrast 2.5, where advice to bide his time is given to someone unnamed (possibly H. himself) who is pursuing a girl still too young for love; there too the girl is compared to a young animal.

24

Metre: 'second' asclepiad (see Introduction 7)

1–4 A dear friend has died, and H. asks the Muse Melpomene to help him sing a dirge in his honour. The poetic dirge formalized the ritual lament that was customary on anyone's death. Pindar, for example, wrote in this manner, cf. 4.2.21–4 *iuuenemue raptum | plorat et uires, animumque moresque | aureos educit in astra nigroque | inuidet Orco.*

1–2 Quis ... sit: the question implies more bleakly than any statement that there can be no way to put any restraint (*pudor*) or limit (*modus*) upon the sense of loss (*desiderium*). The subjunctive is potential (G–L §259, Roby §1538), and the dative case, *desiderio*, is owed to *modus* (as at 36.11), rather than *pudor*. **tam cari capitis:** alliteration underscores the strongly emotional expression. *caput* 'person' (*OLD* 7) is much less abstract in Latin (and in Greek) since the head is our most vital part (as Austin suggests on Virg. *Aen.* 4.354 *capitis ... cari*, English would use 'soul').

2 praecipe 'teach' (*OLD* 5b), a basic function of the Muse in an oral society: she sings first, and the poet repeats the song.

3–4 cui ... dedit: H. hints that Melpomene has the necessary means to help him. Sometimes the expression is more blunt, as at *Epod.* 17.45 *potes nam.*   **liquidam** 'clear' (*OLD* 6), a sense found chiefly in poetry; it is perhaps a loan-shift from λιγύς / λιγυρός.   **pater:** Jupiter; her mother (indeed of all the Muses) was Mnemosyne 'Memory'.

5–8 H. now begins the dirge, and names the deceased, pronouncing a eulogy over him.

5 ergo 'so, then' expresses resigned confirmation (*OLD* 4), as at *S.* 2.5.101–2 *ergo nunc Dama sodalis | nusquam est?*   **Quintilium:** his identity is uncertain, but he is generally agreed to be the Quintilius, a helpful critic, at *AP* 438–44, as well as the Quintilius whose name is restored in texts of Philodemus recovered upon Herculaneum papyri in association with the name of Virgil (Gigante 2002: 47); they were bound together by an interest in Epicureanism. Traditionally he is given the cognomen Varus, and so sometimes identified with the more shadowy dedicatee of 18. This is pretty certainly mistaken, and the identifications are likely to have been generated by the name of the notorious general, P. Quintilius Varus, whose three legions were annihilated in Germany in AD 9.   **sopor:** a mainly poetic synonym for *somnus*, though it can imply a deep sleep, especially euphemistically of death (*OLD* 1b).

6 urget: cf. *urgentur* 4.9.27 of the unwept dead, a poetic use of the verb (*OLD* 3b). We may contrast the elevated lyric style of *perpetuus sopor | urget* with the colloquial euphemism *nusquam est* quoted above from a satire.

6–7 The virtues of Quintilius, all of them here civic or social (cf. Latte 1960: 241), are personified as divinities (2.34n.), a literary tradition which, though stretching back to Hesiod and Pindar and reflecting Roman cult practice, still leaves modern readers cold. It may help to bear in mind that the poetic dirge was a public act, and so the social virtues of the deceased mattered more to the *boni* of line 9 than his intimate qualities; as H. said in describing Pindar's dirges (quoted above on 1–4), he sang the *mores aureos*.

Pudor 'Decency' (*OLD* 2), also found at *CS* 57. The name evokes Hesiodic αἰδώς (*Opera* 200).   **Iustitiae soror:** Justice is first personified here (*OLD* 1b); as such she can be figured as the 'sister' of *Fides*, cf. Petron. 84.4 *bonae mentis soror est paupertas* and, less pictorially, Cicero, *De officiis* 1.23 *fundamentum autem est iustitiae fides* with Dyck's n.   **Fides:** an old personification, cf. *OLD* 6d (Enn., Plaut., Cic.), also found at *CS* 57; for her cult on the Capitol see Scullard 1981: 189–90.   **nuda ... Veritas:** Pindar had personified Truth in *Olymp.* 10.4, and fr. 205. She is naked because she has nothing to hide (*OLD nudus* 14).

8 inueniet: for the singular see *iuuat* 2.38n.

9–20 The lament is sustained by *flebilis* and *flebilior*, but it gradually yields in a refocusing movement from the many (*multis*) to a particular mourning friend, Virgil (*nulli ... tibi*), to a tone of consolation, which occupies the remainder of the poem. There is a somewhat similar movement from the many to an individual at 36.4–7.

9 bonis flebilis: the dative of agent with passive verbals in *–bilis* is poetic (G–L §355n., K–S I 325). *bonus* was a fundamental evaluative term in Roman society, and the *uir bonus* provided a moral and social ideal (see Mayer on *Epist.* 1.16.40–62). It is therefore high praise of Quintilius that such men bewailed his death. For the plural *boni* cf. *TLL* II 2085.32.

10 nulli: *nullus* (*OLD* 2) commonly provides the genitive and ablative for *nemo*; the dative is much rarer, cf. 36.6.   **Vergili:** H.'s friend, the poet (cf. 3.6).

11–12 frustra . . . heu: *TLL* VI 2.2673.51–4 collects examples. *frustra* should be taken equally with *pius* and *poscis* in 12. It was a commonplace in antiquity that expressions of grief could not achieve anything.   **non ita creditum:** variously explained. It might mean that Quintilius was not entrusted by the gods to Virgil as a friend to keep forever or (the general view) that Virgil had in circumstances unspecified (a journey perhaps, cf. *Carm.* 3 above and 36.3, or during a serious illness) entrusted Quintilius to the care of the gods, who dealt with him 'on their own terms' (so Quinn).   **poscis** = *reposcis* 'reclaim', as *non ita creditum* suggests. The simple verb for the compound is common in poetry.

13 quid si 'supposing' (*OLD quis*¹ 13).   **Threicio . . . Orpheo:** the form of the epithet is Greek and poetic; it appears first in H. (*Epod.* 13.3, cf. 36.14). Orpheus came from Thrace (12.6). When his wife Eurydice died, he ventured into the Underworld and successfully pleaded in song for her to be restored to life (only to lose her again through his own fault). Virgil had memorably told a version of this tale at the end of his fourth *Georgic*. H. flatters him by comparison with the mythical singer, but he corrects Virgil's fable with another, more realistic one: Mercury herding the irrevocable dead into the Underworld (no Elysian Fields here).   **blandius:** 12.11–12n.

14 moderere 'were you to manage', i.e. play, used of music by Cicero, *Tusculanae disputationes* 5.104 *tibicines . . . cantus numerosque moderantur*. In effect it is used here as a synonym for *modulor*.   **arboribus:** agent dative (1.24–5n.); cf. 12.11 for their 'ears'.   **fidem:** for the singular see 17.18n.

15 num: H. leaves no room for an equivocal answer.   **imagini** 'wraith' (Rudd), a poetic sense (*TLL* VII 1.408.60–71).

16 uirga: 10.18n.   **semel** 'once and for all' (*OLD* 3).

17 non lenis: a litotes (1.19–21n.) H. rather likes, cf. 2.19.15 *non leni ruina* and *S.* 2.7.93 *dominus non lenis* [of Amor]. H. is alone in combining *lenis* with an infinitive (1.18n.), *recludere*; cf. *CS* 13–14 *aperire . . . lenis.*   **precibus fata recludere** 'to open the Underworld to prayers'; as *OLD recludo* 1 allows, the expression is poetic, since *fata* 'death' is here treated as if it referred to a place; cf. the use of *Orcus.*

18 nigro compulerit . . . gregi: the dative of goal (2.1n.) with this verb is rare and poetic, perhaps picked up from Virg. *Ecl.* 2.30 *uiridi compellere hibisco. niger* is the colour associated with death and the Underworld (*OLD* 7).

19 durum: understand *est*. If H. had included the verb, the awful weight of the blunt word would have been lost.

19–20 sed leuius fit patientia | quidquid corrigere est nefas: prover-
bial wisdom (Otto 1890: 134) is given greater impact by the final word; *nefas* implies
an almost religious ban (cf. *OLD* 1). The moralizing maxim (γνώμη) was also used
by Pindar to end poems, e.g. *Olympian* 11.19–20.

*

This austere ode combines features of the poetic lament, *lugubres cantus* (= θρῆνος),
with themes of consolation. Typical of lament is the praise of the departed, with
an indication of his good qualities (nothing is here said of any achievements, and
that keeps the tone personal). The grief of Quintilius' many worthy friends is
then recorded, and one is singled out, Virgil, to whom the ode is now addressed.
Virgil's grief becomes the issue, and it is at this point in the ode that the tone
changes, as H. aims to help his friend to get over their loss. He does so by focusing
on Virgil (*tu* 11), and on the particular friend he cannot recover (*Quintilium* 12). The
pointlessness of the attempt to reclaim the dead is emphasized by *frustra*, but H.
sighs sympathetically (*heu*) nonetheless. He then generalizes his point: it is not just
Quintilius who cannot be recalled, no power of song, no prayer can recover any
dead soul. Realistically, H. admits that coming to terms with this universal truth
is tough (*durum* 19), but making the attempt lightens the burden of what cannot
be changed. Quinn (1980: 168) observes that these final reflections reject the
implied answer to the opening question, so that the poem's structure represents
the movement of the mind from grief to acceptance. This is similar to H.'s attitude
in the nineteenth ode: the impact of the inevitable can be mitigated by a spirit
of acceptance (*lenior* 19.16 and *leuius* 19 strike the same note). Thibodeau 2002–3
offers an attractive analysis and interpretation, but it should be remembered
that plain-speaking between friends was not enjoined only by Epicureans; the
concluding part of Plutarch's essay *Quomodo adulator ab amico internoscatur*, §§26–37,
is devoted to the topic (Loeb ed. vol. 1, pp. 352–95). More specifically *candidus*,
cited from *S.* 1.5.41, does not mean 'forthright' but 'well disposed' (*OLD* 8).

25

Metre: sapphic (see Introduction 8)

1–8 H. draws Lydia's attention to the scarcity of lovers begging for admittance
to her house. It was not always thus.

1 Parcius 'with greater restraint' (*OLD* 2), i.e. importunities are worryingly
less frequent than they once were. The comparative strikes the key note, which
is sustained by *prius* 5, *minus* 6, *magis* 11, 18.   **iunctas:** the window-shutters
are 'joined', and fastened with a bar (*OLD iungo* 2), but once the poem's theme
is known, on a second reading an erotic sense might be in play (*OLD iungo*
8).   **quatiunt** 'beat upon' (*OLD* 6, and cf. 4.7n.).   **fenestras** 'window-
shutters' (*OLD* 1b, Courtney on Juv. 9.104), folded back in the day time, were
closed at night.

2 iactibus: they throw stones or pebbles at the shutters to attract Lydia's attention. Bedrooms (and indeed windows) were upstairs, as we may see, pathetically, at Herculaneum, where the bedsteads are still attached to the walls.   **proterui** 'boisterous', because fuelled by drink. H. has in mind the *comissatio*, a post-symposium revel through the streets on the way to a mistress's place.

3 somnos: poetic plural.   **amat** 'hugs' (*OLD* 4b); but there is no hugging for Lydia.

5 multum 'very' (*OLD multum²* 2, with adjectives) qualifies *facilis* 'obliging' (*OLD* 9); the usage is found in epic, e.g. Lucan 6.687, 9.190, Statius, *Thebaid* 4.800, so the colloquial tone may not be that strongly felt. It is clear that Lydia was not disdainful of her lovers.

7–8 A snatch of the lover's serenade. For the form of the question see 9.1–4n.; the tone here is complaining.

tuo 'your lover' (*OLD* 2d, and cf. 15.32 *tuae*).   **longas ... noctes:** focalization: to her supplicant the night seems long, and to make his case more pathetic, he claims he has been waiting more than one night (the singular was possible here, and proposed by Bentley). The accusative is used of extent of time (G–L §336).   **pereunte:** for the common erotic metaphor see *OLD* 4 and Fantham 1972: 88; cf. 27.11–12. The lover lies at her threshold to demonstrate his devotion, cf. P. Pinotti, art. 'paraklausithyron' in *EO* II 718–21, especially 719 for this poem.

9–20 H. turns from Lydia's worrying present to reflect upon her alarming future (*flebis, saeuiet*) as a common prostitute on the streets at night. The three stanzas form an impressive period.

9 inuicem forms the fulcrum or pivot of the argument: soon it will be Lydia's turn to spend the night alone out of doors; for the threat cf. Propertius 3.25.15 *exclusa inque uicem fastus patiare superbos.*   **moechos** 'lovers'; *OLD* misleads, since the word is not always used to mean precisely 'adulterer'. *moechus* is a colloquial loan-word from the Greek, common in comedy. It finds a natural place in H.'s satires; its sole appearance here in his lyrics clearly suits the tone of the whole poem (*TLL* VIII 1324.15–20); Catullus too had used it in a lyric, 11.17. Its synonym *adulter*, 33.9, is a more elevated word.

10 solo ... angiportu: the deserted (*OLD solus* 3) alleyway recalls Catullus' reflections upon the obscene activities of his absconded mistress in degraded surroundings, 58.4 *angiportis.* H. here preferred the fourth declension termination to avoid the echo with *solo.*   **leuis** 'of no account' (*OLD leuis¹* 10).

11 bacchante 'raging'; H. may have been the first to use the verb metaphorically of a wind (*OLD* 3c, *TLL* II 1664.335); Ovid imitates him at *Tristia* 1.2.29 *Boreas bacchatur.* The verb is peculiarly appropriate to the Thracian wind Boreas, since Thrace was home to bacchants.   **magis:** in this half of the poem too the comparative is telling, and is picked up at 18.

11–12 inter- | lunia: the period of moonless darkness between the old and the new moon; the plural is poetic. This period was commonly regarded as stormy, see Vegetius, *Epitoma rei militaris* 4.40.60 *interluniorum autem dies tempestatibus plenos . . . uulgi usus intellegit.* H. hints that Lydia's sexual hunger (or her need for business) will be so desperate that she is out in all weathers. The darkness would also hide the evidence of her age. The word is divided between the third and fourth 'lines' of the sapphic stanza as at 2.19.

14 furiare 'to madden', apparently a coinage of H.'s, and noticed as such by the scholiasts; it remained poetic diction. The passionate desire of mares was notorious, cf. Virg. *G.* 3.266 *scilicet ante omnes furor est insignis equarum* with Mynors's note.

15 iecur: poetic physiology. The average Roman located love or desire in the heart; H. seems to have been the first to specify the liver on the basis of his reading of Greek texts, e.g., Theocritus 11.16 or 13.71 (*TLL* VII 1.245.71–80; see too 4.1.12 *si torrere iecur quaeris idoneum*). **ulcerosum:** as at *Epist.* 1.18.72 *non ancilla tuum iecur ulceret ulla* the sore is generated by (unrequited) desire.

16 non sine: 23.3n.

17–20 quod . . . | gaudeat . . . | dedicet: after *questu*, this clause virtually reports what Lydia says or thinks to herself, hence the verbs are in the subjunctive. They are moreover linked by adversative asyndeton, the co-ordination of contrasted clauses without a conjunction; English has to add 'but'.

17 pubes 'young males' (Rudd), a collective term for the youth of military age. By H.'s time the word was archaic, and commoner in poetry than in prose (Fordyce on Virg. *Aen.* 7.105, *OLD pubes²*); H. confines it to his lyrics (including *Epodes*). Plautus used it only once (*Pseudolus* 126) in the mock formal context of an edict. Cicero used it only once in a speech (*Pro Milone* 61). Sallust shows no examples, but Livy used it four times, confining it to his first, stylistically poetic, book; all the instances refer to young warriors (*Albanam pubem* 6.1 and 28.8, *Romana pubes* 9.6 and 16.2). Tacitus used it twice, in historical works (*Hist.* 2.47.3 *Romana pubes* (from Livy), *Ann.* 6.1.2), both times with pathetic impact (as Ash notes on *Hist.* 2.47.3). There seems to be a measure of focalization here. H. had called Lydia's suitors *moechi* (9), but in her decrepit state she will see them as heroic young men.

17–18 hedera . . . | gaudeat . . . magis atque myrto 'take more delight in ivy and myrtle'. It is here assumed (*a*) that *atque*, connecting *hedera* and *myrto*, is postponed, exceptionally, to third place (cf. *OLD atque, ac* intro.) and (*b*) that *magis* modifies *gaudeat* (with Porphyrio). Ivy and myrtle are found together, e.g. Virg. *G.* 4.124 *pallentesque hederas et amantes litora myrtos*, and both plants were used in drinkers' chaplets. Granting that they belong together here (Syndikus 2001: 244, n. 32), we have another instance of the *schema Horatianum*. The basic notion is that the young men prefer fresh (even dark) foliage to withered leaves, but H. casts the latter notion into a new sentence.

Rudd, however, follows N–H in taking *magis* to introduce a comparison, so that *atque* means 'than': 'take their pleasure with ivy rather than myrtle'. *atque* after a comparative, common in the satires, is said by Klotz in *TLL* II 1084.57–8 not to be found in H.'s odes or epistles, but there can always be an exception for a sound reason. *atque* thus used tends to follow a negative or negative idea, but H. is the first to depart from this practice (Lejay on *S*. 1.5.5 *altius ac nos*). So its usage is a matter of stylistic register. Since this poem admits less elevated usage, given its theme, N–H's interpretation is possible.

18 pulla 'dusky'. There are two kinds of fragrant myrtle, the white and the black, and the colour term describes the hue of the berries, not the leaves. H. avoids the standard descriptor *nigra*, found in Cato, *De agricultura* 8.2 and Ovid, *Ars amatoria* 3.690. As for N–H's notion that 'dusky myrtle' refers to mature women, it should be remembered that Catullus twice compared very young girls to the plant (colour admittedly unspecified), 61.22 and 64.89.

19 aridas hints by contrast that young women are 'juicy', cf. on the one hand the *sucus* of Europa's cheeks, 3.27.54, and on the other the withered oaks, *aridas quercus*, to which the aging Lyce is compared at 4.13.9–10.   **hiemis:** cf. Virg. *G*. 2.339 *hibernis flatibus Euri*.

20 Euro: this correction for the transmitted *Hebro* was printed in the Aldine edition of 1501; the east wind is much more likely to be styled 'winter's henchman' than the Thracian river Hebrus: cf. 28.21–2 *comes Orionis* | . . . *Notus* and 4.12.1–2 *ueris comites* . . . | . . . *animae* . . . *Thraciae* ('Thracian breezes').

*

The structure of the poem is a straightforward situation-and-response: the first two stanzas describe Lydia's waning influence and the last three predict her grim future, as H. imagines it.

There was a long tradition, as old as Archilochus, *GIP* 188, of the abuse of ageing mistresses or courtesans – to our minds a disagreeable and pointless exercise. West 1995: 116–19 however grants that whilst it may not be an appealing poem, it is vivid and realistic about sexuality; Quinn noted its 'sombre realism'.

H. is somewhat teasing for what he passes over in silence (so Syndikus 2001: 241). He suggests no personal reason for addressing Lydia; a reader might assume that she rejected his advances or brought their relationship to what he felt was a premature end. But we are not told, as we are in the ode to Lyce, 4.13. Nor is a scene set: the tradition of the paraclausithyron is adumbrated in lines 7–8, but it is not H. who stands or lies at her door. Nor does H. indulge, as did many other poets (including Archilochus) in similar circumstances, and as he did in other poems (again, 4.13), in distressing details of Lydia's physical decay (cf. Griffin 1994: 21–2). It is thus all the more shocking that he focuses on her degradation and the physical hunger for the lovers who have moved on to younger women. The point of this grim scenario, according to Commager 1962: 249, is that Lydia is attempting to defy the decorum of nature, and so H. wastes no sympathy upon her. Ancona 1992: 246, n. 3 summarizes helpfully a number of readings of the poem.

The poem might be so placed in the collection as to form a complement to 23: there a girl at the start of her erotic career, here one anticipating its end.

26

Metre: alcaic (see Introduction 8)

1–6 H., as client of the Muses and occupied with song, will be untroubled by faraway matters, which lie beyond his competence; cf. 22.10–11.

1–3 Musis amicus 'as one who is dear to (*OLD* 5) the Muses' = μουσοφίλ-ητος Corinna, *GL* IV 674; Virgil picked up the expression at *Aen.* 9.774. The affection of the Muses guarantees a poet's freedom from care (see Krasser 1995). The notion that a poet should be serene is as old as Sappho, who, in *GL* I 150, admonished her daughter thus: οὐ γὰρ θέμις ἐν μοισοπόλων †οἰκίαι† | θρῆνον ἔμμεν· οὔ κ' ἄμμι πρέποι τάδε 'it is not right that there should be lamentation in the house of those who serve the Muses. That would not be fitting for us.' **tristitiam et metus | tradam ... | portare uentis:** for casting to the winds what is not wanted cf. *Epode* 11.16–17 *ingrata uentis diuidam | fomenta*; Weinreich 1968: 21–2 regards this as a variant on the ἀποπομπή-motif (cf. 21.13–16n.). *metus* sets up the leading idea of the following indirect questions, dread (*metuatur, terreat*).   **tradam ... | portare:** the infinitive expresses purpose, a grecism (K–S I 681(b)). 'To convey' is the strict sense of *portare*, though it is often used as a synonym for *fero*, the preferred verb among better writers (usage is discussed in *TLL* X 2.45.18–33).   **in mare Creticum:** the sea to the south of the island of Crete is 'notorious for the squalls that blow off the high mountains with the prevailing summer winds' (Heikell 1994: 442, and cf. Sophocles, *Trachiniae* 118–19).

3–6 quis ... | rex ..., | quid ... terreat, ... | securus: the indirect questions define the objects of H.'s 'indifference' (*OLD securus* 4b). The construction seems to be peculiarly Horatian, cf. *S.* 2.4.50 *quali perfundat pisces securus oliuo*, and *Epist.* 2.1.176 *securus cadat an recto stet fabula talo* (it is taken up by his admirer, Persius, 6.12).

3–4 sub Arcto 'under the constellation of the Bear'; Aeschines, *In Ctesiphontem* 165 used a similarly hyperbolical expression to suggest that Alexander was 'out of the picture'.   **rex:** attempts to identify this northern sovereign (e.g., the Dacian Cotiso, 3.8.18) founder upon our ignorance of the activities of eastern rulers at the supposed time of this ode's composition; it even seems likely that H. intended the indeterminacy, to underscore his own indifference, the point being that the king's remoteness diminishes his fearsomeness.   **orae** 'region' (12.5n.). N–H ad loc. take the case to be genitive (so too Rudd), but N–R on 3.29.27–8, p. 355, take it to be dative of the agent with *metuatur*. Lucan seems to be imitating a genitive at 5.55 *gelidae dominum ... orae*.

5 Tiridaten: for the termination see 6.15n. Tiridates II and Phraates IV of Parthia were rivals; Octavian settled Tiridates in Syria in 30, but there was a second unsuccessful rebellion, and Tiridates again took refuge with Augustus, this time in Spain *ca* 26–25 (which perhaps provides a date for the poem); he was basically a pawn in the game between the empires (see E. S. Gruen in *CAH* x

158–9).   **terreat:** the northern king was fearsome, Tiridates by contrast feels dread. Either way, H. remains carefree.

5–6 unice | securus: H. often professes, and sometimes urges upon others, an indifference to remote political affairs, cf. 2.11.1–4, 3.29.25–8. The adverb *unice* is colloquial (*OLD*), and the position of *securus* as last word of its sentence but first in its line could hardly be more emphatic.

6–12 H. now invokes the Muse, beseeching her for a crown for a friend (West 1995: 121–2).

6 quae: for the relative clause in hymns or prayers see 2.34n.   **fontibus integris** < Lucr. 1.927 *iuuat integros accedere fontes*; the allusion is live, and H., like Lucretius, draws attention to the novelty of his own literary undertaking, lyric in the Greek manner, cf. *nouis* 10. Springs had long been associated with the Muses and poetic inspiration, but the emphasis upon their purity strikes a Callimachean note (*Hymn* 2.110–12).

7–8 flores | . . . coronam: Lucretius is still in play: *iuuatque nouos decerpere flores | insignemque meo capiti petere inde coronam* (1.928–9). Here the garland is a metaphor, common in Pindar (e.g., *Pythian* 12.4), for an encomiastic poem. *apricos* contrasts with *gelidae* 4. The repetition of *necte* is emphatic.

8 meo Lamiae: the only other man given this warm possessive pronoun is Maecenas (4.11.19), and the word order here, the reverse of the norm, is emphatic, 'my own beloved' (cf. 22.10, Catull. 95.1 *mei Cinnae*, cf. *OLD meus* 2b); Lamia is furthermore styled *dulcis* at 36.7 (again, a term also used of Maecenas). H. liked him, and that gives the poem its content. The friend seems to be L. Aelius Lamia, from a distinguished family based in Formiae; 3.17 is also dedicated to him (where N–R provide an up-to-date account of him in their introductory n.).

9 Piplei 'lady of Pipla', a Greek vocative form (G–L §65, s.v. *Paris*); the Muses inhabited various localities in Greece, and Pipleia (the word's orthography varied in both languages) was a mountain and spring located in Pieria near Mt Olympus (cf. *Pieri* 4.3.18). The locality, unknown to older Greek poetry, became fashionable among Hellenistic writers, e.g., Apollonius Rhodius, *Argonautica* 1.25, Callimachus, *Hymn* 4.7, and Leonidas of Tarentum, *Anthologia Palatina* 5.206.3 = *HE* XLIII.2233; their devotee, Catullus, introduced the locale into Latin poetry, 105.1, where it became popular.

9–10 nil . . . | possunt 'are of no avail' (*OLD* 8), cf. Virg. *Aen.* 9.446 *si quid mea carmina possunt*; for the sense of *nil* see 7.27n. The better part of the tradition offers *prosunt*, which makes sense, but *possunt* suits the religious tone (see Brink on *AP* 410 for the error).   **sine te:** a formula characteristic of hymns and prayers, stressing the god's power, help, or presence as necessary, cf. 30.7 (Norden 1923: 157–9, 349–50).   **mei | . . . honores** 'the praises I bestow', i.e., the encomiastic song, again a Pindaric notion (cf. *Isthmian* 1.34). *mei* is given emphasis by its position (Nisbet 1999: 142).

10–11 hunc . . . | hunc: repetition focuses upon Lamia.   **fidibus nouis:** H. glances again at the originality of his own lyric poetry, but goes on to indicate his debt to a Greek model, Alcaeus (*Lesbio ... plectro* 11). *nouis* reinforces *integris* 6.

11 sacrare 'hallow' (*OLD* 5), a strong word, which suggests 'immortalize' (cf. Brink on *Epist.* 2.1.49). The notion is tactfully introduced here, but will become dominant in his fourth book of lyrics.

12 -que ... -que: high-style connectives, modelled on τε ... τε, 'an archaic idiom prevalent in epic poetry' (so Brink on *AP* 11, with addenda III 580).   **sorores:** ring-composition takes us back to the first idea of the poem, *Musis*.

*

The poem, a prayer to the Muse to provide a song in praise of a friend, is formed of three clear sections, all bound together by references to the Muse(s): *Musis* 1, *Piplei* 9, *sorores* 12. The opening section puts public affairs into an Horatian perspective: what is remote is irrelevant (cf. the opening of 3.19, in honour of Murena). We expect then to be told what does matter to H., and so the next section exalts the personal and immediate over the public and distant (3.19 is rather more circumstantial, since a symposium is to be prepared). The poem effects what it describes (so Kießling's 1884 introduction to the poem, Campbell 1924: 223, Commager 1962: 326–8): the Muse's garland is the present poem. West 1995: 123 agrees with K–H (as against N–H) that this poem is a small masterpiece. But N–H 1970: 302, largely agreeing with Wilkinson 1968: 12, recognized that the poem is not just 'about poetry' but records the poet's pleasure in his ability to celebrate a friend.

27

Metre: alcaic (see Introduction 8)

1–8 H. reprimands his fellow symposiasts for spoiling the party by brawling. These opening stanzas have the same structure, a declarative sentence followed by injunctions. The declaratives both contain loan-words, *scyphus* and *acinaces*, put prominently at the end of the line; they also refer to foreigners – Thracians and Medes – as uncivilized. The injunctions are also similarly cast, each having two imperatives; judgemental terms – *barbarum* and *impium* – occur early, and in the same metrical position (Marouzeau 1949b: 221).

1 Natis 'born' in a metaphorical sense, 'suited to' (*OLD* 14).   **in usum laetitiae:** for the phraseology cf. Tac. *Ann.* 15.44.4 *in usum nocturni luminis*.

2 Thracum est 'is a Thracian habit'; the possessive genitive is here used as a predicate (G–L §366). For Thracian indulgence cf. 18.9 and 36.14. Anacreon *GL* II 356(b).3 sang dismissively of noisy 'Scythian drinking'.

   tollite 'away with ...' (*OLD* 14).

3 uerecundum: cf. the moralizing of 18.7, *modici*. By contrast wine is *inuere-cundus* if taken to excess, *Epod.* 11.13.

5 uino et lucernis: dative with *discrepat*, poetic syntax (K–S I 319, and Brink on *AP* 152, where, it is worth pointing out, *manu* in Apuleius, *Apologia* 69 could be dative rather than ablative). The serious drinking of the symposium followed upon dinner, so lamps would be needed, cf. 3.8.14–15 *uigiles lucernas | perfer in lucem* and 3.21.23 *uiuae . . . lucernae.*   **acinaces:** a short, straight sword, used by Persians, hence *Medus* (a poetic adjective for *Medicus*, see Marsus 1.28n.). The word is apparently Persian, but H. found it in Greek authors, especially Anacreon (*GL* II 465); he is the first to use it in Latin. Romans did arm themselves when out at night, cf. Apuleius, *Metamorphoses* 2.18.5 and 32.4, though it must be supposed that the symposiasts left their weapons at the door. H. means only that barbarians are the sort to bring their weapons to the table.

6 immane quantum: in theory *est* could be understood (G–L §209 N. 2 (omission of copula), and cf. *OLD immanis* 3e), but in practice the expression is treated as adverbial ('utterly', Rudd).   **impium:** their behaviour is insulting to a god, Bacchus.

8 remanete 'stay put' (*OLD* 1b), i.e., on the divans/couches, on which Romans reclined at meals or symposia. Men propped their left elbow on a cushion, hence *presso* (*OLD premo* 3), cf. *S.* 2.4.39 *languidus in cubitum iam se conuiua reponet.*

9–12 The symposiasts have apparently calmed down and invited H. to drink with them, which he will do, on one condition.

9–10 uultis . . . | . . . Falerni?: for the conversational question see *uides* 9.1n., and cf. 13 *cessat.* The interrogative sentence in effect expresses a protasis, 'if you want . . . ', and 10–12 is its apodosis (G–L §593.4); cf. 28.30–1.   **seueri** 'dry' (*OLD* 2), as opposed to sweet, a poetic loan-shift from *austerus*. The elder Pliny says that one variety of Falernian wine, for which see 20.10–11n., was *austerum* (*Nat. hist.* 14.63), and H. himself styles it *ardens* (2.11.19) and *forte* (*S.* 2.4.24).   **partem** 'my share' (*OLD* 8).

10–12 H.'s terms presuppose a common situation: one symposiast guesses from traditional symptoms such as sighs or distractedness (cf. Callimachus, *Epigram* 42 Pfeiffer) that another is in love. H. goes on to try to find out the object of his affection.

10–11 Opuntiae | . . . Megyllae: Megylla is a prostitute from Opus, in Locris opposite Euboea.

11–12 quo . . . | . . . sagitta: the structure of the indirect questions exemplifies double ἀπὸ κοινοῦ (cf. *dirae* 2.1n.): *beatus* belongs as well to the second question, as does *pereat* to the first.   **uulnere:** *OLD* 1d and Pease on Virg. *Aen.* 4.2 illustrate the metaphor, which is chiefly poetic. Placed after *beatus*, *uulnere* produces oxymoron, hinting that love affairs are bittersweet.   **pereat:** see *pereunte* 25.7n.   **sagitta:** Cupid is armed with bow and arrows, cf. 2.8.15 *semper ardentes acuens sagittas.*

13–18 The lad is hesitant, but H. insists on his terms and tries flattery to wheedle the information out of him.

13 cessat uoluntas?: a high-flown expression for tardy compliance with H.'s terms (*OLD cesso* 1c); for the conversational question see *uultis* 9n.

14 quae ... cumque: for the tmesis see 6.3n.   **domat** 'subdues' (*OLD* 3), a usage at home in erotic elegy (cf. Prop. 1.9.6 *quos iuuenes quaeque puella domet*).   **Venus:** used metaphorically of the beloved (*OLD* 1b).

15–16 non erubescendis: understatement (1.19–21n.). The gerundive of an intransitive verb, especially when used adjectivally, becomes common after Cicero (G–L §427 N. 4), cf. 2.10.7 *inuidenda*.   **adurit** 'scorches', metaphorically (*OLD* 1).   **ignibus:** 13.8n.

16 ingenuoque 'respectable' (cf. *OLD* 3b) seems better than 'free-born' (*OLD* 2c) here. H. is ironic: he knows very well the girl's social status.

-que: where a preceding negative goes closely with a single word other than the main verb (*non erubescendis*), the clause as a whole is felt to be affirmative, and so another affirmative clause can be joined to it by *-que*; cf. 28.34, 2.20.4, and 3.30.6.

17 peccas: of sexual liaisons, but not necessarily connoting serious wrong-doing (*OLD* 3b). In this sense the verb may be used either with *in* + ablative or with an instrumental/causal ablative, as here (*amore*) and at 33.9 (see Lejay on *S.* 1.2.63).

17–18 quidquid habes: Catullus tried to get the name of his friend Flavius' mistress out of him in similar terms: *quare quidquid habes boni malique | dic nobis*, 6.15–16.   **age** imparts the urgency of colloquial speech (*OLD* 24a; cf. 32.3, 2.12.23, *S.* 2.7.92).   **tutis** 'trustworthy' (*OLD* 7a); H. won't tell!

18–20 H. on hearing the name expresses mock horror, because the girl is grasping. There is a roughly similar situation in Theocritus 10.15–18: Milon asks Boucaeus the name of his beloved and expresses mock satisfaction that he has got what he deserved.

18 a miser: commonly found together (*TLL* 1 1442.48–59). Fraenkel 1957: 181 n. 1 noted the rarity of this interjection in H., proof of his coolness; here the tone is mocking.

19 laboras in: for the erotic sense see 17.19n. The reading is defended by Brink 1969: 3 against the better attested *laborabas*. The imperfect is some-times seen as an idiomatic use of the tense ('what a mess you've been in all this time!'), but Fraenkel 1957: 324, n. 3 pointed out that the idiom is not well supported for Latin (unlike Greek), and he particularly doubted its suitability here.   **Charybdi:** Circe describes Charybdis to Ulysses as a godlike creature which three times a day sucks in sea water, and then expels it (*Od.* 12.103–6); hence the name could apply metaphorically to a greedy harlot, cf. *OLD* 1b. This is amusing, since H. had just called her *Venus* 14, before he found out who she was.

20 meliore: of social status, cf. 33.13.   **flamma:** for the erotic metaphor, common in poetry, see *OLD* 8a and Fantham 1972: 88. H. is the first to use *flamma* concretely of the beloved; he sustains the metaphor of 15–16.

21–4 H. can see no prospect of release from her clutches. Having likened the girl to Charybdis he keeps up the mythological burlesque with Pegasus and the Chimaera.

21–2 quae saga ... | ... deus: as at 11–12, the questions are structured by means of ἀπὸ κοινοῦ (cf. *dirae* 2.1n.): *te soluere* and *poterit* must be taken with the first clause, *poterit* with the second, and *te soluere* with the third. (But *Thessalis ... uenenis* does not apply to *deus*.) The whole sentence is an example of rhetorical *gradatio*, or climax, reminiscent of the Pindaric opening of *Carm.* 12 above. **saga:** witches were believed capable of releasing from love as well as of inducing it, cf. *Epode* 5.71–2 *solutus ambulat ueneficae | scientioris carmine*.

21–2 Thessalis | ... uenenis: Thessaly was traditionally the home of magic and of the potent herbs (*OLD uenenum* 1) from which drugs or philtres were concocted, cf. Tib. 2.4.56 *quidquid et herbarum Thessala terra gerit*. For the proper adjective see 7.4n. **magus:** strictly speaking the Magi formed a Persian priesthood of dream-interpreters (the 'wise men' of Matthew 2:1; see Fry 1984: 81), but quite early on Greek used the name for 'wizard'; H. introduced it to Latin in this sense (Catull. 90.1, 3 clearly refers to the Persian priesthood).

23–4 triformi: a coinage of H.'s, calqued upon τρίμορφος; poetic diction. **Pegasus:** a mythological flying horse, ridden by Bellerophon when he slew the Chimaera (Hesiod, *Theogonia* 325); cf. 4.11.26–8. **Chimaera:** a mythological creature, described by Homer, *Il.* 6.181–2 as made up of lion, she-goat (the proper meaning of the common noun in Greek), and snaky tail (for securing a victim, hence *illigatum*); its metaphorical use of a grasping prostitute is first found here in Latin.

*

Porphyrio traced the opening motif – the poet's deprecation of a noisy symposium – to a song of Anacreon's, in the third book of the Hellenistic edition, now *GL* II 356(b): ἄγε δηὖτε μηκέτ' οὕτω | πατάγωι τε κἀλαλητῶι | Σκυθικὴν πόσιν παρ' οἴνωι | μελετῶμεν 'come again, let us no longer practise Scythian drinking in this way with clatter and shouting over our wine'. H.'s developing scenario however is altogether more elaborate and makes a characteristic point about good behaviour.

The poem is presented as a dramatic solo in real time, evoking the events of a drinking party at which H. is present. This is an old technique, which became especially popular with Hellenistic poets and with their Roman imitators, e.g., Catullus' wedding song, 61 (see Wheeler 1934: 203–5, and Martin 2002). In this poem the reactions of the other participants are to be gathered as the poem progresses: the rambunctious revellers quieten down after the poet's rebuke and invite H. to drink; he focuses on one of the party, who is clearly lovelorn, and urges him to name his mistress; he evidently refuses at first, so H. gets huffy, and that forces the issue; H. concludes with an exaggerated account of the lad's erotic perils, designedly humorous. The lively conversational tone is superbly maintained.

Porphyrio understood correctly the movement of the poem: 'protreptice est ode haec ad hilaritatem'; H. is coaxing his fellow drinkers in the direction of cheerfulness. Commager 1962: 72–5 demonstrates how this movement from unseemly brawling to civilized erotic banter enacts H.'s ethics of pleasure. He takes charge of the revel and nudges it towards that *laetitia* and *uerecundia* which are in his view alone appropriate to Bacchus. This movement between contrasts has been seen before, especially in the seventeenth ode, where it was the reverse of the present. There H. was reminding Tyndaris of what she could so easily leave behind, here, in real time, H. himself effects the shift from rowdiness to badinage.

Albert 1988: 127–34 provides an analysis of the varied accounts of the scenario.

28

Metre: as 1.7 (dactylic hexameter + dactylic tetrameter) (see Introduction 9)

1–6 A speaker who does not identify himself addresses Archytas, who is buried nearby. The grand opening sentence emphasizes the futility of human endeavour, in Archytas' case, intellectual achievements. It is made up of two parts. The first focuses on the land or earth, which Archytas could measure despite its vastness; by contrast some little dust confines him (*cohibent*). That notion of present confinement is countered in the second half of the sentence: Archytas' mind once ranged throughout the firmament. But again there is a contrast: that did him no good at all since his mind (or he) was doomed to die. *morituro* sets the seal on the sentence.

1 Te: emphatically placed. The speaker will point the (unexpected) similarity to himself with *me*, 21.   **numeroque carentis** 'numberless'. Poets used *carens* either as a synonym of *sine*, e.g., 3.24.27 *matre carentibus* 'motherless' and 27.39 *uitiis carentem* 'blameless', or to represent the privative prefix *in-*, e.g., 2.8.12 *morte carentes* = *immortales*. Cf. 31.20.   **harenae:** counting grains of sand was a proverbial impossibility (Otto 1890: 159).

2 mensorem: there is no evidence that Archytas excogitated means of measuring sea, land, or sand (Archimedes is credited with the final feat); H. just reckons that this is the sort of thing mathematicians do (so N–H 1970: 321).   **Archyta:** the form is the vocative of the Greek first declension (G–L §65). Archytas of Tarentum was a fourth-century philosopher, politician, and mathematician; as an Italian he commanded considerable interest among H.'s philosophically minded contemporaries (see Huffman 2005: 21).

3 exigui ... parua: the adjectives provide an ironic and yet pathetic contrast with the global and indeed cosmic extent of Archytas' intellectual achievement. That even great men end up in small tombs is something of a commonplace, cf. Ov. *Met.* 12.615–16 (Achilles), Juvenal 10.168–73 (Alexander), *Anthologia Latina* 437 Riese (Alexander), 438 (Alexander and Pompey).   **litus ... Matinum:** the location was uncertain in antiquity and remains so. A. Russi, art. 'Apulia' in

EO I 396–7 (a substantial essay, with special bibliography on p. 405b), reckons it was roughly in the middle of Apulia's Adriatic coast. How Archytas died and the place of his burial are unknown (Huffman 2005: 19–21).

4 munera 'tributes' (*OLD* 3); the plural is poetic.

nec quicquam ... prodest: it was a commonplace that the deceased's accomplishments availed him nothing in the face of death.

5–6 Huffman 2005: 22–4 finds H.'s emphasis on Archytas' astronomy surprising, since there is little evidence for it, though he did argue that the universe was limitless.

aerias: a loan-word, and so poetic diction (*TLL* I 1061.83).   **temptasse** 'to have investigated' (*OLD* 3).   **animoque:** take ἀπὸ κοινοῦ with both infinitives (cf. *dirae* 2.1n.). Archytas' experiment was entirely intellectual, so there can be no ground for supposing it audacious or impious (Huffman 2005: 22, n. 10).   **rotundum** 'vaulted' (Rudd), cf. the use of *conuexa* of the heavens (*OLD conuexus* 1b).   **percurrisse:** compounds of *curro* vary in their use of reduplication in the perfect, see G–L §134.III.   **polum** 'heaven' (*OLD* 2), a loan-word, and so poetic diction.   **morituro** 'destined, as it was, to die', is probably to be regarded as ablative with *animo*, though many, including Rudd, take it as dative with *tibi*. The attributive use of the future participle was literary and at first poetic, though taken up in the formal prose of the early principate (N–H on 2.3.4 *moriture*). The position is emphatic and produces a gliding transition to *occidit*.

7–15 In another elaborate sentence, the speaker offers commonplace consolation by listing *exempla* of pre-eminent mortals who have all necessarily died; cf. Lucr. 3.1025–44, with Kenney's introductory n. Like the first sentence, the second has two parts. The first lists three individuals, who are given short descriptive phrases – *conuiua deorum, remotus in auras, Iouis arcanis admissus* – that suggest privileges that might have exempted them from death. The second part (*habentque* 9) introduces a much more important figure, who actually seemed to have cheated death. The speaker focuses on him, because Archytas held him in special regard (*iudice te* 14). The message remains the same as that of the first sentence: death is inevitable, even for those who stand out from the crowd for some reason.

7 occidit et recalls a famous passage in the *Iliad*, 21.107, where Achilles addressed Lycaon: κάτθανε καὶ Πάτροκλος ... 'Patroclus too died ...' For *et* 'too, also' see 4.11n., but Rudd translates 'even' (12.11n.).   **Pelopis genitor** = Tantalus, by the figure antonomasia. *genitor* 'father' is grand poetic diction (*TLL* VI 2.1816.56–9).   **conuiua deorum:** a number of myths related that Tantalus was honoured by the gods as their dinner-guest, a privilege he abused, in some versions, by the betrayal of their secrets (Euripides, *Orestes* 8–10, Ovid, *Amores* 2.2.43–4, with McKeown's n.), for which he was notably punished in the Underworld.

8 Tithonus: a Trojan prince, he was the beloved of the Dawn (Eos, Aurora). He hardly belongs in this list, however, since he did not die: Dawn sought a boon for him, immortality, but she failed to ask for eternal youth, so Tithonus aged eternally, cf. 2.16.30 *longa Tithonum minuit senectus*.   **remotus in auras:** this phrase, 'swept off into the breezes', ought to indicate the nature of the divine favour Tithonus enjoyed, since it parallels *conuiua deorum* and *Iouis arcanis admissus*, which describe the other privileged mortals, Tantalus and Minos. But what exactly H. had in mind is anyone's guess.

9 Iouis arcanis ... admissus: Minos, king of Crete, was described by Hom. *Od.* 19.179 as 'the bosom friend of great Zeus' Διὸς μεγάλου ὀαριστής; ὀαριστής was hard to understand and explained by the writer of the pseudo-Platonic dialogue *Minos*, 319C–E, as proof that every ninth year Minos went for instruction to Zeus. Some such account seems to lie behind H.'s description, which does not refer to his function as lawgiver (rightly *RE* xv 1903.54–9).   **habent** 'holds', a poetic sense (*TLL* vi 3.2431.53–69, and cf. *OLD* 13b and Virg. *Aen.* 5.733–4 *me ... Tartara habent*), perhaps a loan-shift from ἔχω (LSJ ἔχω (A) A.II.7).

10–11 Panthoiden 'son of Panthus', a patronymic; for the termination see 6.16n. and for the figure 6.5–6n. It designates primarily the Trojan Euphorbus, killed by Menelaus, but secondarily the philosopher Pythagoras, who claimed to be a reincarnation of Euphorbus to demonstrate his theory of the transmigration of souls.   **iterum Orco | demissum:** cf. Virg. *Aen.* 2.398 *Danaos demittimus Orco*; as Austin says in his n. ad loc., the dative suggests a personal recipient (dative of goal is less likely). H. uses the adverb to allude to the death of Pythagoras as well.

11–12 clipeo ... refixo: to substantiate his claim to be Euphorbus re-incarnate Pythagoras identified a shield hanging in the temple of Hera at Argos as having belonged to him; cf. Ov. *Met.* 15.153–64. Pausanias, a traveller of the second century AD, said that the shield was still in the Heraeum, 2.17.3, but other sites claimed it too.   **Troiana ... | tempora testatus** 'having called Trojan times to witness', namely that he had lived then. *OLD testor* 1 provides a couple of examples of an appeal to places or inanimate things regarded as cognizant of a fact.

13 neruos atque cutem: down-to-earth language, especially *cutis*, which is rare in any poetry (*TLL* iv 1578.34–9). It is only here in H.'s lyrics, 4x in his hexameter poems.   **atrae:** an emotive word for 'black' (*OLD* intro. s.v. and 7b).

14 iudice te 'in your opinion' (*OLD* 4b); the speaker regards Archytas as a follower of Pythagoras, whose teaching he perhaps imbibed from Philolaus (Cicero, *De oratore* 3.139); see Huffman 2005: 44–5, though he aims to establish the independence of Archytas' thinking. The expression was used by Virgil, *Ecl.* 2.25 (cf. 4.58–9), and then by Gallus, fr. 2.9, so it probably did not sound all that prosaic to H. (cf. Ov. *Met.* 2.428).   **non sordidus** 'not paltry' (*OLD* 5); litotes (1.19–21n.).

15–22 The speaker however challenges the Pythagorean doctrine: death is an absolute end, universal (*omnes* 15) and irrevocable (*semel* 16). It comes in a variety of forms, and no one escapes it, not even the speaker.

15–16 H. appropriates the language of Catullus, 5.5–6: *nobis cum semel occidit breuis lux | nox est perpetua una dormienda*. In addition to the underlined words taken over, H. adopts Catullus' rhythm (*manet nox ∼ breuis lux*), the emphatic monosyllable at line end, and the gerundive (*calcanda ∼ dormienda*).

una 'one common' (*OLD* 3, Rudd), a meaning often found when *omnes* is in the vicinity, here juxtaposed.   **nox** 'death', 4.16n. For the proverbial sentiment see 4.13n.   **calcanda:** supply *est*.   **semel:** 24.16n.   **uia leti:** for the common image of the 'road to death' see *OLD uia* 8b; for *leti* see 3.32–3n.

17–18 The deaths of soldiers and sailors imply a polar idea, since they die on land and sea, i.e., everywhere.

18 exitio 'the ruin of', a common predicative dative (Roby xlvii*a*–*b*); contrast *exitium* 15.21–2.   **auidum:** cf. *auaro . . . mari* 3.29.61.

19 senum ac iuuenum: another polar expression (= 'everyone'), summed up by *nullum*.   **densentur** 'are multiplied'; *denseo* is mainly poetic, picked up by historians (*TLL* v 543.3–4), whereas *denso* was preferred by prose writers.   **nullum:** highly emphatic, placed thus. The rhythm would be exceptional in a Virgilian hexameter, since he rarely began a fresh sentence with a two-syllable word in the sixth foot (e.g., *Aen.* 4.416, 593; see Norden 1927: 389–90); cf. 31. Nor does H. adopt this rhythm in the hexameters in his *Epodes*.

20 caput: this should be taken literally, rather than indicating a person or individual (*OLD* 7), since the poets fancied that Proserpina, or other Underworld divinities, took a lock of hair from those about to die (see Pease's examples on Virg. *Aen.* 4.698).   **fugit** 'has shunned' (*OLD* 11). The perfect tense is gnomic, indicating what has been and what shall be (G–L §236n., Roby §1479, K–S I 132–3), a poetic usage introduced by Catullus (62.42, 44, 53, 55) and taken up by later prose writers.

21 me quoque answers the initial *Te*, but most unexpectedly: the speaker himself proves to be dead, and it is his ghost which has all along been addressing the buried Archytas.   **deuexi . . . Orionis** 'of the constellation Orion at its setting'; cf. 3.27.18 *pronus . . . Orion, Epode* 10.10 *Orion cadit* (with Watson's n.). The constellation sets in November, a stormy month. The hexameter ends with an impressive four-syllable word (often, as here, a Greek proper noun), which also makes the fifth foot spondaic; hence the line was called σπονδειάζων. This was a feature of high-style poetry from Catullus on (see Fordyce on Catullus 64.3 *Aeeteos*, Mankin on *Epode* 13.9).   **rabidus** 'wild' suits *comes*; the better attested *rapidus* is often confused with it by scribes.   **comes Orionis:** cf. *hiemis sodali | . . . Euro* 25.19–20.

22 Notus: 3.14n. This wind, blowing from the south-west, would indeed propel a ship from Italy towards the Illyrian coast; a glance at an atlas will show that the coast (mod. Croatia or Albania) is blockaded by islands, a danger to vessels.

23 at tu: the drama develops as a new character appears. The ghost has spotted a passing ship, and appeals for burial to the captain. The dead required burial, and in difficult circumstances their need could be satisfied symbolically, as in Sophocles, *Antigone* 255–6, 'the dead man . . . was lightly strewn with dust, as by the hand of one who shunned a curse' (Jebb's translation, and he quoted this passage of H. in his note ad loc.).   **ne parce:** this is the commonest form of prohibition in poetry (K–S I 203); it is an archaism not much used by H. (also at 2.7.20 and 3.7.30). The construction of the infinitive (*dare* 25) with *parco* is poetic syntax (*TLL* x 1.332.36–56).   **malignus:** adjective for adverb. The word is rare in prose until the post-Augustan writers (*TLL* viii 183.16–18), so presumably here it is poetic diction.

24 inhumato: to be taken ἀπὸ κοινοῦ with *ossibus*. The hiatus after *capiti* is difficult to defend but emendations have failed to convince, though Peerlkamp's *intumulato* deserves honourable mention.

25–6 sic: 3.1n.   **Eurus | . . . Hesperiis:** the seaman addressed is voyaging along the 'Matine shore' (3) of Italy, so needs the east wind; this is the reverse of the speaker's situation (22). *Hesperia* and its adjective were loan-words from Greek, meaning 'western' land, i.e., from the Greek point of view, Italy. It is poetic diction.

26 Venusinae: these forests are well inland, near H.'s birthplace, Venusia. For the wish that the storm strike elsewhere cf. 21.13–16.

27 te sospite 'leaving you unharmed', a pregnant use of the ablative absolute (cf. *NLS* §50).

28 unde = *a quo / quibus* (12.17n.).   **aequo** 'indulgent' (*OLD* 7), cf. Virg. *Aen.* 6.129–30 *aequus . . . Iuppiter.*

29 Neptuno . . . Tarenti: Neptune (= Poseidon) was the father of Taras, the founder of the city of Tarentum, and hence its protector (see S. Cataldi, art. 'Taranto' in *EO* I 571–2). All cities were regarded as sacred, hence *sacri* here and at 3.19.4 *sacro sub Ilio* (*OLD* 4a).

30–6 The appeal might have ended with the wish for reward, but the monologue takes a final dramatic turn: we surmise that the *nauta* is at first unresponsive, so the ghost, desperate for burial, takes to threats, and closes with a last humble appeal.

30–1 neglegis 'can you be indifferent that' + accusative and infinitive (*te . . . committere* 31) (*OLD* 1b). For the interrogative sentence as virtual protasis see 27.9–10n.; for its scolding tone cf. 15.22n.   **postmodo** modifies *nocituram*. This adverb is adopted by refined stylists, largely poets (*TLL* x 2.237.41–51); *post* or *postea* served others. It has however a threatening connotation (Riese and Ellis on Catullus 30.12).   **fraudem** 'an offence' (*OLD* 3).

31–3 In case the *nauta* really is indifferent to the fate of his descendants, the ghost warns him that retribution may actually befall him (*te . . . ipsum* 33).

fors 'it may be', poetic usage of the noun as adverb (*OLD fors²*, adv., *TLL* VI 1.1136.51-6, K-S I 812). *et* probably here means 'too' (4.11n.), modifying *te* 33; such a separation is uncommon but not impossible (see Housman on Manilius, *Astronomica* 1.780 with addenda). As at 19, the run of the hexameter is unusual.   **debita iura** 'rights (*OLD* 10) unpaid' to you; this is Gow's interpretation of the difficult expression, adopted by N-H. If correct, it is an instance of the construction described on 1.4-5 *meta euitata*, and the emphasis falls on the participle: 'the non-payment of your due'.   **uices** 'requital' (*OLD uicis* 5), a sense first attested by *OLD* in H.

33 precibus 'my curses' (*OLD prex* 2b).   **non ... inultis** 'not unanswered, unfulfilled'; *OLD* 2b and *TLL* VII 2.243.4-5 agree on the unusual sense here.

34 -que: 27.16n.

35-6 The final appeal for burial is more urgent than similar appeals made by epitaphs to travellers to halt briefly and read them.

quamquam festinas: cf. *tam etsi properas* in the epitaph of the tragic poet Pacuvius, preserved by Aulus Gellius, *Noctes Atticae* 1.24.4. The dead when asking a favour of the living show courtesy in acknowledging that they are busy people still.   **ter:** common with reference to ritually repeated acts (*OLD* 1a). **curras** 'you may sail on' (*OLD* 3a).

*

There is nothing like this poem in the lyric collection, though a single persona, Priapus, had been deployed in the satires, *S.* 1.8; this is therefore an experimental piece. It seems now to be agreed that there is only the one speaker, the drowned voyager (see Syndikus 2001: 258, n. 12 for adherents to this view, from which Frischer 1984 vigorously dissents). The poem combines two strands of funerary poetry, a lament on the death of an eminent man and a lament for one unburied (so Williams 1968: 220, and see his analysis on 183-5). Interwoven are strands from the extensive literature of consolation. Such a combination is unique, and the second motif too is unusually handled in that it is the spirit of the dead voyager who begs for burial. The themes derived from consolatory literature too are given a different 'spin', since they serve rather to emphasize the power of death. Like the previous poem, this one too is dramatic and in 'real time'. That is clear from the pause after the request at lines 23-9: the *nauta* must hesitate to act as the ghost requests, and that prompts the threat which precedes the closing appeal.

Why might H. have had recourse to a persona? Syndikus 2001: 263 rightly observes that when H. 'himself' speaks of the inevitability of death, it usually serves as foil to underscore his advice to enjoy the moment. Reflections on the nullity of death are not for him, in his own person. But the adoption of a fictive persona allows him to give voice to a more unsettling view about what awaits us all on 'the other side'. There is no consolatory note, there are no Elysian Fields, even for the virtuous: 'la morte è il nulla'.

29

Metre: alcaic (see Introduction 8)

1–10 Iccius is asked about his plans to enlist for an Eastern campaign and what profit (attractive slaves?) he hopes to gain from it. He also receives an epistle, 1.12, which has a not dissimilar message to the ode's (see Putnam 1995a). There he appears as the land agent (*procurator*) for Agrippa's Sicilian estates. Beyond that he is unknown. The tone of the opening is bantering and ironical: Iccius does not strike H. as cut out for such an escapade.

1–5 The simple direct question without an interrogative particle (cf. 9.1n.) here expresses a measure of surprise.

1–2 nunc hints that some other activity or vocation is 'now' being sidelined. The final stanza clarifies the situation.   **Arabum:** at this time proverbial for their wealth, cf. 2.12.24 *plenas ... Arabum domos*, 3.24.1–2 *intactis opulentior | thesauris Arabum*, and *Epist.* 1.7.36 (Otto 1890: 33–4). Men became soldiers less out of patriotism than as a means to enrichment (cf. the fine story of the soldier of Lucullus at *Epist.* 2.2.26–40). Campaigns had economic motives (Brunt 1990: 440, with n. 11).   **gazis:** a loan-word (not exclusively poetic however), appropriately eastern in origin (apparently); the plural is largely poetic.

3 non ante: a favourite phraseology in H., cf. 3.29.2, 4.9.3, and especially 4.14.41 *Cantaber non ante domabilis.*   **Sabaeae:** understand *terrae*, nowadays the Yemen. The prefect of Egypt, Aelius Gallus, led a bungled campaign against the Sabaeans in 26–25 (or possibly a year earlier), with a view to securing improved trade with India via the port of Aden. Strabo, a friend of his, recorded that booty too was a motive (*Geographia* 16.4.22): 'Another consideration was the report, which had prevailed from all time, that they were very wealthy, and that they sold aromatics and the most valuable stones for gold and silver, but never expended with outsiders any part of what they received in exchange.' Augustus referred to the campaign in *Res gestae* 26.5, insisting that many of the enemy were killed and a number of towns taken; but the Roman army was actually weakened by disease and driven out. H., who presumably had no way of knowing of the real calamity, may also allude to the campaign at 35.31–2. See further E. S. Gruen in *CAH* x 149 (but for 'north-west' read south-western Arabia), and Mayerson 1995.

4 Medo: see 2.51n., and for the singular, *Parthum* 19.12n. It adds purely local colour, since Gallus had no intention of attacking Parthia.

5 nectis catenas: cf. Pliny, *Epist.* 9.28.4 *tibi compedes nectimus.* The chains were prepared and taken along on campaign for the prisoners. Reference to them forms a gliding transition to the notion of prisoners.

5–6 quae ... uirginum | ... barbara: the genitive is partitive with the interrogative pronoun (2.25n.); the transferred epithet, *barbara*, makes the whole phrase an even more exotic departure from the spoken or written norm.   **sponso necato:** by the dashing Iccius, of course; cf. 3.2.8–11 for an enemy maiden worried lest her fiancé challenge a Roman soldier.

7–8 ex aula = *aulicus*; the boy is of a respectable family. The attributive use of a prepositional phrase attached to a noun, here *puer*, is common (see K–S I 214 for *ex*).   **capillis | ... unctis:** see *nitidum caput* 4.9n., and for the plural 12.41n. The boy is clearly imagined as attractive, hence his display at the symposium.   **ad cyathum:** the lad stands 'by (*OLD ad* 13) the ladle' (like Lygdamus in Prop. 4.8.37) to pour wine into cups.

9 doctus ... tendere 'though [he was] trained to aim (*OLD* 1b)'. A concessive idea is to be understood with the participle, since there is a stark contrast between what the boy's training prepared him for (military service) and his ignoble fate as a cupbearer (and probably *concubinus* as well). For the syntax of the infinitive see 1.18n. *Sericas* provides exotic colour (the boy is not Chinese), cf. 12.56.

10 arcu paterno: the boy learned his military skills from his late father (now, pathetically, to no purpose).

10–16 H. now unriddles for the reader the *nunc* of the first line: Iccius' previous interests in philosophy led H. to assume that he had a mind above the lure of wealth and its trappings.

10–12 arduis | ... relabi ... | montibus 'flow back up steep mountains'; *montibus* is local ablative. That streams might flow backward was a proverbial impossibility, adynaton (Otto 1890: 139).   **arduis | pronos:** juxtaposition heightens antithesis. For *pronos* 'down-rushing' cf. *Epist.* 1.10.21 *pronum ... riuum* (*OLD* 5c).   **relabi:** a largely poetic verb, taken up in post-Augustan prose.

12 Tiberim: local colour enlivens the adynaton, as at 33.7.

13–14 tu: emphatic, 'you, of all people!'.   **nobilis:** take with the following proper name.   **Panaeti:** Panaetius of Rhodes was a Stoic philosopher who had lived in Rome with P. Scipio Aemilianus. He became head of that school until his death in 109. Cicero used his treatise on duties as the foundation of his own *De officiis*. For the Stoic wealth was a matter of indifference, so Iccius ought not to have been pursuing it.   **et:** postponed (2.9n.). *domum* 'school' (*OLD* 6b); the term is used loosely of the followers of Socrates, e.g., Plato and Xenophon.

15–16 mutare ... tendis 'are hell-bent on exchanging' (Rudd). *tendo* in this sense and governing an infinitive is initiated by poets, then taken up in prose (K–S I 674, *OLD* 13b).   **loricis Hiberis:** Robinson 1975: 147–86 illustrates Roman breastplates. They were generally made of iron, so securing a source of iron (and other metals) was one reason for the Roman conquest of Spain (see Healey 1978: 63). *Hiberus* is a loan-word from the Greek, and as such poetic diction; the Roman in the street, including H. on occasion, used adjectives derived from *Hispania*.   **pollicitus** 'having led us to expect'. In this sense the word is rarely used of people, as opposed to their qualities or character (see *OLD polliceor* 4 and *TLL* x 1.2553.10–29, especially 13).

*

The poem, formally reminiscent of the eighth ode, to Lydia, is a series of four questions, the final three of which increase in length. What binds the poem into a unity is the teasing adverb *nunc* in the first line. The reader cannot know what Iccius has aspired to before 'now', and it is the final sentence of the poem (10–16) which fills in the gap in our understanding.

The poem is undeniably humorous, but the quality of the humour is open to interpretation. N–H 1970: 339 identified in it the ironic banter of a civilized and serene governing class. West 1995: 136–41, who largely agreed with this line, surveys a number of interpretations which take a more serious view; to them may be added Connor 1987: 151–3, who finds the humour grim. In the main, those who detect, especially in lines 5–10, an anti-militarist critique or an attack on the attitude of Roman society at large expose a post-colonial angst unknown to the Romans of H.'s day (Syndikus 2001: 268, n. 20 lists the paladins of this interpretation). That, however, is not to say that the lines lack an element of pathos: see Wilkinson 1968: 45. H. himself – or at any rate the speakers of a number of his poems – blithely encouraged the expansion of the empire into Britain, India, and China, without a thought for the human cost. It is hard to see that cost seriously taken into account here. Even where H. does describe sympathetically the human cost of warfare, as at 3.2.6–12 (note there *eheu*), he is still on the side of the Roman soldier. Moreover a moral critique of Iccius would be tactless, since he is a friend; a personal failing like envy (*inuides* 1) can fairly be noticed, but a more profound indictment of Roman militarism and its effect on conquered peoples ought not to be centred on him alone. It may be noted for instance that when H. condemns over-extended estates in 2.15, the poem, exceptionally, has no addressee; H. could hardly have criticized a named friend for owning too much property. So here: if he wanted to push an anti-imperial line – in itself scarcely thinkable – he ought not to have pinned the charge on Iccius alone. But criticism there clearly is, nonetheless, and it is personal: Iccius is abandoning the high ground of philosophical ethics. H. states his criticism briefly enough – *pollicitus meliora* – but its reservation to the final line makes it stand out: Iccius has fallen short of his own standard. The poem is amusing, but it has a sting in its tail.

30

Metre: sapphic (see Introduction 8)

1–4 H. invites Venus to leave Cyprus and visit a shrine prepared for her by Glycera.

1 Cnidi: Venus had three cult-sites at Cnidus on a peninsula in Caria (mentioned again at 3.28.13); the cult statue by Praxiteles drew numerous tourists (Pliny, *Nat. hist.* 36.4.20; *LIMC* II 1.49–52 provides discussion of sources, etc., II 2.36–8 illustrations). **Paphi:** Venus/Aphrodite was born in the sea off Old Paphos in western Cyprus; her aniconic image may be viewed online: www.mcw.gov.cy/mcw/DA/DA.nsf/All/D29999253080F9BBC2257199002134BD?OpenDocument; cf. 3.1.

2 sperne dilectam Cypron: a nod to Alcman, *GL* ii 55 Κύπρον ἱμερτὰν λιποῖσα. For the termination *-on* see 21.10n. The gods of antiquity had only local power, Jupiter excepted, and so supplicants in their prayers first mentioned cult-sites where they might be dwelling and then invited them to leave and come to a specific place to provide help. *sperne* is stronger than *linque*, and suggests a measure of repudiation; Venus will surely prefer her new shrine.

2–4 uocantis: 2.25n.   **ture:** 19.14n.; for the expression cf. *multo ... odore*, 3.18.7–8.   **te** does double duty as object both of *uocantis* and then of *transfer*.   **Glycerae:** 19.5n.   **decoram | transfer in aedem:** Venus is invited to take up residence in Glycera's attractive shrine; as a working woman, she honours the goddess who protects her business. The shrine could well be a niche with a statue or mosaic in her house, or something more elaborate, like the shrine (*sacrarium*) belonging to the Sicilian C. Heius, and described in detail by Cicero, *Verrines* ii 4.4 (it contained a statue of Cupid by Praxiteles), or the one Paullus Maximus might build to Venus, cf. 4.1.19–20. For *decoram ... aedem* cf. Lucr. 2.352 *deum ... delubra decora.*

5–8 The goddess is to come not alone, but accompanied by a retinue of congenial divinities, Cupid, the Graces and Nymphs (cf. 4.6), Youth, and Mercury.

5 feruidus ... puer = Cupid, by the figure antonomasia; he is of course himself lusty (*OLD* 7).

5–6 solutis | ... zonis: the descriptive ablative (12.41n.) is to be taken ἀπὸ κοινοῦ with *Nymphae*, since both groups have loosened their girdles, with a view to dancing or perhaps to ease their running.

6 properentque: the verb is common (ἀπὸ κοινοῦ) to all five subject words of this sentence/stanza, as its connection with *–que* suggests (cf. *dirae* 2.1n. and in this case Bo Index 183). It is a characteristic artificiality of H.'s style to connect the verb, rather than the third subject word, *Nymphae*, to the list (cf. *CS* 22 *cantus referatque ludos*). That said, it is natural to put the verb with a subject word that has no (or few) qualifiers, thus balancing the cola of the sentence, as at *S.* 1.3.60 *ubi acris inuidia atque uigent ubi crimina*; this principle was enunciated by Lindholm 1931: 25: 'If a verb has two subjects or objects, one of which is longer than the other, we find that the verb joined with the shorter word or limb forms a counterweight to the longer'.

7 sine te: 26.9n. Here it contrasts with *tecum* 5.   **Iuuentas:** the Roman cult of this personified abstraction was very old, and she had two shrines, one on the Capitol, the other near the Circus Maximus (Richardson 1992: 228); Augustus was keen to revive her cult, which symbolized a new age (Ogilvie on Livy 5.54.6, p. 750, R. Dimundo, art. 'Iuuentas' in *EO* ii 407–8). A prostitute would honour this god because her clients of choice would be young men (cf. 25.2 *iuuenes proterui*) and because she would wish to preserve her own youthful looks (there is no suggestion that Glycera is ageing).

8 Mercuriusque: the various reasons adduced for his presence do not rule each other out. As a god of fair speech and persuasion he finds a place in love-making (cf. *Suadela Venusque* at *Epist.* 1.6.38); likewise, as a god given to lies and tricks he has a role to play in erotic warfare (see Kenney on Apuleius, *Metamorphoses* 6.7.3). But pseudo-Acro noted that he was the god of gain (*lucrum*), and Glycera might want his help for business reasons.

*

This deceptively straightforward poem evokes the 'cletic' hymns of Greek poetry, by which a divinity was summoned to leave one cult site for another. We have examples of such hymns to Venus dating from Alcman, cited on line 2 above, to the Hellenistic Posidippus, *Anthologia Palatina* 12.131 = *HE* 3081–5, whose poem is clearly parodistic of the early lyric. H.'s poem will only be a parody like Posidippus' if we take the presence of Mercury to be a hint at profit from prostitution. There are other problems of interpretation. For instance, who speaks the poem? Is it H., or could it be Glycera herself (admittedly, a unique ploy)? If the speaker is H., is he to be imagined as one of her lovers? West 1995: 144–5 endorses this view, but it was long ago repudiated by Mitscherlich 1800: 281. H.'s supposed involvement with Glycera is not apparent in this poem and has to be imported from *Carm.* 19, where a girl of the same name, but not necessarily the same girl, has reignited erotic fires in the poet (there is yet another Glycera in 33.2). If Glycera is herself the speaker, then the inclusion of Mercury in the final line may not be so much a parody, as a stroke of realism. But if it is H. who speaks, a characteristic note of light irony closes the poem.

31

Metre: alcaic (see Introduction 8)

1–3 H. asks what he is to pray for on a special occasion.

1–2 dedicatum 'consecrated', i.e., handed over to the god so that it becomes his property.   **Apollinem:** by metonymy the name of the god stands for the temple built in his honour (*TLL* v 1.259.38–46, more generally Courtney on Juv. 9.24 *Cererem*). The consecration of a temple to Apollo on the Palatine hill took place on 9 October 28. Richardson 1992: 14 and P. Gros in *LTUR* 1 54–7 describe the temple and its decorations; it is significant for this poem that the statues of Apollo probably represented him as a lyre-player, *citharoedus* (cf. Prop. 2.31.5–6 and 15–16). For the temple's ideological programme – ignored in this poem – see Zanker 1988: 384, Index s.v. 'Rome: Temple of Apollo on the Palatine', and Galinsky 1996: 213–24. It was probably not connected with an alleged vow made by Octavian during the Sicilian war against Sextus Pompeius, but served rather to expiate a prodigy mentioned by Suet. *Aug.* 29.3: a thunderbolt fell upon private land adjacent to his house on the Palatine, and this was interpreted by the *haruspices* as a sign that Apollo wanted a temple there (see Hekster and Rich 2006). Nonetheless the temple came in due course to be associated with the victory at Actium.   **uates:** 1.35n., but here H. does not hesitate to claim the distinction for himself. The word by its placement as last in the sentence and its juxtaposition with *Apollinem* indicates his claim upon the god of poetry, and it prepares us for the final item of his prayer. If the word suggests H. as poet in some official or public capacity (cf. the reference to the *Carmen Saeculare* at 4.6.44 *uatis Horati*), then the purely private nature of his prayer comes as a surprise.

2–3 patera: 19.15n.   **nouum** suggests the Meditrinalia on 11 October, the festival of the new wine (Scullard 1981: 192). Varro, *De lingua Latina* 6.21, derived its name from *mederi* 'to heal', and this would perhaps be in H.'s mind when he prays for health below (Apollo being a god of healing).   **liquorem:** i.e., wine. The word is largely poetic, though technical writers use it of fluids that have no specific name.

3–15 H. rejects traditional sources or tokens of wealth, in a priamel (Race 1982: 128–9, citing Pöschl (originally 1970) 1991: 292–300). Much 'local' colour is provided by place names, which are both Italian and foreign.

3–7 non: the anaphora (4x) emphatically repudiates.

4 Sardiniae: along with Sicily Sardinia was a major source of grain for Rome, see Rickman 1980: 106–7, who notes that there are very few literary references to the island.   **segetes** 'cornfields' (*OLD* 2), rather than the crops.

5–6 grata ... | armenta: Calabria was more famous for its flocks of sheep, but herds of cattle are also referred to. *grata*, regarded by some editors as unacceptable, seems to mean 'thankful', namely for the toil expended on them by the farmer, which they repay with their produce; cf. Pliny, *Panegyricus* 31.1 *omnibus equidem gentibus fertiles annos gratasque terras precor*, and pseudo-Quintilian, *Declamationes* 298.4 *mihi rus paternum erga labores gratissimum* 'I have a family property that gives an excellent return for work' (Shackleton Bailey trans.).

7 Liris: the river served as boundary between Latium and Campania. The plains it cut through were fertile, and notable wines came from the region (cf. *Epist.* 1.5.4–5); see M. P. Muzzioli, art. 'Liri' in *EO* I 498–9, 503. This may form a gliding transition to the next idea.   **quieta** 'unhurried' (*OLD* 3b), cf. *diluuies quietos | irritat amnes*, 3.29.40–1.

8 mordet 'erodes', a metaphorical sense, first found here (*OLD* 4), but cf. the use of *rodo* by Lucr. 5.256 (*OLD* 2a), and *lambit* 22.8n. The phraseology as a whole is derived from Callimachus, *Epigram* 44.4 Pfeiffer ὑποτρώγων ἡσύχιος ποταμός (= *taciturnus amnis*). For *amnis* see 2.20n.

9 premant 'prune' (*OLD* 19b). The phraseology as a whole is owed to Virgil, *G.* 1.157 *falce premes umbras*.   **Calena:** by the figure hypallage the epithet is transferred to *falce*, see N–H on 2.11.23 *Lacaenae ... comae*, and cf. *Sabellis ... ligonibus* 3.6.38, where H. could have written *Sabellas* to agree with *glaebas* in the following line; Porphyrio however read *Calenam* (to go with *uitem*). For its wine see 20.9n., and for the pruning-hook see Mynors on Virg. *G.* 1.157.

10 et: postponed, and defended against *ut* by Brink 1969: 4.

11–12 exsiccet: like the simple verb *sicco*, it is used of the vessel emptied (cf. *S.* 2.6.68 *siccat ... calices conuiua*), and of the liquid drained.   **culillis** 'cups, goblets', a rare word (but presumably not a coinage), only found again at *AP* 434, where Brink discusses its orthography. **uina:** 11.6n. **Syra:** for the shorter gentile name preferred to the adjective *Syriacus* cf. *Marsus* 1.28n. **reparata** 'obtained in exchange for' (*OLD* 2). **merce:** exotic commodities: spices, purple, perfumes, textiles. The ablative is one of price, a sort of instrumental (*NLS* §86).

13–15 dis carus: it was commonly believed that material prosperity was a sign of divine favour. This is a step up from the favour of *fortuna* in 9–10. **quippe** introduces an explanation of how H. is so sure the merchant enjoys divine favour. Many commentators – Orelli, Page, N–H – take this to be ironic or sarcastic, but Kießling (followed by Heinze) fairly observed that H. can still acknowledge the merchant's privilege without wanting his risky way of life. *quippe* used with a participle, rather than the older *quippe qui* with a finite verb, is high style, found also in historians (K–S I 791–2). **ter et quater** 'three and even four times', i.e., 'repeatedly' (*OLD ter* 1b). **aequor Atlanticum:** H.'s merchant now sails beyond the Pillars of Hercules into the Atlantic Ocean, at the opposite end of the Mediterranean world from Syria. He is heading for the Roman province of Baetica in southern Spain, and its ports, Gades (mod. Cadiz) or Hispalis (mod. Seville), where he can trade his exotic wares for grain, wine, honey, fish sauce (*garum*), and olive oil (all mentioned by Strabo, *Geographia* 3.2.6), or perhaps for metals too (see *loricis Hiberis* 29.15n.). For *aequor* see 2.11–12n. **impune:** the crucial point which demonstrates the favour of heaven is given the greatest emphasis.

15–20 Having rejected the common objects of prayer, H. still delays stating his own wishes and first asserts – the anaphora of *me* (15–16) is emphatic, as at 1.29–30 – the simplicity of his own lifestyle. It is that simplicity which conditions his closing prayer. For H.'s plain diet cf. *S.* 1.6.114–15 *inde domum me | ad porri et ciceris refero laganique catinum*. Still, the language chosen to describe it is here elevated in a lyric style.

15–16 oliuae: 7.7n. In a satire, *S.* 2.2.46, H. naturally uses the everyday word, *nigris ... oleis*. **cichorea** 'endive' to Europeans, 'chicory' to Americans, a salad plant of many varieties (one of which is radicchio); see Olck, art. 'Cichorie', *RE* III 2537–41. The word, first found here, is borrowed from Greek – the Roman in the *forum holitorium* asked for *intubum* – and it is given a poetic plural; both the plural and the quantity of the penultimate syllable are exceptionally found in Aristophanes, fr. 293. **leuesque** 'easily digested' (*OLD* 8). Rudd's translation applies the epithet ἀπὸ κοινοῦ to the preceding nouns (cf. *dirae* 2.1n.). **maluae** 'mallow', another common salad; see Steier, art. 'Malve', *RE* XIV 922–7, esp. 923.45–52 for passages relating to its benefits to digestion, e.g., *Epode* 2.57–8 *graui | maluae salubres corpori*. Both there and here the plural seems to be poetic.

17–20 H. finally makes his prayer to Apollo, thus answering the initial questions. The construe is: 'precor, Latoe, dones mihi et ualido et integra cum mente frui paratis, et degere senectam non turpem nec cithara carentem.' *precor* governs the subjunctive *dones* (2.30n.), and *dones* governs the two infinitives, *frui* and *degere*. The word order is not arbitrary, since *precor* emphasizes the part of the sentence in which it is placed: H. sets more store by mental health than physical (*ualido*). The first half of the prayer relates to the present and is positive in form, the second half relates to the future and is negative.

17–18 frui ... | ... dones: the infinitive is rare and poetic with *dono*; even *S.* 2.5.60 *diuinare etenim magnus mihi donat Apollo* is highfalutin.   **paratis** 'what is available', τὰ ὑπάρχοντα (*TLL* x 1.431.25–55, especially 44–5). It was a commonplace of morality that one should be satisfied with what lies to hand, rather than entertain vain desires for remote or impracticable things.

17–19 et ualido mihi | ... et ... integra | cum mente 'to me, being both in good health and of sound mind'; for *integra* see *OLD* 12.

18 Latoe 'son of Leto/Latona' = Apollo; the adjective is here used as a noun.   **et:** Lambinus' conjecture for transmitted *at*, which 'throws the carefully balanced sentence completely out of gear' (Page), is now widely accepted.

19 senectam: originally an adjective with *aetas*, *senecta* alone serves as a synonym, largely but not exclusively poetic, for *senectus*.

20 cithara carentem = ἀκίθαρις (Aeschylus, *Supplices* 681); for *carentem* see 28.1n. The most important thing he prays for comes last, and it is emphasized by alliteration.

*

Structurally considered, the poem presents a situation, framed as questions (1–3), and a response in the form of answers (3–20), which contrast what is not sought (3–15) with what is (17–20). (The opening of 2.18 follows a similar strategy of negative followed by positive.) Between these options is inserted a brief statement of lifestyle (15–16), which prepares for the substance of the concluding prayer. The opening questions and final answering prayer are thematically linked (for the prayer as a closural device see 2.41–52n.). *precor* 18 recalls the questioning verbs, *poscit* and *orat*, of the opening. *Latoe* 18 scrolls back to *Apollinem* 1. The reference to the 'new' wine (2) hints at a festival, the Meditrinalia, which fostered health, something also requested in the final prayer. Most importantly, H. presents himself at the outset as *uates* and so prays at the close that his poetic power may not be lost to him with age.

This is a private prayer on a public occasion (H. would surely endorse Auden's claim that 'Private faces in public places | Are wiser and nicer | Than public faces in private places'). H. might have used that occasion to flatter Augustus, but, unlike Propertius 2.16 or 4.6, he says nothing about the temple itself or its 'meaning'; he commemorates a public occasion in a purely private way (3.14 is similar in this regard). See Miller 2009: 221–6.

The poem seems to be deliberately placed between similar invocations and prayers. This trio of religiously coloured poems is then capped by 34, in which

H. accounts for his renewed sense of divine power. That poem in turn preludes the grand hymn to *Fortuna*, 35.

32

Metre: sapphic (see Introduction 8)

1–12 H. invokes his lyre, and asks it to sing a Latin song. His lyre has a heritage, stretching back to Alcaeus.

1 Poscimur 'we are bidden'. When 'we' is a poet, what he is bidden to do is clear: to sing a song. Thus the song which follows is H.'s response to the abrupt opening. The situation is left vague, and who bids him, or why is not stated; Mitscherlich 1800: 293 suggested that the demand might come from within: 'impelli me sentio ad canendum'.

poscimur is the reading printed by Shackleton Bailey, whose apparatus criticus should be consulted. There is, however, a respectable variant reading, *poscimus*, argued for by Brink 1971b: 17, n.1, and adopted by Rudd. It is however stylistically hard to accept since (*a*) *posco*, which means something like 'demand', is not used in prayers as a synonym of *obsecro/oro/peto/rogo*, and (*b*) it is unusual for the thing prayed for to be introduced in direct speech (though Scheible-Flury in *TLL* x 2.76.26–30 suggests this usage may here be modelled upon Pindar's practice).

1–2 si quid ... | lusimus 'if we have amused ourselves with something' (*OLD ludo* 8, and see Fordyce on Catull. 50.2 *lusimus*); the meaning seems more general than a reference to producing light verse as at 4.9.9 *si quid olim lusit Anacreon*. For the plural see *nos* 6.5n. *si* = *siquidem* 'seeing that', i.e., there is no genuine doubt about what is said, the condition is tactfully diffident (cf. Fordyce on Catull. 14.17 *si luxerit*; the usage is not recognized by *OLD*). Conditional clauses of this sort – in effect saying, 'if ever before now . . .' – are common in prayers and remind the divinity of a previously established bond which encourages the supplicant to make the present appeal (cf. *CS* 37 *Roma si uestrum est opus* and 65 *si Palatinas uidet aequus aras*); for similar Greek usage see Hopkinson on Callimachus, *Hymn* 6.98–9 (the conditional 'serves to reinforce rather than cast doubt on the truth') and the examples cited by Campbell on Sappho, *GL* 1 1.2.   **sub umbra:** shade is provided by a grove (cf. *nemus* 1.30), but it also reinforces the notion of inactivity (*uacui*): real work (fighting battles, pleading cases) is done out under the sun.

2 quod: the antecedent is *quid*, not *carmen* 4.   **in** 'for' expresses expected duration for a given period, cf. 3.11.35 *in omne uirgo nobilis aeuum* (*OLD* 23b).

3 uiuat 'survive' (*OLD* 5), of poetry also at *Epist.* 1.19.2 *nulla placere diu nec uiuere carmina possunt*. The subjunctive is consecutive/result.

3–4 age: 27.17n.   **dic** 'sing' (*OLD* 6b, cf. 17.19 for a related sense). **Latinum, | barbite, carmen:** juxtaposition marks the cultural blend as at 1.35 *lyricis uatibus*. For the *barbitos* see 1.34n.

5 Lesbio ... ciui: for the dative of agent see *matribus* 1.24n. The 'citizen of Lesbos' is Alcaeus; the antonomasia is not inert, since H. hints at that poet's active engagement in the political life of his community, perhaps with a hint of his attacks upon tyrants referred to at 2.13.31 *exactos tyrannos*. For the praise of others on this score see Campbell's *testimonia* 20 citing Dionysius of Halicarnassus, *De imitatione* and 21 citing Quintilian, *Institutio oratoria* 10.1.63.   **primum:** there seems to have been a tradition that Alcaeus invented lyric song (Porphyrio on *Epist.* 2.2.101), but more to the point is the common practice in prayers of referring to the parentage or place of origin of the divinity invoked.   **modulate** 'played' (*OLD* 3); for the passive past participle see *detestata* 1.24n. The vocative participle is grandiloquent and hymnic (N–H on *deducte* 2.7.1 and cf. *amictus* 2.31n.).

6 ferox bello: a concessive idea is latent here, as *tamen* shows. Alcaeus had fought against the Athenians, see *GL* 1 428 (citations from Strabo's *Geographia* and from Herodotus 5.94–5).

7–8 siue = *uel ... si*; see 2.33, 35, 41n.   **religarat:** the pluperfect in the protasis, with the imperfect *canebat* in the apodosis forms a past general condition (*NLS* §193.5): 'whenever he tied up'. For *udo* see 7.13n.   **nauim:** for this form of the accusative see the introduction to the *OLD* article (but delete from it Ov. *Rem.* 569, and correct Cic. *Att.* 7.21.1 to 7.22.1). Since the form is found a few times in Plautus it may have struck H. as archaic.

9–12 The previous stanza focused on the strenuous aspects of Alcaeus' life; *tamen* paved the way to a contrast which this stanza provides: despite his toilsome life Alcaeus was still able to sing of the pleasures of drink and love-making. The divinities of the first two lines are sharply separated from the handsome mortal boy of the last two by the verb, *canebat*. They are uncharacterized, but H. lingers on his description.

9 Liberum: 12.22n.

9–10 illi | semper haerentem puerum = Cupid, by the figure antonomasia. *semper* indicates that this is a standing activity, cf. 35.17 and 2.8.15 *semper ardentes acuens sagittas* (again of Cupid).

11–12 Lycum: 'we still do not have any obviously paederastic verse of Alcaeus' (Page 1955: 294–5), but it was known to exist, according to Cicero, *Tusculanae disputationes* 4.71 *quae de iuuenum amore scripsit*, and cf. *De natura deorum* 1.79 *naeuus* ['a mole, birthmark'] *in articulo pueri delectat Alcaeum*.   **nigris oculis nigroque | crine:** recycled at *AP* 37, where *capillo*, the everyday word, is substituted for *crine*, the more poetic. Prosodic variation of a repeated word was a something of a mannerism as old as Homer, cf. *Il.* 5.31 (Austin on Virg. *Aen.* 2.663, Wills 1996: 464). Here the naturally short first syllable in *nigris* is lengthened before the mute and liquid consonants. *crinis* is a high-style word, usually found in the plural, so the collective singular is poetic (*TLL* IV 1202.2–4).

12–13 decorum. | ... decus: the echo forges a link between the stanzas. For *decorum* see 10.3n.

13–16 H. concludes with a solemn greeting to the lyre.

13–14 o (2x): the repeated interjection elevates the expression, cf. 14.1, 2n.   **decus Phoebi:** Mercury gave Apollo the newly fashioned lyre in recompense for the thieving mentioned in 10.9–11. Given the placement of this poem immediately after the one which refers to the dedication of the new temple of Apollo on the Palatine, the reader might be expected to recall how the god was represented there (see *Apollinem* 31.1n.).   **dapibus** 'sacrificial banquets' offered to the gods, cf. 37.4, 2.7.17 *obligatam Ioui dapem*; some however seem to take it of Jove's feasting in heaven, which seems possible. The word is poetic, by and large; prose writers preferred *epulae*.   **supremi | ... Iouis** = 21.3–4.

14–15 laborum | dulce lenimen: the phrase caught on: see *Anthologia Latina* 887 Riese. *lenimen* is a coinage, picked up by Ovid (*Met.* 6.500 *lenimen dulce*). It is H.'s only venture with a suffix which was proving especially fertile in contemporary poetry (Perrot 1961: 110–12 and 287).

15–16 mihi cumque salue | rite uocanti: the text is usually reckoned to be corrupt, but no solution has proved satisfactory. Tampering with *mihi* is entirely unacceptable (as Munro in his n. on Lucr. 5.313 insisted), because (*a*) it brings H. back into the poem, for a personal ending; if removed, *uocanti* might apply to anyone who invoked (2.25n.) the lyre, and (*b*) the ethic dative (cf. 19.13) evokes (but does not replicate) a Greek salutation, χαῖρέ μοι, unusual with *salue* (cf. Virg. *Aen.* 11.97); thus this construction gives the Latin a Greek colour and is unlikely to have been introduced by scribal error. If this line of argument is accepted, *cumque* alone is the stumbling block. It can either be marked as corrupt, or the sense accorded to it by the *OLD*, 'at any time', can be hesitantly adopted (Wackernagel 1928: II 120 = 2009: 548 took the expression to mean 'mihi salue, quandocumque rite uoco').

*

This poem to the lyre, the symbol of H.'s poetic initiative, parodies hymns or prayers; Fraenkel 1957: 168–70 and West 1995: 152–3 list its elements evocative of a hymn.

H.'s view of the function of poetry is clear, and probably still hard for modernists to take. For the contemporary view of the arts generally is that they should challenge us by addressing serious, even distasteful, issues, or that they should subvert complacently held certainties. H. was not alone however in believing that poetry and music exist to charm and to soothe. The tone is set at once: *uacui sub umbra | lusimus*; the poet himself enjoys freedom from mundane cares (cf. 26.1–6) and, out of the hurly-burly (cf. 1.30–2), he can give himself up to amusement. Alcaeus is then evoked to provide both a model and an authority; he did not forgo the stresses and strains of a citizen's life, but his musical themes reflected life's lighter side, drinking and love-making. The value of song is further enhanced in the final stanza, where it is seen to be favoured by the gods; still, it is an adjunct of their life of pleasure (*dapibus* 13), not a vehicle for the expression of anxieties. All is summed up in the phrase *laborum lenimen*. Song had long been seen as solace of cares (cf. Hesiod, *Theogonia* 55, 98–103), a notion developed by Pindar (cf. *Isthmian*

8.1 λύτρον εὔδοξον … καμάτων 'a glorious recompense for toils' and *Nemean* 4.1–3). (But the Nurse in Euripides, *Medea* 190–8 provocatively challenged this opinion.) H. often endorsed the widespread attitude to song's soothing function, cf. 2.13.37–40, 4.11.35–6 *minuentur atrae | carmine curae, Epode* 13.17 *omne malum uino cantuque leuato,* and *Epist.* 2.1.131 *inopem solatur et aegrum* with Brink's n.

Writing poems was traditionally reckoned by H.'s fellow Romans among life's less exacting activities – Cicero's defence of Archias well illustrates the acceptable view of it – so it was tactful and realistic of Roman poets to belittle their own calling by suggesting that it is not really work at all (*lusimus*). But it is not for that reason trivial. Indeed, it may prove more durable than more strenuous undertakings – people were still reading Alcaeus long after the tyrants of Mytilene were dust. H. glances at this possibility for his own poetry at the outset. The sentiment of *quod et hunc in annum | uiuat et plures* is similar to that in the dedicatory poem of Catullus, 1.10, who referred to his work as *nugae* 'trifles', but he still prayed it would survive, *plus uno maneat perenne saeclo.* This is the first time in the collection that H. expresses a hope for the durability of his poetry, and it will be more emphatically enunciated in the final poems of the succeeding books.

This poem seems to be deliberately placed after its predecessor, though of course each makes perfect sense on its own. In 31 H. stressed his function as *uates* and prayed to Apollo that his old age would not 'lack the lyre', *cithara.* That penultimate word forges a clear link with the prayer to the lyre, *barbitos,* in this poem.

33

Metre: 'second' asclepiad (see Introduction 7)

1–12 H. tries to console a friend who is unlucky in love, by drawing his attention to the erotic mismatches of others, including himself.

1 Albi: an Albius is also the addressee of *Epist.* 1.4; presumably they are the same man. Many identify him with the contemporary elegiac poet Tibullus, whose *nomen gentilicium* they necessarily believe to have been Albius. But the evidence for this lacks cogency. The poet Tibullus is named in antiquity by himself (twice), by Domitius Marsus shortly after his death, by Ovid (frequently), Velleius Paterculus, Quintilian, Statius, Martial, and Apuleius; none of them supplies a *gentilicium*; to them all he is simply Tibullus. Scholars however in antiquity, perhaps those referred to by Porphyrio who wrote *de personis Horatianis* (see his n. on *S.* 1.3.21), somehow divined that the Albius here was Albius Tibullus, and that name (or identification) is found (i) in some of the subscriptions of H.'s MSS to this poem and to the epistle, and in his scholiasts, (ii) in the grammarian Diomedes (*GLK* 1 484.17), and (iii) in the MS tradition of the elegist, which also includes an anonymous life of 'Albius Tibullus' that may derive from Suetonius. But it must be remembered (i) that attempts in antiquity to put more flesh on the

names of H.'s addressees sometimes fail to convince (see e.g. *Vare* 18.1n.), (ii) that
Diomedes obviously knew the scholarship on H., and (iii) that the MS tradition
of the elegist only starts for us in the fourteenth century, when scholarship was
equal to borrowing information from H.'s scholiasts or MSS. It is easy to see how
the link was made, since H. refers to *elegi* in line 3, though he does not say Albius
wrote them, nor is the mistress, Glycera, known to Tibullus. On balance then the
agnosticism of Mayer on *Epist.* 1.4.1 is to be followed.   **ne doleas:** probably
an elliptical purpose clause, 'lest you grieve, think how . . . ' (trans. Wickham), cf.
18.7n. Brink 1969: 4–6 followed Kießling in arguing that there are no independent
second person prohibitions using the present subjunctive in H.'s lyric; the usage
was perhaps too colloquial. Light punctuation after line 4 is adopted by Rudd,
though he translates with a prohibition; Shackleton Bailey prints a full stop at
the end of the stanza.   **plus nimio:** 18.15n. The expression is positioned so
as to be taken ἀπὸ κοινοῦ both with *doleas* and with *memor* (cf. *dirae* 2.1n.).

2 immitis 'sour' literally, 'harsh' used of a person, undermines the Greek
name of Albius' mistress, Glycera, 'sweetie'; for such wordplay cf. *S.* 2.3.142
pauper Opimius. The women in this poem are pretty unpleasant: Pholoe is *aspera*
and Myrtale *acrior*.   **miserabiles** indicates the content of the elegies, self-
pitying laments for lost love.

3 decantes 'drone out' (Rudd, cf. *OLD* 1); the *TLL* article, v 1.117.63, took it to
mean no more than 'chant', but this is an exceptional sense and inappropriate to
the context, which is lightly critical of Albius' reaction to being dumped.   **ele-
gos:** the first appearance of this Greek loan-word in Latin, though *elegeum* is found
in Plautus, *Mercator* 409. It is assumed Albius wrote the elegies he sings, but he
could as easily have been reciting the poems of others.   **cur** 'asking the reason
why' (*OLD* 3, and cf. *Epist.* 1.8.9–10 *irascar amicis | cur me funesto properent arcere ueterno*
and 9.7 *multa quidem dixi cur excusatus abirem*).

4 laesa . . . fide 'having broken her faith' (*OLD laedo* 5), with perhaps a hint
of the notion of a wrong done to a lover (*OLD* 3b).   **praeniteat** 'outshine'
(cf. *nites* 5.12–13n.); the verb may be a coinage of H.'s, cloned on *praefulgeo*; cf. too
Epist. 1.1.83 *nullus in orbe sinus Bais praelucet amoenis*.

5–12 The unreciprocated loves H. lists recall the similar plight of lovers in a
fragmentary poem of Moschus, fr. 2 Gow. The wit of H.'s list turns upon the
crisp descriptions of the unhappy lovers: Lycoris is good-looking, which counts
for nothing with Cyrus, who favours the 'abrasive' (Rudd) Pholoe, but she spurns
the plug-ugly fellow. Love is no respecter of looks or character (*formas atque
animos* 11).

5 tenui fronte: a narrow brow was considered beautiful in girls, cf. Petronius,
Satyrica 126.15 *frons minima* (Circe's), and in boys, cf. Martial 4.42.9 *frons breuis*; at
Epist. 1.7.26 *angusta fronte* is part of a picture of H. in his youth.   **Lycorida:** a
Greek accusative singular termination of the third declension (G–L §65 s.v. *Paris*).

6 torret: for the common erotic metaphor see *OLD* 2b, and Fantham 1972:
88, Williams on Callimachus, *Hymn* 2.49 κεκαυμένος (with further references);

cf. *torrere iecur* 4.1.12.   **Cyri ... Cyrus:** the repetition of the name effects an adversative asyndeton: 'but Cyrus ...'.

7 declinat 'deviates', in a metaphorical sense (*OLD* 2).   **Pholoen:** a Greek accusative singular termination of the first declension (G–L §65 s.v. *Penelope*).

7–8 Apulis adds local colour.   **iungentur:** the coupling of different breeds is a traditional form of adynaton, especially in an erotic context (29.10–11n.). For *iungo* of 'joining' in sexual intercourse see Adams 1982: 179.

9 Pholoe: a Greek nominative singular termination of the first declension (G–L §65 s.v. *Penelope*).   **peccet:** 27.17n.   **adultero:** see *moechos* 25.9n.

10 sic uisum Veneri 'so Venus has decided', supply *est*, and for *uisum* see *OLD uideo* 24c. H. ascribes the cause of the human erotic condition to divine will, tantamount to saying it is inexplicable, as Servius observed on Virg. *Aen.* 3.1–2.

11 iuga aenea: the yoke acquired two metaphorical meanings, subjection and various kinds of partnership (*OLD* 2 and 5, cf. 35.28, and Ferber 2007: 245–7); here the two seem to be combined. The plural is poetic, cf. the singular at 3.9.18 *diductosque iugo cogit aeneo*. *aenea* suggests the yoke's weight and strength.

12 saeuo ... ioco: oxymoron. At 2.33–4 Venus, accompanied by *Iocus*, was described as *ridens*; here her glee takes a nasty turn, cf. *saeua* 19.1.

13–16 In a self-depreciating personal ending (see N–R on 3.14.27–8, comparing 2.4.22, 3.19.28, *Epode* 14.15), H. adduces his own experience of the same regrettable erotic muddle.

13 melior: 27.20n.   **Venus:** 27.14n.

14 grata ... compede: more oxymoron, found again at 4.11.23–4; for *grata* cf. 19.7. The singular is poetic usage.

15 libertina: cf. *Epode* 14.15, *S.* 1.2.48. A slave who had been a prostitute might well stay in the business after manumission, like the *scortum nobile*, Faecenia Hispala (Livy 39.9.5). To define Myrtale's social status in this way marks the realistic H. off from the romanticizing elegists (cf. his use of *scortum* at 2.11.21). There is also a paradox in the freedwoman's 'enslavement' of H.

15–16 For the metaphor see 5.6–8n.   **fretis:** see 15.1n.   **acrior** 'wilder' (*OLD* 10c) of the sea also in Plautus, *Asinaria* 134 *mare haud est mare, uos mare acerrumum*.   **Hadriae:** see 3.15–16n.   **curuantis:** a poetic verb. As N–H say, it does not here describe the action of the sea, making hollows in the coastline; it simply indicates that the coastline curves.   **Calabros:** the 'heel' of Italy, see *Iapyga* 3.4n. The adjective *Calaber*, first attested in Virgil, *G.* 3.425, seems to be poetic diction (but our record of the word's occurrence may be defective).

*

The late Republic witnessed an extraordinary evolution in the character of contemporary poetry: it became personal, rather than public, and it focused squarely on the emotional life of the poet (or his persona). Catullus embodies this change of direction for us, but that is only because the work of his contemporaries, Calvus for instance, has not survived. Such an attitude had become the fashion. After Catullus this intensely self-regarding poetry began to develop most significantly in a particular genre, erotic elegy. Its founding father was Cornelius Gallus; he was followed by H.'s more immediate contemporaries, Tibullus and Propertius. All three of them elaborated what might be called an erotic code appropriate to the elegiac lover. It is this code which H. mildly guys in the present poem (and he guys it elsewhere too, e.g., 2.9). The cornerstone of the elegiac code is devotion to a single mistress, obviously anathema to H., who sings of many girlfriends and is firmly committed to none of them. For H. the elegists' attitude to love is at bottom unrealistic, and this poem administers a dose of realism to one who subscribes to the code (it hardly matters for purposes of understanding this poem whether Albius is or is not the elegist Tibullus, for he clearly 'sings from the same songsheet').

It is made clear in the very first line what the moral issue is: excess (*plus nimio*) is Albius' failing. He is also, in practical terms, rather clueless: a single word, *iunior* 3, indicates his rival's chief attraction for Glycera, but Albius 'doesn't get it'. So H. has to draw his attention to what is going on around them both, namely failures to connect. To formalize this observation as a kind of natural law, H. enunciates his own erotic code: love is like that because Venus (a more considerable divinity than Cupid, cf. 19.1 and 9) has so decreed it. There is no point in trying to evade her ordinance. H. finally shows that he personally has had to bend to the goddess's will, that is to say, his own cheerful (cf. *grata* 14) acceptance of his lot is exemplary.

The past tense of the verbs in the final stanza is perhaps significant (contrast the use of the present in 3.19.28 *me lentus Glycerae torret amor meae*). H. is not only an example of the attraction to an unsuitable partner, he has also survived the experience, which is now part of his history (cf. 5.13–16).

34

Metre: alcaic (see Introduction 8)

1–5 H. claims not to have been much given to formal religious practice, thanks to his philosophical leanings, but now he finds himself compelled to backtrack.

1 cultor 'worshipper', a rare sense, found once before H. in Cicero, *Tusculanae Disputationes* 1.69.

2 insanientis ... sapientiae: an oxymoron: *sapientia* is the Roman name for philosophy (*OLD* 3), and more specifically Lucretius had appropriated it exclusively for Epicureanism at *De rerum natura* 5.9–10 *uitae rationem ... eam quae | nunc appellatur sapientia*. H. thus intimates an attachment to Epicureanism, which he had more expressly avowed at *S.* 1.5.100–3 when he was faced with a natural wonder. Epicurus had denied that the gods are active in human affairs (a doctrine thus abandoned below, 12–16), and he had sought to demonstrate that alleged demonstrations of divine power can be explained by an understanding of the working of nature.

3 consultus erro: more oxymoron! For adjectival *consultus* with genitive see 22.1n. The expression may have been influenced by the common nominal phrase *iuris consultus*, but H. likes combining the genitive of 'respect' with adjectives that indicate knowledge or skill (*AP* 407 *Musa lyrae sollers*), perhaps on the analogy of the use of *peritus*. *erro* parodies Lucr. 2.9–10 *queas . . . alios* [i.e., non-Epicureans] *. . . uidere | errare.* It is the Epicurean who goes astray, not the philosophical ignoramus.

4–5 uela dare: the metaphor is not purely poetic, see *OLD uelum* 2.   **iterare cursus | cogor relictos** 'I am forced to take up again the course I had abandoned', i.e., resume my pre-philosophical attitude (*TLL* VII 2.549.81–4, cf. 7.32n.). *cursus* is poetic plural ('inde a Verg.', *TLL* IV 1529.20). Some editors (N–H, SB) prefer the correction of the Dutch scholar Nicolaus Heinsius (1620–81), *relectos* 'retraced' (Rudd; see Horsfall on Virg. *Aen.* 3.690 *relegens*). Gow, however, and Fredricksmeyer 1976: 161 n. 6 defended *relictos*, feeling that *relectos* produces tautology (admitted by N–H), which seems out of place in such an economical poem. Rudd's translation, 'now I am forced to sail back and repeat my course in the reverse direction', does not get round this: 'back' and 'in the reverse direction' come to the same thing. *cogor* is emphatically placed after a stanza without the main verb: H. is not happy with the state of affairs, but can see no alternative.

5–12 His reason (*namque*) is the experience of a marvel in nature: thunder in a clear sky. This meteorological phenomenon is regularly recorded by Greek and Roman writers (see Pease on Cicero, *De diuinatione* 1.18), and it was always regarded as a portent (good or bad, see Skutsch on Ennius, *Annales* 541). There is no sound reason for supposing H. better informed or more sceptical than, say, Seneca, who mentioned the phenomenon at *Naturales quaestiones* 1.1.15 *sereno quoque aliquando caelo tonat* (and then discussed it at 2.18, following Anaximander), or the emperor Titus (see Suetonius, *Titus* 10). Nor need he have owed the alleged incident to poetic tradition.

5 Diespiter: an archaic name for Jupiter as 'father of the day' (found again at 3.2.29), chosen for its solemn effect.

6–7 igni corusco: a poetic periphrasis for *fulmen* or *fulgur*, neither of which is unpoetic; cf. *OLD ignis* 5b.   **nubila:** Epicureans made the point that thunder and lightning are produced by clouds, and Lucretius specifically attacked the theological explanation of the phenomena, 6.379–422, especially 400–3.   **diuidens:** the participle describes a characteristic activity, as *plerumque* shows, and so is equivalent to a relative clause, as at Catull. 61.17 *colens*, 64.8 *retinens*, and 193 *mulantes*.   **plerumque** 'normally' (Rudd) is emphatic by position. H. goes on to explain that there are exceptions to the general rule. West 1995: 163 however feels that the word undermines H.'s point, and that he ought to have said lightning 'always' comes from a cloudy sky; but that would not have been true to ancient belief. *plerumque* is uncommon in higher forms of poetry, as might be expected: poets tend not to make the nice qualifications of prose writers, didactic poets (Lucretius favours them), or moralists (cf. Brink on

Epist. 2.2.21 *prope*).   **purum** 'clear' sc. *caelum*. *per purum* is headlined so as to contrast with *nubila* 6. The expression, drawn from Lucretius, 4.327 *aera per purum*, is abbreviated, by way of Virg. *G.* 2.364 *per purum* (where the sense is 'through the void'). The adjective thus serves as a noun (*OLD* 6), perhaps on the analogy of *serenum*; Virgil followed suit with *sudum* at *Aen.* 8.529.

7 tonantes: H. describes the alleged incident in pictorial terms derived from the poetic tradition: thunder is caused by the four-horse chariot of Jupiter racing through the sky, cf. 12.58.

9–12 The description of the far-reaching effect of the thunder is drawn from Hesiod, *Theogonia* 839–41, but where Hesiod is elaborate and repetitive, H. is crisp and compact (a lesson learned from the Alexandrians). The description is no mere ornament, rather it serves to demonstrate the vast range of divine power in the physical world. This prepares for the claims made in the final sentence, 12–16.

9 quo 'at which . . . '; the relative is best taken as neuter (so Rudd, 'at that'), referring to the activity of driving (*egit*), though some believe it is masculine, referring to *currum*.   **bruta** 'inert', in contrast with the moving (*uaga*) rivers. *brutus* is uncommon in its literal sense in classical Latin (*TLL* II 2216.9–11), and since H. owes so much in this poem to Lucretius, it is probable that he has picked up this possibly archaic usage from the only other text in which it is found, *De rerum natura* 6.105, *cadere . . . bruto deberent pondere* (of clouds, in the discussion of thunder).

10 Taenari: a promontory of the southern Peloponnese, now Cape Matapan, where there was thought to be a cave leading to the Underworld, hence *inuisi* and *horrida*; cf. Virg. *G.* 4.467 *Taenarias etiam fauces, alta ostia Ditis*.

11 Atlanteusque: poetic diction, unlike *Atlanticus*, 31.14; the epithet replaces a genitive (see 3.36n.). Accounts of the Titan Atlas are various, but commonly he was regarded as a mountain in the remote western Mediterranean (hence *finis*) which supported the heavens. If the allusion is to the support of heaven, there is an appropriately polar contrast with the Underworld just referred to (Fredricksmeyer 1976: 165).

12 concutitur: historical present (G–L §229) for vividness; for the singular see *iuuat* 2.38n.   **ualet** headlines the sentence for emphasis on power. The verb governs the infinitive in poetry from Lucretius, and commonly in H. (K–S I 674); analogy with *possum* presumably eased the usage. For additional passages to those collected by N–H on the power of god to transpose great and small see West on Hesiod, *Opera* 5ff., pp. 139–40. The phraseology of the notion is proverbial (Otto 1890: 335), starting with Lucilius. For the abstract plurals, *ima* and *summis*, cf. Aristophanes, *Lysistrata* 772–3 τὰ δ' ὑπέρτερα νέρτερα θήσει | Ζεὺς ὑψιβρεμέτης 'high-thundering Zeus will put higher things lower'.

12–16 Such power over natural phenomena argues for divine intervention in human affairs as well.

13 mutare 'to transform' (*OLD* 12b). **attenuat** 'reduces in estimation' (*OLD* 4) must be the sense, especially with the object *insignem* 'distinguished' (*OLD* 5); 'impoverishes' (*OLD* 3b) seems inappropriate. H. is translating Hesiod, *Opera* 6 ἀρίζηλον μινύθει '[Zeus] diminishes the conspicuous'. **deus:** the lack of a definite article in Latin could be a virtue. Here H. is designedly elusive and ambiguous, for he might be referring to 'the god', i.e., *Diespiter* just mentioned, or 'god' in the abstract, 'divinity, divine power', as at 3.21 and 18.3. The indeterminacy eases transition to a specific divine power, *Fortuna* 15 (Fredricksmeyer 1976: 169).

14 obscura promens: the debt to Hesiod continues, *Opera* 6 καὶ ἄδηλον ἀέξει 'and he exalts the obscure man', though for variety's sake H. changes from concrete (*insignem*) to abstract.

apicem 'crown' as at 3.21.20, with special reference to the peaked mitre of eastern monarchs.

15 cum stridore acuto: a vivid and unnerving touch, given the austerity of the language in these concluding lines: this is no benevolent divinity at work. The phrase is sometimes taken to refer to the whirring sound made by *Fortuna*'s wings (cf. 3.29.53–4 *celeres quatit | pennas*); this fails however to do justice to *acuto*.

16 sustulit: the perfect is explained either as gnomic or instantaneous. Grammar books barely notice the use of the perfect to describe immediate action, though Hale and Buck 1903: 255 §492 on 'tenses of rapid action', speak of the picturesque present perfect, quoting Virg. *Aen.* 1.90 *intonuere poli* 'instantly the heavens thunder'. Indeed Virgil's commentators frequently draw attention to his use of the tense, e.g., *G.* 1.330–1, 2.81, 210, 4.213–14, and see Fordyce on *Aen.* 7.394 or Page on *Aen.* 5.140. (A number of the Virgilian examples regarded by commentators as 'instantaneous' appear in the discussion of the gnomic perfect in K–S 1 132–3.) The usage thus seems to be poetic and may be borrowed from Greek: see Smyth 1956: 451 §1927 on the 'complexive' aorist, where it is noted that when used 'of rapid or instantaneous action this aorist is often called "momentary"'. **posuisse gaudet:** for the infinitive see 1.11n. Here the perfect tense is not exactly a substitute for the present (1.4n.) but emphasizes an instantaneous action (see N–R on 3.18.15 *gaudet … pepulisse*). *gaudet* personalizes *Fortuna*, whose activities are not claimed to be either just or fair: she represents rather the incalculable forces at work in human affairs. The sentiment is developed at 3.29.49–52: *Fortuna saeuo* _laeta_ *negotio et | ludum insolentem ludere pertinax | transmutat incertos honores, | nunc mihi nunc alii benigna.*

*

This poem is exceptional for two reasons. In the first place, it has no addressee. H. is either addressing the reader directly, or musing to himself ('ad se ipsum' is the superscription in some MSS; 2.5 also seems to be reflective self-address). Heinze felt that one reason for doing so was to dispense with the sort of adaptation of the tone of the poem to the character of the addressee that we find in other odes. This suggests an absence of exaggeration or rhetorical colour designed to impress someone else. The poet instead reflects within himself upon the implications of the event he describes. Secondly, the poem seems to lack any antecedents within the Greek or Roman literary tradition. Commentators reasonably draw attention to Archilochus, *GIP* 122 χρημάτων ἄελπτον οὐδέν ἐστιν 'nothing is unexpected'; the speaker (not Archilochus) adduces an extraordinary phenomenon – solar eclipse – which produced widespread fear. But what little we know of the rest of that poem does not suggest the event had any effect on the speaker. H.'s poem is therefore fundamentally original both for its form and its content. That naturally has produced very various readings.

Fredricksmeyer 1976 and Syndikus 2001: 293–304 provide helpful orientation. Fredricksmeyer 1976: 173, n. 27, and Syndikus 2001: 294, n. 12, list those who take the poem to be a serious account of a kind of conversion. Others are sceptical of any profound reorientation and feel that H.'s story is not to be taken seriously (Fredricksmeyer 1976: 170, n. 23, and Syndikus 2001: 295, n. 13, list them).

The opening line enunciates the theme, worship of the gods (*deorum cultor*). H. was misled (*erro*) by his philosophical studies (*insanientis sapientiae consultus*) into believing that since the gods took no thought for the affairs of men, he could neglect their worship (*parcus, infrequens*). Something happened however that forced upon him (*cogor*) a recantation. That something is alleged to have been the sort of meteorological phenomenon, thunder in a cloudless sky, which mankind had long taken to be a sign of divine suspension of the natural order, but which Epicurean rationalism denied (so Lucr. 6.99 (thunder), 247–8 (lightning), 400–1 (both)). Personal experience of the phenomenon however drove H. to abandon the philosophical argument as empirically invalid. (There is a similar situation related by the Messenger in Aeschylus' *Persians* 495–8: the retreating Persian army is enabled to cross the river Strymon by an unseasonal frost which freezes the river sufficiently to allow passage; the Messenger observes that 'one who formerly thought the gods of no account on that occasion prayed'.) The sheer extent of the disturbing (*concutitur*) event (elaborated over lines 9–12) leads to an inference developed in lines 12–16: god has power (*ualet ... deus*), and indeed deploys it in human affairs, where *Fortuna* is active after all.

The Epicurean philosophy might be reckoned the crowning achievement of pure rationalism in the ancient world (see Greenblatt 2011). H.'s poem demonstrates on a personal level appropriate to the lyric voice that such thorough-going rationalism does not after all explain everything within human experience. There remain frightening mysteries in nature, and equally there are forces at work within human affairs which cannot be denied and which are to be deemed supernatural. The poem subtly confronts competing accounts of experience by drawing upon two didactic poets, Lucretius, the Roman paladin of Epicureanism, and Hesiod. Indeed since Hesiod is the earlier poet, and traditionally regarded as the inventor of didactic epos, H.'s claim to be returning to an abandoned view (*cursus iterare relictos*) is inscribed within the poem itself by drawing upon Lucretius chiefly at the beginning, and upon Hesiod in the second half. Moreover, H. combines elements from two of Hesiod's poems to describe the effect of the thunder and the power of god, the sort of blending (on a lyric scale here) that we see in Virgil's *Aeneid*, which mixes the Homeric epics together to form a new whole. H.'s debt to Hesiod stops short however of asserting the justice of divine power; he is concerned only with its existence and the fact that it is exercised in human affairs. The poem ends with declarative statements of fact; H. does not say how he intends to deal with the facts.

Contemporary events too may have contributed to the ode's genesis (though it is not possible to date it). Suetonius, *Augustus* 29.3, relates that during his Cantabrian campaign in 26 a thunderbolt (*fulgur*) grazed Augustus' litter, and killed his torch-bearer (there is no detail about the state of the sky that night). In thanksgiving for the escape Augustus vowed a very grand temple (for which see Richardson 1992: 226–7) on the Capitoline to Jupiter Tonans, to whom he clearly ascribed his safety; it was dedicated in 22. Is it entirely unthinkable that H. might have turned this situation to poetic advantage, so as to demonstrate his own adherence to the revitalized worship of the gods under the *princeps* (who was, incidentally, terrified of thunderstorms, Suet. *Aug.* 90)?

G. E. Lessing's (1729–81) account of this poem at the close of his *Rettungen des Horaz* (1754) is well worth reading, since like Fredricksmeyer he was establishing its serious tone against the levity ascribed to it by the French commentator André Dacier (1651–1722). Ogilvie 1969: 18 too felt that 'there is no reason to disbelieve H. when he attributed his return to religion to the sudden sense of the overwhelming might of god ... He does *not* say that it made him more virtuous' (and neither does he say that he has returned to religion). That point is worth stressing. The poem does not enunciate a moral, rather it acknowledges the existence and activity of a power H. had learned to ignore. This poem is therefore not unlike the fourteenth, in which H. admits to a change of heart towards the *nauis* (however we interpret that), or the nineteenth, in which he finds himself unexpectedly once again the prey of passion.

This poem served as a springboard for Seamus Heaney's meditation, entitled 'Open Air Strike (11 September 2001)', upon the terrorist attack on the Twin Towers in New York City. If Heaney saw levity in H.'s original, he elided it.

35

Metre: alcaic (see Introduction 8)

1–28 A hymnic preamble to a prayer, which typically rehearses the powers and attributes of the divinity addressed.

1 O diua: oddly, H. never actually names her. But by specifying her cult site at Antium (mod. Anzio) on the coast of Latium south of Rome, he identifies her by the figure antonomasia as *Fortuna*. In fact however the main cult at Antium was dedicated to a double divinity, and there was even a third *Fortuna* called *equestris*.

The actual location of the shrine is uncertain (see M. P. Muzzioli, art. 'Anzio', in *EO* I 494 and 502). For *diua* see 3.1n. **gratum:** to her, because her cult was there, cf. *dilectam* 30.2. **quae:** for the relative clause in a hymn see 2.34n.

2–4 praesens … tollere … | uertere: H. alone attaches an infinitive to *praesens* (*TLL* x 2.844.33–6, *OLD* 3; cf. 1.18n.). Fortune's powers recall those mentioned at 34.12–14. *imo* (see 10.20n.) is prominent and in contrast with the equally prominent *superbos*. *mortale* prepares for *funeribus*.

3–4 superbos | uertere funeribus triumphos: as at 37.31–2. *uerto* here has an unusual sense, 'turn x into y' (*OLD* 23b), found also at *AP* 226 *uertere seria ludo* (where see Brink's n.); the construction with the ablative is similar to that with *mutare* 17.2.

5–16 These three stanzas illustrate H.'s exploitation of the unpunctuated text of antiquity to achieve unmarked transitions of thought. Since there would have been no semi-colon or full stop after *carina* 8, his reader would naturally have assumed, especially thanks to the continued anaphora of *te* 9, that the verb to be supplied in lines 9–11 was *ambit/ambiunt* (as indeed some commentators suggest). It is only with *metuunt* 12 that a new predicate is introduced, and it might induce the reader to re-think the construe of the earlier part of the stanza as well. Be that as it may, the new predicate allows the sentence to continue into the third stanza by giving the substance of the tyrants' fear, *ne* 13. That substance of course only applies to the tyrant, not to any of the other subjects in the stanza; this procedure is found again at 2.8.21–4. The reader is thus moved through the long sentence without any distinct marks of transition, especially thanks to the quick accumulation of copulatives (noted by Wickham) in lines 9–12.

5–8 Fortune is worshipped on land and sea, i.e., everywhere, a polar expression. Since Antium is on the sea, and since Augustus would have to cross the Channel to get to Britain (29–30), there is a special point in the second half of the stanza (see Weinstock 1971: 125–6, but Champeaux 1982: 159 is right to insist that the notion that Octavian had made a vow before a campaign at the shrine of the *Fortunae* of Antium is speculation).

5–6 te … te: for the anaphora see 10.9n. (Norden 1923: 152). **pauper … | … colonus:** cf. *inopes … coloni* 2.14.12. *colonus* means 'farmer' (*OLD* 1), not, despite N–H and Rudd, 'tenant farmer' (cf. *TLL* III 1706.56). **ambit** 'courts'. **prece:** for the singular see 2.26n.

6 ruris: best taken as objective genitive with *colonus*; those who find the expression *ruris colonus* pleonastic will also need to deal with *CS* 64 *corporis artus*. Some take *ruris* with *dominam* (to be understood ἀπὸ κοινοῦ), which will then be in apposition to *te* 5. One argument advanced in favour of this is that it contrasts with *aequoris*. But *ruris* is not a synonym for *terrae*, hence there is no real contrast, and word order too seems to be against this explanation (so Fraenkel 1957: 251, n. 6), though N–H argue for hyperbaton. **aequoris:** see 2.11–12n.

7–8 Bithyna: poetic for *Bithynicus*, cf. Catull. 31.5. Bithynia's forests made it a centre of shipbuilding (Catullus' yacht came from there, *Carm.* 4). **lacessit** 'challenges' (*OLD* 1c takes this as largely poetic when applied to natural forces) suggests the impiety of sailing; see Wachsmuth 1967: 233–4 and cf. 3.24 *non tangenda*. **Carpathium pelagus:** the island of Carpathos, which lies between Rhodes and Crete, gave its name to the surrounding waters. The adjective is not exactly poetic, but Latin poets doted on that sea (see *TLL Onomasticon* II 205.37–55); the same phraseology is found in the satirist Lucilius, fr. 466 Marx = 497 Warmington. For *pelagus* see 3.11n.   **carina** 'ship', a poetic sense (*OLD* 2), by synecdoche (here the part, the ship's hull, stands for the whole vessel).

9–12 The picture widens to include among Fortune's worshippers barbarian peoples (a glance perhaps at the campaigns mentioned in 29–32), civilized communities (*urbes*), the Roman homeland (*Latium*), and exotic kingdoms.

9 te ... te: 5–6n. The pronoun is the object either of *ambit* 5 or, as the whole is usually punctuated nowadays, *metuunt* 12, in which case it anticipates the subject of the *ne*-clause, 13; cf. 17.24n. The line is elegantly composed, with chiasmus of nouns and epithets, and variation of number.   **Dacus asper** 'the savage (*OLD* 9) Dacian'; for the collective singular see *Parthum* 19.12n. The Dacians were a tribe north of the Danube, and their inroads into Roman territory were feared by contemporary poets, e.g., *S.* 2.6.53 *'numquid de Dacis audisti?'* and Virg. *G.* 2.497 *coniurato descendens Dacus ab Histro.* In 29–28 M. Crassus secured a triumph over them (see J. J. Wilkes in *CAH* X 549–50).   **profugi Scythae:** for the Scythians see 19.10n. *profugi*, also found at 4.14.42 *profugus Scythes*, is taken to refer to their supposed strategy of retreat before an invader, rather than their nomadic lifestyle. The word is high style, used mainly in poetry and historiography (*TLL* X 2.1736.33–5).

10 In this line the subject words, denoting civilized communities, are all in antithesis with the barbarian peoples of the previous line. Hence it is assumed that the -*que* attached to *urbes* does not connect the two lines, but rather connects *urbes* with *gentes*, so that -*que* ... -*que* correspond (26.12n.).

10–11 Latium ... | ... barbarorum: another polar expression.

12 purpurei = *purpurati* 'dressed in purple', a poetic sense (*OLD* 1b) first found in H.; purple-dyed fabric symbolized high status, cf. *OLD purpura* 3. H.'s expression has had extraordinary success among English poets. The translator of Abraham Cowley's *Of Plants* 2.330 'The purple tyrant wisely you expel' took it straight from the original Latin version of the poem, line 319; Gray has it in the *Hymn to Adversity* 7 'purple tyrants vainly groan', and Blake probably got the phrase in *The Grey Monk* 34 from Gray.

13–16 This particular fear applies only to the tyrants, cf. 2.8.21–4 for a similar sentence.   **pede proruas:** alliteration emphasizes the brutal action. **stantem columnam:** symbolic of the ruler as the prop supporting his realm, cf. Ennius, *Annales* 343 Skutsch *regni uersatum summam uenere columnam.*

15 ad arma . . . ad arma: the repetition seems to reflect the actual cry (*TLL* II 594.30–5), cf. Ov. *Met.* 12.241 *certatimque omnes uno ore 'arma, arma' loquuntur.* **17–24** The personified associates of *Fortuna* are described. The symbolism of 17–20 is very obscure, and the whole section has long caused difficulties of interpretation. Numberger 1997: 298–300 provides a full, if bewildering, account of attempts to unravel these stanzas.

17 semper: 32.9–10n.   **anteit** scans as two syllables by synizesis. The verb suggests the lictors who walked in front of a Roman magistrate to clear the way or enforce his will.   **Necessitas:** a personification (2.34n.) peculiar to H., perhaps cloned on the Greek Ananke. But there was also an Etruscan goddess, Athrpa (= Greek Atropos), who seems to have had very similar attributes to H.'s *Necessitas*, see *LIMC* I 757–8 and III 1–2 for a mirror on which she is depicted with hammer and nail. For *saeua* see 12.43n.

17–20 *Necessitas* is depicted with the attributes of the building trade: nails, dowels, clamps, and lead, all of which are used to bind, connect, or fasten parts of a structure. For illustrations of nails see D–S 12:1238, for dowels and 'pi' clamps see Adam 1999: 55–6.

18 clauos trabales: nails to hold beams together were long and so proverbial of fixity, cf. 3.24.5–7 *si figit adamantinos | summis uerticibus dira Necessitas | clauos* (Otto 1890: 85, West 1995: 171 and 173). For the fastening wedge or dowel (*cuneus*) see *OLD* 1b.

19–20 seuerus | uncus . . . plumbum: a 'pi' clamp set into a solder of lead was used to bind blocks of stone securely together. *seuerus* is variously translated, but 'immovable' (Rudd) fits the bill.

21–8 'One of the most difficult passages in Horace', justly remarked West 1995: 170, whose account follows Perret 1970. Perret's basic point is that *Spes* and *Fides* are plainly stated to be attendants of *Fortuna* (*colit*), so when she abandons her favourites, they follow her lead (*nec comitem abnegat*). *at* 25 'whereupon' is continuative and moves the picture from the abstract to the human plane, introducing the immediate response of humanity to the departure of *Fortuna*: men too abandon the fallen. Perret endorses the interpretations of the scholiasts, and some pre-Renaissance scholars, who reckoned that *Spes* must here be the hope which hangers-on entertain of *Fortuna*'s pet. *Fides* he takes to be the financial credit men secure in their prosperity; parodistically she is hypocritically veiled, not in a liturgical garment but in a rag (*pannus*). The only problem is that Perret does not account adequately for *rara*. It seems better therefore to take *Fides* to mean 'loyalty' in general, which is a scarce (*OLD rarus* 5) virtue (cf. 18.16).

21–2 albo . . . | uelata panno: commentators cite Livy's account of Numa's (alleged) cult of *Fides*, 1.21.4, whose priests performed sacrifice with a hand covered to the fingers. But Livy does not specify the garment's colour, and H. does not specify a part of the body (he seems to have in mind the veiling of the head, normal for Romans performing sacred rites). The standard interpretation also fails to take any account of *pannus*, which is not the word one would expect to describe a priest's dress, since its primary sense is 'rag' (*OLD* 1); its use upset the ancient commentators (cf. *TLL* x 1.232.32–3), who reckoned its lowly status hinted that the poor honour *Fides* more than the rich.   **colit | ... abnegat:** for the singular see *iuuat* 2.38n. H. borrowed *abnego* from his friend Virgil, who seems to have coined what remained a largely poetic verb (*TLL* i 111.2–7).

22 comitem 'companionship': often in poetry a concrete noun is used instead of one expressing the abstract idea, for vividness' sake (H–S 751); for the phraseology cf. Minucius Felix, *Octauius* 1.4 *non respuit comitem* 'he did not repudiate my companionship'. The basic problem, as stated above, is to know whom *Spes* and *Fides* accompany: *Fortuna* (so Naylor, Ker, Perret, West) or the households which *Fortuna* is abandoning (so most commentators, and Rudd). The interpretation favoured here is that the once-powerful houses are utterly deserted once Fortune removes her support; nothing is left. Cf. Ovid, *Ex Ponto* 2.3.10 *et cum Fortuna statque caditque Fides* with Galasso's n.

23–4 utcumque: 17.10n.   **mutata ... | ueste:** *Fortuna* is imagined as changing into a mourning outfit as she abandons her former favourites. Perret notes that the phrase might evoke the change of dress of the general going out to war.

25–6 at 'whereupon' (*OLD* 2, *TLL* ii 1004.26–83) is here assumed not to be adversative, but continuative, as argued by Ker 1964: 42–4, who supports his interpretation by the use of *at* in *Epode* 5.25, where it is clearly not adversative (see Mankin's n.).   **uulgus infidum:** proverbially so, cf. *mobilium* 1.7n. and Otto 1890: 378; *infidum* clearly harks back to *Fides* 21. Shackleton Bailey and Rudd accept the Scottish scholar Alexander Cunningham's (1650/60-1730) emendation *ut* for *et*, but this produces awkward word order, *retro* being sandwiched between *meretrix* and *periura*.   **cedit:** for the number see *iuuat* 2.38n.

26–8 cadis | cum faece siccatis: for drinking to the lees, cf. 3.15.16. The false friends have taken all they could, then slipped away.   **ferre ... dolosi** 'too cunning to bear' (Rudd), 'evasive about sharing' (Quinn), a unique use of the infinitive with *dolosus* (1.18n., *TLL* v 1.1856.53–4, glossing 'fere id quod dolose recusantes').   **iugum:** a proverbial symbol of sharing a task as equal partners (Otto 1890: 178).

29–32 After the long introduction H. makes his prayer for the success of Roman arms in adding to the empire the remotest quarters of the earth, Britain and the Far East.

29–30 iturum Caesarem in ... | ... Britannos: Augustus is imagined as setting out to (re)conquer the Britons. This points up an uncertainty about their status. They could be regarded as having been conquered by Julius Caesar. Augustus is credited by the historian Dio with a repeated intention to invade the island (49.38.2, 53.22.5 and 25.2), and he may even have claimed it belonged to the Romans (Livy fr. Bk 135 Weissenborn; Servius on Virg. *G.* 3.25). But he never realized the intention (if he ever seriously entertained it), which Claudius in due course carried out. The poets seem to have swallowed the propaganda (and furthered it), without detriment to themselves or to the *princeps* (Syme 1978: 50–1, 1991: 386); N–R on 3.3–4 still insist that they are mouthpieces of official policy (cf. 2.22n.).   **ultimos | orbis** 'out on the world's edge'. *orbis* is a partitive genitive (so *OLD ultimus* 2b, H–S 54): poetic style; for its sense see 12.57n. Poets from Catullus (11.11–12) on enjoyed stressing the remoteness of Britain.

30–2 iuuenum recens | examen 'the fresh swarm of young soldiers'. For the sense of *iuuenum* see *OLD iuuenis²* 1b. *examen* is used metaphorically of any throng, cf. Justinus 25.2.8 *Gallorum ea tempestate tantae fecunditatis iuuentus fuit ut Asiam omnem uelut examine aliquo implerent.*   **Eois ... | partibus** 'eastern quarters' (*OLD pars* 12). *Eous* is a loan-word, and so poetic diction; the Latin for 'eastern' is *oriens*. The dative was naturally used in Latin with the gerundive, here *timendum*, to denote the person for whom the necessity exists (*NLS* §202, G–L §§354–5); it thus in effect came to be regarded as an agent. Here the place-names stand for the inhabitants. For the expression cf. *S.* 2.5.62 *iuuenis Parthis horrendus* and *Epist.* 2.1.256 *formidatam Parthis ... Romam.*   **Oceanoque rubro:** H. may be alluding to the campaign against Arabia, since *rubro* refers to the arm of the encircling Ocean known as the Red Sea; cf. 29.2.

33–40 H. has just referred to new recruits in the Roman army, who will be engaged in foreign campaigns. Since his thought often moves forward by antitheses, he reflects, in an emotional coda, on the criminality of the civil wars in which his own generation was occupied; cf. 2.12–15 and 2.1.29–36 (a very similar passage). By a further antithesis he acknowledges that the younger generation too (*iuuentus* 36) is little better. He prays therefore that Rome's martial energy be directed against eastern enemies, a thought similar to 2.21–2. There is a small problem of interpretation: whom is H. addressing with the verb *diffingas*? The standard interpretation is *Fortuna*, who after all is addressed throughout, and there has been no change of addressee. But Rudd's translation makes it clear he believes the addressee has changed to the *iuuentus*: 'O that you would forge afresh your blunted swords.'

33–4 heu heu: 15.9n.   **cicatricum ... sceleris ... | fratrumque:** for the syllepsis see 8.16n. In effect the three words combine to form a single idea: 'the criminal wounds brothers' have inflicted upon each other in civil war.

34–5 dura ... | aetas 'a hard-hearted generation' (*OLD aetas* 8c), in apposition to *nos. refugimus* and *liquimus* 36 are like *petimus* 3.38 in that H. associates himself with the wrong-doing.

35–6 intactum: cf. *non tangenda* 3.24n.   **nefasti:** first used as a noun here, to supply the genitive of the indeclinable *nefas*.   **liquimus?:** for the pause cf. 37.12 (and N–H on 2.13.7).

36–8 Sacrilege generally is in H.'s mind; N–H collect instances during the civil wars, but strangely neglect Julius Caesar's robbing of the state treasury, kept in the temple of Saturn, which is referred to by Appian, *Civil wars* 2.41, Suet. *Iul.* 54.3, and made much of by Lucan, 3.114–68. Killing fellow citizens was bad, but

sacrilege was, in Roman eyes, equally bad, since it destroyed the *pax deorum*. It is
not that H.'s tone is false (so N–H), rather the Roman mind-set regarded sacrilege
as a capital offence, which Cicero ranked with treason and violence against one's
parents, *De finibus* 3.32 (see N–H on 2.13.2 *sacrilega manu* and Robinson 1973).

36 unde 'from what'.

38–40 o utinam: for the hiatus see 1.2n.   **diffingas** 'refashion', a verb
only found in H. (also at 3.29.47), so presumably a coinage. The prefix *dis-* here
signifies the reversal of a previous process (see *OLD* s.v.).   **retusum** 'blunted'
from excessive use in civil war.   **in** 'against' (*OLD* 9), to be taken with *diffingas*.
The monosyllabic preposition at line-end effects enjambement.   **Massage-
tas:** a nomadic tribe in the region east of the Caspian Sea. H.'s ethnography is
as usual exotic, since the tribe, which Alexander the Great had conquered,
was subsequently absorbed into the Dahae (cf. Virg. *Aen.* 8.728 *indomiti ...
Dahae*).   **ferrum:** 2.21n.

*

It was noted at the outset that H. does not name his divinity. Localizing her
cult at Antium helped to identify her initially as the Italian *Fortuna* (see the *OCD*
art. 'Fortuna/Fors', 606, and Kajanto 1981). But H. then extends the horizon to
include among her worshippers remote barbarian tribes, and he endows her with
something of the capricious and amoral character of the Greek *Tyche* (see the *OCD*
art. 'Tyche', 1566). Champeaux 1982: 168 rightly sees that H. presents a generic
image of *Fortuna*; such lack of specificity indicates that the prayer is literary, not
something appropriate to an actual cult. H.'s *Fortuna* is a world power; composite
in form, she seems here to be more benevolent than in the previous poem, but
she is not without her irresponsible side. In addition to the divinity of cult, *Fortuna*
also played a dominant role in popular morality (see Morgan 2007: 378 Index s.v.
'fortune'), and she was the object of philosophical disquisition, which might be
channelled into literary culture in, say, a tragedy by Pacuvius (fr. 366–75, quoted
by the anonymous *Auctor ad Herennium* 2.36–7). In short, H.'s *Fortuna* is very much
an amalgamation of diverse elements. Perhaps one reason for emphasizing her
wilfulness is that it makes for a more exciting poem. If *Fortuna* were the generally
benevolent Italian power, conciliating her would not perhaps take much trouble.
By adding the more arbitrary use of power characteristic of *Tyche*, H. creates an
agent whose good will may prove harder to secure or maintain. But the arbitrary
behaviour of H.'s *Fortuna* must go deeper, and is to be explained by the unexpected
turn the poem takes at its end. After the long preamble, H. makes his request
to the goddess at lines 29–32, where the poem might end. But the principle of
contrast suddenly asserts itself, and foreign campaigns make him think of the
recent civil wars, during which many men probably thought they saw the hand
of an arbitrary power, which might well be called Chance, directing events. So
whilst the main prayer seems to be for the success of Roman arms abroad, the
emotional weight is found in the concluding prayer for an end to civil conflict
and its attendant crimes against men and gods.

36

Metre: 'fourth' asclepiad (see Introduction 7–8)

1–9 H. announces, in one long sentence, a sacrifice and feast, *cena aduenticia*, in honour of the return from Spain of Numida, who will be welcomed by his loving friends.

1–2 Et ture et fidibus ... | ... et uituli sanguine: polysyndeton links the essential elements of the sacrifice, which will provide food for dinner. For incense see 19.14n.   **iuuat | placare:** for the infinitive see 1.4n.   **debito** 'owed', by reason of the vow made by Numida's friends when he set out so as to ensure his safe return; cf. 2.7.17 *obligatam ... dapem* and *Epist.* 1.3.36 *pascitur in uestrum reditum uotiua iuuenca.*

3 custodes ... deos: for the attributive use of the substantive see 1.1n. *atauis ... regibus.*   **Numidae:** unknown, but he is unlikely to be a fictive character, given his close friendship with Lamia (7).

4 Hesperia ... ab ultima indicates Spain, for *Hesperia* 'the western land' meant Italy (from the Greek point of view, cf. Virg. *Aen.* 1.530 *est locus, Hesperiam Grai cognomine dicunt*). Either way *Hesperia* is poetic diction.   **sospes:** cf. 3.14.9–10 *iuuenumque nuper | sospitum*, of troops returned in 24 from the Cantabrian campaign in Spain with Augustus; Numida may have been one of them.

6 nulli: 24.10n.   **tamen:** suggests an ellipse of the concessive idea in the previous clause: though he will have *many* a kiss for his dear friends, he will nonetheless have yet *more* for Lamia. This move from a group to an individual is also seen at 24.9–10.   **diuidit** 'shares out' (*OLD* 6c). There is a slight zeugma here, since the verb is only really appropriate with line 5.   **oscula:** return from a journey was one of the commonest occasions for a kiss between men; examples are provided by Sittl 1890: 38 or Kroll, art. 'Kuß', *RE* Supplementband v 515.25–48, and see especially Catull. 9.9 *os oculosque sauiabor* (he kisses his friend Veranius on his return from Spain).

7 dulci Lamiae: for Lamia see 26.8; H. too was very fond of him. For *dulcis* see 1.2n. *dulce.*

7–9 memor | ... togae: the appended phrase explains why Lamia is so dear to Numida: they have been close since boyhood.

8 actae ... puertiae 'his boyhood passed' (*OLD ago* 31); this (?colloquial) syncopated form of *pueritia* is unique in the language (*lamna* at 2.2.2 and *Epist.* 1.15.36 is much commoner; so too *soldus* at *S.* 1.2.113 with Lejay's n., 2.5.6; *surpuerat Carm.* 4.13.20, *surpite S.* 2.3.283).   **non alio rege** 'with no other as king'; the reference is much debated, but it seems to indicate Lamia as the acknowledged superior of the two.

9 mutatae ... togae = *mutatio togae* (1.4–5n.). At about the age of fifteen or sixteen, a Roman boy laid aside the purple-bordered *toga praetexta* and donned the pure white *toga uirilis* (D–S v 352–3 provides ample details). He was then formally introduced to his fellow-citizens in the Forum. Whilst this ceremony could be performed at any time, it was traditional for all boys of the appropriate age to celebrate this rite of passage at the festival of the Liberalia on 17 March (Scullard 1981: 92, and see Ovid, *Fasti* 3.771–90), hence here *simul*.

10–16 H. describes in a negative list what is needed to make the party go with a bang.

10 Cressa ... nota: i.e., 'chalk', which produced a white mark symbolizing felicity; more usually the markers were white stones, a custom the elder Pliny ascribed to the Thracians (*Nat. hist.* 7.131); see Otto 1890: 64–5, and Fordyce on Catull. 107.6 *candidiore nota*. It remains unclear what was marked with the chalk: a calendar, perhaps. The Latin word for chalk *creta* had nothing to do with the island of Crete, even in popular etymology (the connection is not found until Isidore, *Origines* 16.1.6). H. thus seems to be making something of a joke. The adjective is poetic (for the normal adjective see 26.2).

11 promptae: of wine, as at 3.21.8 *promere* and 3.28.2 *prome*; cf. 37.5 *depromere*.

12 morem in Salium: *in* expresses manner 'after the fashion ... ' (*OLD* 18); the expression reappears at 4.1.28 *in morem Salium*. *Salius* is less usual than *Saliaris*, being found only twice in H., apart from a single instance in a first-century BC juristic text. The Salii formed one of the priestly fraternities (*sodalitates*) of Rome, associated with Mars. Their ritual dance was, as the name implies, a vigorous leap (*salio*). They were also noted, as indeed were most priestly associations at Rome, for sumptuous dinners (cf. 37.2–4n.). See *OCD* art. Salii and *sodales*.   **requies pedum:** for dancing in private see 9.16n.

13 multi ... meri: the descriptive genitive attached directly to a noun, especially a proper name, is mainly poetic style, cf. 3.9.7 *multi Lydia nominis*, S. 1.1.33 *magni formica laboris*; literary prose tended to favour apposition, 'formica, animal magni laboris', 'Damalis, puella multi meri'; so 3.7.4–5 *constantis iuuenem fidei* | *Gygen*. The development of the descriptive genitive helped Latin get round its reluctance to generate compound adjectives, so characteristic of Greek. For this phrase cf. Ov. *Met.* 14.252 *nimii Elpenora uini*.

14 Bassum: an unknown friend of Numida's, clearly a good drinker.   **Threicia ... amystide** 'at the Thracian draught' i.e., drinking a substantial amount without stopping. For the epithet see 24.13n.; *amystis* is a loan-word, and H. is the first to use it (indeed it is never used again in classical Latin). The whole expression seems owed to Callimachus, *Aetia* fr. 178.11 Pfeiffer.

16 apium: wild celery had a pleasant fragrance (Theophrastus, *Historia plantarum* 1.12.2), and its pliancy (Theocritus 7.68) also made it suitable for garlands, cf. 2.7.23–5 (quoted above in 4.9n.), 4.11.3 *nectendis apium coronis*. It does not wilt rapidly, hence *uiuax*, unlike the short-lived lily.

17 putres 'melting', an unusual sense (*OLD* 1e), picked up by Persius, 5.58 *ille in Venerem putris*; cf. Apuleius, *Metamorphoses* 3.14.5 *oculos ... libidine marcidos*. It seems to be a loan-shift from τακερός as found in, e.g., Ibycus, *GL* III 287.2 τακέρ' ὄμμασι δερκόμενος 'gazing meltingly with his eyes', a poem H. often laid under contribution (see Mayer on *Epist.* 1.1.8 *equum*, to which this passage should be added); LSJ 2 collects more examples of τακερός applied metaphorically to the eyes.

18 deponent 'will rest them upon', an uncommon sense (*OLD* 1b), perhaps a loan-shift from Callimachus fr. 571 Pfeiffer ὦ κούροισιν ἐπ᾽ ὄθματα λίχνα φέροντες 'oh you who rest lustful eyes on boys'.

19 adultero: Numida, her new boyfriend; cf. 33.9n. The simple ablative of separation with *diuello*, rather than *a/ab*, is poetic style.

20 lasciuis 'wanton' is first applied to plants by H., who is followed by the elder Pliny, *Nat. hist.* 17.5 (*TLL* vii 2.985.48–50, and cf. 982.81–3); the word in its erotic sense suits the girl.   **hederis:** for the plural see 1.29n.; here the singular would cause difficulties of scansion. For the erotic comparison cf. *Epode* 15.5 *artius atque hedera* and Ferber 2007: 104–5.   **ambitiosior** 'more embracing'. The use of this word in its literal or original sense is exceptional (as is its comparative degree, see *OLD* 1). Fraenkel in his commentary on Aeschylus, *Agamemnon* II: 90, n. 1, insisted that poets had the right to restore to words an original meaning lost in everyday usage; he noted the present example and compared H.'s use of *euenit* 'emerges' at 4.4.65 (cf. *OLD* 1).

*

H. is something of an absent presence in this poem (Cairns 1972: 195–7, Syndikus 2001: 320), unlike Catullus in a similar situation, warmly described in poem 9. Numida is presumably a friend of his, but the friendship celebrated is between Numida and Lamia, hence the view that the poem might have been commissioned by Lamia. Hence too we should assume the sacrifice of line 2 is Lamia's, not H.'s (*contra* Rudd: 'which I have promised'). If all of this is so, H.'s somewhat detached tone becomes understandable, even appropriate, and is of a piece with the detached tone we find when H. is talking about other people's love-affairs. West 1995: 176–81 emphasizes that H. suggests rather than expresses emotion, and so offers a sympathetic reading of a poem generally marginalized. Esser 1976: 93 draws attention to directive changes of mood and tense: present indicatives (1, 6) describe the moment; past participles (8, 9) establish the bond between Numida and Lamia. Then jussive subjunctives (12, 14, 15) prepare the way for the *cena aduenticia* – in fact here H. seems to be taking on himself the role of master of ceremonies (Murray 1993: 94 and 100 plausibly suggests that the poem could actually have been performed at the celebratory dinner). Final futures (18, 19) focus upon a single guest at the party, the hard-drinking Damalis, entwined about her new boyfriend, Numida.

37

Metre: alcaic (see Introduction 8)

1–4 H. invites his companions (*sodales*) to prepare a celebration (possibly private) in accordance with Roman traditions. The ode opens with a grand tricolon crescendo, each limb of which begins with *nunc* in anaphora and asyndeton, thus stressing that celebration is finally in order.

1 Nunc est bibendum: a motto (12.1n.) drawn from Alcaeus, *GL* 1 332 Νῦν χρῆ μεθύσθην, prepares the learned reader for what is to come, for Alcaeus went on to say that the drinking party was organized to celebrate the death of the tyrant Myrsilus. H.'s celebration will have a similar motive, the death of an enemy, but that is not mentioned yet. The openings of the two poems also differ considerably in tone: μεθύσθην means 'to get drunk', *bibendum* is less drastic (cf. *potabis* 20.1n.), because his celebration is to be more sober (see *ebria* 12n.). Drinking is also to be a keynote of the whole poem; as in 5, the metaphor/image is structural, not ornamental.

libero: a suggestive word. Octavian's propaganda put it about that Cleopatra sought to enslave Rome. By defeating her he championed the freedom of the Roman people, a slogan found on a coin of 28 (E–J 18 = Braund 11).

2–4 Saliaribus | . . . dapibus: the feasts of the priestly colleges and fraternities at Rome were proverbial for their luxury (Otto 1890: 306), cf. 2.14.28 *mero pontificum potiore cenis*. But since the Salii (for whom see 36.12n.) were associated with Mars, their feasting is peculiarly appropriate for the successful end of a war. For *dapibus* see 32.13n., though here it is rather a technical term for religious feasts (*OLD* 1).

3 puluinar: a cushioned couch on which images or symbols of the gods were placed during the occasional ceremony known as *lectisternium*, a sacrificial feast (not originally of thanksgiving, as here) which the gods were invited to share (see *OCD* s.vv. *puluinar, lectisternium* (where private rites are noted) and Dyck on Cicero, *Catilinarian* 3.23.1–2 for the *supplicatio* 'thanksgiving'). Here the singular is poetic, since couches are clearly meant.

4 tempus erat 'it is high time'. In this expression (largely confined to poetry, as Oakley noted on Livy 8.5.3) the imperfect expresses an impatient desire; it is not easily explained. Brink on *AP* 19 *sed nunc non erat his locus* urged that the use of the imperfect in Latin verse needed to be surveyed in greater detail.

5–12 Having ordered an immediate celebration, H. explains why it was not appropriate before: the Roman state was threatened by an enemy, whose recent defeat justifies festivities, private and religious.

5–6 antehac nefas: understand *erat. antehac* scans as two syllables by synizesis, i.e. the *e* is in effect elided. The adverb probably sounded archaic by H.'s time. It had been the preferred word in Plautus and Terence, but it lost favour with Cicero, who advanced the claims of *antea* (*TLL* II 137.73–81). *antehac* appears only here in H. and sparsely in historiography (Sall. *Catil.* 25.4, Livy 40.52.6, 3x in Tac. *Ann.* only). **depromere:** 9.7n. The prepositional prefix *de-* was, for metrical purposes, separable, so there is normal word-break after the fifth syllable, a 'quasi-caesura', cf. 18.16. **Caecubum:** sc. *uinum* (20.9n.). H. urged Maecenas to produce this wine to celebrate the battle of Actium at *Epode* 9.1–4. Against this Italian wine is set an Egyptian at 14. **auitis** 'ancestral', largely a poetic sense, as Ihm acknowledges briefly in *TLL* II 1442.23–5; the evidence is more conveniently set out in the *OLD* article.

6–7 Capitolio | regina: enjambement heightens the shocking antithesis. The Capitol was the most sacred hill of Rome's seven, as the site of the temple of Jupiter Optimus Maximus. To attack it was a sort of sacrilege. Ovid picked up the point at *Met.* 15.828 *seruitura suo Capitolia nostra Canopo* (Canopus was a town and island in the western branch of the Nile's mouth). *regina* = Cleopatra, queen of Egypt, by the figure antonomasia, but it was consistent with contemporary propaganda that she was too abominable to be named (see Nisbet 1984: 1–18, especially 12 = 1995: 161–81, especially 174). *regina*, like *rex*, was hateful to Romans, doubly so, because it also denotes a female, who naturally should have no sway over men. But there is more to it than that. H., again consistently with propaganda, has airbrushed her consort, Marcus Antonius, out of the picture, since victory over a Roman could not be celebrated by a triumph. The emphasis is thus solely on the queen and the trappings of her court (a similar strategy is found in *Epode* 9, where Watson's introduction, pp. 310–14, should be consulted).   **dementes:** the epithet is transferred from the queen to the ruin she was planning; pseudo-Acro recognized the hypallage (cf. K–S I 221, Bell 1923: 326).

8 funus 'destruction', 8.15n.   **et:** postponed (2.9n.).

9–10 contaminato ... | ... uirorum: H. dwells with moral horror on the eunuchs of the royal court (see Balsdon 1979: 277–8), to enhance the awfulness of the queen's designs. It is characteristic of the elevated style of the lyrics that H. avoids plain language; in the iambic style of an epode however he can refer bluntly to 'wrinkled eunuchs' (*spadonibus ... rugosis, Epode* 9.13–14). Tacitus was struck by H.'s expression and recycled it at *Ann.* 15.37.4 to describe the eunuch who 'married' Nero: *uni ex illo contaminatorum grege* (cf. too *Hist.* 2.71.1 with Ash's n.).   **morbo** 'vice' (*OLD* 3b), viz sexual perversion; causal ablative with *turpium*.   **uirorum:** ironic, in the circumstances.

10–11 quidlibet impotens | sperare 'uncontrolled in her hoping for anything at all'. H. alone used the infinitive with *impotens* (*TLL* VII 1.671.26; cf. 1.18n.), but he had good precedent in its use with *potens* (*OLD* 3a).

12 ebria is given maximum emphasis by its position and the strong pause after it (35.36n.); it underscores the theme of drink pervading the poem. Cleopatra's metaphorical 'drunkenness' is in contrast with the sober *bibendum* of the opening line. Her drinking, a slur in the propaganda battle, is also mentioned by Propertius, 3.11.56 *assiduo lingua sepulta mero* (a poem worth comparing with ours, for the crudity of its gloating).

furorem pickes up *dementes* 7.

13 uix una sospes nauis ab ignibus 'the survival from the flames of scarcely a single ship', a construction explained at 1.4–5n. (K–S I 770). This is a reference to Octavian's use of fire against Antony's fleet in the naval engagement at Actium on 2 September 31 (Dio 50.34), but H. may also recall that Antony had burned his superfluous ships beforehand, though he spared some sixty of Cleopatra's (see Pelling on Plutarch, *Life of Antony* 64.1). Moreover, during the battle Cleopatra bolted and so saved the bulk of her fleet (Dio 50.33; see the helpful account of the battle by Pelling on Plutarch, *Life of Antony* 65–6, pp. 278–80 with map, or *CAH* x 59). H. is therefore exaggerating, as Porphyrio recognized.

14 lymphatam 'deranged', a poetic word, which Varro felt needed explaining in *De lingua Latina* 7.87 (the book is devoted to elucidating poetic diction): Latin *lympha* was the same as Greek *nympha*, and just as Greeks believed that those whom the water sprites seized went mad, so Romans spoke of the deranged as *lymphati*. Varro's etymology is apparently correct, see Sommer 1914: 69. It may be noted that the usual 'caesura' after the fifth syllable of the alcaic hendecasyllable is here overridden; the effect may suggest drunken licence (Raven 1965: 146).   **Mareotico:** understand *uino*. The wine came from Lake Mareotis (mod. Mariut) near Alexandria, the Hellenic capital city of the kingdom of Egypt.

16–17 Caesar ab Italia: Caesar's name appears at the mid-point of the poem, and its juxtaposition with *Italia* may be significant. H. on the one hand indicates the threat posed not just to Rome, but to Italy as a whole. On the other he may be hinting at Octavian's claim to have had 'all Italy' sworn to support him (see Syme 1939: 284–8). The first syllable of *Italia* is naturally short, but poets, perhaps even earlier than Catull. 1.5, adopted from Greek verse (e.g., Sophocles, *Antigone* 1119, Callimachus, *Hymn* 3.58) the lengthened *i*.   **uolantem:** understand *reginam* (not *mentem*, obviously). The participle forms a gliding transition to the first part of the following simile.   **remis adurgens** 'closely pursuing with oars'; the verb is perhaps a coinage of H.'s. The panegyrist exaggerates for dramatic effect, since Octavian took nearly a year to pursue his enemy (he had more pressing matters to deal with on the home front).

17–21 The first part of the simile is epic in tone, cf. Virg. *Aen.* 11.721–2 *quam facile accipiter . . . | consequitur . . . columbam.* It derives from Homer, *Il.* 22.139–40. The second part recalls *S.* 1.2.105–6 (itself derived from Callimachus, *Epigram* 31 Pfeiffer).

18 molles 'gentle' (*OLD* 14).   **citus:** a poetic word, found again at 24.

20 Haemoniae: a poetic name for Thessaly first found in H., derived from his reading of Hellenistic poetry; see Mayer 1986: 49–50.

20–1 daret ut catenis 'to put in chains' (*OLD do²* 20); the word order is poetic.   **fatale** 'deadly' (*OLD* 4b).   **monstrum:** commonly used in denigration of a person, especially in Republican political life (*TLL* VIII 1452.39–40, *OLD* 4).

21–2 quae: the pronoun naturally takes its gender from the person, *regina* (resumed at *uolantem*), rather than from the image applied to her, *monstrum*. This is known as *constructio ad sensum* (G–L §211 Rem. 1, K–S I 27). Here it serves to return her humanity to Cleopatra, as the tone of the poem changes.   **generosius | perire quaerens:** i.e., suicide was a nobler death than strangulation by the public executioner after Octavian's triumph. With a single word H. changes the tone and direction of his poem: no more abuse, but admiration for the queen's calm strength in adversity. This too has a panegyrical function: she was a formidable opponent after all (Syme 1939: 299). *generosius* also perhaps sustains the imagery of wine and drink, for *generosus* is used of choice wine at *Epist.* 1.15.18 (with Mayer's n.). The adverbial form is found in H. first, and remains rare; cf. *TLL* vi 2.1802.49–50. For *perire quaerens* see 16.26n.

22–3 nec muliebriter: similarly Velleius Paterculus 2.87 describes her as *expers muliebris metus*. *muliebriter* belongs to a class of adverbs generally avoided by poets (Axelson 1945: 62); it is therefore not surprising that this is its only appearance in classical poetry.   **expauit:** *expauesco* is not found before H. (*TLL* v 2.1600.57), so may be his coinage; the transitive use is also remarkable, though taken up in later prose. For *ensem* see 16.10n. Plutarch, *Antonius* 79.3, relates that when Proculeius entered the monument where Cleopatra was tending the dead Antony she tried to stab herself with a small sword she happened to be equipped with, but H. more probably has in mind that she stood her ground when Octavian invaded Alexandria (Dio 51.9.5–6).

23–4 nec ... | ... oras: Plutarch, *Antonius* 69.3–5, describes an unsuccessful plan to haul ships over the isthmus of Suez and sail to safety in the Red Sea.   **classe cita:** the poetic epithet (18n.) is commonly used of ships (*TLL* iii 1208.70–5); travel by sea was generally quicker in antiquity than by land.   **reparauit** 'reached' (*OLD* 2), sc. by 'exchanging' Egypt for the safe retreat, an unusual sense, if the text is deemed sound. N–H substantiate this meaning by citing *CLE* i 258.1 *quod licuit Iunianos reparare penates*, but the editor of that collection, Buecheler, disagreed with Orelli (an editor of H.), and took *reparare* there to mean the restoration of the house. The linguistic puzzle is intensified just because H. elsewhere uses the verb in perfectly normal senses.

25–6 ausa et ... | ... fortis et: this is not a fresh sentence, the participle and adjective are predicative of *quae* 21, giving the grounds for what H. has just asserted.   **ausa et** 'even with the strength of mind' (Rudd, adapted). *audeo* is probably derived from *auidus*, and so its original sense had nothing to do with boldness, but indicated the subject's will or desire (here admittedly in the midst of adversity); hence the common formula of politeness *sodes* (= *si audes*) 'if you will'. Cf. *Epist.* 1.2.40 *sapere aude*, with Mayer's n., and see *TLL* ii 1252.61–75. For *et*, 'even', see 12.11n.   **iacentem ... regiam** 'her palace brought low' (*OLD iaceo* 5, *TLL* vii 1.26.53–4, and *OLD regia* 1). In fact the palace was not destroyed, but the scene contrasts with the ruin Cleopatra designed for the Capitol (6–7).

26–7 fortis ... | tractare: H. is the first to attach the infinitive to *fortis* (cf. 1.18n.), a construction he fancies: cf. 3.3.50 *spernere fortior* and *S.* 2.7.85–6 *contemnere honores | fortis*; it is taken up by Statius (*TLL* vi 1.1161.32–5) and in W. Whiting's famous hymn, 'Eternal Father, strong to save'.   **et:** probably the simple connective, postponed (2.9n.); it was first recognized by Bentley on 3.4.69, but possibly he was prompted by the layout of the lemma in Lambinus' 1588 edition, which reads *fortis et asperas* ... , though in his text Lambinus put a comma after *fortis*. Some take *et* to be stronger, with the adverbial sense 'even', as in the previous line.

Details of the suicide of Cleopatra were uncertain, and her use of a snake, specifically the asp, was only cautiously reported by, e.g., Suetonius, *Augustus* 17.4 *perisse morsu aspidis putabatur*; there is a full discussion by Pelling on Plutarch, *Life of Antony* 85–6, pp. 318–20, and more briefly in *CAH* x 64–5. If Cleopatra did use a snake, it was probably the Egyptian cobra, the protector of the Pharaohs (its image adorned their crown).

asperas: see 23.9n., and used of a snake cf. Lucr. 5.33; but given the context there may be a hint at the sharpness of their fangs, hence 'sharp-toothed' (Rudd), or even at their species, ἀσπίς 'asp'.

27–8 atrum 'deadly' (*OLD* 9).   **combiberet** sustains the leading image of the poem, drinking.

29 deliberata morte 'having resolved to die', ablative absolute. In the perfect tenses *delibero* not uncommonly means 'decided upon' (after careful thought), *OLD* 3. Cleopatra is no longer in the grip of *furor* (12), nor is her mind crazed (14); she makes a rational choice.   **ferocior** 'more defiant' (*OLD* 3), i.e., than before she made up her mind to commit suicide. Defiance, *ferocia*, was a good quality, 'worthy of a Roman noble' (so Syme 1939: 299); at 6.3 and 35.10 the notion defines the Roman soldier and Latium respectively, and at 32.6 Alcaeus.

30 saeuis Liburnis: dative with *inuidens*. The scholiast, now followed by Sydenham 2010, took it to be ablative of comparison with *ferocior*. *saeuis* is an instance of focalization, since the galleys appear cruel only to one pursued by them; this point was made by Petrus Victorius (Pier Vettori, 1499–1585) in his *Variae lectiones* Lib. x Cap. ix: 'saeua autem liburna ipsa uocat ex affectu animi Cleopatrae'; he was also the first to explain the sentence and punctuate it correctly, pointing out that *liburnis* referred to a kind of ship: 'the liburnian was a fast, two-banked galley adapted from a craft developed among the Liburnians, piratical-minded dwellers of the Dalmatian coast' (Casson 1995: 141–2). Octavian had made successful use of them at Actium, or so the propaganda suggested (see Watson's helpful discussion of *Epode* 1.1–2, pp. 57–9).

30–1 scilicet 'evidently' qualifies a presumption or inference (*OLD* 3); cf. e.g. *Epist.* 1.10.2–3 *hac in re scilicet una | multum dissimiles*. The ironical use of the word (*OLD* 4), as at 3.5.25–6 *auro repensus scilicet acrior | miles redibit*, would be out of place.   **inuidens | ... deduci** 'refusing to be transported'; for the infinitive see 1.18n. *deduci* has a specific sense, of being brought back to Rome (*OLD* 10a).   **priuata:** in Roman public life *priuatus* designated any citizen who did not hold office, whether civil or military. It suggests Cleopatra's loss of her regal status, *regina* 7; cf. *S.* 1.3.142 *priuatusque magis uiuam te rege beatus*.

32 non humilis: for the understatement see 1.19–21n. It is in marked contrast with the preceding *superbo*, but reminds us that she was still in spirit a monarch.   **mulier** forms an internal ring-composition with *muliebriter* 22. By

H.'s day *mulier*, preferred by Plautus and Terence, had lost ground to *femina*, which better suited high style (*TLL* VIII 1571.50–62). The tone is appropriately down-to-earth. **triumpho** 'to/for a triumph' is probably dative (so Kießling); Livy writes *ad triumphum deducere* (28.32.7, 36.39.8, 42.34.10). For *superbo . . . triumpho* cf. 35.3–4.

*

Alcaeus provided no more than the springboard for this poem, a drinking party in celebration of the death of an enemy. The tone of the poems, as hinted in the observation on *bibendum*, is markedly different. The reason for the difference is to be sought in the character of the different enemies.

Alcaeus' Myrsilus was no Cleopatra. At most, he was a local tyrant in Mytilene, about whom all we know is to be derived from the poetry of his opponent. Myrsilus was not a player on the world stage, and such threat as he posed was restricted to his political rivals on the island of Lesbos, who knew him at first hand. His death (and we have no idea how he died) cheered the exiled Alcaeus and his gang, but it probably went unnoticed in the wider world and did not necessarily have any lasting effect on the fortunes of the poet (see Page 1955: 238). Very different was Cleopatra, and very different was H.'s relation to her.

Cleopatra ruled an ancient kingdom. She was unscrupulously adroit, wealthy, and powerful. As a national enemy, she arguably posed the greatest threat to Rome since Hannibal (so Pelling in *CAH* x 63). Her death, strange yet glamorous, marked the end of nearly two decades of civil and foreign wars. It also added virtually the last independent territory on the Mediterranean coast to the Roman empire. All taken in all, the battle of Actium and the subsequent conquest of Egypt decided the future of the Mediterranean world for centuries, and so Cleopatra's story would always figure largely in Roman, that is to say, world history. (Her death indeed has continued to inspire artists (Reni), poets (Shakespeare), and musicians (Berlioz).)

Unlike Alcaeus, H. had no personal knowledge of the individual whose death he celebrated; if he was at the battle of Actium, he may have seen her fleet escape. His knowledge of events and of the key players in them depended on such information as was available at the time (there is no evidence that Pollio's history included events of the 30s). Presumably he had no personal animus against the Queen of Egypt. He speaks rather as a Roman who was relieved that a foreign (and how foreign, cf. *Epode* 9.11–16!) threat to his own community and culture has been permanently removed. He thus sounds a measured tone at the outset, in urging his companions (not a political faction) to prepare a thanksgiving to the gods on the occasion of the death of a national enemy. It needs to be borne in mind as well that the poet's distance from Cleopatra relieves him of the frequently made claim that he is the voice or echo of Augustan propaganda (so, e.g., Pöschl 1991: 94–5, with n. 58). Such a claim assumes that H. knew as much about contemporary events in remote places like Actium and Egypt as modern historians believe they do. It might be said however that H. only knew what the agents chose to tell. There were conflicting stories at the time, and he might more fairly be seen as the victim rather than the echo of propaganda. The only detail which he must have known to be his own exaggeration was the claim that Octavian pursued Cleopatra hotfoot. That said, it is clear that he does endorse some contemporary 'spin', especially in the elision of M. Antonius from the course of events (Propertius too left him out of his 'Actium' poem, 4.6). But that was in conformity with the official *damnatio memoriae*. It is also worth reflecting that H. may personally have felt that had Antony and Cleopatra won at Actium, Roman life would have changed for the worse.

Structurally considered, this poem reverses a common pattern in the odes: it starts with the response ('Let's drink!'), and then proceeds to depict the events which generated it. The antecedent (*antehac* 5) situation is then brilliantly sketched in three sections, which move forward in chronological order. The first section, 5–12, is the earliest in time and describes Cleopatra's hopes and ambitions, with denigration of her character. (It has already been noted that drinking is the key linking theme throughout.) The second section, 12–22, progresses to the battle of Actium and its effects. Annulling Cleopatra's hopes and ambitions, it focuses upon the realities of her defeat (*ueros timores* 15). This is arguably the most important section, spanning as it does the middle of the poem. Caesar is prominent, and the whole is ornamented with epic-style similes. One paradoxical link between the first and second sections is frustrated expectations: Cleopatra was preparing destruction (*funus parabat* 8), which she never achieved, and Caesar aimed to enchain 'the monster of doom', but he never actually caught her. Dashed hopes are emphasized at the outset: both the second and the third section begin with adversatives. The adversative at 12 is manifest, *sed*, but the adversative at 21 is latent within the connecting relative *quae*; Wickham rightly translated this as 'but she'. We thus have come full circle: the first section focused on Cleopatra, the second on Octavian, and the last returns to the Queen of Egypt. That is where we need to be, since it is her death that is celebrated in the opening stanza, the 'response' to the situation set out in the body of the poem. The three sections are woven together very skilfully in that none of them chimes exactly with the stanzaic pattern. We move seamlessly from section to section.

38

Metre: sapphic (see Introduction 8)

1–4 H. tells his slave-boy that elaborate preparations for a drink are unwelcome.

1 Persicos ... apparatus: the prominently placed epithet, evocative of eastern luxury, contrasts with *simplici* 5. *apparatus* 'trappings' (*OLD* 3), thanks to the *ad-* prefix, echoed by *allabores* 5, suggests something superfluous.   **odi** 'have no use for' (cf. *oderit* 8.4n.). For *puer* see 19.14n.

2 coronae: 4.9n. The elaborate chaplets H. rejects were the sort made by professional *coronarii*, flowers woven (*nexae*) on to a strip of bast (*philyra*), the inner bark of the lime-tree.

3–4 mitte 'give up, stop'. *mitto* + infinitive is colloquial (see *OLD* 3b), and its imperative, like *fuge* 9.13n., serves as a substitute for *noli* in poetry; cf. Plautus, *Persa* 207 *mitte male loqui*, Lucr. 6.1056 *mirari mitte*, and Ov. *Met.* 3.614 *mitte precari*.   **sectari** 'go about in search of' (*OLD* 4).   **rosa . . . | sera:** it is clear from *arta | uite* 7–8 that the season is high summer, so in Italy roses would be well past their time.   **quo locorum:** *quo* is here weakened in sense, and virtually = *ubi*; the partitive genitive of *locus* (both singular and plural are found) is idiomatically added; see *TLL* VII 2.1604.55–76, especially 70, H–S 652, and cf. Cicero, *De diuinatione* 2.135 *quo illa loci nasceretur*.

5–8 H. now states his preferred arrangements.

5 simplici 'pure and simple, alone' (*OLD* 4). Prominently placed to contrast with *Persicos*, the epithet sets the seal upon the scene; Pyrrha had embodied the aesthetic quality of *simplicitas* (5.5). For *myrto* see 4.9n.

5–6 nihil allabores | . . . curo 'I'm not bothered about your troubling to add anything'. The now generally accepted interpretation (first proposed by the German schoolmaster, A. Meineke (1790–1870)) dismantled *nihil* so that the negative idea is to be taken with *curo*, and an object, *quidquam*, is to be supplied with *allabores*, thus: *non curo allabores quidquam*. The normal construction would include *ut*, but Lachmann illustrated the present (rare) usage in his note on Lucr. 6.231.   **allabores:** only found in H., here and at *Epod.* 8.20. The *ad*- prefix picks up *apparatus*, with its suggestion of the superfluous.   **sedulus** better suits the slave, eager to please, than H.; cf. the *sedulus hospes* of *S.* 1.5.71, the *strenua* Lyde of 3.28.3. This phraseology finds support in Seneca, *Phaedra* 1109 *sedulus . . . labor*, and Frontinus, *De aquaeductu* 130.2 *sedulo laborauimus*.

6–7 neque . . . | dedecet: for the understatement see 1.19–21n.   **myrtus:** the repetition from 5 in the same metrical *sedes* drives home H.'s point that there is nothing wrong with myrtle; Wills 1996: 389–90 calls it confirmatory.

7–8 me . . . | . . . bibentem: the personal ending, both of the poem and of the book, paints a scene of a solitary drinker attended by a single slave. Such a monoposiast, interpreted as the 'master of his possessions', is occasionally found on Greek vases (see Steinhart and Slater 1997: 207), but it is also a very common sepulchral image in the Roman world, one type of the 'Totenmahl' ('banquet of the dead'), described by Dunbabin 2003: 103–10. A scene of solitary, self-sufficient pleasure closes the book and forms a contrast both with the civic celebrations of the preceding poem and with the programmatic first ode of the collection.   **arta** suggests dense shade (so Porphyrio, and cf. *OLD artus¹* 9) and the restraint of the straggling shoots of the vine: 'tackled' was how Gerard Manley Hopkins translated it.

*

In the first ode H. aspired to a poet's crown of ivy; here we see him wearing the drinker's crown of myrtle: ring composition for the book as a whole. Since a crown was awarded to a victorious athlete and this poem is placed last, it could serve as a closural emblem of the book; cf. 3.30.15–16 (the end of both the poem and the collection), with N–R's final n., and Rutherford 1997: 49–50. But further symbolic interpretations are on offer, ably charted by Lowrie 1997: 164–75 (her own interpretation makes much of this little poem's position between two grander ones, 37 and 2.1, relating to the civil war).

Might the crown also symbolize poetry (so Davis 1991: 118–26, among many others)? If we go back to ode 26, the crown for Lamia is clearly a metaphor, just because it is sought from a Muse and because H. goes on to refer to *mei honores* (i.e., the poem he is writing; cf. 7.7). There is no such clear convertibility in this poem, since H. does not present himself as a singer. He could have written *canentem* as last word if he had wanted to, but the last word is *bibentem*: that projects the final image, the drinker, not the singer.

A related interpretation takes the myrtle's simplicity to have formal and stylistic implications, namely H.'s rejection of the grand and overblown. (Such an interpretation would be well supported if *artus* were ever used of a compact style of writing; but it is not.) Anyway, Fraenkel 1957: 298–9 toyed with this reading, which also has numerous followers, e.g. Murray 1993: 95, who emphasized the decision to end the book with this poem, and Fowler 2000: 259–60. But after all Fraenkel acknowledged that H. too had his grand style, when it was appropriate; an appeal to irony scarcely bridges the gap.

Another symbol is detected by some in the repeated reference to myrtle, a plant sacred to Venus (most recently Davis 1991: 126, West 1995: 191–3, Syndikus 2001: 334, n. 12). But it is hardly the case that whenever myrtle is specified for a crown, e.g., at 4.9 or especially 2.7.25, the context is eroticized. Contrariwise, at 36.16 plants for crowns are specified in an erotic context, but myrtle is not one of them. Once again, a symbolic/metaphoric interpretation seems unlikely; it was long ago rejected by Reitzenstein 1963: 15–16 and is anyway unnecessary.

This is not to say however that the image of the simple crown is inert. The poem repudiates anything unnecessary (*Persicos apparatus*) or unseasonable (*rosa sera*). Persia is remote, and the lingering rose is not easy to find (though that late bloom has become something of a fixation for contemporary critics, e.g., Commager 1962: 118–19). Myrtle on the other hand is commonplace and evergreen. The subtext then is one of H.'s favourites: *frui paratis*, enjoyment of what lies to hand (Nisbet 1995: 421–3 still favours this interpretation over any of the allegorical ones listed above).

For the last time we are faced with an interpretational stand-off. Some are content with an uncomplicated 'ethical' reading. Others find that insufficient (without denying the ethical element) and look for some sort of allegory, whether aesthetic or erotic. There is no way to reconcile these opposed camps.

BIBLIOGRAPHY

1 CITED TEXTS OF OR COMMENTARIES ON HORACE'S ODES

Bentley, R. 1711. Cambridge

Gow, J. 1896. *Q. Horati Flacci Carmina, liber epodon*, Cambridge

Keller, O. and A. Holder. 1899. *Q. Horati Flacci Carminum libri iiii* (edn. 2), Leipzig

Kiessling, A. 1884. *Q. Horatius Flaccus. Oden und Epoden*, Berlin

Klingner, F. 1959 (3rd edn). Leipzig

Lambinus, D. 1588. Paris

Mitscherlich, C. G. 1800. Leipzig

Nisbet, R. G. M. and M. Hubbard 1970. *A commentary on Horace: Odes Book 1*, Oxford

Orelli, I. C., I. G. Baiter, G. Hirschfelder 1886. *Q. Horatius Flaccus* 1: *Odae, Carmen Saeculare, Epodi*, Berlin

Page, T. E. 1895. *Q. Horatii Flacci Carminum libri IV, epodon liber*, London

Plessis, F. 1924. *Oeuvres d'Horace: Odes, épodes et chant séculaire*, Paris

Quinn, K. 1980. *Horace, the Odes*, Basingstoke and London

Shackleton Bailey, D. R. 2001 (4th edn). Munich and Leipzig

Smith, C. L. 1894. *The Odes and epodes of Horace*, Boston and London

Wickham, E. C. 1896 (3rd edn). *Quinti Horati Flacci Opera omnia*, 1: *The odes, carmen saeculare, and epodes*, Oxford

Wickham, E. C. and H. W. Garrod 1912 (2nd edn). Oxford

2 BIBLIOGRAPHICAL STUDIES

Doblhofer, E. 1992. *Horaz in der Forschung nach 1957*, Darmstadt

Draeger, G. and Angermann, M. 1975. *Horaz-Bibliographie*, Berlin

Kißel, W. 1981. 'Horaz 1936–1975. Eine Gesamtbibliographie,' *ANRW* II 31.3, 1485–98

Gesamtbibliographie 1976–1991 in Koster 1994: 154–63

Thummer, E. 1979. 'Horaz: Bericht über die Literatur der Jahre 1963–1975', *Anz. A.W.* 32: 21–66

3 BEST ENGLISH TRANSLATION

Rudd, N. 2004. *Horace*, Odes and Epodes (Loeb Classical Library 33), Cambridge, Mass. and London

4 CITED WORKS

Adam, J. P. 1999. *Roman building: materials and techniques*, London

Adams, J. N. 1973. 'The vocabulary of the speeches in Tacitus' historical works', *BICS* 20: 124–44

1982. *The Latin sexual vocabulary*, London

Adams, J. N. and Mayer, R. G. (eds.) 1999. *Aspects of the language of Latin poetry* (= *Proceedings of the British Academy* 93), Oxford

Albert, W. 1988. *Das mimetische Gedicht in der Antike: Geschichte und Typologie von den Anfängen bis in die augusteische Zeit*, Frankfurt

Aldrete, G. 2007. *Floods of the Tiber in ancient Rome*, Baltimore

Alföldy, G. et al. (eds.) 1995. *Römische Lebenskunst*, Heidelberg

Allan, W. (ed.) 2008. *Euripides, Helen*, Cambridge

Ancona, R. 1992. 'Horace *Odes* 1.25: temporality, gender, and desire' in C. Deroux (ed.), *Studies in Latin literature and Roman history* VI, Brussels, 245–59

Anderson, W. S. (ed.) 1999. *Why Horace? A collection of interpretations*, Wauconda

Auberger, J. 1996. 'Quand la nage devint natation . . .', *Latomus* 55: 48–62

Axelson, B. 1945. *Unpoetische Wörter. Ein Beitrag zur Kenntnis der lateinischen Dichtersprache*, Lund

Babcock, C. L. 1981. '*Carmina operosa*: critical approaches to the "Odes" of Horace', *ANRW* II 31.3: 1560–1611

Bakhouche, B. 2002. *L'astrologie à Rome*, Louvain

Balsdon, J. P. V. D. 1979. *Romans and aliens*, London

Barchiesi, A. 2009. 'Lyric in Rome' in Budelmann 2009: 319–35

Barr, W. 1962. 'Horace, *Odes* i.4', *CR* 12: 5–11

Beard, M. 2007. *The Roman triumph*, Cambridge, Mass., London

Becher, I. 1985. 'Tiberüberschwemmungen: die Interpretation von Prodigien in augusteischer Zeit', *Klio* 67: 471–9

Bell, A. J. 1923. *The Latin dual and poetic diction*, London and Toronto

Bernays, L. 2005. 'Zum text der Horaz-Ode 1.4', *Mnemosyne* 58: 282–4

Bolkestein, A. M. 1996. 'Is "qui" "et is"? On the so-called free relative connection in Latin' in H. Rosén (ed.), *Aspects of Latin: papers from the seventh international colloquium on Latin linguistics*, Innsbruck, 553–66

Bowra, C. M. 1961. *Greek lyric poetry from Alcman to Simonides*, Oxford

Bradshaw, A. 1989. 'Horace in Sabinis' in C. Deroux (ed.), *Studies in Latin literature and Roman history* V, Brussels, 160–86

2008. 'The prophet's warning: Horace, *Odes* 1.15', *MH* 65: 34–43

Braund, D. C. 1985. *Augustus to Nero. A sourcebook on Roman history, 31 B.C. – A.D. 68*, London and Sydney

Brink, C. O. 1969. 'Horatian notes: neglected readings in Horace's Odes', *PCPS* 15: 1–6

1971a. *Horace on poetry: the 'Ars Poetica'*, Cambridge

1971b. 'Horatian notes II: neglected readings in Horace's Odes, Book II', *PCPS* 17: 17–29

1982. 'Horatian notes III: despised readings in the manuscripts of the *Epodes* and a passage in *Odes* Book III', *PCPS* 28: 30–56

Brown, R. D. 1991. '*Catonis nobile letum* and the list of Romans in Horace *Odes* 1.12', *Phoenix* 45: 326–40

Brunt, P. A. 1971. *Italian manpower 225 B.C. – A.D. 14*, Oxford

1990. *Roman imperial themes*, Oxford

Budelmann, F. (ed.) 2009. *The Cambridge companion to Greek lyric*, Cambridge

Buecheler, F. 1915–30. *Kleine Schriften*, Leipzig, etc.

Burck, E. 1966. *Vom Menschenbild in der römischen Literatur*, Heidelberg

Burkert, W. 1985. *Greek religion, archaic and classical*, Oxford

Cairns, F. 1972. *Generic composition in Greek and Roman poetry*, Edinburgh

1977. 'Horace on other people's love affairs (*Odes* I, 27; II, 4; I, 8; III, 12)', *QUCC* 24: 121–47

1989. *Virgil's Augustan epic*, Cambridge

Cameron, A. 1995. *Callimachus and his critics*, Princeton

Campbell, A. Y. 1924. *Horace, a new interpretation*, London

Campbell, B. 1992. 'War and diplomacy: Rome and Parthia, 31 BC–AD 235' in Rich and Shipley 1992: 220–8

Casson, L. 1995. *Ships and seamanship in the ancient world* (revised edn), Baltimore and London

Champeaux, J. 1982. *Fortuna: recherches sur le culte de la Fortune à Rome et dans le monde romain des origines à la mort de César*, Rome

Citroni, M. 2009. 'Occasion and levels of address in Horatian lyric' in Lowrie 2009a: 72–105

Clark, R. J. 2010. 'Ilia's excessive complaint and the flood in Horace, *Odes* 1.2', *CQ* 60: 262–7

Clausen, W. 1994. *A commentary on Virgil Eclogues*, Oxford

Clay, J. S. 2010. 'Horace and Lesbian lyric' in Davis 2010: 128–46

Collinge, N. E. 1961. *The structure of Horace's Odes*, London

Commager, S. 1962. *The Odes of Horace. A critical study*, New Haven and London

Connor, P. 1987. *Horace's lyric poetry: the force of humour* (Ramus Monographs 2), Berwick

Cordray, J. M. 1956. 'The structure of Horace's *Odes*: some typical patterns', *CJ* 52: 113–16

Costa, C. D. N. (ed.) 1973. *Horace* (Greek and Latin Studies: Classical Literature and its Influence), London and Boston

Courtney, E. 2003. *The fragmentary Latin poets*, Oxford

2004. 'The "Greek" accusative', *CJ* 99: 425–31

Cowan, R. W. 2006. 'The land of King Mane. A pun at Horace, *Odes* 1.22.15', *CQ* 56: 322–4

Cucchiarelli, A. 2004. 'La nave e lo spettatore. Forme dell'allegoria da Alceo ad Orazio I', *SIFC* 4 2: 189–206

2005. 'La nave e lo spettatore. Forme dell'allegoria da Alceo ad Orazio II', *SIFC* 4 3: 30–72

2006. 'La tempesta e il dio (forme editoriali nei *Carmina* di Orazio)', *Dictynna* 3: 73–136

Cupaiuolo, F. 1967. *Lettura di Orazio lirico. Struttura dell' ode oraziana*, Naples

Curtius, E. R. 1953. *European literature and the Latin middle ages*, London

Davis, G. 1991. *Polyhymnia. The rhetoric of Horatian lyric discourse*, Berkeley, Los Angeles, Oxford

(ed.) 2010. *A companion to Horace*, Chichester

Dicks, D. R. 1963. 'Astrology and astronomy in Horace', *Hermes* 91: 60–73

Diederich, S. 1999. *Der Horazkommentar des Porphyrio im Rahmen der kaiserzeitlichen Schul- und Bildungstradition*, Berlin and New York

Dionisotti, C. 2007. '*Ecce*', *BICS* 50: 75–91

Doblhofer, E. 1966. *Die Augustuspanegyrik des Horaz in formalhistorischer Sicht*, Heidelberg

Doblhofer, G. and P. Mauritsch 1993. *Speerwurf* (Quellendokumentation zur Gymnastik und Agonistik im Altertum 3), Vienna

Dunbabin, K. M. D. 2003. *The Roman banquet: images of conviviality*, Cambridge

Edmunds, L. 1982. 'The Latin invitation-poem: what is it? Where did it come from?', *AJP* 103: 184–8

1992. *From a Sabine jar*, Chapel Hill and London

2010. 'The reception of Horace's Odes' in Davis 2010: 337–66

Engels, D. W. 1990. *Roman Corinth. An alternative model for the classical city*, Chicago

Esser, D. 1976. *Untersuchungen zu den Odenschlüssen bei Horaz* (Beiträge zur klassischen Philologie, 77), Meisenheim am Glan

Evans, H. B. 1993. '*In Tiburtium usum*: special arrangements in the Roman water system (Frontinus, *Aq.* 6.5)', *AJA* 97: 447–55

Fain, G. L. 2007. 'A Lesbian ending in the *Odes* of Horace', *CQ* 57: 318–21

Fantham, E. 1972. *Comparative studies in Republican Latin imagery*, Toronto

2002. 'Commenting on commentaries: a pragmatic postscript', in Gibson and Kraus 2002: 403–21

Färber, H. 1936. *Die Lyrik in der Kunsttheorie der Antike*, Munich

Farrar, L. 1998. *Ancient Roman gardens*, Stroud

Fears, J. R. 1977. *Princeps a diis electus. The divine election of the emperor as a political concept at Rome*, Rome

Feeney, D. C. 1993. 'Horace and the Greek lyric poets' in Rudd 1993: 41–63 and Lowrie 2009a: 202–31

1998. *Literature and religion at Rome: cultures, contexts, and beliefs*, Cambridge

Fehling, D. 1989. *Herodotus and his 'sources'. Citation, invention and narrative art* (ARCA. Classical and Medieval Texts, Papers and Monographs 21), Leeds

Ferber, M. 2007. *A dictionary of literary symbols*, 2nd edn, Cambridge

Fitch, J. G. 2006–7. 'Horace, *Odes* 1.3: Nature's boundaries', *Eranos* 104: 31–40

Fortuin, R. W. 1996. *Der Sport im augusteischen Rom* (Palingenesia 57), Stuttgart

Fowler, D. 2000. *Roman constructions. Readings in postmodern Latin*, Oxford

Fraenkel, E. 1957. *Horace*, Oxford

Fredricksmeyer, E. A. 1976. 'Horace *C.* 1.34: the conversion', *TAPA* 106: 155–76

   1993/94. 'Horace's Chloe (*Odes* 1.23): inamorata or victim?', *CJ* 89: 251–9

Frischer, B. 1984. 'Horace and the monuments: a new interpretation of the Archytas Ode (*C.* 1.28)', *HSCP* 88: 71–102

Fry, R. N. 1984. *The history of ancient Iran*, Munich

Gaisser, J. H. 2009. *Catullus*, Chichester

Galinsky, K. 1996. *Augustan culture: an interpretive introduction*, Princeton

Garnsey, P. 1979. 'Where did Italian peasants live?', *PCPS* 25: 1–25 = Garnsey 1998: 107–33

   1998. *Cities, peasants and food in classical antiquity. Essays in social and economic history*, ed. W. Scheidel, Cambridge

Gerber, D. 1997. *A companion to the Greek lyric poets*, Leiden, New York

Gibson, R. 2007. *Excess and restraint. Propertius, Horace, and Ovid's Ars Amatoria*, London

Gibson, R. K. and C. S. Kraus (eds.) 2002. *The classical commentary: histories, practices, theory*, Leiden

Gigante, M. 2002. *Philodemus in Italy: the books from Herculaneum*, Ann Arbor

Giuliani, C. F. 1970. *Tibur* I, Rome

Görler, W. 1995. '*Carpere, capere, rapere*. Lexicalisches und Philosophisches zum Lob der Gegenwart bei lateinischen Dichtern' in Alföldy 1995: 47–56

Gold, B. K. 1987. *Literary patronage in Greece and Rome*, Chapel Hill and London

Golden, M. 2004. *Sport in the ancient world from A to Z*, London

Greenblatt, S. 2011. *The swerve: how the Renaissance began*, London (= *The swerve: how the world became modern*, New York)

Griffin, J. 1984. 'Augustus and the poets: *"Caesar qui cogere posset"*' in Millar and Segal 1984: 189–218

   1994. *Latin poets and Roman life*, Bristol

Hadot, P. 1995. *Philosophy as a way of life: spiritual exercises from Socrates to Foucault*, Oxford

Hale, W. G. and C. D. Buck 1903. *A Latin grammar*, New York

Hancock, E. 1925. 'The use of the singular *nos* by Horace', *CQ* 19: 43–55

Handford, S. A. 1947. *The Latin subjunctive, its usage and development from Plautus to Tacitus*, London

Hardie, A. 2003. 'The Pindaric sources of Horace *Odes* 1.12', *HSCP* 101: 371–404

Harrison, S. J. (ed.) 1995. *Homage to Horace: a bimillenary celebration*, Oxford

   2004. 'Lyric middles: the turn at the centre in Horace's *Odes*' in Kyriakidis and De Martino 2004: 81–102

2007a. 'The primal voyage and the ocean of epos: two aspects of metapoetic imagery in Catullus, Virgil and Horace', *Dictynna* 4: 1–17

(ed.) 2007b. *The Cambridge companion to Horace*, Cambridge

Healey, J. F. 1978. *Mining and metallurgy in the Greek and Roman world*, London

Heikell, R. 1994. *Greek waters pilot: a yachtsman's guide to the coasts and islands of Greece*, St Ives

Heinze, R. 2009. 'The Horatian ode' in Lowrie 2009a: 11–32

Hekster, O. and J. Rich 2006. 'Octavian and the thunderbolt: the temple of Apollo Palatinus and Roman traditions of temple building', *CQ* 56: 149–68

Herzog, R. and P. L. Schmidt (eds.) 1997. *Lateinische Literatur der Antike*, vol. 4, Munich

Highet, G. 1957. *Poets in a landscape*, London

Hill, G. 1940. *The history of Cyprus*, Cambridge

Hofmann, J. B. 1951. *Lateinische Umgangssprache*, 3rd edn, Heidelberg

Holzberg, N. 2009. *Horaz, Dichter und Werk*, Munich

Hopkinson, N. 1984. *Callimachus: Hymn to Demeter* (Cambridge classical texts and commentaries 27), Cambridge

1988. *A Hellenistic anthology*, Cambridge

Hornblower, S. 2008. *A commentary on Thucydides*, vol. 3. Oxford

Hubbard, M. 1973. 'The *Odes*' in Costa 1973: 1–28

Huffman, C. A. 2005. *Archytas of Tarentum, Pythagorean, philosopher and mathematician king*, Cambridge

Humphrey, J. 1986. *Roman circuses. Arenas for chariot racing*, London

Hutchinson, G. O. 2001. *Greek lyric poetry*, Oxford

2008. *Talking books: readings in Hellenistic and Roman books of poetry*, Oxford

Hyland, A. 2003. *The horse in the ancient world*, Stroud

Jacobson, H. 1987. 'Horatiana', *CQ* 37: 524–6

Jocelyn, H. 1982. 'Boats, women, and Horace *Odes* 1.14', *CP* 77: 330–5

1999. 'The arrangement and language of Catullus' so-called *polymetra*' in Adams and Mayer 1999: 335–75

Kajanto, I. 1981. 'Fortuna', *ANRW* II 17.1: 502–58

Kalinina, A. 2007. *Der Horazkommentar des Pomponius Porphyrio: Untersuchungen zu seiner Terminologie und Textgeschichte*, Stuttgart

Kaster, R. A. 2005. *Emotion, restraint, and community in ancient Rome*, Oxford, New York

Kenney, E. J. 1983. 'The key and the cabinet: ends and means in classical studies', *Proc. Class. Ass.* 80: 7–18

Ker, A. 1964. 'Some passages from Virgil and Horace', *PCPS* 190: 39–47

Kirkwood, G. M. 1974. *Early Greek monody. The history of a poetic type*, Ithaca and London

Knorr, O. 2006. 'Horace's ship ode (*Odes* 1.14) in context: a metaphorical love-triangle', *TAPA* 136: 149–69

Köchling, J. 1914. 'De coronarum apud antiquos ui atque usu', diss., Giessen

Koster, S. (ed.) 1994. *Horaz-Studien*, Erlangen

Krasser, H. 1995. *Horazische Denkfiguren. Theophilie und Theophanie als Medium der poetischen Selbstdarstellung des Odendichters* (Zetemata, Heft 106), Göttingen

Kröhling, W. 1935. *Die Priamel als Stilmittel in der griechisch-römischen Dichtung*, Greifswald

Kruschwitz, P. 2007. '*Fluctuat nec mergitur*: Überlegungen zu Horaz' Ode 1, 14', *Hyperboreus: Studia Classica* 13: 151–73

Kyriakidis, S. and F. De Martino (eds.) 2004. *Middles in Latin poetry*, Bari

Labarre, G. 1996. *Les cités de Lesbos aux époques hellénistique et impériale.* (Collection de l'Institut d'Archéologie et d'Histoire de l'Antiquité, Université Lumière Lyon 2), vol. 1, Paris

Landels, J. G. 1999. *Music in ancient Greece and Rome*, London

La Penna, A. 1989. '*Cum flore, Maecenas, rosarum*: su una collocazione artistica del vocativo in poesia latina', in G. G. Biondi (ed.), *Mnemosynum, Studi in onore di A. Ghiselli*, Bologna, 335–53

Latte, K. 1960. *Römische Religionsgeschichte*, Munich

Laughton, E. 1964. *The participle in Cicero*, Oxford

Leigh Fermor, P. 1977. *A time of gifts*, London

Lendon, J. E. 1997. *Empire of honour. The art of government in the Roman world*, Oxford

Leo, F. 1878, repr. 1968. *De Senecae tragoediis observationes criticae*, Berlin

Leumann, M. 1977. *Lateinische Laut- und Formenlehre*, Munich

Lind, L. R. 1973–4. 'Roman religion and ethical thought: abstraction and personification', *CJ* 69: 108–19

Lindholm, E. 1931. *Stilistische Studien zur Erweiterung der Satzglieder im Lateinischen*, Lund

Lodge, G. 1933, repr. 1962. *Lexicon Plautinum*, Leipzig, Hildesheim

Löfstedt, E. 1942. *Syntactica*, 2nd edn, Lund

Lowrie, M. 1997. *Horace's narrative odes*, Oxford

(ed.) 2009a. *Horace: Odes and Epodes* (Oxford Readings in Classical Studies), Oxford

2009b. 'A parade of lyric predecessors: Horace. *C.* 1.12–18' in Lowrie 2009a: 337–55

Lucas, H. 1900. 'Recusatio' in *Festschrift Johannes Vahlen: Zum siebenzigsten Geburtstag. Gewidmet von seinen Schülern*, Berlin

Lyne, R. O. A. M. 1980. *The Latin love poets from Catullus to Horace*, Oxford

1995. *Horace: behind the public poetry*, New Haven and London

2007. *Collected papers on Latin poetry*, Oxford

Lyons, S. 2006. *Horace's Odes and the mystery of do-re-mi*, Warminster

Maas, M. and J. M. Snyder 1989. *Stringed instruments of ancient Greece*, New Haven

Maas, P. 1973. 'Studien zum poetischen Plural bei den Römern' in W. Buchwald (ed.), *Kleine Schriften*, Munich, 527–85 = *ALL* 12 (1902) 479–550

MacLachlan, B. C. 1997. 'Personal poetry' in Gerber 1997: 133–220

Maggiani, A. 1986. 'Cilnium genus: la documentazione epigrafica etrusca', *SE* 54: 171–96

Marouzeau, J. 1938. *L'Ordre des mots dans la phrase latine*. II: *Le verbe*, Paris

1946. *Traité de stylistique latine*, Paris

1949a. *L'Ordre des mots dans la phrase latine*. III: *Les articulations de l'énoncé*, Paris

1949b. *Quelques aspects de la formation du latin littéraire*, Paris

Martin, R. 2002. 'Horace in real time: *Odes* 1.27 and its congeners' in Paschalis 2002: 103–118

Mathiesen, T. J. 1999. *Apollo's lyre. Greek music and music theory in antiquity and in the Middle Ages*, Lincoln

Maurach, G. 1992. 'Hor. *c.* 1, 13: einige Methodenprobleme', *Gymnasium* 99: 501–17

Mayer, R. 1986. 'Geography and Roman poets', *G&R* 33: 49–50

1994. *Horace, Epistles, Book I*, Cambridge

1999. 'Grecism' in Adams and Mayer 1999: 157–82

2001. ' "Not" again?', *Glotta* 77: 65–74

Mayerson, P. 1995. 'Aelius Gallus at Cleopatris (Suez) and on the Red Sea', *GRBS* 36: 17–24

McKeown, J. C. 1987. *Ovid: Amores. Text, prolegomena and commentary*. I: *Text and prolegomena*, Liverpool

Millar, F. and E. Segal (eds.) 1984. *Caesar Augustus: seven aspects*, Oxford

Miller, J. F. 2009. *Apollo, Augustus, and the poets*, Cambridge

Miller, P. A. 1994. *Lyric texts and lyric consciousness. The birth of a genre from archaic Greece to Augustan Rome*, London, New York

Miller, S. G. 2004. *Ancient Greek athletics*, New Haven, London

Minarini, A. 1989. *Lucidus ordo. L'architettura della lirica oraziana (libri I–III)*, Bologna

Moles, J. 2002. 'Reconstructing Plancus (Horace, *C.* 1.7)', *JRS* 92: 86–109

Morgan, T. 2007. *Popular morality in the early Roman empire*, Cambridge

Moritz, L. A. 1968. 'Some "central" thoughts on Horace's *Odes*', *CQ* 18: 116–31

Müller, C. F. W. 1908. *Syntax des Nominativs und Akkusativs im Lateinischen*, Leipzig and Berlin

Murray, O. 1993. 'Symposium and genre in the poetry of Horace' in Rudd 1993: 89–105

Musurillo, H. 1962. 'The poet's apotheosis: Horace, Odes 1.1', *TAPA* 93: 230–9

Mutschler, F.-H. 1974. 'Beobachtungen zur Gedichtanordnung in der ersten Odensammlung des Horaz', *RhM* 117: 109–33

Naylor, H. D. 1922. *Horace, Odes and Epodes. A study in poetic word-order*, Cambridge

Nisbet, R. G. M. 1979. Review of Esser 1976 in *CR* 29: 148–9

1984. 'Horace's *Epodes* and history' in Woodman and West 1984: 1–18

1995. *Collected papers on Latin literature*, ed. S. J. Harrison, Oxford

1999. 'The word order of Horace's *Odes*' in Adams and Mayer 1999: 135–54 and Lowrie 2009a: 378–400

2007. 'Horace: life and chronology' in Harrison 2007b: 7–21

Norden, E. 1923. *Agnostos Theos. Untersuchungen zur Formengeschichte religiöser Rede.* Leipzig, Berlin

1927. *P. Vergilius Maro Aeneis Buch VI*, Leipzig

1939. *Aus altrömischen Priesterbüchern*, Lund

Numberger, K. 1997. *Horaz: Lehrer-Kommentar zu den lyrischen Gedichten*, Münster

Ogilvie, R. M. 1969. *The Romans and their gods*, London

O'Hara, J. J. 1996. *True names: Vergil and the Alexandrian tradition of etymological wordplay*, Ann Arbor

Otto, A. 1890, repr. 1962. *Die Sprichwörter und sprichwörtlichen Redensarten der Römer*, Leipzig

Page, D. L. (ed.) 1942. *Select Papyri III: literary papyri, poetry*, Cambridge, Mass. and London

1955. *Sappho and Alcaeus*, Oxford

Paschalis, M. (ed.) 2002. *Horace and Greek lyric poetry* (Rethymnon Classical Studies I), Rethymnon

Pasquali, G. 1920. *Orazio lirico*, Florence

Pearce, T. E. V. 1981. 'Notes on Horace, *Odes* I', *Latomus* 40: 72–87

Perret, J. 1970. 'Fides et la Fortune (Hor. C. 1,35,21–8)' in Wimmel 1970: 244–53

Perrot, J. 1961. *Les dérivés latins en -men et -mentum*, Paris

Pfeiffer, R. 1968. *History of classical scholarship from the beginnings to the end of the Hellenistic Age*, Oxford

Pöschl, V. 1986. 'Horazens Ode an den Weingott (*c.* 1 18). *Nullam Vare sacra*', *WS* 20: 193–203

1991. *Horazische Lyrik*, 2nd edn, Heidelberg

Poinsotte, J.-M. 1979. 'Les Romains et la Chine: réalités et mythes', *Mélanges de l'École française de Rome: Antiquité* 91: 431–79

Putnam, M. C. J. 1994. 'Structure and design in Horace *Odes* 1.17', *CW* 87: 357–75

1995a. 'From lyric to letter: Iccius in Horace *Odes* 1.29 and *Epistles* 1.12', *Arethusa* 28: 193–207

1995b. 'Design and allusion in Horace, *Odes* 1.6' in Harrison 1995: 50–64

Quinn, K. 1963. 'Horace as a love poet. A reading of *Odes* 1.5', *Arion* 2: 59–77

Race, W. C. 1982. *The classical priamel from Homer to Boethius. (Mnemosyne* suppl. 74), Leiden

2010. 'Horace's debt to Pindar' in Davis 2010: 156–62

Ramsey, J. T. 2006. *A descriptive catalogue of Greco-Roman comets from 500 B. C. to A. D. 400*, Iowa City

Raven, D. S. 1965. *Latin metre*, London

Reitzenstein, R. 1963. *Aufsätze zu Horaz. Abhandlungen und Vorträge aus den Jahren 1908-1925*, Darmstadt

Renehan, R. 1988. 'Shackleton Bailey and the editing of Latin poetry: a Latin classic', *CP* 83: 311–28

Reynolds, L. D. (ed.) 1986 (corrected edn). *Texts and transmission. A survey of the Latin classics*, Oxford

Rich, J. and G. Shipley (eds.) 1992. *War and society in the Roman world*, London

Richardson, L. 1992. *A new topographical dictionary of ancient Rome*, Baltimore

Richardson, L. J. D. 1936. 'The dative of agent in Horace's *Odes*', *CR* 50: 118–20

Rickman, G. 1980. *The corn supply of ancient Rome*, Oxford

Roberts, D. H., F. M. Dunn, and D. Fowler (eds.) 1997. *Classical closure: reading the end in Greek and Latin literature*, Princeton

Robinson, H. R. 1975. *The armour of imperial Rome*, London

Robinson, O. 1973. 'Blasphemy and sacrilege in Roman law', *Irish Jurist* 8: 356–71

Roddaz, J.-M. 1984. *Marcus Agrippa*, Rome

Ross, D. O. 1969. *Style and tradition in Catullus*, Cambridge, Mass.

Rossi, L. 2009. 'Horace, a Greek lyrist without music', in Lowrie 2009a: 356–77

Rudd, N. (ed.) 1972. *Essays on classical literature selected from* Arion, Cambridge and New York

1993. *Horace 2000: a celebration for the bimillennium*, London

2004. *Horace, Odes and Epodes* (Loeb Classical Library 33), Cambridge, Mass. and London

Rumpf, L. 2009. '*Caelum ipsum petimus stultitia*. Zur poetologischen Deutung von Horaz' c. 1.3', *RhM* 152: 292–311

Rutherford, I. 1997. 'Odes and ends: closure in Greek lyric' in Roberts et al. 1997: 43–61

Saintsbury, G. 1923. *A second scrap book*, London

Schmidt, E. A. 2002. 'Schema Horatianum. Ein horazisches Verdichtungs- und Konstruktionsverfahren' in *Zeit und Form. Dichtungen des Horaz*, Heidelberg: 335–79

Schönberger, O. 1966. 'Horatius, *Carm.* 1.1', *Gymnasium* 73: 388–412

Schrijvers, P. H. 2009. 'How to end an ode? Closure in Horace's short poems', in Lowrie 2009a: 56–71

Schwinge, E.-R. 1965. 'Horaz, Carmen 2, 20', *Hermes* 93: 438–59

Scullard, H. H. 1981. *Festivals and ceremonies of the Roman Republic*, London

Sear, F. 2006. *Roman theatres: an architectural study*, Oxford

Segal, C. 1973. '*Felices ter et amplius*: Horace, *Odes* 1, 13', *Latomus* 32: 39–46

Sellar, W. Y. 1891. *The Roman poets of the Augustan age: Horace and the elegiac poets*, Oxford

Shaw, B. D. 1987. 'The age of Roman girls at marriage: some reconsiderations', *JRS* 77: 30–46

Sherwin-White, S. and A. Kuhrt 1993. *From Samarkhand to Sardis*, London

Simpson, F. P. 1879. *Select poems of Catullus*, London

Sittl, C. 1890. *Die Gebärden der Griechen und Römer*, Leipzig

Smyth, H. W. 1956. *Greek grammar* (revised by G. M. Messing), Cambridge, Mass.

Solodow, J. B. 1986. '*Raucae, tua cura, palumbes*: study of a poetic word order', *HSCP* 90: 129–53

Sommer, F. 1914. *Handbuch der lateinischen Laut- und Formenlehre*, Heidelberg

Spies, A. 1930. *Militat omnis amans. Ein Beitrag zur Bildersprache der antiken Erotik*, Tübingen

Stanford, W. B. 1963. *The Ulysses theme: a study in the adaptability of a traditional hero*, Oxford

Steinhart, M. and W. J. Slater 1997. 'Phineus as monoposiast', *JHS* 117: 203–11

Storrs, R. 1959. *Ad Pyrrham, a polyglot collection of translations of Horace's Ode to Pyrrha (Book I, Ode 5)*, London

van Straten, F. T. 1981. 'Gifts for the gods' in Versnel 1981: 65–151

Sutherland, E. H. 2003. 'How (not) to look at a woman: bodily encounters and the failure of the gaze in Horace's *C.* 1.19', *AJP* 124: 57–80

　　2005. 'Writing (on) bodies: lyric discourse and the production of gender in Horace *Odes* 1.13', *CP* 100: 52–82

Sydenham, C. 2010. 'Punctuating Cleopatra', *CQ* 60: 652–6

Syme, R. 1939. *The Roman revolution*, Oxford

　　1978. *History in Ovid*, Oxford

　　1979. E. Badian (ed.), *Roman papers* I and II, Oxford, 205–17

　　1991. A. R. Birley (ed.), *Roman papers* VI, Oxford, 372–97

Syndikus, H. P. 1995. 'Some structures in Horace's *Odes*' in Harrison 1995: 17–31

　　2001. *Die Lyrik des Horaz: eine Interpretation der Oden*, 3rd edn, Darmstadt

Talbot, J. 2007–8. 'Critical implications of the caesura in Horatian alcaics', *CJ* 103: 41–61

Tarrant, R. J. 1986. 'Horace' in Reynolds 1986: 182–6

　　1995. '*Da Capo* structure in some *Odes* of Horace' in Harrison 1995: 32–49

Tatum, W. J. 2005. 'Teucer's *imperium* (Horace *Odes* 1.7.27)', *Papers of the Langford Latin Seminar* 12: 113–16

Tchernia, A. 1986. *Le vin d'Italie romaine: essai d'histoire économique d'après les amphores*, Rome

　　1999. *Le vin romain antique*, Grenoble

Thibodeau, P. 2002–3. 'Can Vergil cry? Epicureanism in Horace *Odes* 1.24', *CJ* 98: 243–56

Tracy, H. L. 1951. 'Thought-sequence in the ode', *Phoenix* 5: 108–18

Traill, D. A. 1982. 'Horace *C.* 1.3: a political ode?', *CJ* 78: 131–7

Tyrrell, R. Y. 1895. *Latin poetry*, London

Vahlen, J. 1907. *Opuscula academica*, Leipzig

Versnel, H. S. 1976. 'Two types of Roman *deuotio*', *Mnemosyne* 29: 365–410

　　1981. *Faith, hope and worship: aspects of religious mentality in the ancient world*, Leiden

Wachsmuth, D. 1967. ΠΟΜΠΙΜΟΣ Ο ΠΛΟΥΣ: *Untersuchung zu den antiken Sakralhandlungen bei Seereisen*, Berlin

Wackernagel, J. 1926, 1928. *Vorlesungen über Syntax*, Basle

　　2009. *Lectures on syntax: with special reference to Greek, Latin, and Germanic* (D. Langslow, ed., tr.), Oxford

Watkins, T. H. 1997. *L. Munatius Plancus. Serving and surviving in the Roman revolution*, Atlanta

Watson, L. C. 2003. *A commentary on Horace's* Epodes, Oxford

Watson, P. 1983. 'Puella and virgo', *Glotta* 61: 119–43

1985. 'Axelson revisited: the selection of vocabulary in Latin poetry', *CQ* 35: 430–48

Weinreich, O. 1968. *Religionsgeschichtliche Studien*, Darmstadt

Weinstock, S. 1971. *Divus Iulius*, Oxford

West, D. 1967. *Reading Horace*, Edinburgh

1973. 'Horace's poetic technique in the *Odes*' in Costa 1973: 29–58

1995. *Horace Odes I: carpe diem*, Oxford

West, M. L. 1992. *Ancient Greek music*, Oxford

2005. 'The new Sappho', *ZPE* 151: 1–9

Wheeler, A. L. 1934. *Catullus and the traditions of ancient poetry*, Berkeley and Los Angeles

White, K. D. 1967. *Agricultural implements of the Roman world*, Cambridge

1970. *Roman farming*, London

1984. *Greek and Roman technology*, London

White, P. 1993. *Promised verse: poets in the society of Augustan Rome*, Cambridge, Mass., London

Wilkinson, L. P. 1966. *Golden Latin artistry*, Cambridge

1968 (first edn 1945). *Horace and his lyric poetry*, Cambridge

Will, E. L. 1982. 'Ambiguity in Horace *Odes* 1.4', *CP* 77: 240–5

Willcock, M. M. 1995. *Pindar, victory odes*, Cambridge

Williams, C. A. 1999. *Roman homosexuality: ideologies of masculinity in classical antiquity*, New York, Oxford

2004. *Martial, Epigrams, Book Two*, Oxford

Williams, G. 1968. *Tradition and originality in Roman poetry*, Oxford

Willis, J. 1972. *Latin textual criticism*, Urbana, Chicago, London

Wills, J. 1996. *Repetition in Latin poetry: figures of allusion*, Oxford

Wimmel, W. (ed.), 1970. *Forschungen zur römischen Literatur: Festschrift zum 60. Geburtstag von Karl Büchner*, Wiesbaden

1983. 'Der Augusteer Lucius Varius Rufus', *ANRW* II 30.3: 1562–1621

Wissemann, M. 1982. *Die Parther in der augusteischen Dichtung*, Frankfurt

Woodman, A. J. 1972. 'Horace's odes *Diffugere niues* and *Soluitur acris hiems*', *Latomus* 31: 752–78

Woodman, T. and D. West (eds.) 1984. *Poetry and politics in the age of Augustus*, Cambridge

Wyke, M. 2002. *The Roman mistress. Ancient and modern representations*, Oxford

Yardley, J. C. 1976. 'Lovers' quarrels: Horace, *Odes* 1.13.11 and Propertius 4.5.40', *Hermes* 104: 124–8

Zanker, P. 1988. *The power of images in the age of Augustus*, Ann Arbor

INDEXES

1. LATIN WORDS

2. GENERAL

References to the *Enciclopedia oraziana* (*EO*) and Bo Index will be found in the commentary wherever the information provided is specific to the passage under discussion; but wherever the *EO* and Bo Index provide useful but non-specific information a reference will be consigned to the following index.

CPSIA information can be obtained
at www.ICGtesting.com
Printed in the USA
LVHW051954121218
600232LV00023B/312/P